A BOOK OF WALES

A Book of Wales

An anthology selected by Meic Stephens

J. M. Dent & Sons Ltd
London Melbourne

First published in Great Britain 1987

Preface, Selection and Notes copyright © J. M. Dent & Sons Ltd 1987

This book is set in 10½/12 Linotron Ehrhardt by Gee Graphics, Gee Street, London EC1

Printed and made in Great Britain by
MacKays of Chatham Ltd
for Phoenix House, an imprint of
J. M. Dent & Sons Ltd
Aldine House
33 Welbeck Street
London W1M 8LX

British Library Cataloguing in Publication Data

A Book of Wales
    1. English literature ——— Welsh authors
    2. Welsh literature ——— Translations into English
    3. English literature ——— Translations from Welsh
    I. Stephens, Meic
    820.8'09429
l5ISBN 0-460-07002-9

Contents

X

Preface

Wales is a country which has two languages and two literatures. Welsh literature, that is literature in the Welsh language, has its beginnings in the sixth century and its tradition is as illustrious as it is long. It flourishes in our own day, despite the fact that only a fifth of the population (about half a million people) now speak the national language, by virtue of a genius that is remarkable not only for its tenacity in difficult circumstances but also for its quality and range. The second literature of Wales, sometimes called Anglo-Welsh if only to distinguish it from the other, consists mainly of writing by Welsh men and women in English. Much the younger of the two, it has antecedents in the sixteenth century but began to gather strength only about a hundred years ago, and lacked any real continuity until the present century.

This anthology draws on the two literatures of Wales, both Welsh and Anglo-Welsh, on verse and prose, in almost equal measure, but it does not pretend to be fully representative of either. There are several reasons for the omission of certain important prose-writers for instance, chief among them being the dearth of satisfactory translations from the Welsh. More generally, the exigencies of space ruled out a good deal of verse and prose that would doubtless have found a place in a much larger anthology based on historical principles. No less relevant was the peculiar fact that some prose-writers, notably those who work on a large canvas, do not lend themselves easily to the anthologist's purpose, which is to select fairly short, lively, narrative passages that can be read out of context with little or no explication of character and plot. I shall therefore have to disappoint readers who expect a thorough survey of the field and, with regard to the verse at least, refer them to any of the excellent specialist anthologies already available.

Nevertheless, the work of some hundred and twenty writers is to be found here, to an extent that may be taken as a rough indication of their reputations, albeit with the provisos noted. They include many of the most distinguished names in the literary pantheon of Wales, together with others whose more modest contributions are still not without merit and interest. As for those among my contemporaries in the republic of Welsh letters who will feel put out at having won no laurels on this occasion, there might be only cold comfort in their knowing that I saluted them all affectionately before complying with the constraints necessarily imposed upon me, but that is most certainly what I did. An old hand at feats of editorial balance, I am aware that in the task of selection an anthologist has to rely mainly on his own taste and judgement, which are never infallible but which, however diligently exercised, may even be thought contentious, especially in a small country that is linguistically divided, culturally fractious and politically frustrated, and where literary opinion (like much else besides) sometimes tends to be fervently held and resolutely defended. If that were not so, life in Wales – and the anthologist's dilemma – would probably be far less complicated; it would certainly be much more wearisome. So perhaps I ought to emphasize that what follows hereafter is a selection made largely according to my own lights, of material that seems to *me* to have significance, and for reasons which I, too, might be prepared to argue but should be loath to relinquish.

It would be tedious of me to go into detail about those reasons here. Suffice it to say, not too portentously I hope, that my anthology attempts to hold up a mirror to the land and people of Wales in all their rich diversity, and sometimes to reflect the one whole Wales that has fired the imaginations of Welsh writers over the centuries. The purview takes in the backward glance of the expatriate and, in two or three instances, the curious gaze of the English and American visitor. The material has been selected from all periods but I have looked with particular favour on the work of twentieth-century writers, on account of its accessibility and relevance for the contemporary reader. I have avoided, for the most part, the overly erudite and the obscurely personal, and my footnotes will throw some light on certain allusions which may puzzle the non-Welsh and the younger reader who are unschooled in the history, topography and society of Wales. Old favourites will be found rubbing shoulders with less familiar matter in a book designed to please that most genial of readers, the browser. For ease of reference the contents are listed by author in alphabetical order, rather than thematically, although the attentive reader will discern that they might just as effectively have been arranged under several broad heads, as was the anthology of the same title that was published under the editorship of D.M. and E.M. Lloyd in 1953.

Like its predecessor, the present *Book of Wales* ranges freely over a wide gamut of subject, style and mood, now joyful and now sombre, touching in turn upon most of the prime facets of human experience such as birth and childhood, courtship and marriage, work and leisure, kinship and friendship, community and solitude, love of country and the natural world, war and peace, old age and religion and death. If there are any recurrent themes they include a keen sense of the past and the numinous, a warm regard for people, a close attachment to place, a distrust of remote authority, a passionate concern for social justice, a prodigal delight in antitheses of language and sentiment, and mercifully, a liking for colour, song and laughter. It is no wonder that such a vivid, ebullient people has attracted more than its fair share of caricature and vilification. My hope is that the portrait presented in the following pages will make a small contribution towards a better understanding of Wales and the

Welsh, as much among the Welsh themselves as beyond their country's borders.

Lastly, I have to thank those who helped me in the preparation of this book. My sickle has been put deep into other men's corn, and so I must first express my gratitude to the writers, translators, editors, publishers and trustees who have given permission for copyright material to be reproduced here. Thanks are also due to Dr Glyn Jones and Mrs Ann Saer for their kind interest and, in particular, for their valuable comments on the text as it existed in draft form. To several other friends whose advice I sought during the period of compilation, but was not always able to accept, I express my gratitude now; they are Professor Gwyn Jones, Mr Raymond Garlick, Dr Roland Mathias, Professor Joseph P. Clancy, Mr Sam Adams, Dr Glyn Tegai Hughes, Mr Michael Parnell, Professor David Smith, Mr Gerald Morgan, Mrs Sally Jones, Mr R. Gerallt Jones, Dr John Rowlands and Mr J.P. Ward. In turning my hand to the work of translation I was advised by the following: Mr Islwyn Ffowc Elis, Dr Gweneth Lilly, Miss Jane Edwards, Mrs Nan Griffiths and Lady Amy Parry-Williams. The proofs were read with the help of my wife Ruth. For their assistance with administrative chores I thank Mrs Gwyneth Evans and Miss Angela Howells. I should also like to put on record my appreciation of the part played by Mr Bill Neill-Hall of Phoenix House (J.M. Dent & Sons Ltd), on whose enthusiasm, courtesy and expertise I depended at all stages of production.

Meic Stephens
Whitchurch, Cardiff
January 1987

DANNIE ABSE (1923–   )

Return to Cardiff

'Hometown'; well, most admit an affection for a city:
grey, tangled streets I cycled on to school, my first cigarette
in the back lane, and, fool, my first botched love affair.
First everything. Faded torments; self-indulgent pity.

The journey to Cardiff seemed less a return than a raid
on mislaid identities. Of course the whole locus smaller:
the mile-wide Taff now a stream, the castle not as in some black,
gothic dream, but a decent sprawl, a joker's toy façade.

Unfocused voices in the wind, associations, clues,
odds and ends, fringes caught, as when, after the doctor quit,
a door opened and I glimpsed the white, enormous face
of my grandfather, suddenly aghast with certain news.

Unable to define anything I can hardly speak,
and still I love the place for what I wanted it to be
as much as for what it unashamedly is
now for me, a city of strangers, alien and bleak.

Unable to communicate I'm easily betrayed,
uneasily diverted by mere sense reflections
like those anchored waterscapes that wander, alter, in the Taff,
hour by hour, as light slants down a different shade.

Illusory, too, that lost dark playground after rain,
the noise of trams, gunshots in what they once called Tiger Bay.[1]
Only real this smell of ripe, damp earth when the sun comes out,
a mixture of pungencies, half exquisite and half plain.

No sooner than I'd arrived the other Cardiff had gone,
smoke in the memory, these but tinned resemblances,
where the boy I was not and the man I am not
met, hesitated, left double footsteps, then walked on.

Lol

Lol was three years older than I. Seventeen years from his shadow he stood,
tall and well built, with a lolling massive head full of air, instead of brains, and

---

[1] Tiger Bay, the city's notorious dockland.

with no neck at all worth talking about. If Modigliani had painted him, he would have just looked about normal. As Keith had said – if Lol was blessed with a neck he would have been a giant almost. Lol's father who'd recently come out of jail had become rich suddenly, so now Lol, dressed in big-shouldered suits and gaudy extravagant ties, lounged round street corners talking to newspaper boys.

I was lying down on the grass near the quarry, chewing a blade of grass when I heard his voice.

'Hello,' he called. Lol sat down beside me, pulled a stem of grass from the earth and started chewing at it like me.

'Whassermarra with your brother Leo?' asked Lol. 'Saw 'im in town with a white thing round his leg.'

'Broke it,' I said. 'Mam's pleased because that's stopped him going to Spain.'

'What's wrong with Spain?' demanded Lol.

'Don't you know, Lol? – there's a war going on.'

He looked at me incredulously. We sat there awhile: looking over the rooftops at the distant Bristol Channel shimmering in the sun that shone out of a bald blue sky. Below us the dark primitive quarry with its rusted stone jutting in and out savagely. Stone abandoned, cold, cruel, ancient . . .

'Why ar't you at school?' he asked me finally in his Canton[1] accent.

'Don't feel like it,' I replied.

'Wish I was you,' he said miserably.

'Why?'

'Dunno. Wish I was anybody but me.'

Lol pulled his creased trousers up from his suède shoes revealing gay yellow socks.

'What do you do all day?' I asked him.

'Goes to the pitchers venyer every afternoon,' he said. 'Likes gangsters best.' He made a fist of his right hand, then slowly extended his index finger like a gun. 'Bang, bang, bang!' he said.

'What else do you do?'

He frowned, trying to think. 'In the mornin', these weathers, I likes goin' for a walk early. Picks mushrooms.'

'On your own, Lol?'

'Oh yes, in the mornin', very early. Sometimes I takes a bus to Rhwbina[2] – I gets up especially early – and I takes a threepenny bus ride. They gives you a blue ticket for threepence. I collects 'em. Tickets. I got lots. And I goes walking in the 'ills. It's dirty, misty I mean, early mornin' and you know, sort of true. Know what I mean? Fresh air, when you breathes. Very good for you, fresh air, Dad says.'

---

[1]Canton, a district of Cardiff.
[2]Rhwbina (*recte* Rhiwbina), a green suburb.

Lol began to breathe violently in and out, in and out, expanding his chest, making a noise like an engine with brakes on, until his face was red.

'Good for you,' he explained. 'Fresh air.'

'You pick mushrooms, Lol?'

'Yes. It's easy. You find 'em, then you pick 'em.'

'And you're on your own?'

'Natcherly. It's nice, mun. Fresh air. Mist. Bloody birds singing.' I laughed and he smiled at me benevolently.

'What you going to do when you grow up?' I asked him.

'I'm 'aving elecuit lessons.'

'What lessons?'

'You knows, for speaking proper,' he said.

'You mean elocution lessons,' I said.

'Yes, 'em,' he nodded vaguely.

'What for?' I asked.

He took the blade of grass out of his mouth once more and looked at me with bright eyes.

'Goin to be a film star,' he said proudly and he threw back his head, closing his eyes, pointing his finger at me. 'Bang, bang, bang!' he bellowed.

'What do you want to be a film star for?' I asked him.

'Go away,' he said. 'You're 'aving me. Leave me be.'

'No, serious, Lol. Why do you want to be a film star?'

'Garn,' he answered.

'I'm interested. Honest.'

Lol looked at me suspiciously. His brow puckered, and his big head lolled forward on his chest.

'They gets their pitchers in the papers.'

'And . . .?' I asked.

'Shut your gob,' he ordered. 'You're 'aving me.'

'No, I'm not, really, Lol.'

'You knows Lydia Pike,' he shouted. He stood up and looked around at the house across the street. Fiercely, he said, 'If you touches 'er, I'll do you in, proper.' He pointed a finger at me. 'Bang, bang, bang!' he screamed. 'Bang, bang, bang!'

'Don't be silly, Lol. Sit down.'

'Shurrup!' he yelled. 'You're 'aving me.' And he walked away leaving me there, on the sparse grass, near the old disused quarry, under a sun that was too dazzling to look at.

from *Ash on a Young Man's Sleeve* (1954)

Epithalamion

Singing, today I married my white girl
beautiful in a barley field.
Green on thy finger a grass blade curled,
so with this ring I thee wed, I thee wed,
and send our love to the loveless world
of all the living and all the dead.

Now, no more than vulnerable human,
we, more than one, less than two,
are nearly ourselves in a barley field –
and only love is the rent that's due
though the bailiffs of time return anew
to all the living but not the dead.

Shipwrecked, the sun sinks down harbours
of a sky, unloads its liquid cargoes
of marigolds, and I and my white girl
lie still in the barley – who else wishes
to speak, what more can be said
by all the living against all the dead?

Come then all you wedding guests:
green ghost of trees, gold of barley,
you blackbird priests in the field,
you wind that shakes the pansy head
fluttering on a stalk like a butterfly;
come the living and come the dead.

Listen flowers, birds, winds, worlds,
tell all today that I married
more than a white girl in the barley –
for today I took to my human bed
flower and bird and wind and world,
and all the living and all the dead.

RUTH BIDGOOD (1922–   )

Little of Distinction

Little of distinction, guide-books had said –
a marshy common and a windy hill:
a renovated church, a few old graves
with curly stones and cherubs with blind eyes:
yews with split trunks straining at rusty bands:
and past the church, a house or two, a farm,
not picturesque, not even very old.
And yet, the day I went there, life that breaks
so many promises gave me a present
it had not promised – I found this place
had beauty after all. How could I have seen
how a verandah's fantastic curlicues
would throw a patterned shadow on the grass?
or thought how delicate ash-leaves would stir
against a sky of that young blue? or known
trees and grey walls would have such truthful beauty,
like an exact statement? And least of all
could I have foreseen the miles on hazy miles
of Radnorshire and Breconshire below,
uncertain in the heat – the mystery
that complements precision. So much sweeter
was this day than the expectation of it.

GEORGE BORROW (1803–81)

A Bard of Anglesey

'I believe you are an Englishman, sir,' said the man in grey, speaking English. 'I will therefore take the liberty of answering your question in the English tongue. The name of this place is Dyffryn Gaint.'

'Thank you,' said I; 'you are quite right with regard to my being an Englishman; perhaps you are one yourself?'

'Sir,' said the man in grey, 'I have not the honour to be so. I am a native of the small island in which we are.'

'Small,' said I, 'but famous, particularly for producing illustrious men.'

'That's very true indeed, sir,' said the man in grey, drawing himself up; 'it is particularly famous for producing illustrious men.'

'There was Owen Tudor?'[1] said I.

[1] Owen Tudor (*c.* 1400-61), the husband of Catherine de Valois.

'Very true,' said the man in grey, 'his tomb is in the church a little way from hence.'

'Then,' said I, 'there was Gronwy Owen,[1] one of the greatest bards that ever lived. Out of reverence to his genius I went yesterday to see the place of his birth.'

'Sir,' said the man in grey, 'I should be sorry to leave you without enjoying your conversation at some length. In yonder house they sell good ale, perhaps you will not be offended if I ask you to drink some with me and my friend?'

'You are very kind,' said I, 'I am fond of good ale, and fonder still of good company – suppose we go in?'

We went into the cottage, which was kept by a man and his wife, both of whom seemed to be perfectly well acquainted with my two new friends. We sat down on stools, by a clean white table in a little apartment with a clay floor – notwithstanding the heat of the weather, the little room was very cool and pleasant owing to the cottage being much protected from the sun by its situation. The man in grey called for a jug of ale, which was presently placed before us along with three glasses. The man in grey, having filled the glasses from the jug which might contain three pints, handed one to me, another to his companion, and then taking the third drank to my health. I drank to his, and that of his companion; the latter, after nodding to us both, emptied his at a draught, and then with a kind of half-fatuous leer, exclaimed, 'Da iawn, very good.'

The ale, though not very good, was cool and neither sour nor bitter; we then sat for a moment or two in silence, my companions on one side of the table, and I on the other. After a little time the man in grey looking at me said:

'Travelling I suppose in Anglesey for pleasure?'

'To a certain extent,' said I; 'but my chief object in visiting Anglesey was to view the birth-place of Gronwy Owen; I saw it yesterday and am now going to Holyhead chiefly with a view to see the country.'

'And how came you, an Englishman, to know anything of Gronwy Owen?'

'I studied Welsh literature when young,' said I, 'and was much struck with the verses of Gronwy: he was one of the great bards of Wales, and certainly the most illustrious genius that Anglesey ever produced.'

'A great genius I admit,' said the man in grey, 'but pardon me, not exactly the greatest Ynis Fon[2] has produced. The race of the bards is not quite extinct in the island, sir, I could name one or two – however, I leave others to do so – but I assure you the race of bards is not quite extinct here.'

'I am delighted to hear you say so,' said I, 'and make no doubt that you speak correctly, for the Red Bard[3] has said that Mona[4] is never to be without a poet – but where am I to find one? Just before I saw you I was wishing to see a poet; I would willingly give a quart of ale to see a genuine Anglesey poet.'

[1]Goronwy Owen (1723-69), a poet.
[2]*Ynis Fon* (recte *Ynys Môn*), the Island of Anglesey.
[3]the Red Bard, Hugh Hughes (1693-1776), a poet.
[4]Mona, an archaic name for Anglesey.

'You would, sir, would you?' said the man in grey, lifting his head on high and curling his upper lip.

'I would, indeed,' said I, 'my greatest desire at present is to see an Anglesey poet, but where am I to find one?'

'Where is he to find one?' said he of the tattered hat; 'where's the gwr boneddig[1] to find a prydydd? No occasion to go far, he, he, he.'

'Well,' said I, 'but where is he?'

'Where is he? why there,' said he pointing to the man in grey – 'the greatest prydydd in tîr Fon[2] or the whole world.'

'Tut, tut, hold your tongue,' said the man in grey.

'Hold my tongue, myn Diawl,[3] not I – I speak the truth,' then filling his glass he emptied it exclaiming, 'I'll not hold my tongue. The greatest prydydd in the whole world.'

'Then I have the honour to be seated with a bard of Anglesey?' said I, addressing the man in grey.

'Tut, tut,' said he of the grey suit.

'The greatest prydydd in the whole world,' iterated he of the bulged shoe, with a slight hiccup, as he again filled his glass.

'Then,' said I, 'I am truly fortunate.'

'Sir,' said the man in grey, 'I had no intention of discovering myself, but as my friend here has betrayed my secret, I confess that I am a bard of Anglesey – my friend is an excellent individual but indiscreet, highly indiscreet, as I have frequently told him,' and here he looked most benignantly reproachful at him of the tattered hat.

'The greatest prydydd,' said the latter, 'the greatest prydydd that – ' and leaving his sentence incomplete he drank off the ale which he had poured into his glass.

'Well,' said I, 'I cannot sufficiently congratulate myself, for having met an Anglesey bard – no doubt a graduate one. Anglesey was always famous for graduate bards, for what says Black Robin?[4]

"Though Arvon graduate bards can boast,
 Yet more canst thou, O Anglesey."

'I suppose by graduate bard you mean one who has gained the chair[5] at an eisteddfod?' said the man in grey. 'No, I have never gained the silver chair – I have never had an opportunity. I have been kept out of the eisteddfodau. There is such a thing as envy, sir – but there is one comfort, that envy will not always prevail.'

'No,' said I; 'envy will not always prevail – envious scoundrels may chuckle for a time at the seemingly complete success of the dastardly arts to which they

[1] *gwr bonheddig*, a gentleman . . . *prydydd*, a poet.
[2] *Tir Fon*, the land of Anglesey.
[3] *myn Diawl*, by the Devil.
[4] Black Robin, Robin Ddu ap Siencyn Bledrydd (*fl.* 1459), a poet.
[5] Chair, a traditional prize for poets . . . *eisteddfod*. A cultural festival usually organized on a competitive basis

have recourse, in order to crush merit – but Providence is not asleep. All of a sudden they see their supposed victim on a pinnacle far above their reach. Then there is weeping, and gnashing of teeth with a vengeance, and the long melancholy howl. O, there is nothing in this world which gives one so perfect an idea of retribution as the long melancholy howl of the disappointed envious scoundrel when he sees his supposed victim smiling on an altitude far above his reach.'

'Sir,' said the man in grey, 'I am delighted to hear you. Give me your hand, your honourable hand. Sir, you have now felt the hand-grasp of a Welshman, to say nothing of an Anglesey bard, and I have felt that of a Briton, perhaps a bard, a brother, sir? O, when I first saw your face out there in the dyffryn,[1] I at once recognised in it that of a kindred spirit, and I felt compelled to ask you to drink. Drink sir! but how is this? the jug is empty – how is this? – O, I see – my friend, sir, though an excellent individual, is indiscreet, sir – very indiscreet. Landlord, bring this moment another jug of ale.'

'The greatest prydydd,' stuttered he of the bulged shoe – 'the greatest prydydd – Oh – '

'Tut, tut,' said the man in grey.

'I speak the truth and care for no one,' said he of the tattered hat. 'I say the greatest prydydd. If any one wishes to gainsay me let him show his face, and Myn Diawl – '

The landlord brought the ale, placed it on the table, and then stood as if waiting for something.

'I suppose you are waiting to be paid,' said I; 'what is your demand?'

'Sixpence for this jug, and sixpence for the other,' said the landlord.

I took out a shilling and said: 'It is but right that I should pay half of the reckoning, and as the whole affair is merely a shilling matter I should feel obliged in being permitted to pay the whole, so, landlord, take the shilling and remember you are paid.' I then delivered the shilling to the landlord, but had no sooner done so than the man in grey, starting up in violent agitation, wrested the money from the other, and flung it down on the table before me saying: –

'No, no, that will never do. I invited you in here to drink, and now you would pay for the liquor which I ordered. You English are free with your money, but you are sometimes free with it at the expense of people's feelings. I am a Welshman, and I know Englishmen consider all Welshmen hogs. But we are not hogs, mind you! for we have little feelings which hogs have not. Moreover, I would have you know that we have money, though perhaps not so much as the Saxon.' Then putting his hand into his pocket he pulled out a shilling, and giving it to the landlord said in Welsh: 'Now thou art paid, and mayst go thy ways till thou art again called for. I do not know why thou didst stay after thou hadst put down the ale. Thou didst know enough of me to know that thou didst run no risk of not being paid.'

---

[1] *dyffryn*, a vale.

'But,' said I, after the landlord had departed, 'I must insist on being my share. Did you not hear me say that I would give a quart of ale to see a poet?'

'A poet's face,' said the man in grey, 'should be common to all, even like that of the sun. He is no true poet, who would keep his face from the world.'

'But,' said I, 'the sun frequently hides his head from the world, behind a cloud.'

'Not so,' said the man in grey. 'The sun does not hide his face, it is the cloud that hides it. The sun is always glad enough to be seen, and so is the poet. If both are occasionally hid, trust me it is no fault of theirs. Bear that in mind; and now pray take up your money.'

'The man is a gentleman,' thought I to myself, 'whether poet or not; but I really believe him to be a poet; were he not he could hardly talk in the manner I have just heard him.'

from *Wild Wales* (1862)

EUROS BOWEN (1904–   )

The Swan

To see intimating and mystery
Is a sanctum's art today –
To see colour and muscularity, to see a candid
Visitor from heaven among our time's bare hills:
His solitude swims in water's stillness
A pilgrim in familiar sedges,
And his form washes the lake's weather
Like a slim shaft that clothed the passion
Of a soul's breath with its light
On a slow bare course in March's cold:
His neck floated, a look-out there,
An immaculate hunting arm,
Stabilizing, – his eyes poising,
And plunged in the pool the flame of his beak:
The mountains a sulky look,
He goes on to slide, glide on the flow:
Tremors of his wing, then a waiting,
And in one bold stroke he breaks from the water:
Slowly he lifted, lofting to the sky,
And draws a soul from its coldness with the fire of his wings.

trans. Joseph P. Clancy

Blackthorn

The bush, a gathering smoke
on blackthorn. Yesterday a sharp wind
blew over its cold impoverished branches,
and like solitariness
turning into a slow thaw when the sun warms,
it just melted today
on the sun's return into a mass of white.
By the time of the evening blaze
all its feathered branches were scorched
with the heat from the fire,
like the solitariness
we ourselves know in the world
as a burning bush,
burned, but not consumed.

                                                    trans. the author

DUNCAN BUSH (1946–   )

Summer 1984

Summer of strike and drought,
of miners' pickets standing on blond verges,
of food parcels and

hosepipe bans . . . And as (or so
the newspapers reported it) five rainless
months somewhere disclosed

an archaeology of long-evicted
dwellings on a valley-floor, the reservoir
which drowned them

having slowly shrunk towards
a pond between crazed banks, the silted
houses still erect,

even, apparently, a dusty
bridge of stone you might still walk
across revealed intact

in that dry air, a thing not seen
for years; just so (though this the papers
did not say)

the weeks and months of strike saw
slowly and concurrently emerge in shabby
river-valleys in South Wales

– in Yorkshire too, and Durham,
Kent and Ayrshire – villages no longer
aggregates of dwellings

privatised by television, but
communities again, the rented videos and tapes
back in the shop,

fridge-freezers going back
– so little to put in them, anyway – and
meetings, meetings in their place,

in workmen's clubs and miners' welfare
halls, just as it had been once, communities
beleaguered but the closer,

the intenser for it, with resources
now distributed to need, and organised to last,
the dancefloors stacked

with foodstuffs like a dockside, as if
an atavistic common memory, an inheritance
perhaps long thought romantic,

like the old men's proud and bitter
tales of 1926,[1] was now being learnt again,
in grandchildren and

great-grandchildren of their bloodline:
a defiance and a unity which even sixty years
of almost being discounted never broke.

[1] 1926, the year of the General Strike.

Brenda Chamberlain (1912–71)

Bardsey

From the end of the peninsula, the island which has been my home for fourteen years, wears an austere aspect. On the eastward side the mountain drops sheer to the sea. The kindly westward side with its scattered farmhouses is not visible from here. Between mainland and sea-rock run the inconstant waters of the Sound. It is the end of our world.

Paul and I came to live here in the spring of 1947. In those days it was easy to rent houses on the island. Several were in disrepair and had not been lived in for years. At first sight, the architecture of the eighty-year-old farmhouse was a disappointment and a surprise. I had expected something more romantic, a crofter's cottage on the strand; fishing nets before the door, in keeping with the extreme simplicity of the limited landscape. Now that I live here, in a four-square granite house that no winds can shake, I feel differently. It is good to have a little distance between the house and the sea; even so, on winter nights the roaring of the surf is monstrous. It booms as if under the foundations. There is no escape from the raving of wind and water.

A house on an island is not quite like other homes; one feels impossibly far when away from it; and when there, it is sometimes a prison, and sometimes a sanctuary. It has its own calm atmosphere, something to do with the silent and remote island air; but perhaps it has more to do with the fact that the house is built from the ruins of the sixth-century abbey. The roof is cleverly broken up and there are no eaves. The south-wester simply streams over it; there is no plucking at the slates as there was in the cottage in the mountains where I lived during the war.

There are no dark corners. At breakfast-time, the living-room is bright with the sun shining over the mountain; and supper-time on a summer evening in the little study facing west across the Irish Sea to the horns of the Wicklows, is a time of molten gold and flame-coloured water, and of a beneficent peace. The living-room has a fireplace which is a joy to use. It was made a few years ago, out of old bricks from a pulled-down chimney. The wood fire is laid on an iron basket which, being high up, throws out a good heat. The iron oven beside it is large enough to accommodate a goose and a week's baking of bread. The oven is stoked by a separate fire underneath: it has an excellent draught, and is economical of wood.

The house has eight rooms; a dairy, kitchen, children's room, study; and four bedrooms, one of which I use as a studio. Upstairs, there is a wide landing lit by a skylight.

At the north side of the house is a small walled garden. The well is only a few yards away from the door; the outlet stream is completely hidden by watercress. We are seldom at a loss for salad; lettuce, watercress, and dandelion in the early spring.

We have no electricity. For lighting, we use paraffin lamps and candles; for heating, wood fires and a paraffin radiator. We have no need of coal since driftwood is easily obtainable; and at times one can find quantities of paraffin wax washed up by the tide. The wax we mould into candles which are then threaded with fishing line for wicks; and the result gives out a quite special kind of radiance, a votive flame.

We are a small community, only about twelve now, interdependent but at the same time independent. Our neighbours are fisher-farmers with feet on the earth and hands in the sea. To a great extent, we live off the fruits of our environment: lobster, crab, crayfish, mackerel and pollack in the summer, and rockfish caught from the rocks in calm weather the whole year round.

Life on this, as on every small island, is controlled by the moods of the sea; its tides, its gifts, its deprivations.

from *Tide Race* (1962)

JOSEPH P. CLANCY (1928–   )

A Cywydd [1] *for Kate*

Twenty years since I waited,
A first-time father, afraid
For you, climbing the winding
Stair to the lintel of life,
Afraid of those fragile steps,
Fearful of your exposure
To light and air, the wearing
Years to come, fearing that I
Would fail you in performing
A father's role, unrehearsed,
No script to follow, no cues.
Then from those pangs of waiting
The birth of wonder and joy,
The moment of your entry,
Wrinkled and pink and bawling
And utterly beautiful.

[1] *Cywydd*, one of the major forms of Welsh prosody, some aspects of which, such as a seven-syllable line, are featured here.

Reduced, now, to my proper
Bit player's role, quite content
To speak a prelude and yield
Center stage to you, linger
In the wings, I wait once more,
Feeling no father's envy
Of your leading man, finding
The wonder and joy reborn
As you, serene and lovely,
No girl, but a woman grown
Pledge yourself to a new life.
Yours, now, is the unwritten
Play, the improvisation,
But mine again the first fears
For you, knowing that marriage
Is an art that none can teach,
How false it would be for me
To offer you direction.

No paternal platitudes
From me, then – but permit me
Merely a benediction.
A happy marriage? For you,
That wish would be unworthy.
May you live your marriage vow
To the full, its joy, its grief,
Unregretful, forgetting
Not one word you speak today,
But learning more each moment
What the words mean by making
The word flesh as you embrace
The man, the world you marry.
May you celebrate each day
Creation, crucifixion,
And each day's blessing of birth.

Dear daughter, may Love in you
Learn a new incarnation.

GILLIAN CLARKE (1937–   )

Birth

On the hottest, stillest day of the summer
A calf was born in a field
At Pant-y-Cetris; two buzzards
Measured the volume of the sky;
The hills brimmed with incoming
Night. In the long grass we could see
The cow, her sides heaving, a focus
Of restlessness in the complete calm,
Her calling at odds with silence.

The light flowed out leaving stars
And clarity. Hot and slippery, the scalding
Baby came, and the cow stood up, her cool
Flanks like white flowers in the dark.
We waited while the calf struggled
To stand, moved as though this
Were the first time. I could feel the soft sucking
Of the new-born, the tugging pleasure
Of bruised reordering, the signal
Of milk's incoming tide, and satisfaction
Fall like a clean sheet around us.

Harvest at Mynachlog

At last the women come with baskets,
The older one in flowered apron,
A daisied cloth covering the bread
And dappled china, sweet tea
In a vast can. The women stoop
Spreading their cups in the clover.

The engines stop. A buzzard watches
From the fence. We bury our wounds
In the deep grass: sunburnt shoulders,
Bodies scratched with straw, wrists bruised
From the weight of the bales, blood beating.

For hours the baler has been moulding
Golden bricks from the spread straw,
Spewing them at random in the stubble.
I followed the slow load, heaved each
Hot burden, feeling the sun contained.

And unseen over me a man leaned,
Taking the weight to make the toppling
Load. Then the women came, friendly
And cool as patches of flowers at the far
Field edge, mothy and blurred in the heat.

We are soon recovered and roll over
In the grass to take our tea. We talk
Of other harvests. They remember
How a boy, flying his plane so low
Over the cut fields that his father

Straightened from his work to wave his hat
At the boasting sky, died minutes later
On an English cliff, in such a year
As this, the barns brimming gold.

We are quiet again, holding our cups
In turn for the tilting milk, sad, hearing
The sun roar like a rush of grain
Engulfing all winged things that live
One moment in the eclipsing light.

Lunchtime Lecture

And this from the second or third millenium
B.C., a female, aged about twenty-two.
A white, fine skull, full up with darkness
As a shell with sea, drowned in the centuries.
Small, perfect. The cranium would fit the palm
Of a man's hand. Some plague or violence
Destroyed her, and her whiteness lay safe in a shroud
Of silence, undisturbed, unrained on, dark
For four thousand years. Till a tractor in summer
Biting its way through the long cairn for supplies
Of stone, broke open the grave and let a crowd of light
Stare in at her, and she stared quietly back.

As I look at her I feel none of the shock
The farmer felt as, unprepared, he found her.
Here in the Museum, like death in hospital,
Reasons are given, labels, causes, catalogues.
The smell of death is done. Left, only her bone
Purity, the light and shade beauty that her man
Was denied sight of, the perfect edge of the place
Where the pieces join, with no mistakes, like boundaries.

She's a tree in winter, stripped white on a black sky,
Leafless formality, brow, bough in fine relief.
I, at some other season, illustrate the tree
Fleshed, with woman's hair and colours and the rustling
Blood, the troubled mind that she has overthrown.
We stare at each other, dark into sightless
Dark, seeing only ourselves in the black pools,
Gulping the risen sea that booms in the shell.

ANTHONY CONRAN (1931–   )

Elegy for the Welsh Dead
in the Falkland Islands, 1982

Gwŷr a aeth Gatraeth oedd ffraeth eu llu;
Glasfedd eu hancwyn, a gwenwyn fu.
– 'Y Gododdin'[1]

Men went to Catraeth, keen was their company;
They were fed on fresh mead, and it proved poison.

Men went to Catraeth. The luxury liner
For three weeks feasted them.
They remembered easy ovations,
Our boys, splendid in courage.
For three weeks the albatross roads,
Passwords of dolphin and petrel,
Practised their obedience
Where the killer whales gathered,
Where the monotonous seas yelped.
Though they went to church with their standards
Raw death has them garnished.

---

[1] *'Y Gododdin'*, a poem attributed to Aneirin which commemorates the heroic deeds of a British war-band who died in a disastrous battle near Catraeth (Catterick, Yorks) about 600; several lines in Anthony Conran's poem echo the earlier elegy.

Men went to Catraeth. The Malvinas
Of their destiny greeted them strangely.
Instead of affection there was coldness,
Splintering iron and the icy sea,
Mud and the wind's malevolent satire.
They stood nonplussed in the bomb's indictment.

Malcolm Wigley of Connah's Quay. Did his helm
Ride high in the war-line?
Did he drink enough mead for that journey?
The desolated shores of Tegeingl,[1]
Did they pig this steel that destroyed him?
The Dee runs silent beside empty foundries.
The way of the wind and the rain is adamant.

Clifford Elley of Pontypridd. Doubtless he feasted.
He went to Catraeth with a bold heart.
He was used to valleys. The shadow held him.
The staff and the fasces of tribunes betrayed him.
With the oil of our virtue we have anointed
His head, in the presence of foes.

A lad in Tredegar or Maerdy. Was he shy before girls?
He exposes himself now to the hags, the glance
Of the loose-fleshed whores, the deaths
That congregate like gulls on garbage.
His sword flashed in the wastes of nightmare.

Russell Carlisle of Rhuthun. Men of the North
Mourn Rheged's[2] son in the castellated Vale.
His nodding charger neighed for the battle.
Uplifted hooves pawed at the lightning.
Now he lies down. Under the air he is dead.

Men went to Catraeth. Of the forty-three
Certainly Tony Jones of Carmarthen was brave.
What did it matter, steel in the heart?
Shrapnel is faithful now. His shroud is frost.

With the dawn men went. Those forty-three,
Gentlemen all, from the streets and byways of Wales,
Dragons of Aberdare, Denbigh and Neath –
Figment of empire, whore's honour, held them.
Forty-three at Catraeth died for our dregs.

[1] Tegeingl, a district in north-east Wales (Englefield).
[2] Rheged, a kingdom in 'the Old North' of Britain, now southern Scotland.

B.L. COOMBES (1894–1974)

My First Night Underground

About nine-thirty that night I started to dress for my first night underground. There are no rules as to what you shall wear, only an unwritten one that you must not bring good clothes unless you do not mind being teased about what you are going to do for Sunday or 'how's it looking for the old 'uns?' Clothes must be tough and not too tight; dirtiness is no bar, because they will soon be much dirtier than they have ever been before. The usual wear is a cloth cap, old scarf, worn jacket and waistcoat, old stockings, flannel shirt, singlet, and pants. Thick moleskin trousers must be worn to bear the strain of kneeling and dragging along the ground, and strong boots are needed because of the sharp stones in the roadways and the other stones that fall. Food must be protected by a tin box, for the rats are hungry and daring; also plenty of tea or water is necessary to replace the sweat that is lost. . . .

As soon as we entered under the mountain I was aware of the damp atmosphere. Black, oily water was flowing continually along the roadway and out to the tip. It was up to the height of a man's knees, and to avoid it we had to balance carefully and walk along the narrow rails. I slipped several times, and then tried crouching up on the side and swinging myself along by the timber that was placed upright on either side. Suddenly I remembered that this timber was supposed to be holding the roof up and that I might pull it out of place and bring the mountain down on to us. I did not touch the timber after that.

We were not more than ten minutes reaching the coal-face – that is the name given to the exact part where coal is being cut. This was a new level, so it had not gone far into the mountain. This seam was a small one, not a yard thick, and was a mixture of steam- and house-coal.

When I had been shown where to hang my clothes I went to see our working place. It was known as the Deep. We were the lowest place of all, because this Deep was heading into the virgin coal to open work. Every fifty yards on each side of our heading other headings opened left and right, but they would be working across the slope, and so were running level. From these level headings the stalls were opening to work all the coal off.

Our place was going continually downhill. Every three yards forward took us downward another yard. It was heavy climbing to go back, and every shovelful of coal or stone had to be thrown uphill. Water was running down the roadway to us and an electric pump was gurgling away on our right side. We were always working in about six inches of water, and if the pump stopped or choked for ten minutes the coal was covered with water. There is nothing pleasant about water underground. It looks so black and sinister. It makes every move uncomfortable and every stroke with the mandril splashes the water about your body.

It takes some time to be able to tell coal from the stone that is in layers above and below it. Everything is black, only the coal is a more shining black and the stone is greyer. It is difficult to tell one from the other, especially when water is about, but the penalty for putting stone – miners call it 'muck' – into a coal tram is severe.

I tried very hard to be useful that night, but was not successful, nor do I believe that any beginner ever has been. Things are so different and there is so much to learn. For several weeks lads of nowhere near my size and strength could make me look foolish when it came to doing the work they had been brought up in. I had used a shovel before, but found that skill was needed to force its round nose under a pile of rough stones on the uneven bottom, turn in that narrow space, and throw the shovelful some distance and to the exact inch.

The need to watch where you step, the difficulty of breathing in the confined space, the necessity to watch how high you move your head, and the trouble of seeing under these strange conditions are all confusing until one has learned to do them automatically. It takes a while to learn that you must first take a light to a thing before you can find it. I started several times to fetch tools, then found myself in the solid darkness and had to return to get my lamp.

My mate lay on his side and cut under the coal. It took me weeks to learn the way of swinging elbows and twisting wrists without moving my shoulders. This holing under the coal was deadly monotonous work. We – or rather my mate – had to chip the solid coal away fraction by fraction until we had a groove under it of an inch, then six inches, then a foot. Then we threw water in the groove and moved along to a fresh place while the water softened where we had worked.

John hammered continually for nearly three hours at the bottom of the coal. He cut under it until he was reaching the full length of his arms and the pick-handle. At last he slid back and sat on his heels while he sounded the front of the coal with the mandril blade and looked closely at where the coal touched the roof to see if there showed the least sign of a parting.

'Keep away from this slip,' he warned me as he moved farther along, 'it'll be falling just now.'

It did, in less than five minutes, and after I had recovered from my alarm and most of the dust had passed I did my best to throw the coal into the tram. I soon found that a different kind of strength was needed than the one I had developed. My legs became cramped, my arms ached, and the back of my hands had the skin rubbed off by pressing my knee against them to force the shovel under the coal. The dust compelled me to cough and sneeze, while it collected inside my eyes and made them burn and feel sore. My skin was smarting because of the dust and flying bits of coal. The end of that eight hours was very soon my fondest wish. . . .

By four o'clock in the morning the shovel felt to be quite a hundredweight and I winced every time I touched my knees or back against anything. I got sleepy too, and felt myself swaying forward on my feet. I dropped some water in my eyes and revived for awhile, then I pinched my finger between two stones and was wide awake for some time after.

I had thought that night and day were alike underground, but it was not so.

It is always dark, but Nature cannot be deceived, and when the time is night man craves for sleep. When the morning comes to the outside world he revives again, as I did.

Even the earth sleeps in the night and wakens with perceptible movement about two o'clock in the morning. With its waking shudders it dislodges all stones that are loose in the workings. It is about that time that most falls occur, at the time when man's energy is at its lowest.

Somehow that shift did end, although I felt it lasted the time of two. . . .

How glad I was to drag my aching body toward that circle of daylight! I had sore knees and was wet from the waist down. The back of my right hand was raw and my back felt the same. My eyes were half closed because of the dust and my head was aching where I had hit it against the top, but I had been eight hours in a strange, new world.

The outside world had slept while we worked, and the dew of the morning sparkled from a thousand leaves when I looked down on the valley. It was beautiful after that wet blackness to see the sun, and the brown mountain, and the picture that the church tower made peeping out over the trees.

As we went down the incline, the day-shift came up. They called their 'Good morning' or 'Shu mai?'[1] as they hurried past with their tea-jacks in their hands.

from *These Poor Hands* (1939)

ALEXANDER CORDELL (1914–   )

The Execution of Dic Penderyn[2]

When the hangman came in and pinioned his arms behind him, Dic said:

'The hangmen are younger than I expected. Where do you come from?'

The man tied the knots, saying: 'I come from Bristol, but all last night I travelled from London, and arrived here at three o'clock this morning.'

'It were a pity you did not arrive later, I think.'

Later it was known that the authorities had scoured the neighbouring counties for a hangman without success, and that the professionals in London would not undertake the task. This hangman was a novice, and had undertaken this hanging because of poverty.

Dic said, before they opened the cell door that led to the gallows:

'Morgan, I do not want to die.'

'We all have to die,' replied Morgan Howells. 'Do you but precede us by a year or two.' In Welsh he said this, which was their mother tongue.

---

[1]'*Shu mai?*' (*recte* '*Shw mae?*'), How are you?

[2]Dic Penderyn (Richard Lewis, 1808-31), martyr, was hanged in Cardiff for his alleged part in the Merthyr Rising of 1831.

At the door Dic paused, and said: 'You will care for my baby son, and my wife, to whom I have not been good, because of the drinking?'

'She sends to you her love,' said Morgan Howells. 'If this is the punishment for drinking then many stand condemned. Your sister Gwen says that she will be united with you, both now and in death. Your mother and father are in prayer for you; Wales itself is in prayer for you.'

And Dic Penderyn said again: 'My God, for all, and for me, this is a bloody hard measure. Thank God I have had the Sacrament.' With this he turned to Morgan Howells, who had been joined by the sheriff and said: 'I am going out to suffer unjustly. God, who knows all things, knows it is so.'

With this he walked to the scaffold. The Reverend Edmund Evans walked one side of him, the sheriff walked on the other; behind came Mr Woods, the prison governor and he was with Morgan Howells; after them came the hangman and a gaoler. Nor did he lose his composure as he mounted the steps to the platform, but looked around the crowd as if seeking friends, while the hangman tied his ankles. It is said, also, that the rain increased and that thunder began to roll in from the sea; many of the people knelt, and bowed their heads. Perhaps he was looking for Sun, perhaps for his sister Gwen, but these he did not see, nor even the face of Molly Caulara, who knelt and prayed alone on the distant street. But, near the scarlet uniforms of the Red-coats on guard against disturbances he saw one face upturned, and it was that of Mistress Morfydd Mortymer, the young agitator of Blaenafon whom he had insulted in the Long Room above the bar of Tafern Uchaf, at the meeting of the Oddfellows Lodge. And he remembered her face with its glowing, dark eyes, and the way she held herself. Suddenly, she clenched her hand and swept back her hair, and as the hangman placed the noose about him, she cried, her voice shrill:

'Die hard, Dic Penderyn. You are dying for Wales. Die hard, Dic Penderyn!'

Legend would have us believe that lightning split the sky and that thunder roared as Dic Penderyn died; it is known only that it was raining, and that, in the moment before the trap was pulled, he cried with his face to the sky:

'O Arglwydd, dyma gamwedd! O Arglwydd, dyma gamwedd!'

Which, being translated, means:

'O Lord, what an iniquity! O Lord, what an iniquity!'

And the thunder rolled over the town and the people bowed their heads, for they were afraid.

from *The Fire People* (1972)

Tony Curtis (1946–   )

Preparations

In the valley there is an order to these things:
Chapel suits and the morning shift called off.
She takes the bus to Pontypridd to buy black,
But the men alone proceed to the grave,
Neighbours, his butties, and the funeral regulars.
The women are left in the house; they bustle
Around the window with a hushed, furious
Energy that keeps grief out of the hour.

She holds to the kitchen, concerned with sandwiches.
It is a ham-bone big as a man's arm and the meat
Folds over richly from her knife. A daughter sits
Watching butter swim in its dish before the fire.
The best china laid precisely across the new tablecloth:
They wait. They count the places over and over like a rosary.

Cynddelw Brydydd Mawr (*fl.* 1155–1200)

Poem on his Deathbed

I salute God, asylum's gift,
    To praise my Lord, bounteous, benign,
Sole Son of Mary, source of morn and eve
        And teeming river-mouths,
    Who made wood, and mead, and true measure,
    And harvests, and God's overflowing gifts,
Who made grass and grove and mountain heather, . . .

I salute God, I solicit acclaim
    For the piece I perform:
    There are thousands praise you, High Prince,
    And your hosts to the highest bounds.
I would beseech, my Lord, with your blessing,
    In your love I believe,
    You, song-renowned, I celebrate,
    Grant a gift, let me not be lost.
    More than needful, the greatest grace,
    Lord, was saving the strong at last.
    The thought terrifies me, thinking
    Of the sinning that Adam sinned.

Vile exile, I, if I shun your fair land,
    And your fair host around me,
The bards of the glorious church,
Their support has been my portion,
Pleasant the path to the place I search for,
Hope in the High Judge, fellowship I seek:
Monarch of all, salvation for me,
After leaving the world, my reward,
By the Father's favour, most royal,
And the Son's, and the Spirit's, pure splendour.
In sanctified glory I shall be,
In angels' charge, innocent, gentle,
In a fair land, Lord, heaven I beg for. . . .

Almighty Ruler, when of you I sang,
    Not worthless the piece that I performed,
    No lack of fine style in His lyric,
    No little largesse have I obtained,
    Not fashioned was I by changeless God
    For devising folly, fraud, or force.
No unfaithful man may have faith in God,
    Not he foulness dwells with, sewer's filth,
    Not he whose heart is slow to waken,
    Not for him, heaven, who will not seek.
    Not easy the form I have fashioned,
    No excessive reward have I earned,
No bearing of boldness has my heart dared,
    No bearing of penance have I craved.
    For the Lord's asylum have I longed,
    My soul's freedom, this need have I sought.

    Almighty Ruler, deign to receive,
    Reverent request, harmonious,
    Flawless in formation of language,
    My song in your praise, fair land's candle.
Since you are master, since you are monarch,
    Since you are prophet, since you are judge,
    Since you are kind, since you are benign,
Since you are my teacher, banish me not,
    In your wrath, from your fair land.
    Refuse me not your grace, exile's Lord,
    Scorn me not amidst the wretched crew,
    Spill me not from your hand, vile dwelling,
    Throw me not to the black loveless throng.

                                    trans. Joseph P. Clancy

DAFYDD AB EDMWND (*fl.* 1450–97)

A Girl's Hair

He who could win the girl I love
would win a grove of light,
with her silken, starry hair
in golden columns from her head,
dragon fire lighting up a door,
three chains like the Milky Way.
She sets alight in one bush
a roof of hair like a bonfire.
Yellow broom or a great birch tree
is this gold-topped girl of Maelor.[1]
A host coloured like angels,
her armour's many-branched,
a peacock-feather pennon,
a tall bush like the golden door,
all this lively looking hair
virtued like the sun, fetter of girls.
Anyone would know, were he a goldsmith,
who owns this fine strong hair.
In summer she has on her head
something like the Golden Hillside.
This fair growth is the girl's garment,
a tent for the sun, or harp strings,
ears of corn closed in above,
reed peelings as ornaments for the breast;
a peahen constantly carrying
hair of broom from head to ground,
a noose of woven amber,
the gold of corn like twig-chains;
her hair's a tree-high woodland,
a twig-crown of new wax.
Labour of bees has ripened
the seeds of warmth from a girl's flesh,
saffron on the herb eyebright,
cherries of gold, like the stars of night.
A good band round its coming growth,
fresh water-grass, golden water-hair,
lye water wets it like sweet herbs;
yellow-hammer head, bush of silk;

---

[1]Maelor, a district of north-east Wales.

a sheaf of Mary Magdalen's broom
is the gold band that binds her hair.
If we let it down all glowing,
she'll wear a gown of golden hair.
It covers her two breasts
from its roof of gold in two fathoms,
fair ringlets, load of a girl's head,
flax before bush of yellow.
If spread out, the bush is gold:
was ever bush so yellow?
In order that from the christening font
the oil of faith should mark her head,
giving life to the sun's bush,
there's no such bush now under the sun.

trans. Gwyn Williams

DAFYDD AP GWILYM (*fl.* 1320–70)

The Girls of Llanbadarn [1]

I am one of passion's asses,
Plague on all these parish lasses!
Though I long for them like mad,
Not one female have I had,
Not a one in all my life,
Virgin, damsel, hag, or wife.
What maliciousness, what lack,
What does make them turn their back?
Would it be a shame to be
In a bower of leaves with me?
No one's ever been so bitched,
So bewildered, so bewitched
Saving Garwy's[2] lunatics
By their foul fantastic tricks.

So I fall in love, I do,
Every day, with one or two,
Get no closer, any day,
Than an arrow's length away.
Every single Sunday, I,
Llanbadarn can testify,

[1] Llanbadarn, a church and parish near Aberystwyth, Cards.
[2] Garwy, a legendary warrior and lover.

Go to church and take my stand
With my plumed hat in my hand,
Make my reverence to the altar,
Find the right page in my psalter,
Turn my back on holy God,
Face the girls, and wink, and nod
For a long, long time, and look
Over feather, at the folk.
Suddenly, what do I hear?
A stage whisper, all too clear,
A girl's voice, and her companion
Isn't slow at catching on.

'See that simple fellow there,
Pale and with his sister's hair
Giving me those leering looks
Wickeder than any crook's?'

'Don't you think that he's sincere?'
Asks the other in her ear.
'All I'll give him is *Get out*!
Let the Devil take the lout!'

Pretty payment, in return
For the love with which I burn.
Burn for what? The bright girl's gift
Offers me the shortest shrift.
I must give them up, resign
These fear-troubled hopes of mine:
Better be a hermit, thief,
Anything, to bring relief.
Oh, strange lesson, that I must
Go companionless and lost,
Go because I looked too long,
I, who loved the power of song.

trans. Rolfe Humphries

The Seagull [1]

Gracing the tide-warmth, this seagull,
The snow-semblanced, moon-matcher,
The sun-shard and sea-gauntlet
Floating, the immaculate loveliness.
The feathered one, fishfed, the swift-proud,
Is buoyant, breasting the combers.
Sea-lily, fly to this anchor to me,
Perch your webs on my hand.
You nun among ripples, habited
Brilliant as paper-work, come.
Girl-glorified you shall be, pandered to,
Gaining that castle mass, her fortalice.
Scout them out, seagull, those glowing battlements,
Reconnoitre her, the Eigr [2] - complexioned.
Repeat my pleas, my citations, go
Girlward, gull, where I ache to be chosen.
She solus, pluck up courage, accost her,
Stress your finesse to the fastidious one;
Use honeyed diplomacy, hinting
I cannot remain extant without her.
I worship her, every particle worships!
Look, friends, not old Merlin, [3] hot-hearted,
Not Taliesin [4] the bright-browed, beheld
The superior of this one in loveliness.
Cypress-shapely, but derisive beneath
Her tangled crop of copper, gull,
O, when you eye all Christendom's
Loveliest cheek – this girl will bring
Annihilation upon me, should your answer
Sound, gull, no relenting note.

trans. Glyn Jones

[1] This poem uses the traditional device of *llatai* – the sending of a bird (or some other creature) with a message for the beloved.
[2] Eigr, the wife of Uthr Pendragon and mother of Arthur, renowned for her beauty.
[3] Merlin, a legendary poet and prophet.
[4] Taliesin (*fl.* late 6th cent.), a poet and character in folk-tale.

In a Tavern

I came to a choice city,
Behind me my handsome squire.
High living, a festive place,
I found, swaggering youngster,
A decent enough public
Lodging, and I ordered wine.

I spied a slim fair maiden
In the house, my pretty dear,
Set wholly, hue of sunrise,
My heart on my slender sweet.
I bought roast, not for boasting,
And costly wine for us two.
Playing the game young men love,
I called her, sweet girl, over.
I whispered, bold, attentive,
That's for sure, two magic words:
I made, love was not idle,
A compact to come to her
When the others had fallen
Fast asleep; dark-browed was she.

After all were, sad journey,
Asleep but the girl and me,
Painstakingly I sought for
The girl's bed; and then came grief.
I had, loud it resounded,
A hard fall, no skill at all;
I could rise, wicked it was,
More clumsily than quickly.
I bumped, by jumping badly,
My shin, and how my leg hurt,
Against, an ostler left it,
The side of a noisy stool.

In coming, penitent tale,
Above, may Welshmen love me,
I struck, great lust is evil,
The place was, not one free step,
A trap where blows were traded,
My head on a table top
Where there lay a loose basin
And a booming pan of bronze.

From the table fell, wild room,
All it held and both trestles,
Raising clamour from the pan
After me, far-flung racket,
And clanging, I was helpless,
From the basin, and dogs barked.

Next the thick walls there lay in
A stinking bed three Saxons
Bothered about their bundles,
Hickin and Jenkin and Jack.
Whispered the filthy-mouthed lad,
Angry speech, to the others:
'A Welshman's, din to dupe us,
Stalking here treacherously;
He'll steal, if we allow it;
Take heed, be on your guard.'

Then rose a crowd of ostlers
Thronging, a terrible tale.
Frowning they were around me,
Searching for my hiding place,
And me, with ugly bruises,
Keeping quiet in the dark.
I prayed, in no bold fashion,
Hidden, like a timid girl,
And by prayer's wondrous might,
And by the grace of Jesus,
I gained, a sleepless tangle,
Unrequited, my own bed.
I escaped, the saints were kind:
Of God I ask forgiveness.

trans. Joseph P. Clancy

E. TEGLA DAVIES (1880–1967)

Nedw and his Nuts

'Nedw,' said Wmffre, 'will you come picking crab-apples instead of going to school this afternoon?'

So that you'll know what's going on, I'm Nedw and Wmffre is my cousin.

It was the season for picking nuts and crab-apples in the Tyno. There were no trees in the Tyno, except nut-trees and crab-apple-trees. And at this time

of year it's like heaven on earth with us, as they sing in chapel. It would take
nothing more to make it completely heaven, if it were not for Joseph the
Teacher. We pick nuts at mid-day and me and Wmffre are the two best
pickers. I got it awful from Joseph one day and that's why picking nuts and
crab-apples is not all heaven. The schoolmaster himself happened to be ill.
He's a better sort than Joseph. Wmffre and me had been picking, with a lot of
others, and were coming back to school with our pockets full – both pockets of
our jackets so that each one of us looked like the thing they call a balloon, like
in the picture in Standard IV's book. Luckily, we were early enough for school
that afternoon and so Joseph had nothing to say, although he eyed us closely as
he saw the boys coming in like half-shot pigeons with their wings drooping and
their legs swollen. He had warned us before about cracking nuts in school and
said what the punishment would be. When he wasn't looking there would be a
lot of cracking and stuffing the shells into the hinges of the desks, and when we
had to stand up and lower the desk there was trouble. We went into school the
afternoon before the one I'm going to tell you about, and all was well. After the
singing came the handing out of slates to start writing. Suddenly I went white
and broke out in a sweat.

'Edward Roberts,' said Joseph, 'are you ill?'

Edward Roberts is my real name, you see; but I never hear it except from
him, and from Jane Jones of Tyddyn Derw when I go there to fetch milk. I
couldn't tell Joseph I was ill, because I wasn't; and I couldn't say I wasn't,
because I felt as if I was. I'll tell you what was the matter. My pencil was at the
bottom of my pocket, under all my nuts, and the nuts packed in so tightly that I
couldn't for the life of me get at it. All the boys saw immediately what the
matter was, because it wasn't anything new; but they couldn't offer to lend me
a pencil without Joseph seeing. There was nothing for it but to remain as I was
– looking at him without saying anything. Joseph thought I was going to faint
and he sent me out into the fresh air. And out I went as quickly as I could. In
this I failed. Old Joseph probably suspected as I was on my way out that I didn't
look as if I was going to faint at all, since I'd gone in two bounds. Off I went to
the back of the school out of sight, and I did my best to feel for the pencil on
the outside of the bottom of my trousers, until I was sweating. And I was
groaning and sweating when a shadow passed by me. I raised my head and I
very nearly did pass out. Who was standing over me, watching every move, but
Joseph. 'Ho, so this is the illness', he said. He caught hold of my ear and
leading me by the ear he took me inside. The other boys were afraid and
trembling by now. Joseph took me up to the desk.

'Find your pencil,' he said.

'I can't, sir,' said I.

'Where is it?' said he.

'In the bottom of my pocket, sir', said I. It's important to call Joseph 'sir' at
times like this.

I stressed the 'sir', for the future's sake, as they say. He made me take out all
the nuts, anyway; and with each fistful of nuts, I got a new pinch in my ear,

until I was howling, like Jinny my elder sister when Mam was piercing her ears with a darning needle, in order to give her elegant ear-rings ...

I emptied all the nuts by and by, but there was no pencil.

'Empty the other pocket', he said, changing his grip from one ear to the other. Well, there was no choice but to empty the other and place the nuts with the rest on his desk, and scream like a piglet in a pen at every pinch. After emptying them all out, the pencil wasn't there, either. I didn't know what to do, because I was beginning to see that the nuts in the other pockets, my jacket pockets, were in danger of going. And go they did, until there was one big pile of nuts on the teacher's desk, but after all this there was no pencil. I searched and I searched, with Joseph by now gripping me from behind by both my ears. Then I put a hand in the pocket where I usually kept my pencil; I pulled the pocket out, and to my surprise, what was in the bottom but a hole, and the pencil must have slipped through it. When Joseph saw the hole he let go my ears. I then had to hold out my hands and have two slaps, but not before he missed several times, because you see it's very natural for a creature to pull back his hand without knowing it, as the cane comes down, and to lift the knee on the same side as the hand at the same time. They must work on the same string, like the legs and arms of a monkey on a stick. I didn't stop doing that, either, until I felt that a blow on the knee hurts more than on the hand. The string must have broken after that blow, because I didn't raise my knee after that as I pulled my hand away. After I had gone to my place, Joseph addressed the whole school. He's stricter than the schoolmaster. They say he's expecting to become a schoolmaster himself before very long.

'Well,' he said, 'I've said what the punishment would be if I caught someone, and I've caught Edward Roberts. (He'd had it in for me for a long time, I'm sure.) 'The punishment is that I will fill my pockets with these nuts and throw the rest out into the road for everyone to pick up.'

He turned to the desk, filled the two back-pockets of his jacket, and walking back and fore in the school that afternoon he was for all the world like the pictures you see of women a long time ago when they used to wear what Mam calls a bustle.

Four o'clock, the children are let out, the load of nuts are collected from the desk and all hurled into the road, and Joseph stands in the school-door smiling, to watch the boys scrambling for them, and me leaning on the school-wall watching – I too was smiling, because I knew the boys better than Joseph did. After picking them all up, with not one left, my cousin Wmffre came up to me, and each one of the boys after him, and they gave me back all my nuts, stuffing them into my pockets. I raised my head to look at Joseph, and I saw him closing the door and going inside the school.

That's why Wmffre and I played truant the next afternoon. We knew Joseph wouldn't dare to do much to us, because he had seen that he wouldn't get the boys on his side.

from *Nedw* (1922), trans. Meic Stephens

IDRIS DAVIES (1905–53)

One Day by the Sea

Let's go to Barry Island,[1] Maggie fach,[2]
And give all the kids one day by the sea,
And sherbert and buns and paper hats,
And a rattling ride on the Figure Eight;
We'll have tea on the sands, and rides on the donkeys,
And sit in the evening with the folk of Cwm Rhondda,[3]
Singing the sweet old hymns of Pantycelyn[4]
When the sun goes down beyond the rocky islands.
Come on, Maggie fach, or the train will be gone
Then the kids will be howling at home all day,
Sticky with dirt and gooseberry jam.
Leave the washing alone for today, Maggie fach,
And put on your best and come out to the sun
And down to the holiday sea.
We'll carry the sandwiches in a big brown bag
And leave our troubles behind for a day
With the chickens and the big black tips
And the rival soup-kitchens, quarrelling like hell.
Come, Maggie fach, with a rose on your breast
And an old Welsh tune on your little red lips,
And we'll all sing together in the Cardiff train
Down to the holiday sea.

from *The Angry Summer* (1943)

Land of my Mothers

Land of my mothers, how shall my brothers praise you?
With timbrels or rattles or tins?
With fire.
How shall we praise you on the banks of the rhymneying[5] waters,
On the smoky shores and the glittering shores of Glamorgan,
On wet mornings in the bare fields behind the Newport docks,
On fine evenings when lovers walk by Bedwellty Church,
When the cuckoo calls to miners coming home to Rhymney Bridge,
When the wild rose defies the Industrial Revolution
And when the dear old drunken lady sings of Jesus and a little shilling.

[1]Barry Island, a seaside resort near Cardiff.
[2]*fach* (lit. 'small'), a term of endearment.
[3]*Cwm Rhondda*, the Rhondda Valley.
[4]Pantycelyn, William Williams (1717-91), one of the greatest of Welsh hymn-writers.
[5]rhymneying, from the river Rhymney in south-east Wales.

Come down, O girls of song, to the bank of the coal canal
At twilight, at twilight
When mongrels fight
And long rats bite
Under the shadows of pit-head light,
And dance, you daughters of Gwenllian,[1]
Dance in the dust in the lust of delight.

And you who have prayed in golden pastures
And oiled the wheels of the Western Tradition
And trod where bards have danced to church,
Pay a penny for this fragment of a burning torch.
It will never go out.

It will gather unto itself all the fires
That blaze between the heavens above and the earth beneath
Until the flame shall frighten each mud-hearted hypocrite
And scatter the beetles fattened on the cream of corruption,
The beetles that riddle the ramparts of Man.

Pay a penny for my singing torch,
O my sisters, my brothers of the land of my mothers,
The land of our fathers, our troubles, our dreams,
The land of Llewellyn[2] and Shoni bach Shinkin,[3]
The land of the sermons that pebble the streams,
The land of the englyn[4] and Crawshay's[5] old engine,
The land that is sometimes as proud as she seems.

And sons of the mountains and sons of the valleys
O lift up your hearts, and then
Lift up your feet.

[1]Gwenllian (d. 1136), a warrior-lady.
[2]Llewellyn, Llywelyn ap Iorwerth (1173-1240) or his grandson, Llywelyn ap Gruffudd (c. 1225-1282), Princes of independent Wales.
[3]englyn, a four-line verse written according to traditional rules of prosody.
[4]Shoni bach Shinkin (lit. Little Johnny Jenkins), used here to represent the common people.
[5]Crawshay, Crawshay Bailey (1789-1872), iron-master, commemorated in the song 'Cosher Bailey's Engine'.

Do You Remember 1926? [1]

Do you remember 1926? That summer of soups and speeches,
The sunlight on the idle wheels and the deserted crossings,
And the laughter and the cursing in the moonlit streets?
Do you remember 1926? The slogans and the penny concerts,
The jazz-bands and the moorland picnics,
And the slanderous tongues of famous cities?
Do you remember 1926? The great dream and the swift disaster,
The fanatic and the traitor, and more than all,
The bravery of the simple, faithful folk?
'Ay, ay, we remember 1926,' said Dai and Shinkin,
As they stood on the kerb in Charing Cross Road,[2]
'And we shall remember 1926 until our blood is dry.'

from Gwalia Deserta (1938)

Consider Famous Men, Dai Bach [3]

Consider famous men, Dai bach, consider famous men,
All their slogans, all their deeds,
And follow the funerals to the grave.
Consider the charlatans, the shepherds of the sheep!
Consider the grease upon the tongue, the hunger of the purse!
Consider the fury of the easy words,
The vulgarity behind the brass,
The dirty hands that shook the air, that stained the sky!

Yet some there were who lived for you,
Who lay to die remembering you.

Mabon[4] was your champion once upon a time
And his portrait's on the milk-jug yet.
The world has bred no champions for a long time now,
Except the boxing, tennis, golf, and Fascist kind,
And the kind that democracy breeds and feeds for Harringay.
And perhaps the world has grown too bitter or too wise
To breed a prophet or a poet ever again.

from Gwalia Deserta (1938)

---

[1]1926, the year of the General Strike.
[2]Charing Cross Road, in London, where unemployed miners were to be seen singing and begging.
[3]Dai, a diminutive of David . . . *bach* (lit. 'small'), a term of endearment.
[4]Mabon, William Abraham (1842-1922), miners' leader.

J. KITCHENER DAVIES (1902–52)

A Prayer

Supreme Doctor,
who carve with Your scalpel between the bone and the marrow,
hold Your hand from the treatment that would carve me
free from my fellows and my neighbourhood,
wholly apart from my household and family.
    Pilgrim of the wilderness,
do not set my steps on the martyrs' wandering path
and the loneliness of the soul's pilgrimage.
    O Father of Mercies, be merciful,
leave me my comrades' company, and my acquaintances' trust,
and the strength that is mine in my wife and children.
    Familiar of grief, do not grieve me
by baring the soft soul, leaving it skinned
of the protective shell that has been settling for half a century
as a layer of sloth over the spirit's daring,
so that not a grain of sand would disturb the core of my ego.
    I am too old and too weak and too happy in my world,
too comfortable, too self-satisfied,
to be shaken into the unknown in the teeth of Your whirlwind.
Let me lurk in the shelter of my hedges, and the nooks in my dyke.
    King of kings, legions of angels flying at Your summons,
volunteers glorying in Your livery — Your crown of thorns and Your five
    wounds —
stop pressing me and conscripting me to the hosts that are Yours
on the Sea of Glass and in the Far Country.
    Atonement who purchased freedom,
leave me in the cocktail parlour to shake them and share them
with the trivial customs of my civility
and the manners in fashion among my people.
Do not tangle me in my prayers like Amlyn[1] in his vow,
do not kill me at the altar by whose horns I have blasphemed, —
but let me, I pray, despite each wound, however hideous,
fail to be a saint.
    'Quo vadis, quo vadis,' where are you going?
Stop pursuing me to Rome, to a cross, my head towards the ground.
O Saviour of the lost,
save me, save me, save me,

[1]Amlyn, a friend of Amig (known in English as Amis and Amile), characters in a tale popular in
the Middle Ages.

from Your baptism that washes the Old Man so clean:
keep me, keep me, keep me,
from the inevitable martyrdom of Your elect.
Save and keep me
from the wind that is blowing where it will.
So be it, Amen,
   and Amen.

        from *'Swn y Gwynt sy'n chwythu'* (1953), trans. Joseph P. Clancy

JOHN DAVIES (1944–   )

The Bridge

Gareth, this photograph you sent
records August when we met again —
in a city this time like a rocket base.
White clusters judder at the sky.
Our vantage point's a spur of rock
and ahead a bridge, the Golden Gate,
takes off through floes of mist.

I was your second-in-command.
Talking, we watched all afternoon
quick ferry boats pay out the distances
that would always haul them back.
Now that you're at ease in sunlight west
of everywhere, roads you took
return east to Colorado then freeze up.

And we talked of another place,
the bleak hometown ten months before.
Rain rinsed the streets. Our father dead,
we'd gathered in an emptied house
to mourn new space between us all.
Comings, goings, made less sense.
Distance ahead blurred out the focus.

A year from now, ten years, let this bridge
still be there still strung firm
across flotations and coldwater miles,
this connection our father tightened
in a town of steel to show us
the meeting-point survives
and wherever we rediscover it is home.

PENNAR DAVIES (1911–   )
Gravity

Generous space and cunning time and cheerful energy
and light – yes, the light that manages
to travel consistently around six million million
miles per year – conspired
to fashion
today in Kingsway in Swansea
a meeting to really please them.

Today in the busy and noisy street
nine year old Owain gave a mischievous nod
full of unconditional friendship
to a brown-skinned, lively, comely-faced
slender and supple youth,
with leopard-like gait,
a youth from India or from Pakistan.
After a moment of astonished hesitation his smile
came as a generous and happy reply to the cheerful greeting.
For a pregnant second
the colours and continents were joined.
The first-born gravity,
that draws consciousness to consciousness,
vivacity to vivacity, body to body,
was revealed.
There flowed from the eyes of the one to the eyes of the other
the holy joy.
Between them leaped the victorious power
that proclaims
that our humanity is both one and various,
that each living soul is both unique and universal.

Is it not in this greeting,
in the gravity of the soul,
that our hope lies?
Was it not to reveal this gravity
that the lad was placed in the middle?
Was this not why we were told
to accept the kingdom like a child?
Is it not the most loathsome foolishness
that our fears and jealousies
and the tyranny of our maturity
prevent us from acknowledging each other
in such a droll and kind manner?

When they foresaw this greeting
the morning stars sang together.
In order to join in this greeting
Euclid the Pure laboured
and Holy Newton and Einstein the Blessed.

trans. Gwilym Rees Hughes

RHYS DAVIES (1903–78)
The Courting of Esther

We had nearly two years of peace after the twelve-month dispute.[1] And it was soon after our colliery began working that Esther allowed herself to be courted by a pit butty of her brother, a lodger needing to settle down in the usual way. His name was Gwilym. He had not taken part in any of the rioting, belonged to the Cambrian Male Voice Choir (eisteddfod[2] winners in their day), and was afflicted with a patience which, had it not derived from the respected virtue love brings to some men, could be called wishy-washy. To Esther his dogged wooing brought eighteen months of sombre procrastination, and if she did not really break a man's heart, this was because men's hearts in our heavily masculine world are not easily broken over baulked love. Silent about the courtship's preliminaries for some time, the whole affair bred an amount of strange humbug and evasions in her. I thought she spent her Wednesday evenings off at her brother's lodgings, where she was friendly with the landlady. Then one Wednesday she obtained my mother's permission to take me to the Empire Theatre in Tonypandy. I had not been there before; neither had Esther. In the street she whispered, 'You can keep your shilling for the seat. A friend will pay. But don't tell anyone, will you?' Her face had a hunted look under a straw hat decorated with flowers, and her person smelled of carbolic soap which she believed had a safe-guarding property against nasty things – I came to realize presently that for her I possessed the same property on these occasions.

Outside the chemist's shop on Tonypandy Square, an area busy enough for the assignation not to be noticed, her young man viewed me with surprise. Esther gave no explanation to him, and he courteously accepted my presence. Wearing a stiff collar and tie instead of a criss-crossed muffler, he did not speak much, looking steadily ahead out of pale grey eyes. He asked my age before buying the Empire tickets, and I was allowed in for half-price. We sat on a long hard bench in the pit. Esther placed me between her and Gwilym. She kept her eyelids down as if they would never lift in such a place. The seats became packed. An attendant bawled 'Close up', and, tightly wedged between Esther's rigid thigh and Gwilym's warmly thick one, I was too excited to be

[1] The twelve-month dispute, the Cambrian Strike (1910-11), during which the Tonypandy Riots occurred.
[2] *eisteddfod*, a cultural festival usually organized on a competitive basis.

bothered by the palpitating silence of the two courters. Great cerise curtains parted to reveal the only fairytale magic I knew in my upbringing . . . .

I always sat between the courters, and Esther's eyelids were always down, though she missed nothing. When we walked home, she told Gwilym outside our closed shop door, 'Next Wednesday,' nodded, and he stood there with a pinched smile until we vanished within. Proper courters went for their doting into the back lanes, where the mountain sheep wandered at night foraging for cabbage stalks and potato peelings. Allowing Gwilym to walk home with us after dark was Esther's only concession.

We were found out. A friend of my mother's had seen us twice in the Empire with the lovesick young man. Esther confessed, and my profitable chaperonage ceased. But my mother encouraged the courtship. She made it her responsibility to discover Gwilym's reputation. The report was sound. Esther, if inclined to choose a collier, couldn't do better. A first-class servant would be lost, but no doubt her married name would adorn a fresh double page of our black ledger; she and Gwilym would be trustworthy, teetotal and clean-minded.

Esther remained both inclined and not. Her Wednesday evenings became a privacy beyond my ken. But I was love's messenger for Gwilym, thus making some return for his Empire treats. He would hang about the collier's gossiping corner opposite the Central for hours, waiting for me to appear and take a folded scrap of paper to Esther. She would read the notes with a frown, and, never putting anything in writing for anyone, give me a verbal message to take back – 'Tell him I wasn't in a temper,' or 'Say I don't like menageries or concerts'. I found myself with a contempt of Gwilym's abject slavery to a girl familiar to me as the horse in our stable. Once or twice I avoided returning to him with her message. On some Saturday evenings, still waiting at the corner, he would hand me a quarter-pound bag of her favourite sweets, Rowntree's fruit gums. She would count the sweets and give me exactly half; if there was an odd number I had the extra one.

But at last she took to going into our back lane with him on Wednesday nights. This promising move began more than a year after my Empire treats. I knew about it because she came in that way, sharp at ten o'clock, instead of by the shop door. But nothing was said. The courtship went on for a further long while without incident. Once Gwilym handed me a brooch in a tiny box for her. Esther gave it a shrewd glance, said he must have won it at a hoopla stall in the fair, and later handed it to the woman who combed the gigantic Cambrian waste tip for saleable bits of coal. My contempt of Gwilym increased. I felt certain that he had never fingered Esther's mysterious bush.[1] However bad the winter weather he seemed to be waiting oftener at the corner, and I noticed his voice had become hoarse. Esther told me he had been missing choir practice. But he did not take to any drinking. This would have given her reason to arrive at the hard decision.

[1]Mysterious bush, a reference to the experience of the boy-narrator, who had often slept in the same bed as Esther.

Her flat-iron, while I sat at the other end of the table on homework evenings, would plunge down with more force than she had supplied formerly, her gob of testing spit issue more virulently. She tended to talk of Gwilym oftener, and derogatively. 'He comes from North Wales,' she would say. Or, 'He plays quoits in that field down by the river.' Or even, 'He sings in the Male Voice Choir.' These criticisms seemed undeserved even to me. Months had gone by when she said, 'Your father says there's going to be another strike. The bums I might have in if I get married.' Few disgraces were more terrible than bailiffs removing household possessions. A crowd of sightseers would gather to view the dramatic act, news of it passing rapidly from street to street.

'We're always having strikes,' I pointed out, not displeased at the prospect of another. Esther shook out a rolled bodice with an impatient flapping, and I added, 'Gwilym can find someone else.' Our chapel was full of unmarried girls, most of them singing louder and sweeter than anyone else.

Esther drew herself up, her eyelids shooting up too. 'He wants *me*!'

The predicted strike came. It was a more orderly one this time, and, for a while, all our Cambrian men did not come out. Gwilym remained in work. Yet this promising sign was of no avail. One Wednesday night Esther returned as usual through the back lane. But this time she entered our living-room with drama in her face. Her bared eyes looked distraught as eyes that have seen the supernatural. Panic lay in them, as it had when she returned from among the rioters. My mother was in the living-room. After a hard swallow and a jerking back of her shoulder, Esther announced at once, 'I must go back to the country now.' It was a month's notice. She had come to a decision at last. I heard no explanation of it. I did not ask her for one. Time was changing our old association, and I was to look at her with a new curiosity.

My mother attempted to make Esther think more carefully over the miserable retreat from courage. Herself critical of the coalmining life, none the less she had a deep admiration for most colliers' wives, and also (when she forgot the Ledger of Old Accounts) for the men's important struggles for better conditions and rewards. Besides, Esther hailed from a very poor Cardigan home; her farm-labourer father earned only eighteen shillings a week. My mother reminded her that there were plenty of other young men to choose from. But Esther would not budge. Her brother came to see her and failed in persuasions; and she refused to go out during the month's notice. Somewhere far away in me I felt an oddly welcome acceptance of her going. She departed with her roped tin trunk while – to my relief – I was at morning school.

It was a long time before I stopped missing her. My mother found a Clydach Vale girl to come in daily; she stole cocoa and soap from the shop, putting them up her elastic-edged knickers. We had three or four girls in quick succession, but not one was of the order of Esther, and each tried to impose her will on me by the usual method of accusation, to attempt to reduce confidence by inducing guilt. Except for a silver-frosted Christmas card one Christmas, Esther did not write to us. When I thought of her I imagined her milking in some lonely green fastness where a policeman was rare as a butterfly on an iceberg. She wore a thick flannel skirt, checked shawl and stout boots as she trudged with two pails to the stone dairy of a whitewashed farmhouse tucked away on a hymn-pure hillside. She had forgotten all the English words picked up so nimbly with us. She would marry a farmhand who put an X to documents requiring his signature, as some country-born colliers did, asking my father to witness it.

I was wrong. It must have been three or four years later – the Kaiser's war had begun – when one September afternoon I arrived home from the intermediate school at Porth to which I had passed by then, and found a lady visitor seated at the tea-table with my mother. Under a wide hat containing a sharp-eyed bird with outspread wings, she sat with an erectness conveying not only the discipline of a lengthy corset but correct visitor's manners. She looked altogether dressily well-off. It was Esther. She had given a cry when I slouched in with my satchel hanging from a shoulder:

'He's grown!'

My adolescent embarrassment lasted throughout tea. I ate and drank in an agony of uncertainty. Formerly it was her eyelids that were nearly always lowered, and mine up; mine kept down now, and her eyes shone on me without stint. My fingering of her bush had returned. Again I heard her grunt as she turned over. Had she *known?* I could scarcely accept that I had done such an act to this well-spoken lady whose corset made a tiny noise of creaking as she leaned forward to take a piece of sponge cake.

'Esther is married now,' my mother had said, and they soon resumed talk appropriate to their mutual status.

She had married into Insurance. Her husband, much older than herself, was district superintendent for one of the impressive companies, his area in West Wales extensive. They owned a bay-windowed house in a Cardiganshire coastal town, well away from the unbridled sea. The Welsh husband bore the astonishing Christian name of Alfonso. He went to London four times a year, but Esther had never gone with him there. Perhaps it was effort to be his contemporary – even to my furtive glance her clothes seemed too old for her – that made her look fifty or more to me, thus deepening my embarrassment. There was even a slight trace of compassionate patronage of my mother. As a married woman Esther was not only her equal but lived immune to the insecurities of such a place as the Rhondda, our everlasting strikes beyond the aid even of Insurance.

'Alfonso,' she said, 'is always praising my sponge cakes.' This was a salutation to my mother.

'Alfonso can't be a Cardigan name,' my mother remarked.

'No. Belonging to his family it is. He says there was a Spaniard long ago that was shipwrecked in Cardigan Bay and married his great-grandmother. A long, thin nose my Alfonso's got, and hair black and shiny as a beetle, forty-five though he was last birthday. A mop of hair he's got like you don't see anywhere in Cardigan.'

I stared hard at my plate, listening. I did not hear of any children. Esther had come to Clydach Vale that day to visit the brother she had once attempted to rescue from policemen's truncheons; he too had married, and a child had been born the week before. Gwilym was not mentioned while I sat at the table; but I already knew he had left Clydach Vale, to work in Cwmparc pits. I gladly escaped into the shop when my father came in for a quick cup of tea, and when he returned I went out for a walk. Esther had left by the time I returned. In the manner of visitors coming from the country, she had brought us a present. It was a plucked duck, and, since the weather was warm, she had stuffed it discriminately with sage leaves and a quartered onion.

from *Print of a Hare's Foot* (1969)

W.H. DAVIES (1871–1940)

The Kingfisher

It was the Rainbow gave thee birth,
  And left thee all her lovely hues;
And, as her mother's name was Tears,
  So runs it in my blood to choose
For haunts the lonely pools, and keep
In company with trees that weep.

Go you and, with such glorious hues,
  Live with proud Peacocks in green parks;
On lawns as smooth as shining glass,
  Let every feather show its marks;
Get thee on boughs and clap thy wings
Before the windows of proud kings.

Nay, lovely Bird, thou are not vain;
  Thou hast no proud, ambitious mind;
I also love a quiet place
  That's green, away from all mankind;
A lonely pool, and let a tree
Sigh with her bosom over me.

Leisure

What is this life if, full of care,
We have no time to stand and stare.

No time to stand beneath the boughs
And stare as long as sheep or cows.

No time to see, when woods we pass,
Where squirrels hide their nuts in grass.

No time to see, in broad daylight,
Streams full of stars like skies at night.

No time to turn at Beauty's glance,
And watch her feet, how they can dance.

No time to wait till her mouth can
Enrich that smile her eyes began.

A poor life this if, full of care,
We have no time to stand and stare.

Days that have Been

Can I forget the sweet days that have been,
    When poetry first began to warm my blood;
When from the hills of Gwent[1] I saw the earth
    Burned into two by Severn's silver flood:

When I would go alone at night to see
    The moonlight, like a big white butterfly,
Dreaming on that old castle near Caerleon,
    While at its side the Usk went softly by:

When I would stare at lovely clouds in Heaven,
    Or watch them when reported by deep streams;
When feeling pressed like thunder, but would not
    Break into that grand music of my dreams?

Can I forget the sweet days that have been,
    The villages so green I have been in;
Llantarnam, Magor, Malpas, and Llanwern,
    Liswery, old Caerleon, and Alteryn?

[1]Gwent, a region (now a county) in south-east Wales.

Can I forget the banks of Malpas Brook,
  Or Ebbw's voice in such a wild delight,
As on he dashed with pebbles in his throat,
  Gurgling towards the sea with all his might?

Ah, when I see a leafy village now,
  I sigh and ask it for Llantarnam's green;
I ask each river where is Ebbw's voice –
  In memory of the sweet days that have been.

CLIFFORD DYMENT (1914–70)

The Romance of Caerleon

The place I was taken to, at one month old, was the place in which I should like to have been born: my private and adopted native town, Caerleon-upon-Usk.

Caerleon, city and village, Isca Silurum. Isca Silurum, a name honouring the Silures, the intolerant mountain men of Monmouthshire and Glamorgan, whose land the Romans seized but had to hold in a grip of iron; Isca Silurum, garrison of the Second Legion of Augustus, six thousand soldiers, where generals composed victory marches on maps stretched over desks of marble, where the proud legionaries looked down on the mere auxiliaries and where glamorous legionary and glamorous auxiliary took the local girls from the local boys with a beam of bronze, silver, and gold; Isca Silurum, eyrie of the Roman eagle, crowded and loud with men, horses, and engines of war, where arrived baskets of quail, pheasant, peacock, thrush, dormice, and snails, trays of figs and cakes sweetened with honey, jars of wine and oil, nets of mullet, bags of shellfish, wagons of corn and pork sent in by the grumbling farmers, unpaid feeders of the army of occupation; Isca Silurum, along whose famous Roman roads walked goldsmiths, tinsmiths, armourers, wheelwrights, masons, glaziers, bakers, confectioners, cooks; walked soldiers to Mithraic caves; walked sporting men to the amphitheatre to watch chariot races, wild boar hunted in real woods and naval engagements fought on real water, gladiator killing gladiator, beast killing beast, gladiators and beasts killing each other. Isca Silurum, Britannia Secundus, outpost of Empire: Caesar, Consul, tribune, centurion, lictor; Julius, Claudius, Nero, Trajan, Hadrian; Suetonius, Frontinus, Agricola; aqueducts, highways, arches, villas; pottery, mosaic, enamel, fresco, bracelets, brooches.

Caerleon-upon-Usk, where King Arthur held his court and received tribute from vassal kings, earls, and barons, where mass for his household was celebrated in thirteen churches, where the courtiers slept on satin and fur, dined at silver tables inlaid with gold and pearl and ate off dishes of gold, silver,

and buffalo horn, where there was roast buck and flagons of mead and
minstrelsy and games; Caerleon-upon-Usk, where on festal days the flowers of
the field were outmatched in colour by the striped tents and flying pennants
and by the ladies' gowns and the lords' surcoats and the knights' glinting
armour and jewel-hilted swords; Caerleon-upon-Usk, where you walk on
grass over which the knights galloped to crash with each other in the jousts;
Caerleon-upon-Usk, where the daily round of polishing of shields, sharpening
of swords, washing of armour, shoeing of horses, where the ambitions were
tournaments and quests, where the talk was of sieges, brachets, harts, and
palfreys, of griffins, dragons, and the Sangreal, where the gossip was of
chivalrous knights and false knights and virtuous women.

Caerleon-upon-Usk, home, chapel, and workshop of Cistercians, who
ploughed, planted, and reaped in white habits that were streaked with loam
and the grease of sheep's wool and were thin at the knees from canonical hours
of kneeling; Caerleon-upon-Usk, where the years passed and the monastery
bell marked time across the fields until the monks departed and the iron rusted
and the tower toppled and there was no marking of time in Caerleon's fields.

from *The Railway Game* (1962)

MARION EAMES (1921–   )

Learning to Read

Rowland[1] had almost forgotten that this was Ellis's[2] first night at Bryn Mawr.
Observing the boy's thin face and his shyness, he smiled encouragingly at him.

'Welcome, Ellis Puw. I am rather late saying that, aren't I? You will be happy
at Bryn Mawr with Dafydd – and Huw,' he added hastily, seeing Huw Morris's
frown.

Ellis must be about sixteen. He had worked for seven years at Tyddyn
Garreg with Rowland's cousin, Lewis Owen. Knowing Lewis, Rowland was
sure that the lad would be well-grounded in farm work in spite of his youth.
Lewis, himself a good farmer, demanded full value, and more, from his
servants.

'Ellis Puw is a scholar, master.'

Rowland saw how the boy flushed at the sarcasm in Huw Morris's voice.

'Oh, good,' he replied lightly.

But Huw was not for letting the matter rest there.

'You should see the books we have in our loft now. Like a priest's cell, it is.'

'Leave the boy alone,' growled old Dafydd.

Not for the first time did Rowland regret having hired Huw Morris for
another season. Whenever the man opened his mouth the words struck like a
serpent's tongue. But he was a good worker and physically in his prime. Even

[1]Rowland, Rowland Ellis (1650-1731), Quaker leader, of Bryn Mawr, near Dolgellau, Mer.
[2]Ellis, Ellis Pugh (1656-1718), Quaker and author.

so, Rowland Ellis was unwilling to allow anyone to upset his household and it was obvious that the boy had already been harassed by Huw.

Meg laughed. 'Well, that's something new, for sure. Never before have we had a servant who could read. Who taught you, Ellis?'

The boy's flush deepened.

'Go on, tell your mistress, Ellis Puw,' goaded Huw.

'I cannot,' the boy whispered, his eyes fixed on the bottom of his empty bowl.

'Come, come, Ellis Puw,' Meg's urging was kindly enough. She smiled at Huw. 'Why can't you tell me?'

'No, it is not that I can't tell you.'

The boy raised his eyes and looked directly at her.

'I cannot read, mistress.'

After a moment's silence, Meg looked around in mock astonishment. 'Well, upon my word, what's all the fuss about?'

'That's enough of this teasing.'

Rowland turned deliberately to Dafydd.

'Did you see anything of the fair, Dafydd Jones?'

The old man caught the hint.

'A little, master, but not much. As soon as the leaves begin to change colour, this rheumatism of mine turns up like an old friend, and the journey to town is beginning to tell on the old bellows by now, too.'

The conversation took a new turn and the boy looked gratefully at Rowland Ellis, but he knew he had not heard the last of Huw Morris's teasing.

The men were leaving the kitchen for their own quarters when Rowland Ellis called out to his new servant.

'Wait a moment.'

Ellis turned back, and Rowland said to Meg, 'Your pardon, my love. I'd like to have a word with Ellis on his own.'

Meg raised her eyebrows and her voice betrayed her displeasure. 'Oh, very well.'

'I shall not be long.'

He opened the door for her and having closed it behind her, walked slowly towards the fireplace. Then he turned to the boy.

'Are you fond of books, Ellis Puw?'

'Yes, sir.'

'But you can't read.'

'Not – not yet, sir!'

'Have you any books?'

'Oh, yes, one or two.'

'Do you know what they are?'

'Oh, yes, Morgan Llwyd[1] – the one about the birds talking. The *Bibl Bach*. And *Llyfr y Resolusion*.'

---

[1] Morgan Llwyd (1619-59), Puritan and author.

Rowland smiled. 'Not many who *can* read really understand those books.'

'No, sir, I don't quite understand them either. But if someone reads to me, somehow I can remember the words. And by repeating a passage to myself over and over, the meaning comes. I don't know whether it's the right meaning or not. But I'm learning to read that way, too.'

'Where did you get these books, Ellis Puw?' asked Rowland curiously.

The boy's face reddened again and his lips tightened uncharacteristically. 'I'm afraid I cannot tell you, Rowland Ellis.'

'Why not? No one need be ashamed of having books.'

He laughed but was suddenly struck with dismay. Surely the boy had not stolen the books? As if sensing Rowland's suspicions, Ellis Puw said quickly, 'There's nothing wrong, master. Only ... only perhaps you wouldn't understand.'

'Very well then.' Rowland could see it was better to allow him to explain in his own good time ... 'Tell me, what about the works of Morgan Llwyd? Do you know anything about him?'

'Oh, yes,' said the boy eagerly. 'He died about forty years ago. He was a famous preacher in the time of the Commonwealth. Don't you know about his work, master?'

'I've heard a little,' said Rowland cautiously.

'Listen to this passage. This is one I have come to understand through repeating it over and over again.'

He took a deep breath, fixed his eyes on the dresser behind Rowland and began to recite in a low, excited voice.

'There is need for neither Bible nor preacher. The true preacher stands in the pulpits of our hearts and the Book within us will serve if we follow it as the Word, or a Candle burning inside us in a dark place. Instead of hearkening to voices from without, we should follow the Light and obey the Voice that is within.'

Rowland Ellis felt cold. He could listen to no more. These were dangerous words, dangerous ideas. Did Ellis Puw realise this? ...

'Don't you feel a freedom, a kind of promise in those words, master? Don't you?'

The boy's eyes and the unnaturally red spot on each cheek reminded Rowland of his brother Guto during the early days of his consumption. He turned to speak lightly.

'Were those the words of Morgan Llwyd? More likely the ramblings of a Quaker. Take care, Ellis Puw, or you could find yourself following the Dolserau family into Caetanws jail.'

Ellis looked as if Rowland had struck him.

'I'm sorry. I thought ... I heard that your father, Ellis Rees, in his day, sympathized with the Friends.'

Rowland noticed that the boy had used the original name for the strange sect that had earned the contemptuous title of 'Quaker'.

'My father was never one of those, Ellis Puw,' he said tersely. 'He once heard Vavasor Powell[1] preach in Dolgellau many years ago, and that had some influence on him, but as for those extremists – oh, no.'

Ellis shifted from one foot to another, waiting uncomfortably for leave to go.

'That is all,' said Rowland curtly. Then suddenly he felt ashamed. 'No. Wait a minute. Would you like to learn to read?'

Rowland was not likely to forget the intensity in the swift reply. 'More than anything else in the world.'

Almost before he had had time to think, he heard himself say, 'Very well. We'll start our first lesson tomorrow night before bedtime. Bring your books down here.'

The boy's face showed his gratitude more eloquently than words. Rowland almost regretted his impetuous offer so great was Ellis's pleasure. Let's hope I have not started something that will prove to be a snare, he thought.

from *Y Stafell Ddirgel* (1969), trans. Margaret Phillips, *The Secret Room* (1975)

TOM EARLEY (1911–   )

Rebel's Progress

When idle in a poor Welsh mining valley,
Dissatisfied with two pounds five a week,
I got invited to a marxist rally
And found to my amazement I could speak.

I soon could spout about the proletariat,
The bourgeoisie and strikes and lockouts too,
Could run an AGM or commissariat
As well as boss-class secretaries do.

At first I joined Aneurin Bevan's[2] party
But soon got disillusioned with all that.
Joined Harry Pollitt and became a commy,
They turned down all my pacifism flat.

The hungry thirties found me hunger marching
To squat with Hannington inside the Ritz.
Then PPU. For just this I'd been searching
Before the war and long before the blitz.

[1]Vavasor Powell (1617-70), Puritan preacher and author.
[2]Aneurin Bevan (1897-1960), Labour politician.

I liked the people in the Peace Pledge meeting
But found that they were holier than me,
So marched with Collins and quite soon was greeting
My former comrades in the CND.

To sit with Russell next became my hobby,
Vanessa Redgrave's fame I hoped to share,
Got thrown around in Whitehall by a bobby
And then a broken arm in Grosvenor Square.

So now I'll leave the politics to others
And not be an outsider any more.
I'll go back to the valley, to my mother's,
And never set my foot outside the door.

Except to go to chapel on Bryn Sion
And maybe join the Cwmbach male voice choir,
I'll sit at home and watch the television
And talk about the rugby by the fire.

JANE EDWARDS (1938–)

Only for a Walk

'Where did you get that pink lipstick?' I asked Margaret.

'Borrowed some from Helen next door,' she said. 'I'm going to buy some next time I go to Woolworth. Outdoor Girl: only costs tenpence.' I'd be ever so glad if Mam believed in buying a new one instead of that red thing that tastes old like Adam.

'Are you ready now?' Margaret asked. She was looking at her watch as if she was on tenterhooks.

'What's the hurry? Nothing calls,' said Mam.

'Doesn't she know then?' said Margaret when we were out of the entry.

'Gracious me no, or none of my feet would be out. Does your mother know?'

'She never bothers.'

We walk for a while without saying a word. That's the effect talking about mothers has on you.

Margaret said: 'That pink suits your suntan.'

'It's a bit big though.'

Margaret is a tall well-built girl and I'm a small skinny scrag. And when we walk together everyone turns his head to look at us. But because it's Saturday night there aren't so many about. Neli Harriet as usual is in the telephone kiosk. 'Looking for lovers, that's what she's doing,' said Margaret, 'they call it Neli Harriet's bungalow.'

Then Deina Jones Tyddyn toddles out of her house, a stained shawl over her shoulders. She stands stunned-like in our path, thrusts her nose into our faces. 'And where are you two going on a Saturday night like this, all made up as there never were a pair?'

'Date,' Margaret boasted.

'Points at your age! Home scrubbing floors or learning verses, that's your place. Does your mother know?' she asked me.

'She will now,' said Margaret, stepping out of her way.

'Is that a choir frock you're wearing?' she asked, feeling the stuff with her forefinger and thumb.

'Cheek!' I said to Margaret.

'A real busybody.'

It was beginning to get chilly by now. The sun had gone behind a cloud, and a breeze was blowing a leaf or two across the street.

'Where's that pretty green frock with long sleeves you had?' said Margaret.

'The one that made a paper noise? Gone too small.' It was Bill who liked that frock. 'I like your frock,' he said one afternoon as we stood by Nelson's Tower[1] looking at the others throwing stones into the river. 'It makes a noise like tissue paper.' His voice was different as if he were hoarse, or as if it were nearly breaking. 'Mam made it,' I said shyly, and left him. We didn't speak to each other for weeks afterwards. And we're still a bit bashful.

'I've got a pen-friend,' said Margaret. She pulled a piece of paper from her pocket. 'Through Radio Luxembourg. Perhaps I'll write to him tomorrow. Terry's his name, Terry Wayne O'Brien. Here's his address.'

'I like your handwriting,' I said.

'From London.'

'So I see. Gee, you've got good handwriting. Much better than mine. Everyone's saying you should have passed scholarship.'

'No one to push me.'

A kick for me, that one.

'Would you like Terry to find you a pen-friend?'

She was saying the name *Terry* as if she'd known him all her life. I honestly didn't like the way she said it.

'I wouldn't dare. Mam would half murder me.'

'Needn't worry, he could put his letter in with Terry's. We wouldn't be any the worse for trying. Perhaps he'd get a student for you.'

A student. Like Mr Harrington, who came to teach us Scripture and biology. Mr Harrington from somewhere far away like Surrey, his hair yellow as gold, his eyes blue and soft. Mr Harrington who was always so kind and tender. Mr Harrington who would duck under the desk every time he heard an aeroplane. Mr Harrington.

Margaret said, 'You're very quiet.'

'I was thinking.'

[1]Nelson's Tower, a monument near Llanfairpwll, Ang.

'Thought so. Perhaps you're nervous.'

'A little.'

'You're shivering.'

'Cold.'

'You should eat more. I get two dinners every day. School dinner and another when Dad gets home.'

That's why she's bonny. I can't stand food. That's why I'm scraggy. 'Perhaps I'd better nip home and fetch my cardigan.'

'There's no time. The boys won't wait for us. Hey, do you like my scent? It's Evening in Paris.' She lifts her hair so that I can sniff behind her ear.

'Mmm . . . nice. Nain had some of that from Auntie Meri as a Christmas box. A small blue bottle with the Eiffel Tower on it. Nain only uses it for chapel. Two spots on her handkerchief.'

'You're not supposed to put scent on clothes.'

'Leusa says the nuns say that only people who don't wash use scent,' I said, to stop her having the last word every time.

'Huh! They need it. Do you know what I hear?'

'What?'

'That they go to bed in their clothes.'

'Never!'

'Do you know what else I heard? They daren't look at themselves in a glass or in a shop-window, or look at their breasts when they change underwear.'

'I don't either,' I said shyly.

'Well, you should. How will you know one isn't bigger than the other? Or that you haven't got three like that woman in the *News of the World*?'

The *News of the World* is terrible. It's got stories to raise the hair on your head, and keep you awake all night. True stories about women turning into men and men turning into women, and every calamity that could hit you.

I've got goose pimples all over me. My inside is shaking like a jelly. My feet are like ice blocks and my scalp is tight and hard. My nose is red. Red and ugly as usual.

I said, 'What about turning back?'

'Turning back? No fear. Afraid or something?'

It's easy for her to talk: she knows this Frank boy. Been with him before. But not one of us has ever seen Henri, though she seems to think he's a farm-hand.

A farm-hand! My dreams don't include farm-hands. My dreams turn round students. Tall handsome students with long scarves around their necks. Students with piles of books under their arms. Merry, noisy students like those I see from the bus at Bangor. Nice respectable students – ministerials like the ones who come for a walk with us to Llyn Rhos Ddu before evening service. Like Mr Harrington.

'How old is this Henri?' I asked as we neared Fern Hill.

'Same age as Frank, I suppose.'

'How old is Frank?'

'Twenty-one.'

'Twenty-one. Heavens above, that's old.'

'You've moaned enough about schoolboys being too young for you. Don't worry. Everything will be all right as long as you don't let Henri put his tongue in your mouth.'

'Put his tongue in my mouth? Ugh!'

'It's a boy's place to try, a girl's place to refuse him.'

'Does Frank try?'

'Every boy tries.'

'What did *you* do?'

'Tell him not to.'

'And he listened?' If anyone tried it on me he'd never see the colour of me again.

'Of course he did. Do you know Olwen? Do you know what Olwen did to a boy from Llangefni way last Saturday night?' She looks into the quick of my eyes and smiles. 'She bit off a piece of his tongue.'

'Bit it off?' I can't swallow because there's a lump like a potato in my throat.

'He had to go to hospital for four stitches.'

I feel quite ill, am cold all over from thinking what I'd do should this boy Henri try such nonsense. Henri's a silly name. An old-fashioned, ugly name. A name to put anybody to shame. How can anyone with a name like that be handsome?

'Why?' I asked coyly, 'why do boys want to put their tongues in your mouth?'

'To make you sleep, of course.'

'Oh!'

'And while you're asleep they lift up your clothes, pull down your knickers and give you a baby.'

I feel my legs giving under me. I feel my inside caving in. I was always a one for jibbing it.

'I'm not coming,' I said, looking in the roadside for a comfortable place to sit.

'Don't talk rot. Come on,' said Margaret, taking hold of my cold hand with her warm white hand. It was like a picture of a hand in a catalogue.

'I'm shivering,' I said and showed her my arms. 'Look how cold I am. I'd better go home before I catch pneumonia.'

'You won't, stupid. Henri'll warm you up like a piece of toast. Anyway, it's too late for you to turn back now.'

It's never too late. Never ever ever too late. I can run as if the devil himself was after me.

'I can hear a motor bike coming,' said Margaret. 'It's them, I tell you. Here, straighten your frock.'

It's Frank who owns the motor bike. 'Hello, girls,' he says after slapping the pedal with his heel and raising his goggles to have a look at us. He's trying to smile like a film star.

'Here's my friend,' said Margaret. And she gave me a shove towards the boy on the pillion.

'Has she got a tongue?' Frank asked.

'A tongue! Do you hear that?' said Margaret, laughing and winking at me.

'Henri, give Mags your helmet, and then we'll leave you two in peace,' said Frank.

'You needn't go,' I said sheepishly.

But away they went, and before I knew where to turn I was in Henri's arms, my head out of sight in his armpits. And I'd have stayed there all the time, even though his coat was coarse and smelled, like someone's breath in the morning. But in a while he asked, 'What about a kiss?' 'What about a kiss?', he said a second time, and put his thumb under my chin.

He had a red face and red hair and a voice that made you think of manure and pigs and muck-raking and the like.

'You're much too tall for me. I've got a crick in the neck,' I said, fed-up with his wet kisses.

'What about going to lie down in the fern?' he said.

Only lovers with bad intentions lie in the fern. 'We'll sit on the roadside,' I said.

And there we sat for I don't know how long without speaking or looking at each other.

'A motor bike's lovely,' Margaret said after the boys had turned for home. 'Would you like to have a go some time?'

'You were a long time,' I said, close to tears. 'I'd got tired of waiting for you.'

'You've got grass stains on your frock,' she said. 'Grass stains are difficult to get off. Your mother'll be raving when she sees it.'

Mam was in the wash-house, carrying hot water from the boiler and was in a lather of sweat.

'Where have you been, girl?' she asked, though she couldn't see anything through the steam.

'Only for a walk,' I said, 'only for a walk.'

from 'Blind Date', trans. Derec Llwyd Morgan

OWEN M. EDWARDS (1858–1920)

Owain Glyn Dŵr [1]

But the common people of Wales did not lose their respect and their love of the leader in his day of misfortune. For years he wandered among his people and he was never betrayed. Owain Glyn Dŵr's career can be summed-up in two phrases – defender of the common people, and the incarnation of love of country. Love of country prepared him for his life's work; the common people's love for him, and their faith in him, gave him strength to pursue it

[1]Owain Glyn Dŵr (*c.* 1354 – *c.* 1416), national hero, known in English as Owen Glendower.

from day to day. He drew his inspiration from the history of Wales; he saw the splendour, half-imagined it is true, of her ancient kings. His letters to the king of Scotland and to the Irish princes are redolent of the dreams of a student of history. He saw the common people of his country writhing under oppression, enduring the tyranny of lordling and official, and with a keener edge on their suffering for having had a glimpse of a better life. He gave them a nobler ideal than merely that of hanging stewards and burning manorial rolls, the pedigree charts of their subjection. He gave a direction to blind resentment – national unity and a university. And no one has ever been loved as the common people of Wales loved Owain Glyn Dŵr. Llywelyn[1] is a figure in history, but Owain Glyn Dŵr is as if he were still alive with the nation, and it is no wonder that like Moses and Arthur,[2] the location of his grave is not known. The poets sang their longing for his return, and the common people awaited his coming. They believed they would encounter him again on their way, that he would lead them to a higher freedom; they would not have it that he was dead.

from *Llynnoedd Llonydd* (1922), trans. D.M.Lloyd

The Welsh Not

The school was in Y Llan,[3] a few miles from where I lived. It belonged to the landowner, as did almost the entire district, and his wife, a tall dignified lady, took a great interest in the education of the locality. When I first went to the school it had a schoolmistress. I was taken to the school-house; school had already begun and not a child was to be seen in Y Llan. The schoolmistress appeared, a small woman with piercing eyes, her hands held folded in front of her. She spoke a little Welsh, the common people's language, with an English accent; her language, obviously, was English, the gentlefolk's language, the language of the parson from Cardiganshire. She could smile only when speaking English. Her face was very sour because she was obliged to degrade herself by speaking Welsh; indeed, it was sourness I always saw in her countenance, except when her thin face wore a smile to meet the generous lady who paid her wages. I did not listen to her words, and I did not like her face; it brought to mind the nose of the she-fox that I saw once, close up, after dark.

'My boy,' said my mother, 'here is your new teacher. Look at her, take the peak of your cap from your mouth, she is going to teach you everything. Shake hands with her.'

She offered me her hand, with a weak smile dying on her face – 'Oh, we shall,' she said (in Welsh), 'we'll teach him everything he needs to know; we'll teach him how to behave.'

[1] Llywelyn, Llywelyn ap Gruffudd (*c.* 1225-1282), the last Prince of independent Wales, killed by Anglo-Norman forces near Builth.
[2] Arthur (late 5th cent. – early 6th cent.), British military leader about whom there exist many tales which have been incorporated into English literature.
[3] Y Llan, Llanuwchllyn, near Bala, Mer., the author's birth-place.

It was not to learn how to behave that I wanted, but how to make a bridge and build a chapel. A great desire came over me to go home with my mother; but it was with the schoolmistress I had to go. The school's door was opened; I heard a strange din, and I could see children packed tight together on many benches. There were two open spaces on the floor of the school, and I could see two people on their feet, one in each open space. I understood later that they were the assistant master and mistress. The schoolmistress took me to one of them, but I only recall the words 'a new boy' from what she said. I could read Welsh quite well by then, and I was put in a class of children who were beginning to read English. The reading-book was one of the SPCK's, and I still loathe those letters, on account of the cruelty I suffered while trying to read from that book. The teacher was a pleasant fellow, and he was kind to me, but after the reading-lessons he went back to his other pupils. The word soon went around that someone new, and ridiculous at that, had come to the school. Several of the cruel children had their eye on me – I knew about them all, loud-mouthed children from Y Llan most of them were, and they never amounted to much. The teacher had whispered to me not to speak a word of Welsh; but these naughty boys did all they could to make me raise my voice, and in the end they succeeded. I lost my temper and I began to speak my mind to the treacherous busybody who had contrived to torment me. As I began to speak my rich Welsh everyone laughed, and a cord was put around my neck, with a heavy wooden block attached to it. I had no idea what it was, I had seen a similar block on a dog's neck to stop it running after sheep. Perhaps it was to prevent me from running home that the block was hung around my neck? At last it was mid-day, the time to be released. The schoolmistress came in with a cane in her hand. She asked a question, and every servile child pointed a finger at me. Something like a smile came across her face when she saw the block around my neck. She recited some long rhyme at me, not a word of which could I understand, she showed me the cane, but she did not touch me. She pulled off the block and I understood then that it was for speaking Welsh that it had been hung around my neck.

That block was around my neck hundreds of times after that. This is how it was done, – when a child was heard uttering a word of Welsh, the teacher was to be told, then the block was put around the child's neck; and it was to stay there until he heard someone else speaking Welsh, when it was passed on to the next poor child. At school's end the one who was wearing it would be caned on his hand. Each day the block, as if by its own weight, from all parts of the school, would come to end up around my neck. Today I take comfort from the fact that I never tried to seek respite from the block by passing it on to another. I knew nothing about the principle of the thing, but my nature rebelled against this damnable way of destroying the foundation of a child's character. To teach a child to spy on a smaller one who was speaking his native language, in order to pass on the punishment to him! No, the block never came off my neck and I suffered the cane daily as school drew to its close.

from *Clych Atgof* (1906), trans. Meic Stephens

The Old Chapel

I confess that I am no objective critic. Childhood impressions are indelible; I am forced to feel that more and more. Although I am no singer the music of Welsh airs and hymn-tunes is part of my soul; in spite of myself I find that I appreciate every other music according as it resembles or differs from these. You have not seen the old chapel at Llanuwchllyn, by the still water, the roof no higher than that of the villagers' houses around it. Its walls were bare, except where patches of damp had given a slight variation to the colour; the benches were sometimes comfortable and sometimes hard – according to the sermon; the windows long and narrow and without ornament, save when the frost drew pictures on them. And yet, that is the most beautiful place where I have ever been. It is the place where I began to think, it was there I fell in love for the first time, there I felt the dread of damnation and the joy of forgiveness; my ambition was first aroused there, and my pride laid low by having it enforced on me that I was wholly without merit – every thought and feeling of greater profundity than the course of daily living, human and divine, direct me back to that old grey chapel. It was void of all architectural and pictorial beauty, but through a window opposite our bench I could see the rain driven by gusts of wind across the mountain-slopes, and a roan tree curved by the prevailing winds into a form of such elegance that it would be the despair of any artist to reproduce the delicate beauty of its branches. The old chapel and its people are greatly changed, now, but when thoughts of heaven visit my unsettled mind, – you will probably smile to hear me say so – but paradise to me is exactly like the old chapel at Llanuwchllyn – the people seated in families on their benches, everyone just the age they then were, the preaching, the jubilant singing, and the plaintive sigh of the wind, and that old roan tree.

from *O'r Bala i Geneva* (1889), trans. D.M. Lloyd

ISLWYN FFOWC ELIS (1924–   )

The Old Woman of Bala [1]

'Oh, while I remember,' said Seeward, sitting in his seat at the steering-wheel. 'I happened to ask in the office just now whether there was anyone around here who might be able to speak Welsh. Everyone looked at me oddly at first, but then one of the men told me there's an old woman living in this street who's more or less off her head and who sometimes founders in a strange language. Would you like to see her, just in case?'

The Professor looked at me anxiously and then nodded to Seeward who drove the car on a little way, stopped in front of a chip-shop and went inside.

[1] By means of a time-machine, Ifan Powell, the narrator, is projected into the Wales of the future and is taken on a visit to Bala in the year 2033.

He came out after a minute or two and signalled to us. We went through the chip-shop into a small dark room at the back. There, in the corner, an old woman was sitting, with her head lolling back in a half-sleep. A woman of about forty, of a quite dirty appearance and an impatient air, was standing by her.

'I don't know,' she said. 'We've always lived 'ere, but I never 'eard any of your Welsh. My mother-in-law 'ere gabbles something sometimes my 'usband and me can't understand. You can try 'er if you like.'

Richards sat down right in front of the old woman and said in Welsh, 'How are you, my dear? Are you feeling well?'

The old woman opened her eyes and looked at him lifelessly.

'Mm? Who are you?' she said, in English.

'I am speaking Welsh to you, old woman,' said the Professor. 'Can you speak Welsh?'

'Eh? I don't know you,' said the old woman, again in English.

The Professor made several more attempts, but in vain. Then I asked whether I could try. The Professor got up and I sat in his place, holding the old lady's hands. I wanted to hear her say just one word of Welsh more than anything in the world, she was someone who had lived in my own time and spoken my language ... I wanted to hear her say *something* that would show that the vandals had not *completely* destroyed my Wales for ever, especially not in Bala ...

'Old woman,' I said in Welsh, 'Do you know this? Try to remember.' And I recited slowly in Welsh: 'The Lord is my Shepherd; I shall not want. He maketh me to lie down in green pastures ...' The old woman's eyes closed. Well, that's it, I said to myself. But I went on. 'He restoreth my soul. He leadeth me ...' Suddenly, I realized that the old woman's lips were moving. She was reciting the Welsh words with me. She opened her eyes and her voice grew stronger and stronger ... 'Yea, though I walk through the Valley of the Shadow of Death, I shall fear no evil ...' And when she came to the last words of the Psalm she uttered them with a force in her voice and a light in her eyes such as I never saw before or have seen since.

'And I shall dwell in the House of the Lord for ever ... Who are you, my boy?' She turned her shining eyes upon me, still speaking in Welsh. 'Are you Meri Jones's boy? They've moved Thomas Charles's[1] statue from by the chapel, you know ... it was those English who ...' She gripped the arms of her chair and sat bolt upright. 'They did it, with their old noise and their wood and their regulations ... it was them ...' And then, in English, she said, 'But I don't know you, do I?' She sank back once again, her eyes glazing over. 'I don't ... know anything now ...'

I got up and left the room. I had seen with my own eyes the death of the Welsh language.

from *Wythnos yng Nghymru Fydd* (1957), trans. Meic Stephens

[1] Thomas Charles (1755-1814), Methodist leader.

Before I Go

If I had only a month to live, and knew it, and that month were wholly and absolutely mine, what would I do? I could sit out of sight in my chair to wither away, or I could go out into the highways and hedges to preach hell fire. But neither is a good way to prepare for the world to come.

I think I would spend the month bidding farewell. Not to people – that is distressing – but to the places that have been woven into my fabric, to extricate myself from them one by one.

I would go to my old school. Not because my days there were happy ones. They were not. But because I cannot forget the knocking of the wind in its windows and the rattling of its doors as they closed. I gazed so often at the trees and high pastures before it that they might well follow me from this world unless I go back to them and demolish them in my eyes. The window seat is warm beneath my thighs and the trees quiver about the stream in the June heat. The grass is tall and I am burrowing through it at the tail end of a row of rough-hewn children. I am eating my lunch on the school yard and have no appetite for it. I am fighting someone by the wall, my pink legs stung by nettles. It is raining, and we are acting a silly play in the cloakroom, each with his jersey over his head as if we were doing a masque. I say the Lord's Prayer recklessly in the sun and the girls say hush. The bell is tinkling . . . I must go back, and everything will have changed. There will be other pictures on the wall and other voices in the yard, and the sun will be twenty years older. Good-bye, old school; I am grateful now that I was not happier in you.

I would go to Trofa Celyn. There the brook talks to itself under a big holly tree; children laugh by the wooden shop a hundred yards away. There stands the stile where the path past Y Gelli begins. I wonder if the Ty'n y Celyn bull will be on that path when I walk it for the last time? I tore my trousers on the thorn bushes once as I scrambled through the hedge out of its way, although it did not so much as raise its head; it was only my fear. There were primroses on the path past Y Gelli long ago, and wild strawberries in the hedge, and sloes among the hawthorns. I played many a game of football there on my way from school, with myself as captain, and led my bloody crew through Arctic ice and across the Sahara. And later I lay there with the lads to talk about girls, the pine trees making the slope across the river a little Switzerland. There are blackberries every August where the sun draws shadows from the tall oaks, and the rivulets never dry up in the bog. I shall go there again when I have only a month to live, and I must not stay too long.

I would go to Hafod y Garreg bridge, to hear the water stumbling over the stones and drop a stone deep into the pool. The water is warm under the larches and small grass grows along the edges of the cart-track. Only once did I ever try fishing, and that near Hafod y Garreg bridge; I hooked one of the branches above and broke my heart. I was there often at sheep-washing time. Once a farmer fell in, the water reaching to his waist; he stood there smiling broadly, and I felt sorry for him. The sheep bounce wet up the road, throwing

off showers of droplets that form brief rainbows in the sunlight, and the dogs
go crazy. I am there again with a friend, then with a sweetheart, the purring of
the water heard far away.

From there, up the green path towards Craig y Pandy. No one walks along
the green path. The grass upon it is tall with moss at its base, and the gate has
sunk deep into the nettles under the hazels. I cross the hard road and start on a
second green path, rising above the valley which I leave askew below me.
Sunlight winks on the rock; sheep chew their cud in the hollows. I am standing
on the rock, the valley like a map beneath me. Toy lorries snail along the
winding road past the dolls' houses and little black figures go in and out under
the public house eaves. I grow on the rock; I am ten years old with a family
crowd, seventeen with Chaucer in my lap and an aeroplane in the blue above,
twenty-two with a friend beneath the moon, twenty-five with my *fiancée*, and
the map remains the same. When I am gone, someone else will be here with
my map.

Up through the ferns – shy little curls in June, a rust-red carpet in October –
up through the gorse to the Windy Stile, where I lay my hand on the gate by the
tree. I see myself going through it a hundred times, turning my head to where
the sun drops like an orange into the saddle between the two mountains.
There, in the wind, I am thrown against the gate and fight with it to open it,
and I see the trees up the valley bent like horses' manes over the pastures. And
the sheaves are ungathered still.

I would go again to gather whinberries on the slopes of Y Foel, below the
Tower ruin. I would tire my feet as I tired them so often long ago, the hems of
my shorts blue-black from the whinberry bushes. We wander, each his own
way, fanning out apart; the hours pass without a word; I lift my head and see
the others out of earshot. I fall on my knees and drink the clear water of the
Dramhouse Stream; we open the hamper and eat our lunch in the shelter of
one of the shooting butts, and our tea on Craig Williams lawn in the shade of
the trees. Here is mile upon mile of heather, a forgotten land, its silence
unbroken except by the croak of grouse in the heath-clumps. And in the midst
of it all, a bare-legged boy with a quarter-filled can in his hand; his lips are
black and his name is mine.

But maybe my calendar is wrong. Maybe I ought to visit these places last, as
it is they that I knew first. Their roots are stouter within me and harder to
extract; it would be better to destroy myself in these places in the last hours
before I go. There are other places that are not so much a part of me, but I
could not leave those either without bidding them farewell.

There is a spot in the commote of Eifionydd,[1] on the road between
Llanaelhaearn and Four Crosses, where I am walking on a May afternoon.
There are two of us, our young breasts swelling with spring, our talk drunk
with larks and gorse bloom. Never did gorse bloom as it did that year, aflame in
every hedge, its scent like that of coco-nut in the merest breeze. I do not

[1]Eifionydd, a commote in north-west Wales.

remember what we talked about, but I do remember how blue the sky was, and how blue the sea in the distance, and I remember the yellow fire in the hedgerows. We turned off the road and plunged into a copse above the river, where we could not walk without treading on bluebells. I remember being intoxicated with a couplet by Williams Parry[1] –

> For the earth and water and air
> of Eifionydd are my peace

– and lashing out later at someone who failed to see its glory. But he had not been in Eifionydd that day. The road between Four Crosses and Llan-aelhaearn also awaits my return, and I am not sure that I wouldn't kiss the tarmac, so sacred is it to me.

I would go to see Anglesey once more. Not because there is much beauty in its flat, treeless miles, but because of the ancient tranquillity on its acres. The shippons that sleep in the stillness and the blueness from the top of Mynydd Eilian on a summer's day. I would have to go by train over the Suspension Bridge between the four fat lions, then change and travel in a rickety little car along the road to Llangefni. But there is beauty in Anglesey too. There is beauty in Benllech, and for all I know the caravan may still be there where we fried fish fresh from the bay with new potatoes and peas, and slept so heavily in the salt air, the sun an itch in our skins. There is beauty on the road from Menai Bridge to Beaumaris between the woods and the Spanish-style wall, from which the mountains of Arfon appear heads down in the blue waters of Menai. I would go again to Anglesey. And I would stop only a moment by Branwen's[2] grave and doff my hat in the sunset and leave quietly, lest I too suffer her fate before I finish my round of farewells.

I would go again to Soar. Of all the Soars that stand grey-walled on the slopes of Wales there is only one Soar for me. My grandfather is not in the elders' pew today with his white beard and black velvet cap, but the organ emits the same old squeak and the pew under my nose the same smell of paint during the prayer. They are still singing in Soar; the doors are open on a June evening and the swallows twitter in the eaves. I sing alto, a boy among the women, exulting in the lah-te-doh at the end of the tune 'Capel Tygwydd'. I still see the Mount of Olives in the trees through the window and Jesus teaching his disciples by the fence in the wood. The Apostle Paul stands before Felix in the elders' pew; Palestine fills the chapel. The afternoon preacher goes on and on, and the clock is too tired to move its hands. The congregation rises to sing and I, my voice breaking, sing tenor an octave too low and think about the row in school next day for failing to finish my maths. Soar. It would be sad if I turned back at the door and failed to go in lest I break the holy pictures at memory's gates. But I might well turn back, for Soar is my testimonial that however

---

[1]Williams Parry, R. Williams Parry (1884-1956), a poet.
[2]Branwen, a heroine in *The Mabinogion*, the wife of Matholwch, King of Ireland, reputed to have been buried in Anglesey.

complex I may be today and however difficult, I loved my Saviour dearly when I was only a youngster between its walls.

I could visit these places with my eyes quite dry, if life has become a burden. But that is brave talk. When the day comes to cross the stile at Trofa Celyn, to pluck blackberries for the last time on the path past Y Gelli, to drop a stone into the water from Hafod y Garreg bridge and to stand with my hair in the wind on Craig y Pandy, my eyes could well be as moist as a rose after a shower. I rather think that these places are embedded more deeply within me than I know, and that the fate which gave me a month's warning before I go would be less than kind.

from *Cyn Oeri'r Gwaed* (1952), trans. the author

CARADOC EVANS (1878–1945)

Be This Her Memorial [1]

Mice and rats, as it is said, frequent neither churches nor poor men's homes. The story I have to tell you about Nanni–the Nanni who was hustled on her way to prayer-meeting by the Bad Man, who saw the phantom mourners bearing away Twm Tybach's coffin, who saw the Spirit Hounds and heard their moanings two days before Isaac Penparc took wing–the story I have to tell you contradicts that theory.

Nanni was religious; and she was old. No one knew how old she was, for she said that she remembered the birth of each person that gathered in Capel[2] Sion; she was so old that her age had ceased to concern.

She lived in the mud-walled, straw-thatched cottage on the steep road which goes up from the Garden of Eden, and ends at the tramping way that takes you into Cardigan town; if you happen to be travelling that way you may still see the roofless walls which were silent witnesses to Nanni's great sacrifice–a sacrifice surely counted unto her for righteousness, though in her search for God she fell down and worshipped at the feet of a god.

Nanni's income was three shillings and ninepence a week. That sum was allowed her by Abel Shones, the officer for Poor Relief, who each pay-day never forgot to remind the crooked, wrinkled, toothless old woman how much she owed to him and God.

'If it was not for me, little Nanni,' Abel was in the habit of telling her, 'you would be in the House of the Poor long ago.'

At that remark Nanni would shiver and tremble.

'Dear heart,' she would say in the third person, for Abel was a mighty man and the holder of a proud office, 'I pray for him night and day.'

---

[1] The dialogue in this story purports to imitate (to some extent) the syntax and vocabulary of spoken Welsh.
[2] *Capel*, chapel.

Nanni spoke the truth, for she did remember Abel in her prayers. But the workhouse held for her none of the terrors it holds for her poverty-stricken sisters. Life was life anywhere, in cottage or in poorhouse, though with this difference: her liberty in the poorhouse would be so curtailed that no more would she be able to listen to the spirit-laden eloquence of the Respected Josiah Bryn-Bevan. She helped to bring Josiah into the world; she swaddled him in her own flannel petticoat; she watched him going to and coming from school; she knitted for him four pairs of strong stockings to mark his going out into the world as a farm servant; and when the boy, having obeyed the command of the Big Man, was called to minister to the congregation of Capel Sion, even Josiah's mother was not more vain than Old Nanni. Hence Nanni struggled on less than three shillings and ninepence a week, for did she not give a tenth of her income to the treasury of the Capel? Unconsciously she came to regard Josiah as greater than God: God was abstract; Josiah was real.

As Josiah played a part in Nanni's life, so did a Seller of Bibles play a minor part in the last few days of her travail. The man came to Nanni's cottage the evening of the day of the rumour that the Respected Josiah Bryn-Bevan had received a call from a wealthy sister church in Aberystwyth. Broken with grief, Nanni, the first time for many years, bent her stiffened limbs and addressed herself to the living God.

'Dear little Big Man,' she prayed, 'let not your son bach religious depart.'

Then she recalled how good God had been to her, how He had permitted her to listen to His son's voice; and another fear struck her heart.

'Dear little Big Man,' she muttered between her blackened gums, 'do you now let me live to hear the boy's farewell words.'

At that moment the Seller of Bibles raised the latch of the door.

'The Big Man be with this household,' he said, placing his pack on Nanni's bed.

'Sit you down,' said Nanni, 'and rest yourself, for you must be weary.'

'Man,' replied the Seller of Bibles, 'is never weary of well-doing.'

Nanni dusted for him a chair.

'No, no; indeed now,' he said; 'I cannot tarry long, woman. Do you not know that I am the Big Man's messenger? Am I not honoured to take His word into the highways and byways, and has He not sent me here?'

He unstrapped his pack, and showed Nanni a gaudy volume with a clasp of brass, and containing many coloured prints; the pictures he explained at hazard: here was a tall-hatted John baptizing, here a Roman-featured Christ praying in the Garden of Gethsemane, here a frock-coated Moses and the Tablets.

'A Book,' said he, 'which ought to be on the table of every Christian home.'

'Truth you speak, little man,' remarked Nanni. 'What shall I say to you you are asking for it?'

'It has a price far above rubies,' answered the Seller of Bibles. He turned over the leaves and read: '"The labourer is worthy of his hire." Thus is it written. I will let you have one copy – one copy only – at cost price.'

'How good you are, dear me!' exclaimed Nanni.

'This I can do,' said the Seller of Bibles, 'because my Master is the Big Man.'

'Speak you now what the cost price is.'

'A little sovereign, that is all.'

'Dear, dear; the Word of the little Big Man for a sovereign!'

'Keep you the Book on your parlour table for a week. Maybe others who are thirsty will see it.'

Then the Seller of Bibles sang a prayer; and he departed.

Before the week was over the Respected Josiah Bryn-Bevan announced from his pulpit that in the call he had discerned the voice of God bidding him go forth into the vineyard.

Nanni went home and prayed to the merciful God: 'Dear little Big Man, spare me to listen to the farewell sermon of your saint.'

Nanni informed the Seller of Bibles that she would buy the Book, and asked him to take it away with him and have written inside an inscription to the effect that it was a gift from the least worthy of his flock to the Respected Josiah Bryn-Bevan, D.D., and she requested him to bring it back to her on the eve of the minister's farewell sermon.

She then hammered hobnails into the soles of her boots, so as to render them more durable for tramping to such capels as Bryn-Bevan happened to be preaching in. Her absences from home became a byword, occurring as they did in the haymaking season. Her labour was wanted in the fields. It was the property of the community, the community which paid her three shillings and ninepence a week.

One night Sadrach Danyrefail called at her cottage to commandeer her services for the next day. His crop had been on the ground for a fortnight, and now that there was a prospect of fair weather he was anxious to gather it in. Sadrach was going to say hard things to Nanni, but the appearance of the gleaming-eyed creature that drew back the bolts of the door frightened him and tied his tongue. He was glad that the old woman did not invite him inside, for from within there issued an abominable smell such as might have come from the boiler of the witch who one time lived on the moor. In the morning he saw Nanni trudging towards a distant capel where the Respected Josiah Bryn-Bevan was delivering a sermon in the evening. She looked less bent and not so shrivelled up as she did the night before. Clearly, sleep had given her fresh vitality.

Two Sabbaths before the farewell sermon was to be preached Nanni came to Capel Sion with an ugly sore at the side of her mouth; repulsive matter oozed slowly from it, forming into a head, and then coursing thickly down her chin on to the shoulder of her black cape, where it glistened among the beads. On occasions her lips tightened, and she swished a hand angrily across her face.

'Old Nanni,' folk remarked while discussing her over their dinner-tables, 'is getting as dirty as an old sow.'

During the week two more sores appeared; the next Sabbath Nanni had a strip of calico drawn over her face.

Early on the eve of the farewell Sabbath the Seller of Bibles arrived with the Book, and Nanni gave him a sovereign in small money. She packed it up reverently, and betook herself to Sadrach Danyrefail to ask him to make the presentation.

At the end of his sermon the Respected Josiah Bryn-Bevan made reference to the giver of the Bible, and grieved that she was not in the Capel. He dwelt on her sacrifice. Here was a Book to be treasured, and he could think of no one who would treasure it better than Sadrach Danyrefail, to whom he would hand it in recognition of his work in the School of the Sabbath.

In the morning the Respected Josiah Bryn-Bevan, making a tour of his congregation, bethought himself of Nanni. The thought came on him on leaving Danyrefail, the distance betwixt which and Nanni's cottage is two fields. He opened the door and called out:

'Nanni.'

None answered.

He entered the room. Nanni was on the floor.

'Nanni, Nanni!' he said. 'Why for you do not reply to me? Am I not your shepherd?'

There was no movement from Nanni. Mishtir Bryn-Bevan went on his knees and peered at her. Her hands were clasped tightly together, as though guarding some great treasure. The minister raised himself and prised them apart with the ferrule of his walking-stick. A roasted rat revealed itself. Mishtir Bryn-Bevan stood for several moments spellbound and silent; and in the stillness the rats crept boldly out of their hiding places and resumed their attack on Nanni's face. The minister, startled and horrified, fled from the house of sacrifice.

GEORGE EWART EVANS (1909–   )

A True Story

The landlord, an oldish man with a thoughtful face, came out and took the farmer's place on the bench. He wore a black denim jacket. Ragtime and Seth got up and went inside, and for a while the landlord sat smoking. He pointed out the air quivering above the sun-baked road, and when he had broken the silence I asked him who was the old man in the picture in the bar. He pulled his pipe slowly from his mouth and then said deliberately: 'That's a picture of old Doctor Price[1] of Llantrisant. Ever heard of him?' Arthur said excitedly: 'Yes. My father knew him. He's told me a lot about him. When he was a boy he lived near Doctor Price.' 'Who is your father, *bach*?'[2] 'William Pritchard.' 'The Shop?' He tapped his pipe vigorously on the seat: 'Oh, your father and me are

[1]Doctor Price, William Price (1800-93), doctor, radical, eccentric and pioneer of cremation.
[2]*bach* (lit. 'small'), a term of endearment.

old butties; I was born in Pentyrch the same as your father. Well, well. Like him in the face you are, the both of you. Your father and me have talked to the old Doctor many times.'

The other two came back and Ragtime asked: 'Telling the lads about the picture, Davey?' The landlord nodded and Ragtime leaned over towards us: 'He didn't tell you how much he was offered for that photograph of Doctor Price?' We looked at the landlord who was smiling with amusement. 'No, he wouldn't tell you. But I'll tell you,' Ragtime said with emphasis. 'An American up here last summer offered Ten Pounds for that bit of a picture and Mr Lewis here wouldn't take it. Too much money you've got, Davey!' The landlord said: 'Ay, that's the trouble no doubt, Jack. But I don't mind telling you this: if he offered me a Hundred Pounds I wouldn't have taken it.' Ragtime argued: 'He was a good man was Doctor Price. I grant you that, Davey, but that's a lot of money for a bit of a picture.'

Ginger had never heard of Doctor Price and asked: 'Did he cure many people?' The landlord said quietly: 'He was a good doctor, only fifty years before his time. If a man was ill with a bad stomach, he'd set to work to cure the man first and his stomach – if it still needed it – afterwards. He wasn't particular about the fee either.' Ragtime agreed, 'He was a good doctor, Davey, no doubt about it, and on the side of the people.' Then he turned to us: 'Did you ever hear how he cured the young boy from Crumlin? Did you, Davey?' Mr Lewis said: 'No, I can't say that I have. What is it, Jack?' Seth interrupted: 'We better have another drink, Mr Lewis, before he starts; because if he gets going, it will be stop-tap before he finishes.' The landlord went inside and returned with the beer. Ragtime took a sip and started: 'This is a true story.' Seth made a noise but Ragtime carried on without taking notice. 'About thirty years ago a man from Crumlin had a son; just like one of you boys by here now. Only this boy was wasting away. Nothing they gave him would turn into flesh, and he was like a reed that the wind was threatening to bend over. The father took him to the doctors down in Newport, and they all took a walk round him and said: "He's getting thin. Feed him up. Milk and eggs! Milk and eggs!" They gave the lad enough milk and eggs to start a shop with, but he still didn't put on flesh; though he had enough appetite to eat a horse between two bread vans. Then somebody told his father: "Take the lad over to Llantrisant; old Doctor Price will cure him if anybody will." So he took his son down to Llantrisant, and although it was late when they got there, the Doctor didn't keep them waiting. He had a look at the boy and asked his father a lot of questions like the doctors do, then he told him: "I'll cure your son if you do this one thing: take him home now and bring him back in three days' time; but from the time he leaves here till the time he returns he's not to touch a bite of anything to eat, and he's only to have a sip of water to drink." The father was a bit uncertain about this, because the lad was pretty thin already and three days on fresh air would take any stuffing he had left, right out of him entirely. But he made up his mind suddenly and said: "I'll do it, Doctor. It's his only chance!"'

'They went home and after three lean days he brought his son back. He had to carry him, just: the lad was on his last legs and ready to eat up anything he put his eyes on. When Doctor Price saw him he said: "Right! Well done, bring him into this room, by here." They went into a room with a big table covered with a white cloth; it was just an ordinary room except there was a big double-barrelled gun standing in the corner. Doctor Price put the boy to sit up to the table facing the gun, and he told his father to sit alongside him. He told the lad he must do everything he said, and he warned the father to keep a close eye on his son. Then he rang a bell. A few seconds later a woman came in carrying a plate covered with a white cloth. Doctor Price said: "Put it down on this side of the table, Mary." The woman left the room and the Doctor uncovered the plate and showed one of the finest dinners that had ever been cooked on a Thursday; and the smell of it soon filled the room. The boy was almost starting out of his skin when he saw the meal in front of him. But Doctor Price fixed him with his eye and said in a firm voice: "If you make one move towards the plate I'm going to shoot. Stay still where you are." And he put his hand on the gun. Then he said to the father: "Push the plate gently towards the boy." The father pushed the plate slowly across the table until it was right under the boy's nose and he was staring at it as though he'd been hypnotised. As the plate came closer his mouth opened and closed just as though he were eating and his face showed the agony he was going through.'

Ragtime took a glance at us, as much as to say: Now I've got you where I want you. Then he went on: 'In a minute the sweat began to show on the boy's forehead, and his jaw dropped and his mouth stayed open. Doctor Price was watching him all the time. Then the boy started to shiver and the Doctor said: "Hold it, *bach*. It won't be long now." And suddenly something dropped out of the boy's mouth on the plate and he screamed loud when he saw it. But Doctor Price went over the other side of the table and lifted the boy off the chair on to the sofa, and said: "Well done, *bach!* Well done! You shall have a proper dinner now." Then he picked the thing off the table and examined it. It was a small lizard, and it had been slowly eating the boy away.'

He paused again for exactly the right length of time. 'Well, there's nothing to tell after that. Doctor Price kept the lad and his father with him that night and he fed the lad up on the right things and in the morning he was as fit again as a hare, though still a bit spare around the ribs. But he was strong enough to walk the fifteen miles back to Crumlin. The lad is still alive to-day, though getting on, of course. He's driving a bread-van in Crumlin. He'll tell you that every word I've said is true – if you ask him.'

Seth said seriously: 'The first time I've heard that one, Jack, and I've heard a few of the Doctor's doings.' The landlord puffed at his pipe and smiled quietly: 'Who told you that one, Jack?' 'Oh, I heard it somewhere, Davey; a long time ago, before going into the Army. I'm pretty good at remembering stories.' 'You are, but you sure that wasn't a home-made story now?' Ragtime pretended to look hurt: 'Come now, Davey. Me, make it up! How could you expect a bloke like me to do that? It takes a poet to make a story now, doesn't it?

And take a look at me: do I look like a bard?' He screwed up his face to his toughest fighting leer to disprove any claim they might give him to words. The landlord chaffed him: 'Well, Jack, if you don't make them up, you know a good place to find them.' He winked and answered, 'Perhaps so.'

from The Voices of the Children (1947)

The Gypsies

I had more work to do in the evenings and on week-ends. I was able to haul sacks of meal and corn from the goods station, and sometimes to serve in the shop. I was serving when the gypsies came. Father got on well with the gypsies. They came to the village two or three times a year and camped on a narrow strip of ground just under the big rock that jutted out from the mountain. They came to the shop in a drove this Saturday afternoon, with baskets and babies in arms and a small girl holding her mother's skirt. Although there were only three women, with their babies and baskets they filled the shop. They came in silently and placed the baskets down on the floor. Two of the women nursed babies in the folds of their shawls. The third, a much older woman, carried two baskets. She was a big woman and her cheekbones were high and her creased skin was like yellow parchment. One of the mothers was beautiful with black glistening hair and full, red lips. Her back was very straight and she held her head high as though she carried an invisible pitcher. She wore thick gold ear-rings. The second mother, a thin woman, with hollow cheeks and a broad mouth showing widely-spaced teeth, set the little girl to sit down on her basket which was still half full of clothes pegs. The big woman looked around the shelves and the counter without showing much interest, as though there was little in the shop to make the money burn in her pocket. A thin cry came from the dark Queen's baby and she undid her dress and gave it the breast with the same dignity she had shown when she first entered and looked around the shop. They waited silently until Father had finished with a regular customer. They stood by the provision counter near the bacon and cheese. Father moved over towards them and the bargaining started. The big woman said abruptly without greeting: 'Some pegs left, mistah, only a few.' Her voice was hard and better made for threats than persuasion. Father knew the moves and wasn't to be hurried. 'Well, we've not seen you for a long time.' He rearranged the pieces of bacon on the counter as he spoke. 'Near a year now. We've been up in England. Will you have the pegs, mistah?' 'Where are you camping?' 'Same place. Have a look at the pegs, sir.' She glanced down at the little girl and with a small movement of her hand waved her aside. The girl got up and the big woman pointed to the bundles of pegs, made from ash wood and thin strips of tin for binding. The pegs were threaded on long strips of bark or osier. Father glanced, a bare glance over the counter. 'But I've got a box full of pegs here.'

'Just a few. Don't let us take them home. Only ninepence.' Her voice became softer. 'Just a few coppers, sir.' Father handed over the money out of the till. 'You'd sell coal to the colliers.' The big woman shrugged her shoulders and kept the coins in her hand while the little girl, without waiting to be told, gathered up the pegs and placed them on the counter. 'Got any bacon, mistah?' Father pointed with a wave of the hand to the counter, 'There we are.' But he knew what she meant and brought out some odd pieces – ham-bones and ends – from behind a pile of tin stuff. She bargained for them trying to get as many pieces as she could for sixpence; Father was slow to close the bargaining, merely for the sport of it, and to avoid the appearance of being overridden, because he really wanted to get rid of the accumulation of scrap ends. The gypsy woman knew this and kept on the attack, 'A piece more, sir. Just another piece, special for my man.' Father put another piece on the pile and flicked the counter with his apron. 'There, you've got them all. You can have boiled bacon for a week.' The thin-faced mother nodded her head towards the cheese. But the big woman still did the talking; the other was content to watch her practised bargaining. She cajoled all the small pieces of cheese on to the counter and at last handed over the threepence, not forgetting to tell Father that he was really having his money back. Father asked her: 'And how much will I get for your pegs?' 'Get as much as you can, mistah. They're good pegs; all made by hand, and they'll bring the women luck.' Father caught my eye and whispered to me, 'Some broken biscuits in a bag,' nodding towards the little girl. She became alive as I filled the paper bag. The big woman nodded to Father: 'You'll live a long time, sir, and your wife will bring you many children.' Father pretended to smooth his moustache as he said, 'Thank you. You are very kind.' I too saw the joke[1] and had so far lived down the family as to be able to laugh at it.

from *The Voices of the Children* (1947)

HUGH EVANS (1854–1934)

What will you have for Supper?

The story goes that Beti Jones had tired of cooking different kinds of food for her very numerous children. She had twenty-five of them, and each one demanded a different supper. This was too much and Beti Jones, her patience exhausted, resolved to teach her brood a lesson. She was a woman of character and originality, and the method she adopted to solve the supper problem was characteristic. She asked the children, beginning with the eldest and ending with the youngest, what they would like for supper.

[1] The joke; the joke is that the grocer already has a large brood of children.

'Robin, what will you have for supper tonight?' 'Porridge,' said Robin.
'Nel, what will you have?' '*Siot*.'[1]
'Mari, what will you have?' 'Posset.'
'Dic, what will you have?' 'Hot buttermilk and bread.'
'Sian, what will you have?' 'Whey.'
'Twm, what will you have?' 'Flummery,' said Twm.
'Sionyn, what will you have?' 'Cold *siot*.'
'Cit, what will you have?' 'Bread and milk.'
'Dei, what will you have?' 'Milk gruel.'
'Abraham Ephraim, what will you have?' 'Bread soaked in small beer.'
'Jacob Henry, what will you have?' 'Potatoes in buttermilk.'
'Hannah Deborah, what will you have?' 'Oatmeal gruel.'
'Ruth Salomi, what will you have?' '*Picwsmali*' (oatcake soaked in hot buttermilk, another form of *siot*).
'Charles Edward, what will you have?' 'Turkey pie' (Bread, with a little butter, pepper and salt, and boiling water added).
'Humphrey Cadwaladr, what will you have?' 'Junket.'
'Claudia Dorothy, what will you have?' 'Bread and water.'
'Margaret Alice, what will you have?' 'Water posset.'
'Goronwy, what will you have?' 'Cold buttermilk and bread.'
'Arthur, what will you have?' 'Caudle.'
'Blodwen, what will you have?' 'Broth.'
'Gwladys, what will you have?' '*Brewis*.'
'Rhys, what will you have?' 'Siot posset.'
'Corwena, what will you have?' 'Wheat flour gruel.'
'Caradoc, what will you have?' 'Toast and milk.'
'Llewelyn, my little one, what will you have?' 'I'll have porridge, like Robin.'
'Good lad,' said Beti Jones, 'you'll make a man yet.'
'No, I'll have whey, like Sian. No, flummery, the same as Twm.'
'You shall have it, my boy.'
Having thus ascertained the wishes of all her children Beti Jones disappeared into the back-kitchen without making any kind of comment and without the usual scolding, which surprised the family, for it was quite out of character. However, Beti remained out of sight in the back-kitchen for a considerable time, and when she reappeared in the living kitchen it was with the baking pan in her arms. This she placed on the kitchen table, and then she began carrying in the vessels in which she had prepared the various foods demanded by her brood. When all had been collected she poured the contents into the baking pan, stirring the whole mess up with the porridge stick, a job calling for a good deal of muscular strength. This done, she spooned the resulting mess into the bowls from which the children ate, filling each bowl according to her knowledge of each child's requirements and capacity, and finally placing them along the table before her astonished offspring. There

---

[1] *Siot . . . picwsmali . . . brewis*, traditional Welsh dishes.

were some faint attempts at rebellion, but Beti was a resolute woman and stood over her brood, porridge stick in hand like a truncheon, until all had been eaten. That cured them of finicky fancies about their food, and the story was a standing warning to us children of a later generation.

from *Cwm Eithin* (1931), trans. E. Morgan Humphreys, *The Gorse Glen* (1948)

ALBERT EVANS-JONES (Cynan; 1895–1970)

Aberdaron

When I am old and honoured,
    With silver in my purse,
All criticism over,
    All men singing my praise,
I will purchase a lonely cottage
    With nothing facing its door
But the cliffs of Aberdaron
    And the wild waves on the shore.

When I am old and honoured,
    And my blood is running chill,
And watching the moon rising
    Stirs in my heart no thrill,
Hope will be mine thereafter
    In a cottage with its door
To the cliffs of Aberdaron
    And the wild waves on the shore.

When I am old and honoured
    Beyond all scorn and acclaim,
And my song goes by the rubric
    And gone is its passion's flame,
Hope will be mine thereafter
    In a cottage with its door
To the cliffs of Aberdaron
    And the wild waves on the shore.

For there I will discover
    In the stormy wind and its cry
Echoes of the old rebellion
    My soul knew in days gone by.

And I will sing with the old passion
While gazing through the door
At the cliffs of Aberdaron
And the wild waves on the shore.

trans. Joseph P. Clancy

Anonymous

Olwen

She was sent for. And she came, with a robe of flame-red silk about her, and around the maiden's neck a torque of red gold, and precious pearls thereon and rubies. Yellower was her head than the flower of the broom, whiter was her flesh than the foam of the wave; whiter were her palms and her fingers than the shoots of the marsh trefoil from amidst the fine gravel of a welling spring. Neither the eye of the mewed hawk, nor the eye of the thrice-mewed falcon, not an eye was there fairer than hers. Whiter were her breasts than the breast of the white swan, redder were her cheeks than the reddest foxgloves. Whoso beheld her would be filled with love of her. Four white trefoils sprang up behind her wherever she went; and for that reason was she called Olwen.[1]

from *The Mabinogion* (1948), trans. Gwyn Jones and Thomas Jones

Trevor Fishlock (1941–)

Remember Tryweryn

Capel Celyn was a small village in the quiet Tryweryn valley in the hill country between Bala and Ffestiniog in North Wales. In and around it lived about seventy people and the community was steeped in the Welsh tradition. The people earned their merely modest living through farming, and their social life, with its strong cultural stream and chapel base, followed an old and rich pattern. The village was in the Penllyn district, the home of *penillion*, which is the singing of verses to the accompaniment of the harp, and there were many harps in the valley. People met for hour upon hour of singing, poetry, reading and the special verse-arts of the Welsh language. Indeed, Capel Celyn, although an obscure settlement, was a precious and largely unspoiled nugget of

---

[1]Olwen, taken by the author to be *ôl wen* ('white track'), but the name probably means 'beautiful'.

Welsh values. Today, however, the name of the valley, Tryweryn, is, for many people in Wales, a shorthand expression for a whole chapter of emotions, and the word is painted on walls and bridges up and down Wales. So is the slogan *Cofia Drywaryn* – Remember Tryweryn. For the corporation of Liverpool, with measured arrogance, and without consulting anyone involved, announced that it would have the valley as a reservoir and proceeded to do just that. The harps have vanished, for Capel Celyn no longer exists; farms, school, chapel, store, cottages, are at the bottom of a silent lake.

The episode of Tryweryn was a traumatic one and it is one of the keys to what has been happening in Wales in recent years. From it sprang a great anger and a hardening of resolve; for many men and women it was an awakening, the first indication that the values of Wales were in danger and were meaningless to the authorities in England; it started people thinking and, for a small group of men, it was the last straw that made them channel rage into a cold determination to strike blows for Wales with stolen gelignite and time switches. The bomb attacks on water pipelines and government offices went on for more than four years, but the reverberations of Tryweryn are being felt still. 'Tryweryn', wrote Gwynfor Evans, the Welsh Nationalist Party leader, 'will become a word of fateful significance for Wales. It may become as well known as a verb as Quisling has become as a noun.'

from *Wales and the Welsh* (1972)

J.O. FRANCIS (1882–1956)

Conversation in a Train

If any impartial inquirer wishes to test the assertion that Englishmen are English and Welshmen Welsh, he has but to make the journey from Paddington to, say, Ystrad-Rhondda. Then, if he has eyes to see and ears to hear, he will not be seduced by any of these heretics of race who go about the country behaving like glorified phrenologists.

The man who goes aboard the Fishguard express with a carriage full of Englishmen knows exactly what to expect. They will be stiff, reserved, and silent. They will put up their newspapers as a fortification against familiarity . . . .

When the train pulls up at Newport the atmosphere grows a little warmer. One feels that the glacial period is done. If a Western Valley train is in the bay the world takes on a new verdure of cheeriness, and man is heard to hail his brother man. Newport Station evokes a little thrill of sympathy in the Celtic heart. If it dared, Newport would like to linger and chat and ask about the people at home. But, as there are many silent Saxons on its platforms, in the courtesy of its compassion it assumes an unbending attitude which is not native to it. To the Welshman, however, it gives a little hospitable smile and whispers to him that he is now within the Cymric border. He knows at once that the new-comers on the train are of his kindred. The icicles begin to melt, and he can now summon up courage enough to ask a neighbour if he may look at the Newport *Argus* or the *Western Mail*.

It would be vain effort to try to compress the Great Western Railway Station at Cardiff into a paragraph. Such a gathering ground for all classes, creeds, and clans demands either a full-length treatment or else a respectful silence. The reader must straightway put himself into a third-class compartment of a Taff Vale Railway train bound for the Rhondda Valley. Then, passing Castell Coch[1], he swings through the gates of Glamorgan and up towards Pontypridd – that Mecca of the Valley Pilgrims – and there, if he be a true-blue South Walian, he has but to look through the window to see an uncle, or a cousin, or an aunt upon the platform. . . .

Moving up the valley of the Rhondda, the traveller finds a sharp contrast to those cold companions of Paddington. In spite of measured heads and Cephalic Indexes, he knows full well that there is still a mystery of race at work in the souls of men. Conversation flows easily through the carriage. It deals with everything and with nothing. The terms of address are altered. In place of the frigid 'sir' of the Great Western comes the friendly 'Well, no mun,' of the Taff Vale Railway. The former is a barrier to easy conversation; the latter is a bridge.

Imagine yourself, in such circumstances, face to face with some hard-bitten old collier, who sits before you with a pungent cloud of 'Ringer' or 'Franklin' trailing across the pallor of a blue-scarred visage. He must, of course, be one of the real old Valley breed, who remembers the 'Glorans'[2] – not a member of the new invading hosts of anywhere. He has been down to Pontypridd, and is now returning, dressed in his 'evening clothes' ('dillad dwetydd'). Soon, whether you will or not, you will be deep in some such dialogue as this: –

He: 'Nice weather for the time of year we're having.' (Or seasonable equivalent.)

You: 'Yes, very!'

He: 'Going far?'

You: (knowing he would despise an easy victory): 'Just up the Valley.'

He: 'Oh, aay!'

(A pause. Do you think he has abandoned the attack? It is the silence of the strategist.)

He: 'Coming up from Cardiff, I suppose?'

You: 'Well, I changed there.'

He: 'Oh, aay! Busy place Cardiff, too. I haven't been there now this long

---

[1] *Castell Coch* (lit. 'Red Castle'), near Tongwynlais, a little to the north of Cardiff.
[2] *Glorans*, a nick-name for the indigenous inhabitants of the Rhondda Valley, those whose origins in the valley pre-dated industrialization.

time.' (With sudden suspicion, politely veiled.) 'Down from North Wales you are, p'r'aps?'

You (swift in denial): 'Oh no! I've just come from London.'

He (accepting the lesser of the two evils): 'Oh, aay! I was up in the Crystal Palace once to a brass band competition. Abertillery pretty near won, too. The 'Beer and 'Bacco Band' people used to call it. Going up to Treherbert you are, I dare say?'

You: 'No, only as far as Ystrad.'

He (with renewed enthusiasm): 'Ystrad? Jawch,[1] mun, that's where I'm living. There aren't many people I don't know in Ystrad. On business, I suppose?'

You: 'Well, no. I'm going to see a relation.'

He: 'Oh, aay! Tidy people in Ystrad, too. P'r'aps you're belonging to Mr. Rees Price up there? You're both the same stamp, however.'

You: 'No, I'm afraid I don't know Mr. Rees Price.'

He: 'That's strange! Aay, as I was saying, I know pretty near everybody in Ystrad. I shouldn't be surprised if I'd known your relations there for years.'

Sooner or later you reach a point when you feel it would be impolite to maintain your defence any longer. Having given him good sport, not allowing too swift a victory, you yield and gratify him with the name he seeks.

On a railway line in England a traveller would resent these queries because they would violate a taciturn tradition. Amongst the friendly South Welsh he would, if he knew his anthropology, expect and revel in this deep concern for other people's destinies. And, remembering those easy gossiping moments of the Taff Vale Railway, he will maintain that, in despite of all the measuring of heads, there is a great gulf fixed between the spirit of Paddington and the spirit of the Valleys that converge on Pontypridd.

from *The Legend of the Welsh* (1924)

RAYMOND GARLICK (1926–   )

Agincourt

Seven of the Welsh archers
whose arrows eclipsed the sun
in icy susurrations
when Agincourt was done
had gone there from Llansteffan.
When that day's death was won

---

[1] *Jawch*, by the Devil, an expletive.

if any of them lived
I wonder what they thought.
I live in Llansteffan
and I know Agincourt –
the bonemeal verdant meadows
over which they fought:

green places, both of them now,
but then, in 1415,
at Agincourt the blood
clotted the buttercups' sheen
and the earth was disembowelled
where stakes and hooves had been.

And far off, in Llansteffan,
castle, village and shore
flowered in the marigold sun.
Did those seven men explore
the contrast of this peace
with another English war?

Matters Arising

No doubt what you say is right.
In Wales we shall never see
a terrible beauty born.
No rose of tragedy,
petalled in crimson and black,
will sway on this post office roof.
Swansea gaol will receive
no heroes, unshaven, aloof,
for the cells' chill liturgy
and the rites of the firing-squad.
Whatever beauty's in blood
will not bloom here, thank God.

I met an Easter man
in Dublin long ago,
Senator, Minister now,
who told me: 'You will know
when you find yourself picking off,
like roses whose day is done,
from behind a garden wall
the soldiers of Albion –

you'll know as you see them fall,
and you feel the frost of fear
icing your ambushed spine,
that what you hope for is near.'

I have lived where blood
had flooded down men's hands.
Though I look for a Wales
free as the Netherlands,
a freedom hacked out here
is a freedom without worth,
a terror without beauty.
Here it must come to birth
not as a pterodactyl
flailing archaic wings,
but the dove that broods on chaos –
wise as a thousand springs.

Anthem for Doomed Youth

Abertawe, 22 Tachwedd 1971[1]

My hope is on what is to come.
I turn in anguish from the servile, dumb

present – from an indifferent people, shut
to justice, crouching in the heart's dark hut.

I turn to the future, to a Wales hung
with the names, like garlands, of today's young.

Outside the court the three stood in the sun,
poised, at ease, in the soft chrysanthemum

light of Swansea, the bitter city. They
alone knew freedom on that icy day.

Policemen, advocates, recognised in those
the radiance of the uncorrupted rose

glowing above their court well's mantled scum.
Even the judge, that perched geranium,

[1] *Abertawe, 22 Tachwedd 1971*, Swansea, 22 November 1971, when members of *Cymdeithas yr Iaith Gymraeg* (The Welsh Language Society) were brought to trial. The first and last line of this poem are a quotation from a poem by Siôn Cent (*c.* 1400-30/45).

saw it; and traded on it – to retail,
after the verdict, his unheard of bail,

honouring their integrity's claim
which he would deny when sentence came.

O unjust judge, mere expert in the sleight
of hand of law, do you sleep at night?

Be sure your victims sleep sounder than you
in the bitter place you comdemned them to.

And you, Mr Secretary of State,
setter up of committees, what fate

have the history books in store for you,
who can watch while the young are spitted through?

who can wait on a touring troupe's report
while conscience is crucified in court?

My rhyme tolls for you all, beats its slow drum.
My hope is on what is to come.

Geoffrey of Monmouth (*c.* 1090–1155)

Brutus [1] *Names the Island*

In the meantime Brutus had consummated his marriage with his wife Ignoge. By her he had three sons called Locrinus, Kamber and Albanactus, all of whom were to become famous. When their father finally died, in the twenty-third year after his landing, these three sons buried him inside the walls of the town which he had founded. They divided the kingdom of Britain between them in such a way that each succeeded to Brutus in one particular district. Locrinus, who was the first-born, inherited the part of the island which was afterwards called Loegria after him. Kamber received the region which is on the further bank of the River Severn, the part which is now known as Wales but which was for a long time after his death called Kambria from his name. As a result the people of that country still call themselves Kambri today in the Welsh tongue. Albanactus, the youngest, took the region which is

[1] Brutus, the legendary progenitor of the British people. Geoffrey's explanation of how Loegria (England), Kambria (Wales), Albany (Scotland) and Britain came to be named is now thought to be onomastic.

nowadays called Scotland in our language. He called it Albany, after his own name. . . .

When they had explored the different districts, they drove the giants whom they had discovered into the caves in the mountains. With the approval of their leader they divided the land among themselves. They began to cultivate the fields and to build houses, so that in a short time you would have thought that the land had always been inhabited.

Brutus then called the island Britain from his own name, and his companions he called Britons. His intention was that his memory should be perpetuated by the derivation of the name. A little later the language of the people, which had up to then been known as Trojan or Crooked Greek, was called British, for the same reason.

from *Historia Regum Britanniae* (*c.* 1136), trans. Lewis Thorpe, *History of the Kings of Britain* (1966)

The Death of Arthur [1]

Arthur was filled with great mental anguish by the fact that Mordred had escaped him so often. Without losing a moment, he followed him to that same locality, reaching the River Camblam,[2] where Mordred was awaiting his arrival. Mordred was indeed the boldest of men and always the first to launch an attack. He immediately drew his troops up in battle order, determined as he was either to win or to die, rather than run away again as he had done in the past. From his total force of troops, about which I have told you, there still remained sixty thousand men under his command. From these he mustered six divisions, in each of which he placed six thousand, six hundred and sixty-six armed men. From those who were left over he formed one single division, and, when he had assigned leaders to each of the others, he placed this last division under his own command. As soon as they were all drawn up, he went round to encourage each of them in turn, promising them the possessions of their enemies if only they stood firm and were successful in battle.

On the other side, Arthur, too, was marshalling his army. He divided his men into nine divisions of infantry, each drawn up in a square, with a right and left wing. To each he appointed a commander. Then he exhorted them to kill these perjured villains and robbers who, at the request of one who had committed treason against him, the King, had been brought into the island from foreign parts to steal their lands from them. He told them, too, that this miscellaneous collection of barbarians, come from a variety of countries–raw

[1] Arthur (late 5th cent. – early 6th cent.), British military leader about whom there exist many tales which have been incorporated into English literature.
[2] Camblam (*recte* Camlan), variously identified as Camelford in Cornwall, by Malory as a place near Salisbury and more recently as Camboglanna, the fort now called Birdoswald on Hadrian's Wall.

recruits who were totally inexperienced in war–would be quite incapable of resisting valiant men like themselves, who were the veterans of many battles, provided always that they made up their minds to attack boldly and to fight like men.

While the two commanders were encouraging their men in this way in both the armies, the lines of battle suddenly met, combat was joined, and they all strove with might and main to deal each other as many blows as possible. It is heartrending to describe what slaughter was inflicted on both sides, how the dying groaned, and how great was the fury of those attacking. Everywhere men were receiving wounds themselves or inflicting them, dying or dealing out death. In the end, when they had passed much of the day in this way, Arthur, with a single division in which he had posted six thousand, six hundred and sixty-six men, charged at the squadron where he knew Mordred was. They hacked a way through with their swords and Arthur continued to advance, inflicting terrible slaughter as he went. It was at this point that the accursed traitor was killed and many thousands of his men with him.

However, the others did not take to flight simply because Mordred was dead. They massed together from all over the battlefield and did their utmost to stand their ground with all the courage at their command. The battle which was now joined between them was fiercer than ever, for almost all the leaders on both sides were present and rushed into the fight at the head of their troops. On Mordred's side there fell Chelric, Elaf, Egbrict and Bruning, all of them Saxons; the Irishmen Gillapatric, Gillasel and Gillarvus; and the Scots and Picts, with nearly everyone in command of them. On Arthur's side there died Odbrict, King of Norway; Aschil, King of Denmark; Cador Limenich; and Cassivelaunus, with many thousands of the King's troops, some of them Britons, others from the various peoples he had brought with him. Arthur himself, our renowned King, was mortally wounded and was carried off to the Isle of Avalon,[1] so that his wounds might be attended to. He handed the crown of Britain over to his cousin Constantine, the son of Cador Duke of Cornwall; this in the year 542 after our Lord's Incarnation.

from *Historia Regum Britanniae* (*c.*1136), trans. Lewis Thorpe, *History of the Kings of Britain* (1966)

---

[1] Avalon, a magic island, a land of perpetual youth, with which Glastonbury, Som., has been associated in English tradition.

GERALD OF WALES (c. 1146–1223)

The Boy who Stole a Golden Ball

A short time before our days, a circumstance worthy of note occurred in these parts, which Elidorus, a priest, most strenuously affirmed had befallen himself. When a youth of twelve years and learning his letters . . . in order to avoid the discipline and frequent stripes inflicted on him by his preceptor, he ran away, and concealed himself under the hollow bank of a river. After fasting in that situation for two days, two little men of pigmy stature appeared to him, saying, 'If you will come with us, we will lead you into a country full of delights and sports.' Assenting and rising up, he followed his guides through a path, at first subterraneous and dark, into a most beautiful country, adorned with rivers and meadows, woods and plains, but obscure, and not illuminated with the full light of the sun. All the days were cloudy, and the nights extremely dark, on account of the absence of the moon and stars. The boy was brought before the king, and introduced to him in the presence of the court; who, having examined him for a long time, delivered him to his son, who was then a boy. These men were of the smallest stature, but very well proportioned in their make; they were all of a fair complexion, with luxuriant hair falling over their shoulders like that of women. They had horses and greyhounds adapted to their size. They neither ate flesh nor fish, but lived on milk diet, made up into messes with saffron. They never took an oath, for they detested nothing so much as lies. As often as they returned from our upper hemisphere, they reprobated our ambition, infidelities, and inconstancies; they had no form of public worship, being strict lovers and reverers, as it seemed, of truth.

The boy frequently returned to our hemisphere, sometimes by the way he had first gone, sometimes by another; at first in company with other persons, and afterwards alone, and made himself known only to his mother, declaring to her the manners, nature, and state of that people. Being desired by her to bring a present of gold, with which that region abounded, he stole, while at play with the king's son, the golden ball with which he used to divert himself, and brought it to his mother in great haste; and when he reached the door of his father's house, but not unpursued, and was entering it in a great hurry, his foot stumbled on the threshold, and falling down into the room where his mother was sitting, the two pigmies seized the ball which had dropped from his hand, and departed, shewing the boy every mark of contempt and derision. On recovering from his fall, confounded with shame, and execrating the evil counsel of his mother, he returned by the usual track to the subterraneous road, but found no appearance of any passage, though he searched for it on the banks of the river for nearly the space of a year. But since those calamities are often alleviated by time, which reason cannot mitigate, and length of time alone blunts the edge of our afflictions, and puts an end to many evils, the youth having been brought back by his friends and mother, and restored to his right way of thinking, and to his learning, in process of time attained the rank of priesthood. Whenever David II, bishop of St David's, talked to him in his advanced state of life concerning this event, he could never relate the particulars without shedding tears.

from *Itinerarium Kambriae* (1191), trans. R.C. Hoare, *Itinerary through Wales* (1806)

The Birds of Llyn Syfaddan [1]

When Gruffydd,[2] on his return from the king's court, passed near this lake, which at that cold season of the year was covered with water-fowl of various sorts, being accompanied by Milo, earl of Hereford, and lord of Brecheinoc, and Payn Fitz-John, lord of Ewyas,[3] who were at that time secretaries and privy councillors to the king; earl Milo,[4] wishing to draw forth from Gruffydd some discourse concerning his innate nobility, rather jocularly than seriously thus addressed him: 'It is an ancient saying in Wales, that if the natural prince of the country, coming to this lake, shall order the birds to sing, they will immediately obey him.' To which Gruffydd, richer in mind than in gold, (for though his inheritance was diminished, his ambition and dignity still remained), answered, 'Do you therefore, who now hold the dominion of this land, first give the command;' but he and Payn having in vain commanded, and Gruffydd, perceiving that it was necessary for him to do so in his turn, dismounted from his horse, and falling on his knees towards the east, as if he had been about to engage in battle, prostrate on the ground, with his eyes and hands uplifted to heaven, poured forth devout prayers to the Lord: at length, rising up, and signing his face and forehead with the figure of the cross, he thus openly spake: 'Almighty God, and Lord Jesus Christ, who knowest all things, declare here this day thy power. If thou hast caused me to descend lineally from the natural princes of Wales, I command these birds in thy name to declare it;' and immediately the birds, beating the water with their wings, began to cry aloud, and proclaim him. The spectators were astonished and confounded; and earl Milo hastily returning with Payn Fitz-John to court, related this singular occurrence to the king, who is said to have replied, 'By the death of Christ (an oath he was accustomed to use), it is not a matter of so much wonder; for although by our great authority we commit acts of violence and wrong against these people, yet they are known to be the rightful inheritors of this land.'

from *Itinerarium Kambriae* (1191), trans. R.C. Hoare, *Itinerary through Wales* (1806)

[1]Llyn Syfaddan, Llangorse Lake, near Brecon, Brecs.
[2]Gruffydd, the son of Rhys ap Tewdwr (d. 1093), king of south-west Wales.
[3]Milo . . . Payn Fitz-John, Norman conquerors of parts of mid-Wales.
[4]Ewyas, a commote in the Black Mountains in south-east Wales.

The Old Man of Pencadair [1]

If the Welsh were more commonly accustomed to the Gallic mode of arming, and depended more on steady-fighting than on their agility; if their princes were unanimous and inseparable in their defence; or rather, if they had only one prince, and that a good one; this nation, situated in so powerful, strong, and inaccessible a country, could hardly ever be completely overcome. If, therefore, they would be inseparable, they would become insuperable, being assisted by these three circumstances; a country well defended by nature, a people both contented and accustomed to live upon little, a community whose nobles as well as privates are instructed in the use of arms; and especially as the English fight for power, the Welsh for liberty; the one to procure gain, the other to avoid loss; the English hirelings for money, the Welsh patriots for their country. The English, I say, fight in order to expel the natural inhabitants from the island, and secure to themselves the possession of the whole; but the Welsh maintain the conflict, that they, who have so long enjoyed the sovereignty of the whole kingdom, may at least find a hiding place in the worst corner of it, amongst woods and marshes; and, banished, as it were, for their offences, may there in a state of poverty, for a limited time, perform penance for the excesses they committed in the days of their prosperity. For the perpetual remembrance of their former greatness, the recollection of their Trojan descent, and the high and continued majesty of the kingdom of Britain, may draw forth many a latent spark of animosity, and encourage the daring spirit of rebellion. Hence during the military expedition which king Henry II made in our days against South Wales, an old Welshman at Pencadair, who had faithfully adhered to him, being desired to give his opinion about the royal army, and whether he thought that of the rebels would make resistance, and what would be the final event of this war, replied, 'This nation, O king, may now, as in former times, be harassed, and in a great measure weakened and destroyed by your and other powers, and it will often prevail by its laudable exertions; but it can never be totally subdued through the wrath of man, unless the wrath of God shall concur. Nor do I think, that any other nation than this of Wales, or any other language, whatever may hereafter come to pass, shall, in the day of severe examination before the Supreme Judge, answer for this corner of the earth.'

from *Descriptio Kambriae* (1193), trans. R.C. Hoare, *Description of Wales* (1806)

---

[1]Pencadair (Pencader), a village in Dyfed, where the Old Man's proud statement is commemorated by a monument.

GERAINT GOODWIN (1903–41)

The Red Lion

Spring came to the Red Lion in a hundred ways, which Beti knew and awaited.

There was the kingfisher, and the fine sheen of green on the scrub which reached up behind the house, so fine and evanescent that it seemed as though the scraggy, twisted blackthorn had been tarnished overnight. It seemed less substantial than a shadow – but it was there. And then in the meadow over the brook, her father's horses had gone wild. They went charging over the turf, tails up, the booming of their hoofs in the distance coming over to her in the still air like far-away thunder.

The snowdrops had gone from the old lawn – their patterns slowly mouldering in the earth. They had been planted no one knew how many years ago and they were a part of the house. They formed a clumsy crown and sceptre and below, in bold letters, the word: WELCOME. They were white and chill as the winter itself, though Beti would not have been without them.

But the daffodils were different – not the large, ornate daffodil of the town garden, but the little wild plant, small and sturdy, which shot up in clusters around the borders. It had no more to do with the grand, cultivated plant than the shaggy mountain pony, which her father had on the hill, had to do with a show horse. It belonged to the earth, in its vivid colour, its small flaming cup of gold, rain-washed and clear and violent in its beauty. Those, too, had been planted before anyone remembered, but they were always the same; they neither spread nor died away. They were always there, in their brilliant clusters, with the first thin sun of the early spring.

And with it all the old house awoke. The place was atremble with the high piping chorus of birds. The doves were back in the beeches, with their soft muted cooing, their endless unseen fluttering in the tall branches; the chaffinches and the tits were in the bushes; the missel thrush with her speckled belly met one, head cocked, at every turn. The swallows had come back to their sun-baked mud nests under the eaves, throwing a spike of shadow beneath them, as, with a shrill twitter, they darted to and fro against the spring sky.

The Red Lion slumbering there under its down-blown smoke, fenced around with trees which reached out, but never encompassed it, was a place of birdsong. It was more felt than heard, as the dropping tinkle of the waterfall at the bottom of the garden. And that, too, taking one abandoned leap through space, from the moss gully above, had its own especial noises. In still weather it came down like a fine shred, breaking on the rocks in that almost soundless tinkle, to shoot up in a cascade so fine that one only saw the sun glisten in it. But a wind blew it backwards and forwards, causing it to play a tune of its own.

For there was no traffic at the Red Lion, and the natural peace possessed it. One was conscious of a motor car, but one was never conscious of the birds. The motor car broke into the quiet and shattered it, destroyed the unsensed rhythm of it all. And for that reason a motor car seemed ten times as noisy, its engine ten times as spiteful as it was. This faint, unalterable twittering of the birds which merged into a cloud of sound, the low hum of the mill and the sharp, metallic tinkle of the brook, were the only real sounds the house knew. Everything else happened; these never happened, for they were always there.

No one knew how old was the house. New wings had been built since the original foundation, and it spread itself out in its warm-coloured brick amongst the trees, with no beginning and no end. And then, bordering it, were the barns and stables and outhouses, the cobbled yard, the sties. One could wander about all day long and there was always something fresh. It was too big for an inn, and yet it was not an hotel; no modern embellishment touched it.

But its rude comfort was very real. Those who went there went again. Its ham and egg teas were a byword among the townsfolk. Nowhere in all Wales were there such ham and egg teas. That was the only speciality it made, and that was one forced upon it. More flitches and more hams went up on the rafters until, early in the year, the great stone-floored tap-room looked like a street overhung with pennants. A tall man could not walk upright among them. The ham and bacon was, of course, home-cured. How, or why, it should attain its particular flavour no one knew, any more than how water in one district is so very much better than in another.

But there was no ham like it – it had the sharp rich tang of the earth in it. The great hams hung up there with their coarse-cut borders, the saltpetre glistening in the lamplight, and then, cut to the horseshoe, showed a moist gleaming pink of lean, a colour all its own, deeper and richer than a salmon cut. It was cut off in thick slices, and the eggs were searched for in the nests; then all put on the great pan that hung from the spit. Over a fire of pine and peat it slowly compounded its own flavour, filling the house with its pungent smell.

Everything in the Red Lion 'happened'. The visitors came and went as night followed day. However noisy they might be – as the char-à-banc full of *shonihois*[1] from the South who had remained for two days when the axle broke on the corner – they could not touch it. The peace, so rudely broken, settled down again like the sea opening and closing. The life went on with the seasons, in time with the seasons – the full violent flowering of the wild daffodils with the first thin sun of the spring; then the deep heavy leaf of summer, when the trees came up to the house as in a flood; the rich bronze and gold of autumn with its thousand tints, and winter with its dark fragile network of branches, the pale, shooting flower of the snowdrops on the frost-gleaming lawn.

Beti watched her mother down the garden hanging out the linen. It had come out of the ottoman above the stairs, where it had lain through the winter all interleaved with sprigs of lavender. It had that dull white texture which rain-water gives and it was going on the shrubs, face to the sun, to give it that bleaching that only the sun can give. And with her Gwenno, the maid of all

[1]*shonihois*, a nickname for men from the industrial valleys of south Wales.

work, was struggling with the feather beds, the soft breast-down plucked from their own geese at Michaelmas and Christmas. There were no hair and spring mattresses at the Red Lion.

from *The Heyday in the Blood* (1936)

LL. WYN GRIFFITH (1890–1977)

Learning English

I can remember when I began to learn English. There was a period when I knew of it as a secret speech used by grown-ups, a thin and pinched language spoken between half-closed lips, but I cannot remember that I had any desire to learn it. Nor can I see why I should be eager to acquire it at that age, for I could say all I wished to say in Welsh, and I had not met anyone who could not understand me. It came of going to school, and it happened a little later than the elements of arithmetic. Fortunately no one attempted in those days, in the name of education, to bewilder the mind of a child with explanations. An alphabet was an alphabet, to be mastered by repetition, and there the matter ended but for the long unison sing-song of 'aye-bee-see' on a summer afternoon in a small classroom.

'A' was not even an archer for a Welsh boy: no doubt wisely, for the picture of a man with a bow would have quickened another word in another language and made teaching difficult for the teacher. After the alphabet came the usual string of monosyllables; the cat, no doubt, sat on the mat, but I do not remember it. English was not a matter of books, and my tears, if they fell, did not fall upon the leaves of a reader. The short words were printed on a large cloth fastened at each end to a wooden roller, and they ran in a prickly black column from the top to the bottom. The cloth was unrolled and thrown over the top of a black-board standing on an easel, with two hillocks where the easel pegs jutted out from the frame. A wooden pointer moved along the column of words, now up, now down, and where it halted it drew out a chord of young voices in response. When the lesson ended, and the varnished cloth was rolled up and taken off the blackboard, English disappeared suddenly: it ceased to be, for children who had no need for it in their daily lives, as completely as if it had never existed. It could not cross the threshold into the playground, nor could it reach the home; it was an affair of black marks under the cracked varnish on a faded cloth between the rollers. Out of the silence into the bright treble of children's voices, then back again into silence, impersonal as a note of music torn from a melody, these monosyllables burst upon the air and died, unassimilated into the rest of our thinking and playing. While the lips were learning to turn h-e-n into hen, the creature itself refused to wear the English word; where the pointer touched the cloth, h-e-n was hen, but elsewhere, in the real world of speech and play, h-e-n meant old.

Slowly, imperceptibly almost, these English words crept into the mind, holding their position precariously as outposts in enemy country, then strengthening their hold and consolidating into a small garrison. They joined themselves into sentences, and they began to live from one lesson into another. 'How arr ewe?' 'Yess pleece' . . . Suddenly an English book moved from the vague background of goods in general (there were hundreds of books in the house) to become unique. It was my book. I cannot remember its name, but in its uniqueness it had no need of title nor of author's name. Its text has now dwindled into – Henry was a good boy. He . . . and thus it remains mirrored in the eye. But the ear has its own memory of the words, a private sound crossing the years and betraying the struggle of the tongue with a strange language. The consonants are harsh, the vowels open, the words moving in a slow and rising tune:– Hennrree wass aye goood boi. Hee . . . I know no more of Henry, and if I were to ask now where it is, this book I called *Hennrree Wass*, no one can tell me.

from *Spring of Youth* (1935)

Silver Jubilee

1939

Faint now in the evening pallor
answering nothing but old cries,
a troop of men shouldering their way
with a new tune I recognise

as something near to Flanders, but far
from the dragon years we killed
to no purpose, scattered seed
on land none but the devil tilled.

That a poet sings as his heart beats
is no new word, but an ancient tale.
Grey shadows on the pavement
and Europe sick of its own bale.

I have no answer, no rising song
to the young in years who are old
with our arrogance, our failure.
Let it be silence: the world is cold.

ANN GRIFFITHS (1776–1805)

Lo, between the Myrtles [1]

Lo, between the myrtles standing,
    One who merits well my love,
Though His worth I guess but dimly,
    High all earthly things above;
        Happy morning
    When at last I see him clear!

Rose of Sharon, so men name Him;
    White and red His cheeks adorn;
Store untold of earthly treasure
    Will His merit put to scorn;
        Friend of sinners,
    He their pilot o'er the deep.

What can weigh with me henceforward
    All the idols of the earth?
One and all I here proclaim them,
    Matched with Jesus, nothing worth;
        O to rest me
    All my lifetime in His love!

                         trans. H. Idris Bell

---

[1]This hymn, in the original Welsh, is sung to the tune 'Cwm Rhondda', as is William Williams'
   'Guide me, O Thou great Jehovah'.

GRUFFUDD AB YR YNAD COCH (*fl.* 1280)

Elegy for Llywelyn ap Gruffudd [1]

Heart cold in the breast with dread,
    Grief-stricken for a king, oak door, of Aberffraw.[2]
    Bright gold was bestowed by his hand;
    He deserved his gold diadem.
Golden king's gold cups! No more merriment,
    Llywelyn; no gay garb may I wear.
I grieve for a prince, hawk beyond reproach,
    I grieve for the ill that befell him.
I grieve for the loss, I grieve for the lot,
    I grieve to hear how he was wounded.
Cadwaladr's[3] stronghold, bulwark from spear waves,
    Lad with red lance, gold-handed linch-pin.
He lavished riches – he gave each winter
    The garments he wore for my wear.
    Lord rich in herds – he aids us no more,
    May a life everlasting be his!
Mine rage at the Saxon who reaved me,
    Mine the need, before death, to lament.
Mine, with good reason, to rave against God
    Who left me without him.
    Mine to praise him, unstinting, unstilled;
    Mine ever, henceforth, his remembrance.
Mine, for my lifetime, is sorrow for him.
    Since mine is the woe, mine the weeping.
    A lord I have lost, long will I fear;
    A lord of high court, a hand killed him.
A lord constant and true, listen to me,
    How loudly I wail! Wretched wailing!
      A lord thriving till eighteen died.
      A lord who gave – low is he laid.
A lord like a lion guiding a land;
    A lord eager to wreak destruction.

[1] Llywelyn ap Gruffudd, (*c.* 1225-1282), the last Prince of independent Wales, killed by
  Anglo-Norman forces near Builth.
[2] Aberffraw, now a village in the south-west of Anglesey, the seat of the House of Gwynedd to
  which Llywelyn belonged.
[3] Cadwaladr (d. 664), Prince of Gwynedd, a traditional hero.

A lord who prospered, till he left Emrais[1]
   No Saxon would venture to strike him,
A lord – stone his roof, mighty king of Wales –
   Of the right line to rule Aberffraw.
     Lord Christ, how I sorrow for him!
     Lord who is true, save us with him
   From the heavy sword-stroke, his downfall;
   From the long swords that had him hard-pressed;
   From the wound for my prince, my distress
   From the word of Bodfaeaw's lord's fall.
Perfect the lad slain by hostile men's hands!
   Perfect his fathers' honour in him!
Candle of kings, strong lion of Gwynedd,[2]
   Throne of honour: he was much needed.
   From Britain's death – rampart of Cynllaith –
   From Nancoel's lion killed – Nancaw's mail –
Many a tear gliding fast down a cheek;
   Many a side made red with gashes;
   Many a puddle of blood, feet soaked;
   Many a widow wailing for him;
   Many a mind burdened and broken;
   Many a son left without father;
Many a home black in the firebrand's track;
   And many a place pillage lays waste.
Many a sorry cry – as at Camlan;[3]
   Many a tear-stained cheek since the fall.
   From a prop cut down – gold-handed prince –
   From Llywelyn's death, lost my man's mind!
   Heart frozen in the bosom with fear!
   Lust for life like dried sticks decaying!
   See you not the rush of the wind and rain?
   See you not the oaks thrashing each other?
See you not that the sea is lashing the shore?
   See you not that the truth is portending?
See you not that the sun is hurtling the sky?
   See you not that the stars have fallen?
Do you not believe in God, foolish men?
   See you not that the world is ending?
Ah, God, that the sea would cover the land!
   What is left us that we should linger?

[1]Emrais . . . Cynllaith, districts in mid-Wales.
[2]Gwynedd, a kingdom in north-west Wales (now a county).
[3]Camlan, the battle in which Arthur was said to have been killed.

No place of escape from terror's prison,
No place to live: wretched is living!
No counsel, no clasp, not a single path
   Open to be saved from fear's sad strife.
      All retainers, true to his trust;
      All warriors, his defenders;
      All strong men once swore by his hand;
      All leaders, all lands were his own.
   All counties, all towns are now troubled;
   All households, all clans now collapse;
   All the weak, all the strong he kept safe,
   All children now cry in their cradles.
   Little good it did, to deceive me –
   Leaving me my head, left headless.
      Head cut off, no hate so dreadful,
      Head cut off, thing better not done,
      Head of a soldier, head of praise,
      Head of a warlord, dragon's head,
Head of fair Llywelyn: harsh fear strikes the world,
        An iron spike through it.
      Head of my prince – harsh pain for me –
      Head of my soul rendered speechless.
Head that owned honour in nine-hundred lands,
        Nine hundred feasts were his.
      Head of a king, his hand hurled iron,
      Head of a king's hawk, forcing a gap.
      Head of a kingly wolf out-thrusting,
      Head of heaven's kings, be his haven!
Blessed king, rule over him, Lord of hosts,
        Whose hopes stretched to Llydaw,[1]
      King right royal of Aberffraw,
      May heaven's fair land be his home.

                                   trans. Joseph P. Clancy

---

[1] Llydaw, Brittany.

IFAN GRUFFYDD (1896–1971)

The Hiring Fair

One of the great days of my life was when I was allowed to go to the hiring fair at Llangefni for the first time.

I set out early on a May morning in the year 1909 to look for a place for myself. I strode like a two-year old foal through Rhostrehwfa, delighted to be thinking of the day that would shortly arrive when I would be allowed to wear corduroy trousers, bell-bottoms and London yorks, with shining buckles and the straps fastened on the outside in a curly link at both knees. Many an old inhabitant of Rhos looked pitifully at my small size and puniness to think that I was ready to go out into the world, and Mary Price the Coal tried to persuade me to look for something better and lighter than serving farmers. But nothing could stand in the way of my determination to become able enough one day to follow a pair of well-fed horses from headland to headland, and turn the peaty bog of Morfa Deugae into long furrows ready for seeding.

There was nothing for it but to walk every step, of course, and the three miles to town was nothing to us in Llangristiolus. I had been there several times before, either driving cattle for a wage of threepence or sixpence, or helping to carry baskets of chicks for some neighbour or other for twopence, and glad of the money to take it to Nan Roberts the Shop towards a pair of boots.

But when that day came for which I had yearned for so long, I felt a degree of independence and thought of being respectable from now on. People would soon forget that I was such a naughty boy after I had started working, and perhaps they would come to recognise me as being as good as most my age if only I were given my chance, and to take that chance was my intention that morning.

I put myself on the market, as it were, in front of the Bull Hotel, among scores of the county's young men, as was the custom at a hiring-fair. It was a lovely experience to be one who counted in the agricultural tradition, and I felt that I was one of those who sustained the world. The farmers, great and small, walked at their leisure through the ranks, weighing up the size and strength of the candidates as was necessary. If it was a bailiff that a man wanted, he had to have one who was capable and clever in his work, who was ready to get up early and go to sleep late – one who could organize his work and take a deep interest in his master's affairs. If it was a horse-handler, well, a strong young man was needed, with broad shoulders, a cap on the side of his head, and a straw in his mouth. The same qualifications, more or less, were required in a feeder and a farmhand, namely that they were prepared to do a bit of everything – some things that would degrade a bailiff and a waggoner, perhaps, but which were necessary to make a team and to ensure a successful season for the master.

The hiring had been brisk and had gone on for hours before anyone noticed that I was there at all, and although I stood up straight and stuck my chest out as best I could, they all passed me by somehow or other. Plenty wanted bailiffs and waggoners, but almost none seemed to be wanting a farmhand, and I was so willing.

I began to lose heart, fearing that I would be left 'on the clout', as Anglesey people say. A man from Llangristiolus came by, one whom I knew well, whose children had got on in the world.

'Are you hired?' he said.

'No, I'm not,' said I.

'You're too naughty a boy, my lad, aren't you, who would take you?' I never had much love for that man for the rest of his days, to my shame perhaps.

If it started badly, my subsequent fate in the fair was even worse – perhaps the man had spoken truly after all, and perhaps he, and others like him, had warned the farmers against burning their fingers by hiring one who was as much of a wastrel as me.

It was now late in the afternoon and most of the lads had been hired, the ranks had thinned, only about three or four were left on the square waiting for someone from somewhere to take pity on them. The street was beginning to empty, the farmers' wives, having filled their butter-baskets with goods, were making for the stables at the back of the Bull, and Huw Jones the ostler was tying the horses to traps, and the pig-carts were hurrying home. For all I know, I had never felt so lonely – there had been such brisk hiring all afternoon and I had been rejected. I had sooner go to Davies the Kennels to clean out the hounds than be without a place to serve, because it was not respectable in those days to be left out. I saw Dafydd Evans of Tyddyn Lleithig coming – towards whom, I wondered? Yes indeed, towards me came the short-legged, handsome smallholder, with his air of authority, who had decided to keep some slip of a lad to run a bit in his stead, because he was getting on in years, he said. With him was Owen Evans of Penrhos, an old neighbour who had showed a bit of fatherly concern for me, fair play to him, and this is how the conversation went from then on.

'Here's Ifan, Dafydd Evans, he's very keen to find a place and I've no doubt he'll be the right lad for you.'

'But I've heard he's a naughty boy.' He turned to me and asked, 'Are you a naughty boy?'

Because of my guilt about a few pranks that I couldn't deny, I could say nothing except lower my eyes and scratch my toe-cap on the edge of the pavement. I ventured to raise my head on hearing Owen Evans say, 'No, he's not, this lad's all right, a bit mischievous perhaps, as some strapping lads like this are when they have nothing to do. Give him plenty of work and he'll settle down.'

Dafydd Evans paused, and then asked, 'If you're allowed to come to my place, will you promise to change your ways?'

'I will,' I said.

'If I say something sharp to you, you won't answer me back?'

'I won't,' and before I had a chance to finish, Owen Evans broke in with 'He won't ever, even if you kick him he'll only go off like a dog with his tail between his legs'.

'Hm', said the smallholder. 'I'm glad to hear that about you'. He put his stick under his arm, and reached for his cherry-wood pipe and filled it with Amlwch tobacco, and as he threw away the match after lighting up, he asked amid a cloud of smoke, 'After finishing your work, will you help the girl with the hens and the chicks in the evenings, and not go larking about with those daft boys up the lane?'

'I will,' I said once again, lest I be without a place. He drew himself up and pushed out his belly as if he owned a thousand acres: 'Well, I'll give you two pounds this first season, and if you behave I'll raise it by a crown by the time winters comes, what do you say, Owen Evans?'

'Well, yes, but aren't you rather hard with the wages, Gaffer?'

'Hard? What's the matter with you, man? Isn't it enough for him and to have his belly full of food into the bargain? What else does the bugger want? I don't know what the lads these days think they are. Where do they expect a farmer to get money to pay them?'

In the end it was agreed on two pounds, with a down payment of sixpence to clinch the bargain and all the conditions that went with it. So, about eighteen pence a week was my wage, when I first went to work, and I was glad of the job.

from *Gŵr o Baradwys* (1963), trans. Meic Stephens

W.J. GRUFFYDD (1881–1954)

Gwladys Rhys

Prayers, Dorcas,[1] Fellowship, and Children's Groups!
And day and night my father's mournful tone
Tiresome as wind, the wind that day and night
Blew shrill through pine twigs round the manse. And mother,
Seeking the speech of heaven, knew no speech
But talk of meetings, Fellowship, and Dorcas.
What could I ever do, I, Gwladys Rhys,
The Reverend Thomas Rhys's eldest child–
The Minister of Horeb on the Moor?
What but to yearn, and ever listlessly
Cast weary eyes across the down's bare slope,
And rise at mornings to await the nights,
And toss through endless nights longing for morn?
And winter, Oh my God, drawing the blinds
O'er windows at four in the afternoon,
And hear the wind bewailing through the pines,
And listen to my father's talk and mother's!

[1]Dorcas, a society for women who made clothes for the poor.

And then one day, Someone drew nigh the house,
And Something strange I felt within my heart;
The wind bewailed no longer through the pines,
Nor listlessly were weary eyes now cast
Across the down's bare slope. I felt the cool
Touch of a playful breeze from brighter lands,
I drew the blinds across the window-pane,
Nor made reply to father's weariness,
I heard my mother render long account
Of North Wales Women's Temperance League, and then
Through snow I sallied forth without a word,
Although the wind was sighing through the pines
And it was Fellowship and Dorcas Night.

And therefore, wayfarer, 'tis here I lie
By Horeb Chapel's walls – I, Gwladys Rhys,
Aged thirty years; father and mother pass
To services, and Fellowship, and Groups,
Dorcas, Prayer Meetings, and Committees of
The North Wales Women's Temperance League; yes, here
In dark Oblivion's Vale, because the gust
Of that light playful breeze from brighter lands
Was nothing but the sigh of wind through pines.

trans. D.M. Lloyd

Exile in Cardiff

The second consequence is that my mind turns more and more to the old things and the old folk. The truth is that I have never lived in a community since I left Llanddeiniolen for Cardiff a quarter of a century ago. Here I simply reside – sleeping, working and eating. I do not *live* here. At home in the village where I was reared I was part of one large community. I knew all about Elin Owen next-door, and her husband, Gruffydd Owen the sailor; when I heard laughter through the window, I knew for certain who was there; when a child passed by on the road, I could tell the history of its father and mother and grandparents; I knew where its great-grandparents lay buried, to what chapel they went, and I could relate many of their sayings. When I was a child, I could describe the mantelpiece of almost every house in the whole neighbourhood; I knew the houses where there was a portrait of Garibaldi painted on glass, where a set of the *Gwyddoniadur* (Welsh Encyclopaedia) was to be found, who had a yellow cat called Sam, and where there was a glass rolling-pin up on the wall. I knew how all the neighbours would react in given circumstances, where I should be most likely to receive a favour and where it would be unwise of me to say too much about myself.

Things are very different indeed for me now. Most of my neighbours are English or Scots, and the native Glamorgan blood flows pretty thin by this time through the veins even of those who call themselves Welsh. No one around me speaks my language or thinks the thoughts I think; they are all rootless people and none of them will be buried with his fathers. In a way it is more comfortable to live thus; there is such a vast continent between me and my neighbours that they never interfere, and I dislike interference. But how sad it is that a Welshman should be an exile in Wales, for every Welshman living in Cardiff or its suburbs is an exile. When I first came here, the farmers around and even the petty squires were Welsh-speaking; by today they have all gone. . . . The last of the old Welsh farmers, Mr George, of the Deri, died a few years ago, and by today most of his land is covered with all kinds of monstrosities of houses and bungalows, with names no less monstrous.

Sometimes, in my bed when I cannot sleep, I bring to mind the homes of my native place, and I repeat the name of everyone who lived in each of them in my time or in the time of my parents; and after dropping off to sleep, I dream of the old people who have gone, my father and mother, my grandfather and my grandmother, my aunt Elin Huws of Cae Meta, Dafydd and Lewis Huws; and for a moment on awaking, I feel overwhelming happiness because I can still have their company. I don't know what Freud and Jung would say about this, and I don't care.

from *Hen Atgofion* (1936), trans. D.M. Lloyd, *The Years of the Locust* (1976)

ANONYMOUS

The Hunting of Twrch Trwyth [1]

Arthur[2] summoned to him Gwyn son of Nudd[3] and asked him whether he knew aught of Twrch Trwyth. He said he did not. Thereupon all the huntsmen went to hunt the pigs as far as Dyffryn Llychwr. And Grugyn Silver-bristle and Llwydawg the Hewer dashed into them and slew the huntsmen so that not a soul of them escaped alive, save one man only. So Arthur and his hosts came to the place where Grugyn and Llwydawg were. And then he let loose upon them all the dogs that had been named to this end. And at the clamour that was then raised, and the barking, Twrch Trwyth came up and defended them. And ever since they had crossed the Irish Sea, he had not set eyes on them till now. Then was he beset by men and dogs. With might and with main he went to Mynydd Amanw, and then a pigling was slain of his pigs. And then they joined with him life for life, and it was then Twrch Llawin

---

[1] Twrch Trwyth, a ferocious wild boar, the hunting of which takes his pursuers across south Wales and into Cornwall.
[2] Arthur (late 5th cent.-early 6th cent.), British military leader about whom there exist many tales which have been incorporated into English literature.
[3] Gwyn ap Nudd, a mythological figure, King of Annwn, the Otherworld.

was slain. And then another of his pigs was slain, Gwys was his name. And he
then went to Dyffryn Amanw, and there Banw and Benwig were slain. Not one
of his pigs went with him alive from that place, save Grugyn Silver-bristle and
Llwydawg the Hewer.

From that place they went on to Llwch Ewin, and Arthur caught up with him
there. Then he stood at bay. And then he slew Echel Big-hip, and Arwyli son
of Gwyddawg Gwyr, and many a man and dog besides. And after that they
went on to Llwch Tawy. Grugyn Silver-bristle then parted from them, and
Grugyn thereafter made for Din Tywi. And he proceeded then into
Ceredigiawn, and Eli and Trachmyr with him, and a multitude along with
them besides. And he came as far as Garth Grugyn. And there Grugyn was
slain in their midst, and he slew Rhuddfyw Rhys and many a man with him.
And then Llwydawg went on to Ystrad Yw. And there the men of Llydaw met
with him, and he then slew Hir Peisawg king of Llydaw, and Llygadrudd Emys
and Gwrfoddw, Arthur's uncles, his mother's brothers. And there he himself
was slain.

Twrch Trwyth went then between Tawy and Ewyas. Arthur summoned
Cornwall and Devon to meet him at the mouth of the Severn. And Arthur said
to the warriors of this Island: 'Twrch Trwyth has slain many of my men. By the
valour of men, not while I am alive shall he go into Cornwall. I will pursue him
no further, but I will join with him life for life. You, do what you will.' And by
his counsel a body of horsemen was sent, and the dogs of the Island with them,
as far as Ewyas, and they beat back thence to the Severn, and they waylaid him
there with what tried warriors there were in this Island, and drove him by sheer
force into Severn. And Mabon son of Modron went with him into Severn, on
Gwyn Dun-mane the steed of Gweddw, and Goreu son of Custennin and
Menw son of Teirgwaedd, between Llyn Lliwan and Aber Gwy. And Arthur
fell upon him, and the champions of Britain along with him. Osla Big-knife
drew near, and Manawydan son of Llŷr, and Cacamwri, Arthur's servant, and
Gwyngelli, and closed in on him. And first they laid hold of his feet, and
soused him in Severn till it was flooding over him. On the one side Mabon son
of Modron spurred his horse and took the razor from him, and on the other
Cyledyr the Wild on another horse, plunged into Severn with him and took
from him the shears. But or ever the comb could be taken he found land with
his feet; and from the moment he found land neither dog nor man nor horse
could keep up with him until he went into Cornwall. Whatever mischief was
come by in seeking those treasures from him, worse was come by in seeking to
save the two men from drowning. Cacamwri, as he was dragged forth, two
quernstones dragged him into the depths. As Osla Big-knife was running after
the boar, his knife fell out of its sheath and he lost it; and his sheath thereafter
being full of water, as he was dragged forth, it dragged him back into the
depths.

Then Arthur went with his hosts until he caught up with him in Cornwall.
Whatever mischief was come by before that was play to what was come by then
in seeking the comb. But from mischief to mischief the comb was won from

him. And then he was forced out of Cornwall and driven straight forward into the sea. From that time forth never a one has known where he went, and Aned and Aethlem with him. And Arthur went thence to Celli Wig in Cornwall, to bathe himself and rid him of his weariness.

from *The Mabinogion* (1948), trans. Gwyn Jones and Thomas Jones

GEORGE HERBERT (1593–1633)

Love

Love bade me welcome; yet my soul drew back,
　　Guilty of dust and sin.
But quick-eyed Love, observing me grow slack
　　From my first entrance in,
Drew nearer to me, sweetly questioning,
　　If I lacked anything.

'A guest', I answered, 'worthy to be here.'
　　Love said, 'You shall be he.'
'I, the unkind, ungrateful? Ah, my dear,
　　I cannot look on thee.'
Love took my hand, and smiling did reply,
　　'Who made the eyes but I?'

'Truth, Lord, but I have marred them; let my shame
　　Go where it doth deserve.'
'And know you not', says Love, 'who bore the blame?'
　　'My dear, then I will serve.'
'You must sit down', says Love, 'and taste my meat.'
　　So I did sit and eat.

NIGEL HESELTINE (1916–　)

Hero of his Village

Though you are missing from the shelf
where your family coffins rot in the vault,
your cross is on the church wall
decorated with a button or two from your coat.

So the children coming with the hymn-
books in their hands see that you died
for liberty or some cause and hang
above where the parish magazine is displayed.

Though there is nothing of you but the buttons,
those in the cricket-team you taught to bowl
remember you; the girls you looked aside from
lest you become entangled, married now
look beyond their solid husbands, remember you well.

Though you left no child, nor a wife
nor ploughed land save once on leave
as relaxation; though the parson leaving
his church in a hurry now never sees
your cross, yet given a proper occasion the man
could preach a sermon on your dying that would make
futile in comparison the longest life.

JOHN CEIRIOG HUGHES (1832–87)

Still the Mighty Mountains Stand

Still the mighty mountains stand,
    Round them still the tempests roar;
Still with dawn through all the land
    Sing the shepherds as of yore.
Round the foot of hill and scar
    Daisies still their buds unfold;
Changed the shepherds only are
    On those mighty mountains old.

Passing with the passing years
    Ancient customs change and flow;
Fraught with doom of joy or tears,
    Generations come and go.
Out of tears' and tempests' reach
    Alun Mabon[1] sleeps secure;–
Still lives on the ancient speech,
    Still the ancient songs endure.

                     from *Alun Mabon* (1862), trans. H. Idris Bell

[1] Alun Mabon, the farmer whose marriage and idealised way of life are the subject of Ceiriog's
poem.

Richard Hughes (1900–76)

The Glass-Ball Country

In a country where I was once walking there was an enormous castle on the top of a rock. It was all ruined; but it was very difficult to climb the rock, and there was still enough of the walls left to make it quite hard to get in. And inside the walls an old charcoal-burner had built himself a cottage, to live there with his wife and his little girl.

At the time he built it there were a tremendous lot of wars. Not just one big war, like we have nowadays sometimes, but any number of little ones going on at the same time and in the same country, so that sometimes you would find as many as three separate battles going on in the same field, and armies falling over each other to get at their own enemy.

The old charcoal-burner did not like this, so he thought if he built his cottage up inside the ruined castle, the armies wouldn't find him and he would be out of the way of all these wars. So he built it, and was very careful not to tell anyone where he lived, in case they went and told one of the armies.

But one night late as he was coming back from the town, he met an old pedlar on the high road. The pedlar was very old and wobbly on the pins, and he asked the charcoal-burner how far it was to the town.

'Ten miles,' said the charcoal-burner.

The old pedlar groaned. 'Dearie me,' he said, 'I don't feel as if I could walk another step.'

Now the charcoal-burner was in a great difficulty. If he left the old pedlar, he might die before ever he got to the town; but if he took him to his cottage, he might be a spy, who would tell an army where he lived.

But all the same, he thought it would be kinder to take the old man home and risk it.

So he took him up to his cottage and gave him supper; and then the old pedlar, who was very tired, went to bed.

No sooner was he in bed, however, than the charcoal-burner's wife began to row him. 'You silly idiot!' she said. 'I'm sure he isn't a real pedlar at all, but a spy who will tell the armies where we are, and we shall all be killed!'

'Well, let's go and look at him,' said the husband.

So they went up to the pedlar's room and looked at him; and sure enough he had taken off his white beard and hung it at the end of his bed, and was really quite a young man.

'What are we going to do now?' said the charcoal-burner.

'We must kill him!' said his wife. 'You go and get your axe, and cut him in half while he is asleep.'

So the old charcoal-burner went and got his axe and came back, but when he saw the stranger lying asleep he found it very difficult to make up his mind to do it.

'My axe wants sharpening,' he said.

'Then sharpen it,' said his wife.

So he went down to the grindstone and sharpened and sharpened it till it was sharp as a razor. Then he came back.

'Now do it,' said his wife.

'I can't,' he said. 'You do it.'

So the charcoal-burner's wife took the axe, but before she could do anything the stranger woke up, and they only just had time to get out of the room before he should see them.

'Never mind,' said the old woman. 'I will do it as soon as he is asleep again.' But, instead, while she was waiting she fell asleep herself, and didn't wake up till the morning, when the pedlar had already got up and put on his beard and was ready to start on his journey.

But before he went he took a big glass ball, bigger than a football, out of his pack.

'That is a present for your little girl,' he said: 'Thank you for being so kind to me'; and away he went.

'Oh dear, oh dear,' said the old charcoal-burner to his wife, 'now he will tell the armies, and they will come and kill us all!'

But the little girl took the glass ball and put it on the mantelpiece, and loved it dearly. And as a matter of fact the stranger was not a spy at all, so it was very lucky they hadn't killed him. But it *did* happen that a few days later one of the armies fighting about the place saw the old castle, and so they said, 'Let's go up there and have a rest, where the enemy won't find us.'

So a whole lot of soldiers began to climb the rock.

'Here they come!' said the old woman. 'Now we shall all be killed. Oh, where can we possibly hide?'

'Haven't you seen there is a whole country inside the glass ball?' said the little girl. 'It's ever so tiny, only about an inch across: but we might hide there.'

'Good idea,' said her father: so they all three made themselves absolutely tiny and got into the country inside the glass ball. They made themselves so tiny they were just the right size for the country.

Meanwhile the soldiers reached the cottage, and they ate all the food, and put their muddy feet on the beds, and laughed and drank and behaved perfectly horribly. At last one of them said, 'Look at that glass ball: what fun it would be to throw it from the top of the rock, and watch it smash to little bits in the valley below!'

So he took the ball, with the country inside it, and the three people inside the country, and went to the edge of the rock and threw it over. And it fell down, down, down into the valley beneath, where it hit a big stone and was smashed to atoms!

But when the ball was smashed the country that was inside fell out, and lay on the ground. It was about as big as a small frog, and first it was hidden under a leaf. But then it began to grow. That was a curious thing; by the afternoon it was quite three feet across. Of course the people grew with it, so they didn't notice what was happening, except that the leaf that at first covered the whole world had now shrunk until it only covered two fields. And all that night the country grew, till by morning it filled all the meadow where it was lying.

Just then a wounded soldier came hobbling along, with another soldier after him trying to kill him.

'Come in here,' called the little girl. So the wounded soldier got into the country, but when the one who was chasing him tried to get in he couldn't do it. And lo and behold, who should the wounded soldier be but the very stranger who had given the little girl the glass ball.

'What country is this?' she asked him.

'It's the Peace Country,' he said; 'No one can fight inside here.'

No more they could. Some of the farmers who were trying to get out of the way of the wars came in, but the armies couldn't.

And still the country went on growing, till now it covered the whole county, and the armies found themselves getting rather cramped for space to fight in. But still they went on fighting and still the country went on growing, till at last there was no room for them at all, and they were all pushed into the sea and the whole lot were drowned. But the Peace Country grew till it covered all the old warry country, and there the farmers and other quiet people all lived together happily, and they made the charcoal-burner and his wife king and queen and the little girl princess.

'Now I am a princess,' she said, 'I think I will marry the stranger who gave me the lovely ball.'

But he had disappeared for good.

T. ROWLAND HUGHES (1903–49)

Thrown into the River [1]

That evening Gwyn, with a number of other small boys, was sitting on the river bank fishing for tiddlers with the usual stick, thread, bent pin and worm, when he felt an elbow being dug into his back. Looking up, he saw Will Parry bending menacingly over him.

'You got plenty of sport 's morning, didn't you?' he remarked in a surly tone.

A small boy named Meurig jumped up.

'You leave Gwyn alone,' he said. 'He's been ill and in his bed.'

'Not too ill to go round with Harry Rags yesterday,' replied Will, pushing the other aside and gripping Gwyn by the shoulder. 'You were enough of a lad last night, weren't you, Gwyn Evans?'

[1] The background to the novel from which this extract was chosen is the Penrhyn Lock-out which took place in the quarrying district of Bethesda, Caerns., in 1896-97 and 1900-03.

Gwyn tried to ignore the bully and carry on with his fishing, but Will
dragged him backwards and jerked him to his feet.

'Say you're sorry,' he told him.

'For what?'

'For what? For knocking at our door and shouting "Traitor".'[1]

'I didn't shout "Traitor".'

'Say you're sorry.'

'I'll tell Os when I see him.'

'Will you, the little blab!' Will tightened his grip on Gwyn's shoulder,
making him wince with pain. 'Say you're sorry.'

'I'm *not* sorry.'

'Uh?'

'I'm *not* sorry.'

'Nor me neither,' put in Meurig, putting down his rod and getting up, his
little fists clenched daringly.

Will realised his danger and rather than stand up to both of them, small as
they were, he chose the bully's way out. A moment later Gwyn was hurled over
the bank and he fell full length into the river. Luckily the water was not deep,
and the terrified boy managed to struggle to his feet and clamber back on to the
bank.

'That'll learn you to blab,' said Will, but half-heartedly, as though knowing
himself to be in the wrong.

'And this'll learn *you*, too, you Will Cuckoo!' rejoined Meurig furiously,
dispensing with his fists and making good use of his feet instead. The pain
inflicted by Oswald's fists on Will's mouth and nose that noon was as nothing
compared with the agony of iron-shod boot on his leg now, and he flopped to
the ground, nursing the injured limb and squealing dolefully like a pig being
pegged.

Gwyn and Meurig hurried back to the village and up Tan-y-bryn. There
was nobody in 'Gwynfa', for Edward Evans was at a meeting of the Fund
Committee, and the boys waited miserably outside the house, not knowing
what to do. The next house up the hill . . . Idris' house . . . was unoccupied, as
was also the next house down, for the owner, Owen Williams, Owie-the-Wern
. . . had found work in Liverpool. And as his cousin Ceridwen was so ill Gwyn
would not go across the road for fear of bothering his uncle John.

'Come up to our house, Gwyn,' said Meurig. 'You shall have a lend of my
best clothes.'

'No, Dadda won't be long, see.'

When Edward Evans arrived about half an hour later Gwyn was shivering in
his wet clothes and his father promptly sent him to bed.

'Run up to Albert Terrace, my lad,' he told the other boy, 'and ask Megan
. . . Mrs Davies . . . to come down here for a bit.'

---

[1]'Traitor', the name given by the strikers to the blacklegs who returned to work against the
wishes of the Union.

He then busied himself with lighting the lamp and re-kindling the fire to boil some milk for Gwyn. ''S nothing like hot milk with pepper in it,' he told himself. 'I hope to goodness the boy won't be any the worse, and Martha coming home end of the week.'

When he took the milk up to the front bedroom . . . father and son shared the same room now . . . he saw by the light of the candle he had left burning that Gwyn was sweating and in pain.

'Come, drink this, my lad. You'll feel better then.'

'Terrible old pain in my side, Dadda.'

'Where, Gwyn *bach*?'

'Here, where it was before when I was in my bed for a week.' And he put a hand to his heart.

'Your limbs hurting?'

'Yes, same as before. My ankles and knees.'

'Got a pain in your head?'

'Yes, Dadda.'

'Try this hot milk, now. And here's a bit of that currant cake from Price's shop for you. You are a terror for this, aren't you?'

But, fond though he was of Price's currant cake, Gwyn could not touch it, his throat was too painful for him to swallow even a morsel. He managed, however, to sip the milk slowly, after which Megan, who had just arrived, turned him gently over on his side and tucked in the bedclothes. She then hurried downstairs, followed slowly by her father.

'Dadda?'

'Yes, my boy?' He went back to the bed.

'I didn't tell him I was sorry.'

'Tell who?'

'Some big boy down by the river.'

'Who was he?'

'He's not in our school.'

'Sorry about what?'

'He'd seen me with Harry Rags yesterday and I knocked on his door. His father's a Traitor, and he was wanting me to say I was sorry. But "I'm *not* sorry", I said.'

'Try and sleep now, Gwyn *bach*.'

'When will you be coming to your bed, Dadda?'

'I won't be long, my boy. Shall I leave the candle for you?'

'No, got to be sparing with candles, Mam said.'

'Try to sleep now, my boy.'

Downstairs in the kitchen Megan and her father looked anxiously at one another: the symptoms were the same as those of three months before, when Gwyn had been laid up for more than a week.

'If he is not better in the morning,' said Edward Evans, 'I'll ask Doctor Roberts to have a look at him.'

'I would like to get hold of that Tom Parry's son,' exclaimed Megan angrily.

'Tom Parry's boy? Why?'

'It was him pushed Gwyn into the river.'

'How d'you know?'

'The little boy who came to fetch me told me.'

There was silence for a while: Edward Evans gazed pensively into the fire.

'It *is* a pity, isn't it?'

'What, Dadda?'

'That this dispute is going among the children like this. Workman against workman, partner against partner, woman against woman, family against family.' He shook his head sadly as he went on, 'And now, children against children, school against school. What will be the end of the whole trouble, I wonder. Its influence will be like poison all through this place for many years, I am afraid. Not one of us thought at the start that things would come to this, that families would be scattered, homes broken up, the whole district split in two, bad feeling everywhere ... on the street, in the shops, in school among the children, even in chapel. Pity there wasn't some way to keep the children unspotted from it. And the chapels. Last Sunday in Siloh there was old William Parry passing by Mike Roberts' seat when taking round the Communion.

'I heard about that. Because he is a Traitor, isn't he?'

'Aye. And when Mr Edwards spoke with him afterwards he was unrepentant altogether, like if he had performed some great deed. I don't know, I don't indeed, what will become of us if this old affair goes on a long time yet.'

                    from *Chwalfa* (1946), trans. Richard Ruck, *Out of their Night* (1954)

ANONYMOUS

The Assembly of the Wondrous Head

And then Bendigeidfran[1] commanded his head to be struck off. 'And take the head,' he said, 'and carry it to the White Mount in London, and bury it with its face towards France. And you will be a long time upon the road. In Harddlech you will be feasting seven years, and the birds of Rhiannon[2] singing unto you. And the head will be as pleasant company to you as ever it was at best when it was on me. And at Gwales in Penfro[3] you will be fourscore years; and until you open the door towards Aber Henfelen, the side facing Cornwall, you may bide there, and the head with you uncorrupted. But from the time you have opened

[1]Bendigeidfran (or Brân), legendary King of the Isle of Britain, who was of gigantic build.
[2]Birds of Rhiannon, legendary birds which were said to waken the dead and send the living to sleep.
[3]Gwales in Penfro, the island of Grassholm, about eight miles off the coast of Pembrokeshire.

that door, you may not bide there: make for London to bury the head. And do you cross over to the other side.'

And then his head was struck off, and they set out for the other side, these seven, and the head with them, and Branwen[1] the eighth. And they came to land at Aber Alaw in Talebolion.[2] And then they sat down and rested them. Then she looked on Ireland and the Island of the Mighty,[3] what she might see of them. 'Alas, Son of God,' said she, 'woe is me that ever I was born: two good islands have been laid waste because of me!' And she heaved a great sigh, and with that broke her heart. And a four-sided grave was made for her, and she was buried there on the bank of the Alaw. . . .

And at the end of the seventh year they set out for Gwales in Penfro. And there was for them there a fair royal place overlooking the sea, and a great hall it was. And they went into the hall, and two doors they saw open; the third door was closed, that towards Cornwall. 'See yonder,' said Manawydan,[4] 'the door we must not open.' And that night they were there without stint, and were joyful. And notwithstanding all the sorrows they had seen before their eyes, and notwithstanding that they had themselves suffered, there came to them no remembrance either of that or of any sorrow in the world. And there they passed the fourscore years so that they were not aware of having ever spent a time more joyous and delightful than that. It was not more irksome, nor could any tell of his fellow that he was older during that time, than when they came there. Nor was it more irksome having the head with them then than when Bendigeidfran had been with them alive. And because of those fourscore years it was called the Assembly of the Wondrous Head. The Assembly of Branwen and Matholwch[5] was that wherewith they went to Ireland.

This is what Heilyn son of Gwyn did one day. 'Shame on my beard,' said he, 'if I do not open the door to know if that is true which is said concerning it.' He opened the door and looked on Cornwall and Aber Henfelen. And when he looked, they were as conscious of every loss they had ever sustained, and of every kinsman and friend they had missed, and of every ill that had come upon them, as if it were even then it had befallen them; and above all else because of their lord. And from that same moment they could not rest, save they set out with the head towards London. However long they were upon the road, they came to London and buried the head in the White Mount. And when it was buried, that was one of the Three Happy Concealments, and one of the Three Unhappy Disclosures when it was disclosed, for no plague would ever come across the sea to this Island so long as the head was in that concealment.

from *The Mabinogion* (1948), trans. Gwyn Jones and Thomas Jones

[1]Branwen, a heroine in *The Mabinogion*, the wife of Matholwch, king of Ireland.
[2]Talebolion, a district in Anglesey.
[3]Island of the Mighty, Britain.
[4]Manawydan, the brother of Bendigeidfran.
[5]Matholwch, King of Ireland.

E. MORGAN HUMPHREYS (1882–1955)

Salem

A few weeks ago there were some interesting articles in *Yr Herald Gymraeg* about the picture known as *Salem*, and someone asked me whether I knew anything about it. Most of us have seen that picture at some time or another – the simple country chapel with its window in the background opening on the countryside; the old woman in her tall hat and Paisley shawl, going to her seat; a bearded, middle-aged man, pressing his forehead on his hands, and another in the same pose near the farthest wall; a small boy with lowered head in another seat, and a few other neighbours here and there in the old-fashioned seats. As it happens, I know of the chapel, and of some of the people in the picture, which was painted about forty years ago by an artist whose name was Curnow Vosper. Salem is a Baptist chapel in Cefncymerau, above Llanbedr and Gwynfryn in Ardudwy, and the figures in the picture are the people of those hills.

The old lady in her Paisley shawl is Siân Owen of Ty'n y Fawnog and later of Ffordd Groes, Llanfair, near Harlech. The old man with his hand at his ear is Owen Siôn of Carleg Coch, and Laura William of Ty'n y Buarth is sitting at his side. The boy is Evan Edward Lloyd of Ty'n yr Aelgerth and the bearded man is William Siôn of Carleg Coch, with Mrs Mary Rowlands, later of Dolgellau, sitting nearby. The man siting under the clock is Robert Williams of Cae'r Meddyg. I remember him well. A farmer and carpenter was Robert Williams, living in a cottage within sight of Y Moelfre and Y Rhiniog on one side, and in view of the sea and all the splendour of Caernarfonshire's mountains, from Snowdon as far as Bardsey, on the other. From the gate which leads towards Cae'r Meddyg you can see the length of Dyffryn Artro, a long, wooded valley, with its little, rocky fields and the slopes purple with heather in its season, rising on all sides, and the rocks of Cwm Bychan blocking the view in the distance. The arm of a hill hides Cwm Nancol with its winding river and its green meadows. I know of no more beautiful scene on a summer's evening – the rays of a setting sun streaming across wood and escarpment, over fields and rocks, the slow, pearly smoke of a farmhouse and an unseen cottage rising now and then from the valley like a light mist, and some sweet and magic silence, a gentle stillness, over the whole.

And it is Cae'r Meddyg and that scene, and the people of the rocky cottages and the sunny slopes, that come to my mind whenever I see the picture of Salem. I know a little of their life – as it used to be, at any rate – of their kindness, of their hospitality, of their daily labour and their regular attendance on Sundays. I remember well many a meal in the snug and jolly kitchens of Cae'r Meddyg, Glyn Artro, Allt Goch and Penbryn in the days gone by – many years ago by now – the furniture and crockery gleaming, the scent of a wood fire and bread in the oven sweet to the nostrils, the talk about what went on in the locality, and the atmosphere so neighbourly and so kind. I used the word 'neighbours' deliberately, when referring at the outset to the people in the chapel at Cefncymerau, for that was the great thing about their way of life – they were people of the same background, the same language, the same interests, living together in their own neighbourhood, and it is that, when all is said and done, which amounts to something priceless in the life of a nation. Look at the face of Siân Owen in the picture; you will see there sadness and calm, strength and gentleness, and these were typical of many of the hill-people. Their lives were often hard and they were no more perfect than we are, but they were part of a community and a tradition, and that put mettle in their characters. And hard though their labour was, from those slopes and within the old chapel's walls a few caught a glimpse of Jerusalem's towers in the clouds of the setting sun, and they saw the sea of glass shining between them and the far horizon.

trans. Meic Stephens

EMYR HUMPHREYS (1919–   )

From Father to Son

There is no limit to the number of times
Your father can come to life, and he is as tender as ever he was
And as poor, his overcoat buttoned to the throat,
His face blue from the wind that always blows in the outer darkness
He comes towards you, hesitant,
Unwilling to intrude and yet driven at the point of love
To this encounter.

You may think
That love is all that is left of him, but when he comes
He comes with all his winters and all his wounds.
He stands shivering in the empty street,
Cold and worn like a tramp at the end of a journey
And yet a shape of unquestioning love that you
Uneasy and hesitant of the cold touch of death
Must embrace.

Then, before you can touch him
He is gone, leaving on your fingers
A little more of his weariness
A little more of his love.

The Arrest [1]

It was while they sat in the kitchen drinking it, the police arrived. Mrs Ellis glimpsed a blue helmet moving above the lace curtain.

—They've come, she said. Oh my God . . . they're here.

She stared so wildly at her husband, she could have been urging him to run away and hide. He sat at the table, pale and trembling a little. He spoke in spite of himself.

—Didn't think they would come today, he said.

The peremptory knock on the back door agitated Mrs Ellis so much she pressed both her hands on her grey hair and then against her cheeks.

—I've got fifteen pounds in the lustre jug, she said. Do you think they'll take them, Gwilym, if I offer them?

The colour began to return to his cheeks.

—They don't really want you to go. The prisons are too full anyway. I read that in the paper only a week ago. They're too full you see. I meant to cut it out to show you. They won't have room for you, when it comes to it . . .

The minister breathed very deeply and rose to his feet.

—It's not a place for you anyway. Not a man like you Gwilym. This is your proper place where you're looked after properly, so that you can do the work you have been called to do. A son of the Manse living in the Manse. There isn't a man in the Presbytery who works half as hard as you do . . .

—Olwen! Pull yourself together! Be worthy.

A second series of knocks sent him rushing to the back door. He threw it open and greeted the two policemen with exaggerated geniality.

—Gentlemen! Please come in! I've been expecting you and yet I must confess I'm not absolutely ready to travel, as you can see. Won't you come in?

He led them into the parlour. The room was conspicuously clear but crowded with heavy old-fashioned furniture. It smelt faintly of camphor. In a glass-fronted cabinet there were ceramic objects Mrs Ellis had collected. Two matching Rembrandt reproductions hung on either side of the black marble mantlepiece. The minister invited the policemen to sit down. The senior policeman removed his helmet. A dull groove encircled his thick black hair. Sitting in a low armchair he nursed both the charge-sheet attached to a clip-board and his helmet on his knees. His companion stood at ease in the doorway until he realised that Mrs Ellis was behind him. She recoiled nervously when he turned and pressed himself against the door so that she could pass into the room. He was a young policeman with plump cheeks and wet suckling lips. When she saw how young he was she looked a little reassured. The older policeman twisted in his chair to speak to her. His voice was loud with undue effort to be normal and polite.

—I don't expect you remember me?

---

[1] The background to the story from which this extract is taken is a campaign by *Cymdeithas yr Iaith Gymraeg* (The Welsh Language Society).

She moved forward to inspect his face more closely. His false teeth flashed under his black moustache and drew attention to his pock-marked cheeks and small, restless eyes. The minister's wife shook her head a little hopelessly.

—I am Gwennie's husband. Gwennie Penycefn. You remember Gwennie.

—Gwennie . . .

Mrs Ellis repeated the name with affectionate recognition. She looked at her husband hopefully. He was still frowning with the effort of identification.

—You taught her to recite when she was small.

Mrs Ellis nodded eagerly.

—And Mr Ellis here confirmed her. I don't mind telling you she burst into tears after breakfast. When I told her where I was going and the job I had to do. 'Not Mr Ellis' she said. 'He baptised me and he confirmed me'. Poor Gwennie. She was very upset.

The minister nodded solemnly. He stood in front of the empty fireplace, squaring his shoulders, his hands clasped tightly together behind his back. The armchair creaked as the policeman lowered his voice and leaned forward.

—What about paying, Mr Ellis? You've made your stand. And we respect you for it. It's our language too isn't it, after all. I don't want to see a man of your calibre going to prison. Honestly I don't.

—Oh dear . . .

In spite of her effort at self-control, Mrs Ellis had begun to sigh and tremble. The policeman turned his attention to her, gruff but confident in his own benevolence.

—Persuade him, Mrs Ellis bach. You should see the other one I've got waiting in the station. And goodness knows what else the van will have to collect. The refuse of society, Mrs Ellis. Isn't that so, Pierce?

He invited a confirming nod from his young colleague.

—Scum, Pierce said in his light tenor voice. That one tried to kill himself last night, if you please.

—Oh no . . .

Mrs Ellis put her hands over her mouth.

—Younger than me too. Now he needs a stretch. Do him good.

—Officer.

The minister was making an effort to sound still and formal.

—This man you say tried to kill himself. What was his trouble?

—Drugs.

The older policeman answered the question.

—Stealing. Breaking and entering. Driving without a licence. Drugs.

The policeman spoke the last word as if its very sound had polluted his lips. His colleague had managed to tighten his wet lips to demonstrate total abomination. He made a strange sound in his throat like the growl of an angry watchdog.

—Will you give me a moment to . . . dress and . . . so on?

The policeman sighed.

—You don't need anything, my dear Mr Ellis. You go in wet and naked like the day you were born.

Mrs Ellis moved into the crowded room. Even in her distress she navigated her way between the furniture without ever touching their edges. Her arms floated upwards like a weak swimmer giving in to the tide.

—I'll pack a few things, she said. In your little week-end case.

Her eyes were filling with tears and it was clear that she had not taken in the policeman's last words.

—Wear your round collar, Gwilym, she said.

She spoke in a pleading whisper and made a discreet gesture towards her own throat.

—There's still respect for the cloth, isn't there?

—I go like any other man who has broken the English law, he said. Get me my coat, Olwen. That's all I shall need.

The younger policeman looked suddenly annoyed.

—Look, he said. Why cause all this fuss for nothing? It's only a bit of a telly licence. Why don't you pay the fine here and now like any sensible chap and have done with it?

The minister looked at him.

—You have your duty, he said. I have mine.

from 'The Arrest'

A Pacifist Protest [1]

The Eisteddfod tent was packed. The daylight filtered through the gently flapping canvas roof. In the audience there were eight thousand people. The bards in their robes occupied a steep bank of seats at the back of the wide platform. The chaired bard, who was a small man, leaned sideways in one half of the ceremonial chair. He listened intently to the white-haired orator[2] in a frock-coat, who stood alone in front of his vast, attentive audience. At intervals there were doorways in the semicircular canvas wall and large policemen stood in these areas of bright daylight to keep back the crowds outside in the Eisteddfod field who were straining forward to catch what they could of the orator's words. The policemen's helmets had polished crests and silver buttons gleamed down the dark bulk of their uniform. With one hand holding the lapel of his coat and the other free to make gestures, the orator pitched his voice accurately to reach the furthest rows of the assembly where they were accepted eagerly as much for the effort and skill that went into their sending as for what they said.

Lydia leaned forward so that she could look first down the row beyond Kate's attentive face and then to her left beyond her brother Griff, who was on leave and whose arms were folded high on his chest, partly obscuring her view.

---

[1] This episode is set in the National Eisteddfod about 1915, during one of the ceremonies of the Gorsedd of Bards.
[2] The white-haired orator, David Lloyd George (1863-1945), Liberal politician.

Lydia gave Kate a nudge, but Kate frowned and continued to listen intently to the orator.

—I say again to this assembly of the eisteddfodwyr[1] of Wales, this war is a crusade in the defence of little nations ...

—Don't, Kate said.

Her lips barely moved as she stared intently at the man on the platform.

—J.T.! Lydia said. J.T. Miles. I saw him.

Kate's head remained tilted and her attention never wavered.

—The greatest art of the world was the work of little nations ...

The orator's voice lifted at the end of each statement as if it carried with it the sum of the emotion of all the people present, so that when the orator released the key word from his lips the hands now resting motionless in laps would begin clapping and create a rainstorm of applause.

—The most enduring literature of the world came from the little nations. The heroic deeds that thrill through generations were the very deeds of little nations fighting for their freedom!

The applause broke. Lydia had not been as attentive as others and she was a little late in beginning to clap her hands. She made up for this in extra vigour which also enabled her to turn her head to where J.T. Miles sat away to her right in the row behind them.

—He's not clapping, Lydia said excitedly in Kate's ear. He's not clapping you know. He's not clapping.

Griff touched her arm. She smiled at him. He smiled back and held up a finger to indicate there was another sentence coming.

Ah yes. Ah yes ...

The applause died away into complete silence.

—Ah yes, and the salvation of mankind came through a small nation.

A wave of sighing spread around the audience, and many nodded and muttered approval as if they were in chapel. Griff winked at Lydia as if to say he had told her it was coming.

—Let me ... let me ... the orator said, stuttering, interrupting himself, and at the same time shifting his weight from one foot to the other so that the movement brought him nearer to his audience and in more intimate contact with them.

—Let me tell you of a sheltered valley I know of in my native country, farther than the harps of our bards from the horrid shriek of shot and shell! A beautiful valley, snug, peaceful, comfortable, sheltered from all the bitter blasts. Comfortable, my friends, but sometimes enervating. All the bolder boys would love to climb the hill above the village and glimpse the great mountains in the distance.

The orator paused. A quick gesture showed a lesson was to be drawn. He began again on a note of greater intimacy.

—We, all of us, you and I, have been living in a sheltered valley for

---

[1] *Eisteddfodwyr*, devotees of the Eisteddfod.

generations. Now, out of our selfish comfort the stern hand of war drives us up
the slopes to see the peaks of duty and honour and patriotism clad in glittering
white. And highest of all . . .

He – lifted his arm and looked upwards.

—. . . The peak of sacrifice pointed like a rugged finger to heaven.

His arm came down slowly, the index finger still erect. He bent his wrist
until the same finger was pointing at the audience. Then he opened his arms
wide as if to embrace the long ranks of listeners who sat below him.

—Fellow eisteddfodwyr, young men of Wales, this little nation, your country
calls and I know and you know it will not call in vain.

Heads suddenly began to turn in irritated consternation. Another voice was
calling. An intruder was speaking. J.T. Miles, an angular young man with
untidy red hair had risen to his feet and was stretching out a hand that clutched
a programme of the day's events towards the platform, in an appeal to the
orator.

—But there is another way, sir. There is another way, sir, is there not?

His voice wobbled and trembled with nervous emotion so that at first neither
Lydia nor Kate recognized it. He was pushing a finger down his collar as if to
give himself more voice. Griff turned to look over his shoulder without
unfolding his arms. His eyebrows were raised and his forehead furrowed. Kate
and Lydia looked at each other anxiously, Kate growing pale and Lydia
disapproving and indignant.

After the shocked silence, a buzz of disquiet began to build up, which was
pierced by angry shouts that came with increasing power.

—Sit down!

—Shut up!

—Sit down!

—Throw him out!

—Shame on him!

—Sit down!

J.T. lifted his arm again. A man sitting next to him plucked away at the
bottom of his jacket; but J.T. gripped firmly at the seat in front of him which
was occupied by a stout lady in black. She blushed furiously as her chair
twitched under her and at seeing so many faces turned towards her. Her
husband in a sudden rage hammered at J.T.'s knuckles with a folded
newspaper until shreds of its pages fell away.

On the platform, the orator quickly recovered. He raised his hand
dramatically.

—My friends!

The ringing voice topped the growing disturbance and once again could be
heard clearly at the back of the Pavilion.

—As long as the men and women of this noble generation last, they will
persecute this righteous war, this war for the weak against the strong, this war
of Good against Evil, this war for the honour of this ancient country, until the
summit of glorious victory is finally conquered!

As at a symphony concert a storm of applause broke out as he finished and Kate allowed herself to release a pent-up sigh of relief. Her shoulders, which had been rigid since the moment J.T. first called out, sagged and she bent forward, breathing heavily. This made it easier for Lydia to try and catch J.T.'s eye, so that she could show all her disapproval, but J.T. was still on his feet, looking despairingly towards the platform where the orator had already sat down in the vacant chair near that of the chaired bard. The orator lowered his head as the archdruid conferred with him, and then nodded, giving his blessing to what was being suggested to him. The chaired bard dried his hands on the arms of his chair and lifted his eyes modestly to the roof. He was prepared to be overlooked. The whole canvas pavilion seethed and hummed like a hive that had been disturbed. The archdruid pushed the white folds of his head-dress over his shoulder, lifted his hand, and called upon the assembly to stand up and sing the Welsh national anthem. An experienced conductor in bardic robes stepped forward at an urgent gesture from the archdruid and with hand and voice induced the audience to sing, at first unsteadily and then, as the melodic line struck home to every inattentive ear, with confident harmony and swelling power. The orator himself rose to his feet and with the freedom of a man who has discharged a heavy task, turned first to one side and then the other, willingly submerging his own voice in the united effort, an equal among equals to be seen sharing the pleasure of communal sound.

from *Outside the House of Baal* (1965)

Hide and Seek

'Isn't there a game we can play?' says Les. 'What about hide and seek?'

'Bit childish, isn't it?' Albie lights a cigarette.

'Who cares? Just the place for a game on a big scale. I like the idea. What about it?'

'Oh, yes. Let's.' Dilys and Ann are enthusiastic . . .

Michael now imitates a child counting out. The lot of searcher falls to me. I borrow Les's wrist-watch, and I sit down comfortably to give them all five minutes to disappear. The entire wooded valley is so peaceful and the sounds of peace so soothing to listen to I wait longer than is necessary and get to my feet almost reluctantly.

I walk very slowly in the direction of the old mill. The solitude of my surroundings moves me strangely, and at the same time releases me from my preoccupation with myself. I identify myself with the eccentric shape of an old, isolated thorn tree near the bright green ground with its wet indentations that lies between me and the shallow race of the river as it approaches the mill. Inside the ruined shell of the mill the earth floor has been churned up by the feet of sheltering cattle. Of the second floor, there remains only one stout joist.

Hundreds of initials and names are scrawled over the patches of whitewashed plaster that remain on the stone walls. Some must have climbed up to the joist to write their names in bold illiterate letters on the highest parts of the wall. Alongside the mill, the rotting moss-covered wooden wheel suffers the endless attack of the white foamed eager mill-race.

I move further into the wood, following a sheep track upwards towards the hilltop. Lost in my delicious reverie I have almost forgotten my companions, when suddenly through the bushes I hear a murmur of voices. I stand quite still, and listen. The glow of happiness begins to drain from me before I am certain that it is Michael and Dilys that I can hear. Two voices that are intimate, that have come to some understanding. They draw me on like a spy who creeps up to see and remain unseen. They disturb me into new forms of shame and disgust. Dilys lies on the grass and Michael lies at her side, his hand lying on her breast. As I watch, Dilys lifts a hand to stroke his hair and Michael leans down to kiss her, his body weighing against hers. I tremble with hatred and disgust. My best friend and the girl whom I respected and adored. For the first time in my life I feel the hatred that can kill.

When I turn away I no longer care whether they become aware of my presence, or whether she sits up suddenly, smoothing her hair with her hand to ask him did he hear someone approach. All I know is that I am unbearably unhappy and wretchedly betrayed by one whom I considered my most admirable friend and a girl whom I believed I loved: the two who stood between me and complete isolation. Now I know as certainly as if I were already dead that I am for ever alone.

In my agony, I lose all count of time, and when at last I return to our rendezvous on the wooden bridge near the café-farm house, everyone has reappeared, and Michael is the first to ask, 'Where on earth have you been all this time?' How is it possible for them all not to observe the change that has taken place in me? Is my suffering not visible? I myself, while the others are talking, cannot help looking at Dilys and Michael; looking for some traces of their sin, some evidence of their guilt. How could they ever be the same again? And yet they seem no different. They laugh like everyone else, and for the same reasons.

from *A Toy Epic* (1958)

ROLFE HUMPHRIES (1894–1969)

For my Ancestors

Wales, which I have never seen,
Is gloomy, mountainous, and green,
And, as I judge from reading Borrow,[1]
The people there rejoice in sorrow,
Dissenters, most of them, and cranks,
Surly and churlish, grudging thanks,
Suspicious, dour, morose, perplexed,
And just a little oversexed.
Mostly, however, they go in
More for remorsefulness than sin,
The latter being prior to
The real delight, of feeling blue.
Fellows named Morgan, Evans, Jones,
Sit glumly on the ancient stones,
And men with names in – IES,
Like mine, lurk in the wilderness
With conscience riding on their shoulders
Heavier than the native boulders.
The weather veers from dim to foul,
The letter W's a vowel;
They dig in mines, they care for sheep,
Some kinds of promises they keep;
They can remember warriors found
Dead in green armor on green ground;
They practise magic out of season,
They hate the English with good reason,
Nor do they trust the Irish more,
And find the Scots an utter bore.
However grim their life, and hard,
One thing they dearly love, a bard.
Even the meanest hand at lays
Is plied with ale, and crowned with bays,
And set with honor in their books
Above even liars, thieves, and crooks.
This is the one redeeming grace
That saves them for the human race,
This is their claim to virtue; therefore,
Though there is much I do not care for

[1]Borrow, George Borrow (1803-81), author of *Wild Wales* (1862).

In my inheritance, I own
This impulse in my blood and bone,
And so I bend a reverent knee,
O Cymric ancestor, to thee,—
Wild Wales forever! Foul or fair,
This tribute from a grateful heir.

HYWEL AB OWAIN GWYNEDD (d. 1170)

Exultation

A foaming white wave washes over a grave,
the tomb of Rhufawn Pebyr,[1] regal chieftain.
I love today what the English hate, the open land of the North,
and the varied growth that borders the Lliw.
I love those who gave me my fill of mead
where the seas reach in long contention.
I love its household and its strong buildings
and at its lord's wish to go to war.
I love its strand and its mountains,
its castle near the woods and its fine lands,
its water meadows and its valleys,
its white gulls and its lovely women.
I love its soldiers, its trained stallions,
its woods, its brave men and its homes.
I love its fields under the little clover,
where honour was granted a secure joy.
I love its regions, to which valour entitles,
its wide waste lands and its wealth.
O, Son of God, how great a wonder,
how splendid the stags, great their possessions!
With the thrust of a spear I did splendid work
between the host of Powys[2] and lovely Gwynedd.[3]
On a pale white horse, a rash adventure,
may I now win freedom from my exile.
I'll never hold out till my people come;
a dream says so and God wills so.
A foaming white wave washes over a grave.

---

[1]Rhufawn Pebyr, named in the Triads as one of the Three Fair Princes of the Isle of Britain.
[2]Powys, one of the principal kingdoms of early Wales (now a county).
[3]Gwynedd, formerly a kingdom in north-west Wales (now a county).

A white wave, near the homesteads, foams over,
coloured like hoar-frost in the hour of its advance.
I love the sea-coast of Meirionnydd,[1]
where a white arm was my pillow.
I love the nightingale in the wild wood,
where two waters meet in that sweet valley.
Lord of heaven and earth, ruler of Gwynedd,
how far Kerry is from Caer Lliwelydd!
In Maelienydd[2] I mounted on a bay
and rode night and day to Rheged.
May I have, before my grave, a new conquest,
the land of Tegeingl,[3] fairest in the world.
Though I be a lover of Ovid's way,
may God be mindful of me at my end.
A white wave, near the homesteads, foams over.

trans. Gwyn Williams

ANONYMOUS

Branwen [4]

Bendigeidfran[5] son of Llŷr was crowned king over this Island and exalted with the crown of London. And one afternoon he was at Harddlech[6] in Ardudwy, at a court of his. And they were seated upon the rock of Harddlech overlooking the sea, and his brother Manawydan son of Llŷr with him, and two brothers on the mother's side, Nisien and Efnisien, and besides these, noblemen, as was seemly around a king. His two brothers on the mother's side were sons of Euroswydd by his mother Penarddun daughter of Beli son of Mynogan. And one of those youths was a good youth; he would make peace between the two hosts when their wrath was at the highest: that was Nisien. The other would cause strife between the two brothers when they were most loving.

And as they were seated thus, they could see thirteen ships coming from the South of Ireland and making towards them with an easy swift motion, and wind behind them, and nearing them swiftly. 'I see ships yonder,' said the king, 'and making boldly for the land. And bid the men of the court equip themselves and go and see what their intent is.' The men equipped themselves and

[1]Meirionydd, a region which later became Merionethshire.
[2]Maelienydd, a cantref in mid-Wales.
[3]Tegeingl, a district in north-east Wales (Englefield).
[4]Branwen, a heroine in *The Mabinogion*, the wife of Matholwch, King of Ireland.
[5]Bendigeidfran (or Brân), legendary King of the Isle of Britain, who was of gigantic build.
[6]Harddlech, Harlech, Mer.

approached them below. When they saw the ships from near at hand, certain were they that they had never seen ships in fairer trim than they. Beautiful, seemly, and brave ensigns of brocaded silk were upon them. And thereupon, lo, one of the ships outstripping the others, and they could see a shield lifted up above the ship's deck, with the point of the shield upwards in token of peace. And the men drew near them that they might hear each other's discourse. They put out boats and came towards the land, and they greeted the king. For the king could hear them from the place where he was, upon a high rock over their heads. 'God prosper you,' said he, 'and welcome to you. Whose is this host of ships, and who is chief over them?' 'Lord,' said they, 'Matholwch king of Ireland is here, and the ships are his.' 'What would he?' asked the king. 'Does he wish to come to land?' 'Not so, lord,' said they '—he is come on an errand to thee—unless he succeed in his errand.' 'What errand is his?' asked the king. 'He seeks to ally himself with thee, lord,' said they. 'He has come to ask for Branwen daughter of Llŷr, and if it seem good to thee he wishes to unite the Island of the Mighty with Ireland, so that they become the stronger.' 'Why,' he replied, 'let him come to land, and we will take counsel concerning that.'

That answer went to him. 'I will go gladly,' said he. He came to land, and he was made welcome, and great was the throng in the court that night, what with his hosts and those of the court. Straightway on the morrow they took counsel. What was determined in council was to bestow Branwen upon Matholwch. And she was one of the Three Matriarchs in this Island. Fairest maiden in the world was she.

And a time was set at Aberffraw, to sleep with her, and a start was made thence. And those hosts started for Aberffraw, Matholwch and his hosts in their ships, but Bendigeidfran and his hosts by land, until they came to Aberffraw. At Aberffraw they began the feast and sat them down. This is how they sat: the king of the Island of the Mighty, and Manawydan son of Llŷr one side of him, and Matholwch the other side, and Branwen daughter of Llŷr next to him. They were not within a house, but within tents. Bendigeidfran had never been contained within a house. And they began the carousal. They continued to carouse and converse. And when they perceived that it was better for them to seek slumber than to continue the carousal, to sleep they went. And that night Matholwch slept with Branwen.

from *The Mabinogion* (1948), trans. Gwyn Jones and Thomas Jones

ELISABETH INGLIS-JONES (1900–)
The Black Ram

Among the glories of Peterwell[1] was a roof-garden where on fine summer evenings it pleased the great man to cool himself of his wine, while he enjoyed the prospect of his broad acres with the Teifi flowing through them. And from there he could see, besides, the farms and hovels of the poor, who dwelt like beasts of the field under the shadow of his great house. His greedy heart rejoiced that as far as his eyes could see all belonged to him, with one sole exception. This was an eighteen-acre field plumb in the middle of the Peterwell estate, which was a source of constant exacerbation. It was the proud possession of Shon Philip whose family had owned it from time immemorial. The old farmer was as obstinate as a mule and, although Herbert Lloyd had made frequent offers to buy it, no money would induce Shon Philip to part with it.

The lovely field sloping down to the banks of the river was the pride of his heart, and in it from morning till nightfall he laboured, helped by his good old wife. The gold pieces the squire jingled in his pockets while he tried to persuade him to sell meant nothing to him. The wheat and roots off his field, his pig and his cow, provided all his simple wants. Thus, though Lloyd argued and bargained repeatedly, Shon Philip remained adamant and nothing Lloyd could offer would induce him to part with his property.

Herbert Lloyd decided to see what effect liquor might have in breaking the old man's resistance and gave orders that at every opportunity Shon Philip should be invited to the Peterwell kitchens, and given a good supply of strong home-brewed ale. But wary Shon Philip would scarcely touch it, and was sober and stubborn as ever when Herbert Lloyd waylaid him with fresh offers, on his way home. Early in the winter of 1762, he came to the end of his patience and evolved a plan that would settle the matter once and for all. A rumour was spread about the place that a valuable black ram belonging to him had either strayed or been stolen from his flock, and his servants were sent searching for it all over the country. One moonless night, two of his men removed the animal from its hiding-place. They carried it across the fields to Shon Philip's cottage and, clambering with it on to the roof, dropped it down the open chimney. Then they scuttled back to Peterwell to inform their master that his instructions had been successfully carried out.

In spite of the hour, it was then three o'clock, Lloyd sent at once for the parish constable, and informing him that he had every reason to believe that Shon Philip had stolen the ram, he gave him a warrant and ordered him forthwith to search the cottage. Shon Philip was held in such high esteem that the constable argued violently that such a thing was impossible and finally set off on his distasteful mission most unwillingly.

[1]Peterwell, the home of the infamous squire Herbert Lloyd (1720-69), near Lampeter, Cards.

Tired with their day's work and probably a little deaf besides, the old couple had slept soundly through the descent of the ram down their chimney and were only awakened by the constable's loud drubbing on the door. Bewildered and half-blind with sleep, as they groped their way across the floor, perhaps they took the awkward black creature bounding ahead of them to be some figment of the night – a creature of their dreams. But if they did, the illusion was rudely dispelled by the astonished constable. In vain did they protest, declaring their innocence. The proof was there, black and living, impossible to refute. The poor old people stared hopelessly at one another with terrified, uncomprehending eyes, as the constable read the warrant for Shon's arrest. Then he was dragged away from his weeping wife and marched off to Peterwell where Herbert Lloyd awaited them.

Although the unfortunate old man doggedly persisted that he had never touched the ram and was innocent, Lloyd refused to listen to him, reminding him instead that he would undoubtedly hang for his crime. Then he promised to forget and forgive the whole business if Shon would agree to sell his field, but Shon's passionate pride of possession and his native obstinacy made him continue to shake his head. Finally the furious squire ordered his men to remove him and keep him safe until they could get him to gaol. He spent the rest of that night and half next day in the stocks, until a large band of men armed with staves fetched him and took him off to the county gaol at Cardigan.

There he lay until the following March, while his persecutor pursued his life of pleasure, dicing and drinking with his friends and making his great journey to London to receive his new title. In March Shon Philip was brought before the Assizes. Sir Herbert's case was presented by the Attorney-General, but the prisoner was undefended, all the local attorneys being too timid to speak for him. Nearly every member of the jury was one of Lloyd's men, thus the outcome of the case was inevitable. Shon Philip was condemned to death and hanged outside the town, and a few days later a deed of conveyance was forthcoming that purported to bear his mark, giving the new baronet possession of the field.

from *Peacocks in Paradise* (1950)

The Burning of Hafod [1]

Hafod without its master was never the same place, but all the same it was a very congenial little party that he left behind him. The busy days slipped by contentedly enough. A hard frost had set in, charming the mornings with a crystalline wonder that glimmered and sparkled over the grey fields and woods, and investing the evenings spent by a blazing fire behind closed curtains with a voluptuous satisfaction. Listening to it shivering and crackling outside made

---

[1] Hafod, the home of Thomas Johnes (1748-1816) in Cardiganshire who transformed the house and its estate into a private paradise; the fire occurred in 1807.

their comfortable rooms feel even more luxuriously snug. And so they sat on that memorable evening of Thursday, 12th March, the ladies with their books and sewing, warming themselves and talking in undertones, while the gentleman snored behind his paper. Although, as it turned out, it was an evening that none of them would ever forget, there was nothing outwardly to distinguish it from a hundred similar ones. It was simply a tiny segment of life's ordinary pattern–the snip of scissors and rustle of turned pages punctuating the quiet chatter, and perhaps a little music as well, for there was nearly always music wherever Mariamne was. At nine o'clock the usual pleasant break occurred when the tea and coffee equipages were brought in and probably something a little stronger for Mr Williams. A quiet, homely evening rounding off a quiet, well-occupied day.

For none of them could guess what a heart-breaking, ghastly significance it was destined to assume for all of them. None of them could suspect that every chance word that was spoken that night, each look that was exchanged, would be feverishly sought for afterwards and seized and fitted into the tattered remnants that they strove to piece together, to rebuild the vanished scene. Memories would strain to breaking point in their efforts to recreate this drawing-room where they sat, a room that resembled a glowing flower border with its tapestries, exquisitely painted china and other choice ornaments. Had they but known it, their eyes were resting on many of these things for the last time, whilst others when they saw them again would be so defaced and mutilated that it would have been almost better if they had been totally destroyed. Yet, when at ten o'clock they rose as usual to light their candles and climb the stairs to bed, they were untouched by even the faintest apprehension of disaster. It was quite beyond the bounds of possibility that anything could alter – at least not for many years to come. Everything would go on exactly the same, for none of them could wish it otherwise. The only difference would be that the dear, familiar rooms would constantly be improved as new and beautiful objects found their way there. As they sleepily mounted the stairs towards the gallery above, they little suspected that for years to come they would still be recalling and grieving over their lost treasures. 'If only . . .' they would sigh. 'What a pity it was not saved. But there was no time.' For that was the most dreadful part of it. There was no time at all. The scorching wings of the fiery angel swept across their sky with devastating speed.

It was Jane, always a light and restless sleeper, who was the one who awoke at a quarter past three on the morning of Friday, 13th March – a date already cursed by every inauspicious portent. Strange and ominous sounds made her start up and listen. Then she detected the dreaded smell of smoke growing more potent every instant as the roaring noise drew nearer. She sprang up and rushed next door to waken Mariamne, and scarcely had she roused her and hurried from the room than the ceiling came crashing down. Fire had broken out in the attic; a warming pan in the housekeeper's bedroom was afterwards believed to have caused it; and already it had made such progress that the upper regions were cut off.

The frosty night was their worst enemy. Wells and springs were frozen fast while the fire-sprites leapt and multiplied unhindered in the dry air. There was a fire-engine, but not a man on the place knew how to work it, and the labourers' cottages were too far away from the house for their occupants to reach it in time to be of any help. Jane, fearless and resolute as she always was when faced with danger, took command. Before anything else was done, she insisted that every life must be saved. Maid-servants, scorched and screaming, were trapped on the roof and much precious time was spent bringing them down with ropes and ladders. By the time they were all accounted for the house was doomed. Already half of it was a raging, roaring inferno, with walls and beams crashing into the swirling flames; but, undismayed, Jane was determined that her husband's books should be saved. Although it was in imminent danger, she rushed to the octagon library with Mariamne and Eliza and started emptying the shelves. Then she remembered the priceless, irreplaceable old French manuscripts up in the gallery. Without a thought for her own safety she sped up the little stairway and started to fling them down, but the flames were racing her, heralding their approach with huge gusts of smoke that nearly choked her. She would not give in without resisting for as long as she could, for these most precious possessions of her beloved Mr Johnes, his priceless manuscrips and notes, the labours of a lifetime, must at all costs be saved. She struggled bravely on, pulling down armfuls of ancient vellums and casting them below, while the fearful noise and heat grew ever more oppressive. At last, stifled and blackened by smoke, she could do no more and fell unconscious to the ground. As she was brought into safety the flames broke in and drove them out of the room and out of the house for ever. Showers of lead from the roof fed the great blaze that lit up the mountains and stained the sky a lurid crimson that could be seen for miles around. The force of the fire was such that it carried the burning books high into the sky and tossed them all over the mountains. By the time this fearful conflagration brought helpers running from all directions, no aid could avail the charred skeleton that was all that remained of Hafod.

from *Peacocks in Paradise* (1950)

SIÂN JAMES (1932–   )

Miss Miriam Lewis

At this time, Miriam Lewis was courting. Her sweetheart was a bank clerk from Henblas who used to cycle to Rhydfelen every Sunday afternoon to have tea with her. His name was Gareth Vaughan, and he was hard-working, religious, and bound, people said, to get on. His father, working at the same bank, had got on, so that he was under-manager when he died, and had left his widow with a house and a good annuity.

In a way, Miriam would have liked to marry Gareth; he was gentle and considerate. He was fairly intelligent, or at least not stupid. She even liked his mother.

He spoke of selling his mother's terraced house in the old part of the town and buying one of the new villas being built on the Carmarthen Road. His mother liked the idea; they were double-fronted, detached houses, and she would be perfectly happy, she said, with a sitting-room of her own, and the front garden to potter about in.

Gareth had said they could have a piano and that Miriam could give lessons. They would have a little maid. There was a sizeable garden at the back, he would grow vegetables there; in a few years would be able to afford a greenhouse.

Miriam was never anything but non-committal, she'd think about it, that was the most she'd say. Yet one day she had gone, alone, to the building site and tried to imagine what married life would be like. One or two of the houses were almost completed; solid, square, red-bricked, with square bay windows on the ground floor. Gareth had mentioned the large, airy kitchen with tiled floor and modern range; the scullery behind.

She tried to imagine choosing furniture and curtains, but couldn't. She tried to imagine herself cleaning and shopping and preparing meals for Gareth, but couldn't. The unfinished house she was looking at made her feel nervous and inadequate.

As Miriam Lewis, schoolmistress, she had duties and obligations which she didn't shirk, but they were a result of what she was, and had chosen to become. She felt unfitted, completely unfitted, to undertake Mrs Gareth Vaughan's burdens. Having to conform, doing what the neighbours did, going to chapel on Sunday; being not only a wife, a daughter-in-law, probably a mother, but a member of a respectable, red-bricked society.

'I can't marry you, Gareth,' she had told him, the next time he'd cycled over to see her.

'You may change your mind,' he'd said. Which was what he always said.

One Sunday afternoon shortly afterwards, she had had a surprise visit from Ifan Jenkins her old schoolmaster, and his wife; Mrs Jenkins, it turned out, had relatives living nearby. They met Gareth Vaughan, though very briefly, because he was on the point of cycling home to the evening service at Henblas.

'Who'd have believed it,' Lisi Jenkins had said after he had gone. 'Such an eligible young man.'

'How can you tell how eligible he is?' Old Jenkins had asked sourly, 'and you only clapped eyes on him for five minutes.'

'Such a lovely suit and such good manners. And when I think what a little . . . ' Lisa Jenkins halted. She was a tactless woman, not very bright, and Ifan was getting more hot-tempered than ever in old age.

'Go on,' said Miriam, always amused by Lisi's indiscretions.

'A poor little thing you were, indeed, no more flesh on your bones than a gipsy child. Hair cut off because of the nits. Dressed in shreds and patches. Never mind. People can rise these days and that's not such a bad thing, surely. The lady's maid in Gwynant married Mr Edmund, and her ladyship visits her, they say, though Gladys Pugh who told me isn't the world's most reliable . . . '

Ifan Jenkins got to his feet as though to rise above his wife's chatter.

'Are you marrying this man, then?' he asked.

'I'm considering it,' Miriam said.

'If you have to consider it, don't,' Jenkins said, 'that's my opinion.'

'I'm all right as I am,' Miriam agreed.

'I should just think you are. As right as anyone can be. Your own boss, very near. Someone will come along, no doubt, and you'll marry him because you can't help yourself, but until that time comes, rejoice in your freedom; that's my advice.'

'I think perhaps you're right.'

'Have you ever known me wrong?'

'I'm not going to marry you, Gareth,' she had told him again, the following Sunday. He went on coming to see her, though, went on proposing from time to time, but without much hope. He was not what she wanted; they both knew it.

When Josi came into her life, she realized that he was the someone Ifan Jenkins had warned her about, the one against whom she would have no defences. But he was already married, so what was the good of that?

The married man rode past Miriam's garden often that summer. He and she would usually talk together for a short time under the rowan trees that overhung the path, but he was never again invited into the house; there seemed no excuse for it. I'm a respectable schoolmistress, Miriam told herself. I'm not for him.

The affair languished during autumn and winter, she saw him once at a Christmas concert; a curt nod, that was all.

Gareth continued faithful, and though he made no headway with her, seemed fairly contented.

Miriam put heart and soul into her work. The Inspector of Schools gave her a glowing report. 'The mistress, Miss Miriam Lewis, is a young woman of rare perception and application. Her pupils have responded well to her love of the written word, displaying a mature knowledge of both English and Welsh literature. Arithmetic is taught systematically and thoroughly, the pupils having a commendable grasp of the processes they employ. In Nature Study and Art, a particular measure of excellence has been achieved by the method of taking the children out of doors whenever possible, enabling them to see the wonders surrounding them. They sing harmoniously and joyfully. I have no hesitation in stating that the pupils of Rhydfelen School are being educated in the fullest sense of the word.'

Miriam was gratified by the report, fairly satisfied with the way her life was going.

Yet, when she caught a glimpse of Josi in Llanfryn one Saturday morning in early spring, she waved and rushed to catch up with him; was at his side before she realized what she had done.

'I'll ride over to see you one of these days,' he said, confidence in his voice, entreaty in his dark eyes. He didn't understand her, had been trying to put her out of his mind.

They stood together for a minute or more, and in that time, each accepted his fate. Neither of them smiled. The sun shone in the pale sky above them. It was a cold day, glittering like a jewel.

The following Monday, he rode up to the school as he had done almost exactly a year before. Once again he waited outside for all the children to leave.

When he went in, Miriam was at her desk writing. She didn't seem surprised to see him, perhaps she had heard his horse, perhaps she had been expecting him for the past year.

He stood against the door looking at her. Neither of them spoke.

The distance between them. Neither of them moved. Why doesn't she say something, Josi asked himself, why doesn't she help me, why doesn't she smile? The distance between them seemed like distance in a dream.

Then at last Miriam put down her pen, wiping the nib carefully, and Josi took a deep breath and bridged the distance between them, arrived at her side and drew her to her feet. He felt as though he had swum through a river to save a drowning man; that he was the drowning man. For several moments he held her, held on to her. Then he took off his top-coat and spread it on the floor by the little stove and they lay down together.

'Someone will come,' Miriam said.

'I locked the door.'

They lay together in the cold schoolroom until it was quite dark, until, through the narrow windows, built high in the walls to prevent the children catching sight of the lovely world outside, they could see the first white stars.

from *A Small Country* (1979)

ANONYMOUS

The Gresford Disaster

You've heard of the Gresford[1] Disaster,
   The terrible price that was paid,
Two hundred and sixty-two colliers were lost
   And three of the rescue brigade.

It occurred in the month of September,
   At two in the morning that pit
Was racked by a violent explosion
   In the Dennis where gas lay so thick.

The gas in the Dennis Deep Section
   Was packed there like snow in a drift,
And many a man had to leave that coal-face
   Before he had worked out his shift.

A fortnight before the explosion
   The shotfirer Tomlinson cried,
'If you fire that shot we'll be all blown to hell'
   And nobody can say that he lied.

The fireman's reports are all missing,
   The records of forty-two days,
The colliery manager had them destroyed
   To cover his criminal ways.

Down there in the dark they are lying,
   They died for nine shillings a day,
They've worked out their shift and it's now they must lie
   In the darkness until Judgement Day.

The Lord Mayor of London's collecting
   To help our poor children and wives,
The owners have sent some white lilies
   To pay for the poor colliers' lives.

Farewell, our dear wives and our children,
   Farewell, to our comrades as well,
Don't send your sons down the dark dreary mine,
   They'll be damned like the sinners in Hell.

[1]Gresford, a village near Wrexham, Denbs. The disaster occurred on 22 September 1934.

BOBI JONES (1929–   )

Portrait of a Pregnant Woman

Today she parades her shape like swellings of song,
The wings that free her, her throne, her tower,
She bursts the land with her being, her brand, her blossom,
Her passion's lofty monument, her belly's dance.

The trickling that was a stream to her hope breaks through its banks,
Swirling in floods. Come, everyone, out of the way.
Where's the great mountain that will not be drowned?
What terror! Look at this. There is nothing loftier.

Along the length and breadth of our fields the world makes its way.
O everyone, run to the side. She is spacious as time.
Watch out for your toes. She carries the stresses
Of the season's muse, her mite of a chick's hidden thumping.

And upon her face is the smile of the Almighty.
Who? Has anyone seen this fulfilling before?
On her tomorrow's sunny roof her rapture warbles:
It chirps, a live coal, in the twigs of her breast.

Cautious her step lest she trample the eggs of Creation,
Light her heart lest she weigh down the little one.
She walks, like Peter on water, doubtfully joyful,
Till she beaches her glory's pyramid in a dry Canaan.

trans. Joseph P. Clancy

Having Our Tea

There is something religious in the way we sit
At the tea table, a tidy family of three.
You, my love, slicing bread and butter, and she,
The red-cheeked tot a smear of blackberry jam, and me.
Set apart for the marvellous doting
Of a world's interchange with each other . . . that's tea.
Not proper for us to think of the thing as a sacrament,
And yet all the elements are found to change in our hands.
Because we sit and share them with each other
There's a miracle. There's a binding of unmerited graces
By the cheese, and through the apples and milk is established
A new creation of life, a true presence.

And talking to each other, uttering words over food
Is somehow different from customary chatting.
I know perfectly well that generations have had to,
Of necessity, perform this petty action.
And surely their pattern has long since burrowed
As part of our consciousness. Then too, back beyond the epochs
Is depending, turning back to the fountainhead,
And listening on the connecting wires to a Voice
That is at the same time food – He expresses
Himself here from the beginning. All would acknowledge
The food in itself as a source of pleasure:
He strengthens the spirit too in its wake.
Still tea is not worship . . . But an overflowing
Of things so the spirit may happily hop
In our hearts. So that swallowing heaven's carol
Into our constitutions, we are a choir, our throats
Blending calories and words together in the presence
Of the unseen Leader who laid the table.

trans. Joseph P. Clancy

David Jones (1895–1974)

Dai's[1] Boast

This Dai adjusts his slipping shoulder-straps, wraps close his misfit outsize greatcoat – he articulates his English with an alien care.

My fathers were with the Black Prinse of Wales
at the passion of
the blind Bohemian king.
They served in these fields,
it is in the histories that you can read it, Corporal – boys Gower, they were – it is writ down – yes.

Wot about Methuselum, Taffy?[2]
I was with Abel when his brother found him,
under the green tree.
I built a shit-house for Artaxerxes.
I was the spear in Balin's hand
        that made waste King Pellam's land.

---

[1]Dai, a diminutive of David.
[2]Taffy, a nickname for a Welshman.

I took the smooth stones of the brook,
I was with Saul
playing before him.
I saw him armed like Derfel Gatheren,[1]
I the fox-run fire
          consuming in the wheat-lands;
and in the standing wheat in Cantium made some attempt to form – (between
dun August oaks their pied bodies darting)
And I the south air, tossed from high projections by his Olifant; (the arid
marcher-slopes echoing –
should they lose
Clere Espaigne la bele).
          I am '62 Socrates, my feet are colder than you think
on this
Potidaean duck-board.
          I the adder in the little bush
whose hibernation-end
undid,
unmade victorious toil:
In ostium fluminis.
At the four actions in regione Linnuis
          by the black waters.
At Bassas in the shallows.
At Cat Coit Celidon.[2]
At Guinnion redoubt, where he carried the Image.
In urbe Legionis.
By the vallum Antonini, at the place of boundaries, at the toiling estuary and
strong flow called Tribruit.
By Agned mountain.
On Badon hill,[3] where he bore the Tree.
          I am the Loricated Legions.
Helen Camulodunum is ours;
she's the toast of the Rig'ment,
she is in an especial way our Mediatrix.
          She's clement and loving, she's Friday's child, she's loving and giving;
O dulcis
imperatrix.
          Her ample bosom holds:
Pontifex maximus,

[1]Derfel Gaderen (*recte* Derfel Gadarn), saint, reputed to have taken part in the battle of Camlan.
[2]Coit Celidon, Celyddon Wood, where Merlin lived as a wild man after losing his reason at the battle of Arfderydd in 573.
[3]Badon Hill, a battle (*c.* 516) in which Arthur is reputed to have borne the Cross on his shoulders for three days and three nights.

Comes Litoris Saxonici,
Comes Britanniarum,
Gwledig,[1]
Bretwalda, as these square-heads say.
    She's the girl with the sparkling eyes,
she's the Bracelet Giver,
she's a regular draw with the labour companies,
whereby
the paved army-paths are hers that grid the island which is
    her dower.
Elen Lluyddawc[2] she is – more she is than
Helen Argive.
    My mob digged the outer vallum,
we furnished picquets;
we staked trip-wire as a precaution at
Troy Novaunt.
    I saw the blessèd head set under
        that kept the narrow sea inviolate.
To keep the Land,
to give the yield:
    under the White Tower
        I trowelled the inhuming mortar.
    They learned me well the proportions due –
by water
by sand
by slacked lime.
    I drest the cist –
the beneficent artisans knew well how to keep
the king's head to keep
the land inviolate.
    The Bear of the Island: he broke it in his huge pride, and over-reach of
his imperium.
The Island Dragon.
The Bull of Battle
    (this is the third woeful uncovering).
Let maimed kings lie – let be
O let the guardian head
keep back – bind savage sails, lock the shield-wall, nourish the sowing.
The War Duke

[1]*Gwledig*, a ruler.
[2]Elen Lluyddawc, Elen of the Hosts (4th cent.), the heroine of *The Dream of Macsen Wledig*, one of two historical tales in *The Mabinogion*, said to have ordered the construction of roads across Britain.

The Director of Toil –
    he burst the balm-cloth, unbricked the barrow
(cruel feet march because of this
             ungainly men sprawl over us).
O Land! – O Brân[1] lie under.
The chrism'd eye that watches the French-men
that wards under
that keeps us
that brings the furrow-fruit,
keep the land, keep us
keep the islands adjacent.

I marched, sixty thousand and one thousand marched, because of the
brightness of Flur, because of the keeper of promises
           (we came no more again)
who depleted the Island,
           (and this is the first emigrant host)
and the land was bare for our going.
    O blessèd head hold the striplings from the narrow sea.
    I marched, sixty thousand marched who marched for Kynan and Elen
because of foreign machinations,
           (we came no more again)
who left the land without harness
           (and this is the second emigrant host).
O Brân confound the counsel of the councillors, O blessèd head, hold the
striplings from the narrow sea.
    In the baized chamber confuse his tongue:
that Lord Agravaine.
He urges with repulsive lips, he counsels: he nets us into expeditionary war.
    O blessèd head hold the striplings from the narrow sea.
    I knew the smart on Branwen's[2] cheek and the turbulence in Ireland
           (and this was the third grievous blow).
    I served Longinus that Dux bat-blind and bent;
the Dandy Xth are my regiment;
who diced
Crown and Mud-hook
under the Tree,
whose Five Sufficient Blossoms
yield for us.
    I kept the boding raven
           from the Dish.

---

[1]Brân (or Bendigeidfran), legendary King of the Isle of Britain.
[2]Branwen, a heroine in *The Mabinogion*, wife of Matholwch, King of Ireland.

With my long pilum
I beat the crow
from that heavy bough.
     But I held the tunics of these –
I watched them work the terrible embroidery that He put on.
I heard there, sighing for the Feet so shod.
I saw cock-robin gain
          his rosy breast.
I heard Him cry:
          Apples ben ripe in my gardayne
I saw Him die.
     I was in Michael's trench when bright Lucifer bulged his primal salient
out.
That caused it,
that upset the joy-cart,
and three parts waste.
     You ought to ask: Why,
what is this,
what's the meaning of this.
Because you don't ask,
although the spear-shaft
drips,
there's neither steading – not a roof-tree.
     I am the Single Horn thrusting
by night-stream margin
in Helyon.
     Cripes-a-mighty-strike-me-stone-cold – you don't say.
     Where's that birth-mark, young 'un.
     Wot the Melchizzydix! – and still fading – jump to it Rotherhithe.
               Never die never die
               Never die never die
               Old soljers never die
               Never die never die
               Old soljers never die they never die
               Never die
               Old soljers never die they
               Simply fade away.

from *In Parenthesis* (1937)

D. Gwenallt Jones (1899–1968)

The Dead

After a man has turned fifty he sees rather clearly
  The people and the neighbourhood that have shaped his life,
And the cords of steel that hold me tightest are the graves
  In two cemeteries in one of the villages of the South.

Riding on bicycles that were stolen from the scrap-heap
  And with pig-bladders playing Rugby for Wales,
I did not dream that I would hear of two of these playmates
  Vomiting their lungs, filthy red, into pails.

Our neighbours, a family from Merthyr Tydfil they were,
  'The Martyrs' was the name we gave to them,
Five in turn fired a cough across the garden hedge
  To break into our chat and darken our game.

We slunk to the Biblical parlours to stare in shock
  At the coke of flesh in the coffin, the ashes of a voice;
There we learned above the lids screwed down before their time
  Collects of red rebellion, litanies of violence.

Not the death that walks naturally like a cell-guard
  Sounding a warning with his damp keys' clank,
But the industrial leopard that leaps sudden and sly
  Out of fire and water upon men at their work.

The hootering death: death dusty and smoky and drunk,
  Death bringing with it grey destiny's terror;
Explosion and flooded-pit turned us sometimes to savages
  Fighting loathsome, primeval, catastrophic power.

Brave silent women with fists full of blood-money,
  And buckets of death as lasting memories,
Carrying coal, cutting fire-wood, tending the garden
  And reading more often of the passion on the Cross.

We place on their graves, on Palm Sunday, a bunch
  Of silicotic roses and lilies pale as gas,
And gather between the untimely stones and the unripe verge
  Their funerals' old curses and blasphemies.

Utopia vanished from the summit of Gellionnen,
  The abstract humanity, the world without frontier or class;
And nothing remains today at the bottom of memory
  But family and neighbourhood, man's suffering and sacrifice.

trans. Joseph P. Clancy

Rhydcymerau

Near Rhydcymerau,
On the land of Esgeir-ceir and the fields of Tir-bach,
They have planted the saplings,
              to be trees of the third war.

I call to mind my grandmother at Esgeir-ceir
As she sat, pleating her apron, by the fireside,
The skin yellow and dry on her face
              like a manuscript of Peniarth,[1]
And the Welsh on her old lips the Welsh of Pantycelyn.[2]
A bit of the Puritan Wales she was of last century.
Although I never saw him, my grandfather
Was a 'character' – a brisk and twinkling little creature,
Fond of his pint;
He'd just strayed in from the eighteenth century.
They reared nine children,
Poets, deacons, and Sunday School teachers,
And each, locally, a man of authority.

My Uncle Dafydd used to farm Tir-bach,
And was, besides, a poet, the countryside's rhymester;
His song to the little cockerel was famous in those parts:
              '*The little cock goes scratching*
              In the garden here and there.'
It was to him I went for the summer holidays
To watch the sheep and fashion lines of cynghanedd,[3]
Englynion,[4] and eight-line stanzas of eight-seven measure.
He brought up eight children,
The eldest son a minister with the Calvinistic Methodists,
And he too wrote verses.
In our family we'd a real nestful of poets.

---

[1]Peniarth, a house in Mer., the home of the Wynne family, who owned an important collection of Welsh manuscripts.
[2]Pantycelyn, William Williams (1717-91), hymn-writer.
[3]*cynghanedd*, an ancient and intricate system of alliteration in poetry.
[4]*englynion* (sing. *englyn*), a four-line verse written according to traditional rules of prosody.

And by this time there's nothing there but trees.
Impertinent roots suck dry the old soil:
Trees where neighbourhood was,
And a forest that once was farmland.
Where was verse-writing and scripture
               is the South's bastardized English.
The fox barks where once cried lambs and children,
And there, in the dark midst,
Is the den of the English minotaur;
And on the trees, as if on crosses,
The bones of poets, deacons, ministers, and teachers of Sunday School
Bleach in the sun,
And the rain washes them, and the winds lick them dry.

                                  trans. Anthony Conran

Glamorgan and Carmarthenshire

Tomos Lewis[1] of Talyllychau,
   His hammersound in the forge like bells
Over the village, abbey and the swans on the lake;
   He drew his hymn like a horseshoe from the fire,
   Struck it on the anvil of the Holy Ghost
And in it set the nails of Calvary Hill.

And Williams of Pantycelyn[2] himself
   Would be at my elbow in Llansadwrn
Tutoring my voice in the pattern of his song;
   But I lost the yearning to look on his face
   In the town square up there on my soapbox,
His fine voice drowned by the drum of the crane.

It was not for any industrial worker
   To wander through the plant and mills like a pilgrim
With empty pockets and a pack on his back:
   On Saturday nights we rose for the justice
   Of our cause, and on Sunday sang your hymns:
Mabon[3] and Caeo[4]; Keir Hardie[5] and Crug-y-bar.

[1] Tomos Lewis (1759-1842), hymn-writer and blacksmith.
[2] Williams of Pantycelyn, William Williams (1717-91), hymn-writer.
[3] Mabon, William Abraham (1842-1922), miners' leader.
[4] Caeo . . . Crug-y-bar, hymn-tunes.
[5] Keir Hardie (1856-1915), miners' leader and founder of the Independent Labour Party, Member of Parliament for Merthyr Tydfil.

The span of the Cross is greater by far
    Than their Puritanism and their Socialism,
And the fist of Karl Marx has a place in His Church:
    Farm and furnace are one together in His estate,
    The humanity of the pit, the piety of the country:
Tawe and Tywi,[1] Canaan and Wales, earth and heaven.

                    trans. Ned Thomas and B.S. Johnson

GLYN JONES (1905–   )

The Meaning of Fuchsias

The lush valley, the two golden mares
    loving in the apple orchard,
  The golden-maned for Gwilym, the milky one
    for me,
And through those dark boughs the vast white
    mansion-walls of heaven.
  Why did we not hear, in that treachery
    of sun-varnished windows,
Of handsome clouds, of the fragrant flesh of pears,
    of gull-white moons in their eternal blue,
  And pastures cast out of morning fire
    everywhere brilliant as enamels,
The creeping by of our days, of our time,
    of change –
  Only the thrush's hammering of morning
    in the dapples of that sunlight,
And the cupboards of the trees around us,
    creaking, creaking.

On the slope the still bushes stood in the sun,
    staring down in silence at their shadows.
  'Fuchsias', said Gwilym, 'wild fuchsias' –
    each bush of flowers
The dark glow in my mind still of lit lanterns
    burning crimson through transparencies of wine,
  A new delight then, inextinguishable,
    a heart's enduring wonder.

[1] Tawe and Tywi, rivers in south-west Wales.

In these sleek gardens, where only meaning
　　has no root or blossoming,
　What is it within me stares through its bars
　　at fuchsias,
So that I bear again the sudden burden
　　of my many dead,
　And you, and all our darkened suns,
　　possess me through the doorways of my tears,
You, sanctified listener, who rode by night
　　your golden pony
　Through the graveyard, listening,
　　And hearing nothing.

My Radiant Granny

When I knocked, my granny opened the door, her brown face wet, one eye shut and a bar of red soap in her hand.

She gave me a wet kiss, and welcomed me into her kitchen, dim even in sunshine because a bush of window geraniums always shut out the light. The aromatic air was strong with the scent of resinous firewood baking in the oven, and I could recognize too the acrid smell of drying pit-clothes. On the glowing fire a large iron kettle boiled and a finished meal lay upon the table oilcloth. The dim cosy room had all the furniture common to the cottages of the miners – the floor sacks, the corner 'bosh,' the wire drying-lines, the china dogs, the stand and fender, the row of brass candlesticks, the window-sized friendly-society calendar. . . .

Often in her dim sweet-smelling kitchen we sat as now by the fire together, while she held her mangled hands heavily upon her aproned knees. They were red and rugged, the hands of a labourer, their knotted erubescence evidenced familiarity with the roughest work, they seemed as though the coarse substances at which they had laboured had become an element of their conformation. Often, when I was older, and knew the meaning of those bony and inflexible knuckles, the large inflammatory fingers, I turned my gaze from them with shame and pity and watched my own painter's hand, culpable, indulged, and epicene, as it moved aroitly in the perfect glove of its skin. Often I stared at those hands and remembered the way they sought, in her bitter childhood, the warmth and comfort of her pigs' wash burden. Potato peelings, loaf-ends, plate-scrapings, all pulped together in a wooden pail with an admixture of hot skimmed milk, she carried every morning from Ystrad up to the pigsties isolated on the colliery refuse tips, earning a few pence weekly from a neighbour for doing so. Often, in winter, when the wind was rough and cold on the bare mountain slopes, she rested with her burden beside the steep path, and held for a moment her frozen hands deep in the warm slop of pigs' food.

But it was always with reluctance, seated with me beside her kitchen fire, that she spoke of her childhood's sufferings, her stern, untutored upbringing, the humiliations of her life of youthful poverty; she preferred to divert me then with humorous recitals of her rare girlish pleasures and of her silliness and vanity. She did not wish to recall her childhood's struggles, the grim grammar of the school she had learnt in, instructing herself in loneliness, and in secret even, to read and write; she did not wish me to know how she had sat on her bed night after night, a simple Welsh book on the seat of her chair before her, and the shadows of the bars falling in candlelight across it as she tried to read. She did not wish me to know of the monotonous food, the cast-off clothing, the drudgery of that time, and then the encaustic history of her widowhood, her laundering, her chapel-cleaning, the endless sharing of her home with strangers.

And she hid from me also how she had sensed, with the brooding divination of motherhood, an unusual actuity and promises of intellectual pre-eminence in her younger son, my father, and how she had determined that under God's will nothing in the mastery of her endurance should be left undone on his behalf. She did not describe to me the morning my father entered college, when, at last, she bore his roped-up tin trunk from this hillside cottage in a manner ennobled by the porterage of balanced basket, water-stane, or clothes-bundle, *upon her head*. She walked the path to the railway halt that morning under her heavy burden with the erect bearing of some at last triumphant wet-eyed queen, wearing her jet, her white collar, and her chapel black. She did not tell me how bitter to her was my father's early death, and my mother's within the year. When I came to live with her down in Rosser's Row she would say rather: 'When I could read Welsh quickly I began to learn English, and there was one thing in that language I could *not* understand then. M-o-u-n-t-e-d is *mount-ed*, isn't it? And w-a-n-t-e-d is *want-ed*. What I could never find out was why l-o-o-k-e-d wasn't *look-ed* and p-o-k-e-d wasn't *pok-ed*. There's a stupid little girl I must have been, mustn't I?'

To me my granny was always a warm and visionary being. Sometimes, the whole sky ablaze, and the crimson sunball dissolving hot as rosin upon the hill-top, a tall black figure seemed to float out of that bonfire as though riding a raft of illumination. Her heavy progress was laborious, her shoulders rose and fell against the dazzling hump of hillcrest radiance with the rock of a scalebeam. She shepherded her rolling shadow down the slope; returning from the prayer-meeting she wore over her vast flesh her long black boat-cloak, with the brass buttons like a dramatic row of drawer-knobs down the front of her. Her feet were in clogs, her head in a black cloth hat with hanging tie-tapes and a cart-wheel brim sweeping the broad spreads of her balancing shoulders.

She would reach the rowan at her garden gate and pause there, eyeing with mildness and benediction the wide sweep of the mining valley below in the moments of sunset. Then, as she turned to the cut sun and the afterglow, her lined face became lit up, illuminated as though from within like a rock of clear crystal; her opaque body glowed, momentary starlight inhabited her glistening form. And I, shouting at the sight of her, reached her side with singing limbs, she was my radiant granny, my glossy one, whose harsh fingers lay gently and sweet as a harp-hand upon my curls.

As we stood together, watching the valley, the sun sank, and from behind the hill the invisible ball cast up the powerful glow of its illumination like a huge footlight into the flawless blue sky above us.

from *The Valley, the City, the Village* (1956)

The Common Path

On one side the hedge, on the other the brook:
    Each afternoon I passed, unnoticed,
The middle-aged schoolmistress, grey-haired,
    Gay, loving, who went home along the path.

That spring she walked briskly, carrying her bag
    With the long ledger, the ruler, the catkin twigs,
Two excited little girls from her class
    Chattering around their smiling teacher.

Summer returned, each day then she approached slowly,
    Alone, wholly absorbed, as though in defeat
Between water and hazels, her eyes heedless,
    Her grey face deeply cast down. Could it be
Grief at the great universal agony had begun
    To feed upon her heart – war, imbecility,
Old age, starving, children's deaths, deformities?
    I, free, white, gentile, born neither
Dwarf nor idiot, passed her by, drawing in
    The skirts of my satisfaction, on the other side.

One day, at the last instant of our passing,
    She became, suddenly, aware of me
And, as her withdrawn glance met my eyes,
    Her whole face kindled into life, I heard
From large brown eyes a blare of terror, anguished
    Supplication, her cry of doom, death, despair.
And in the warmth of that path's sunshine
    And of my small and manageable success
I felt at once repelled, affronted by her suffering,
    The naked shamelessness of that wild despair.

Troubled, I avoided the common until I heard
    Soon, very soon, the schoolmistress, not from
Any agony of remote and universal suffering
    Or unendurable grief for others, but
Private, middle-aged, rectal cancer, was dead.

What I remember, and in twenty years have
    Never expiated, is that my impatience,
That one glance of my intolerance,
    Rejected her, and so rejected all
The sufferings of wars, imprisonments,
    Deformities, starvation, idiocy, old age –
Because fortune, sunlight, meaningless success,
    Comforted an instant what must not be comforted.

Summer Camp

'I was telling you about the Traeth Camp, down there on the coast. I'll never forget that Mysie Powell. You don't remember him, Dewi, his mother put him into a home just before you came to the Penn, the bitch. He was a quiet little boy, very shy and pretty, with some sort of fastidiousness about him, you know, the kind of sensitiveness I'm always quick to recognize in other people because I'm such a bloody oaf myself. Anyway, every morning in camp – it was a lovely month we had that year, the sun shining day after day and the weather turning the kids into a gang of half-castes – every morning during the first break all the boys, about fifty or sixty of them, used to gather round the veranda outside my hut to collect their mail. I used to bring all the letters and parcels out on a table and call their names, and throw the stuff down to them as they stood in a crowd at the bottom of the steps. Well, I couldn't help noticing that although Mysie was there every day with the others no letter or parcel ever came for him. A whole week went by and he was the only kid in camp who hadn't received anything at all from home. And I knew he'd written to his mother more than once because I used to collect the boys' letters up every evening and bring them up here into Pontisa in the car to post them. Then one night when I went round the sleeping-huts to see that everybody had settled down I found Mysie wide awake; he was lying on his back in the darkness with his hands under his head, staring at the roof. I felt sure he'd been crying, but he was too shy to tell me what was the matter. I didn't question him, anyway: I let him think I assumed he had a pain. I sat with him a bit, talking in whispers, and at last he said he wanted to sleep now, so I left him. Poor little dab. I felt pretty sorry for him. I had him on my mind all day.

'Another week went by without a letter, and I thought – to hell, I'll send him something myself, so I wrote him a letter with funny drawings in it and comical bits of poetry and that. I watched him getting it the next morning. He seemed pleased, but I could tell that it wasn't what he wanted.

'Later that day Rouse, the deputy camp warden, gave the boys a bit of composition to write on anything they chose. He was so struck with Mysie's he showed it to me. And I must say it was lovely. He had written about his five senses, about what he liked to taste and to touch and hear and so on. You can see what sort of a little kid he was. And what he liked in the way of touching, I remember, was to smooth his mother's fur coat, and the scent he liked best of all in the world was the sweet smell of his mother's bedroom. I was madder than ever, wanting to do something for him, and that afternoon, when he was in the outfield in a baseball match, I sat down near him on the grass.

'"How are things, Mysie?" I asked him.

'"All right, thank you, sir."

'"Enjoying yourself?"

'"Yes, thank you, sir."

'"Everything all right? You like the food?"

'"Yes, sir, the food's lovely, sir."

'I wondered how the devil I could bring up the next thing I wanted to say to him. He fielded the ball and when he had returned it to the pitcher he went and stood a bit farther off from me. I didn't know what to do. At last I called across to him. "Mysie," I said, "come here a minute, will you?"

'"Yes, sir," he said, coming over and kneeling down in front of me.

'"I thought I'd give your mother and father a ring to see how they're getting on. Would you like that? You know, on the phone."

'His eyes filled with tears. "I haven't got a father, sir," he said.

'"Your mother, then. I expect she'll be glad to have a bit of a chat with you. Is she in in the afternoons?"

'He looked at me and then dropped his eyes. "Yes, sir, she's never out in the afternoon."

'"Has she got a telephone?"

'"No, sir."

'"Has anyone near you got one?"

'He thought for a moment. "I think Phillips the Crown Stores have got one, sir."

'"Phillips the Crown Stores. How far is that from your house?"

'"On the corner, sir. Next door but one, sir."

'"Right," I said. "Phillips. A grocer, is he? Will you be here for the next ten minutes, say? I'll slip over to my hut and give Mr Phillips a ring and ask him if he can get hold of your mother for a bit. You stay here. I'll give you a shout."

'I got up and went across to the hut. Honestly, Dewi, I could have gone running, I felt so delighted. Phillips was in the phone-book all right and, yes, he knew Mrs Powell and he was quite willing to slip in to fetch her to the phone. I waited. By God, I was going to tell her a thing or two. Through the window I could see Mysie still kneeling on the grass in the outfield where I had left him, and I wondered how in hell anybody could be indifferent to such a nice and decent little kid as that. After a hell of a long wait Phillips came back to the phone. He'd been to see Mrs Powell and she wanted to know if anything was wrong.

'"Wrong!" I shouted. "Yes, by God, there's plenty wrong. Mrs Powell's little kid has been here over a fortnight and he's the only one in camp who hasn't received a word from home. Why doesn't she come to the phone to have a word with him?"

'Phillips said he had asked her, but unless there was something wrong, an accident or something, she didn't think there was any need. By God, Dewi, I nearly went mad. I told Phillips to tell her she was a heartless bitch, not anywhere near fit to have a kid at all, let alone such a nice one as Mysie. I banged the receiver. What the hell was I going to tell Mysie, anyway? I was stupid to have said anything about it to him. I sat down a bit and then I went over the field towards him, trying to look casual and cheerful.

'"Sorry, Mysie," I said, "we seem to have phoned your mother in her busiest time. But she's fine, boy, and she sends you her love. We'll try again some other time, shall we?"

'Well, I didn't try. And during the whole month all that kid got from his mother was a postcard from somewhere she'd gone for a day trip. And that didn't come until the last day but one because she'd written the address wrong. And yet, do you know, Dewi, the night before we went home from camp the boys showed me, as usual, the presents they'd bought for their families and their girl friends. They laid them out on their beds in the sleeping-huts for me to see. Pretty rubbishy stuff most of it was, cheap and gaudy: alarm clocks, chalk Alsatians, tobacco pouches, bedroom slippers, done up in cellophane to make them look a bit more substantial. And honestly, the outstanding present in the room was the one Mysie had for his mother. I'd noticed he'd been spending a lot of his time in the workshop, even at night when we had our concerts and do's, and what he'd been doing was making a tray for her dressing-table. It really was beautiful; it was oval, of some deep brown wood and with a slender black rim; it was inlaid all over with small spaced-out diamonds of black wood. There was an oblong box to go with it and this was inlaid too with the black diamonds in the same way. Honestly, in the middle of all that gaudy trash on the beds Mysie's presents looked professional, and the other boys recognized it, fair play to them.

'That's what we've to remember, Dewi, boy. I don't say we should never clout a kid, far from it, but when we begin to clout him we ought to remember we're clouting a human being and not a juvenile delinquent or the bottom of the class in arithmetic.'

from *The Learning Lark* (1960)

GWYN JONES (1907–   )
All this is Wales

I have just come down from the hill fronting my home in mid-Cardiganshire. It is like half a hundred hills in this part of Wales, rounding out of a bramble-filled dingle on the southern side, a dingle blue-black with juiced fruit in autumn, with a sun-shot fringe of scrub oak and alder, and a noble ash-tree rearing from the bottom, its roots much exposed and straddling the course of a fast-running brook. Beyond the dingle is gorse-striped rough grazing for a couple of ponies, and in a cleft a hundred yards away a pink-washed farm with squat outbuildings has been sited to miss the prevailing south-wester. Then one skirts a ploughed field much admired of herring gulls and crows, and a short ascent brings one to the overswell of land and to sight of the sea.

In season the hillside is ablaze with gorse and alive with rabbits. Blue and gold, the sea and land: gold and blue, the earth and sky. To the north, over the first hump of ground, one sees the far side of the Clarach valley, then a lovely patchwork hill, downpitched to the sea in eighty-foot cliffs. Further away are the yellow bank of the Dyfi and the dark hills of Meirionydd. Then these are dwarfed by the huge whaleback of Cader Idris, and beyond Cader, unseen, is the tide-washed estuary of the Mawddach. The prospect ends with fitting splendour: the northern claw of Cardigan Bay, the long peninsula of Lleyn, reaches out over thirty miles to Bardsey, and from that western extremity the eye moves back from mountain to mountain, the two summits of Yr Eifl, round Moel Hebog, the spike of Cnicht, to the exquisite cone of Snowdon himself, and the confused masses that buttress his eastern and south-eastern approaches. Now turn the head. Confronting Lleyn to the south, across seventy miles of heaped-up water, is the long rocky headland of Pembrokeshire, running to the claw-tip of St David's Head, with the magic mountains of Prescelly hanging inland like a haze. Turn again, for behind one the Plynlymon massif is displayed in a score of rosy lumps, divagated by green valleys, black woodlands, the silver ribbons of rivers, its fields brown, grey, pink, emerald, until the blunted tops of the five mountains are lost in purple distance half-way to the English border. All this is Wales, and this is half of Wales.

The view, necessarily and properly, is inconstant. Heat haze, cloud or rain turns the peninsulas to a smudge or to nothing at all. In sea mist one is content to see not the next county but the next hummock. Under a bruised sky the seaward horizon encroaches on the beaches, and Plynlymon, like the water, shows a dull-grained navy blue. Conversely, air washed by summer rain and then dried out by a warm breeze gives the coastline the brilliance of glass. Thus one has heard men on the cliffs near Pentrebont claim they can discern Bardsey like a thumb in the water. Maybe they can. Until they claim to see the lighthouse I am with them all the way. For one evening in late July of 1943, sober, solitary, and in my five senses, from the high point of ground this side of Clarach I beheld, fifteen minutes before the going down of the sun, the western mountain wall of North Wales swung forward and westward through thirty degrees of the compass. Every mountain was an island, the point of Lleyn was a finger's breadth from the sun. Between the mountains that were islands the sea poured pale smoky streams, and one saw the sea *behind* them, fluorescent as a fresh-caught mackerel. Each mountain top was gold, their lower slopes were mauve where they were drowned in sea. Never had the sun shown more evening splendour: it hung from long blackish bars of the oncoming dark, a polished copper cauldron. Inshore the water was a milky blue, then came a ten-mile band of salmon-rose, growing tawnier as it receded towards a charcoal horizon. Washes of yellow and red stained the sky behind the black cloud-bars. All along the coast folk must have been exclaiming at the glory of the sunset, but this other and ultimate glory, this dislocation in space, was pure magic and illusion. It lasted the brief third of an hour, but when I forget it wholly, the axe will be laid to the root of the tree.

from *A Prospect of Wales* (1948)

A White Birthday

With their next stride towards the cliff-edge they would lose sight of the hills behind. These, under snow, rose in long soft surges, blued with shadow, their loaded crests seeming at that last moment of balance when they must slide into the troughs of the valleys. Westward the sea was stiffened to a board, and lay brown and flat to the indrawn horizon. Everywhere a leaden sky weighed upon land and water.

They were an oldish man and a young, squat under dark cloth caps, with sacks worn shawl-like over their shoulders, and other sacks roped about their legs. They carried long poles, and the neck of a medicine-bottle with a teat-end stood up from the younger man's pocket. Floundering down between humps and pillows of the buried gorse bushes, they were now in a wide bay of snow, with white headlands enclosing their vision to left and right. A gull went wailing over their heads, its black feet retracted under the shining tail feathers. A raven croaked from the cliff face.

'That'll be her,' said the younger man excitedly. 'If that raven – '

'Damn all sheep!' said the other morosely, thinking of the maddeningly stupid creatures they had dug out that day, thinking too of the cracking muscles of his thighs and calves, thinking not less of the folly of looking for lambs on the cliff-face.

'I got to,' said the younger, his jaw tensing, 'I got reasons.'

'To look after yourself,' grumbled the other. He had pushed his way to the front, probing cautiously with his pole, and grunting as much with satisfaction as annoyance as its end struck hard ground. The cliffs were beginning to come into view, and they were surprised, almost shocked, to find them black and brown as ever, with long sashes of snow along the ledges. They had not believed that anything save the sea could be other than white in so white a world. A path down the cliff was discernible by its deeper line of snow, but after a few yards it bent to the left, to where they felt sure the ewe was. The raven croaked again. 'She's in trouble,' said the younger man. 'P'raps she's cast or lambing.'

'P'raps she's dead and they are picking her,' said the older. His tone suggested that would be no bad solution of their problem. He pulled at the peak of his cap, bit up with blue and hollow scags of teeth into the straggle of his moustache. 'If I thought it was worth it, I'd go down myself.'

'You're too old, anyway.' A grimace robbed the words of their brutality. 'And it's my ewe.'

'And it's your kid's being born up at the house, p'raps this minute.'

'I'll bring it him back for a present. Give me the sack.'

The older man loosed a knot unwillingly. 'It's too much to risk.' He groped for words to express what was for him a thought unknown. 'I reckon we ought to leave her.'

Tying the sacks over his shoulders the other shook his head. 'You leave a lambing ewe? When was that? Besides, she's mine, isn't she?'

Thereafter they said nothing. The oldish man stayed on the cliff-top, his weight against his pole, and up to his boot-tops in snow. The younger went slowly down, prodding ahead at the path. It was not as though there were any choice for him. For one thing, it was his sheep, this was his first winter on his own holding, and it was no time to be losing lambs when you were starting a family. He had learned thrift the hard way. For another, his fathers had tended sheep for hundreds, perhaps thousands of years: the sheep was not only his, it was part of him. All day long he had been fighting the unmalignant but unslacking hostility of nature, and was in no mood to be beaten. And last, the lying-in of his wife with her first child was part of the compulsion that sent him down the cliff. The least part, as he recognized; he would be doing this in any case, as the old man above had always done it. He went very carefully, jabbing at the rock, testing each foothold before giving it his full weight. Only a fool, he told himself, had the right never to be afraid.

Where the path bent left the snow was little more than ankle-deep. It was there he heard the ewe bleat. He went slowly forward to the next narrow turn and found the snow wool-smooth and waist-high. 'I don't like it,' he whispered, and sat down and slit the one sack in two and tied the halves firmly over his boots. The ewe bleated again, suddenly frantic, and the raven croaked a little nearer him. 'Ga'art there!' he called, but quietly. He had the feeling he would be himself the one most frightened by an uproar on the cliff-face.

Slowly he drove and tested with the pole. When he had made each short stride he crunched down firmly to a balance before thrusting again. His left side was tight to the striated black rock, there was an overhang of soft snow just above his head, it seemed to him that his right shoulder was in line with the eighty-foot drop to the scum of foam at the water's edge. 'You dull daft fool,' he muttered forward at the platform where he would find the ewe. 'In the whole world you had to come here!' The words dismayed him with awareness of the space and silence around him. If I fall, he thought, if I fall now ——. He shut his eyes, gripped at the rock.

Then he was on the platform. Thirty feet ahead the ewe was lying on her back in snow scarlet and yellow from blood and her waters. She jerked her head and was making frightened kicks with her four legs. A couple of yards away two ravens had torn out the eyes and paunch of her new-dropped lamb. They looked at the man with a horrid waggishness, dribbling their beaks through the purple guts. When the ewe grew too weak to shake her head they would start on her too, ripping at the eyes and mouth, the defenceless soft belly. 'You sods,' he snarled, 'you filthy sods!' fumbling on the ground for a missile, but before he could throw anything they flapped lazily and insolently away. He kicked what was left of the lamb from the platform and turned to the ewe, to feel her over. 'Just to make it easy!' he said angrily. There was a second lamb to be born.

'Get over,' he mumbled, 'damn you, get over!' and pulled her gently on to her side. She at once restarted labour, and he sat back out of her sight, hoping she would deliver quickly despite her fright and exhaustion. After a while she came to her feet, trembling, but seemed rather to fall down again than re-settle to work. Her eyes were set in a yellow glare, she cried out piteously, and he went back to feel along the belly, pressing for the lamb's head. 'I don't know,' he complained, 'I'm damned if I know where it is with you. Come, you dull soft stupid sow of a thing – what are you keeping it for?' He could see the shudders begin in her throat and throb back the whole length of her, her agony flowed into his leg in ripples. All her muscles were tightening and then slipping loose, but the lamb refused to present. He saw half-a-dozen black-backed gulls swing down to the twin's corpse beneath him. 'Look,' he said to the ewe, 'd'you want them to get you too? Then for Christ's sake, get on with it! At once her straining began anew; he saw her flex and buckle with pain; then she went slack, there was a dreadful sigh from her, her head rested, and for a moment he thought she had died.

He straightened his back, frowning, and felt snowflakes on his face. He was certain the ewe had ceased to work and, unless he interfered, would die with the lamb inside her. Well, he would try for it. If only the old man were here – he would know what to do. If I kill her, he thought – and then: what odds? She'll die anyway. He rolled back his sleeves, felt for a small black bottle in his waistcoat pocket, and the air reeked as he rubbed lysol into his hand. But he was still dissatisfied, and after a guilty glance upwards reached for his vaseline tin and worked gouts of the grease between his fingers and backwards to his wrist. Then with his right knee hard to the crunching snow he groped gently but purposefully into her after the lamb. The primal heat and wet startled him after the cold of the air, he felt her walls expand and contract with tides of life and pain; for a moment his hand slithered helplessly, then his middle fingers were over the breech and his thumb seemed sucked in against the legs. Slowly he started to push the breech back and coax the hind legs down. He felt suddenly sick with worry whether he should not rather have tried to turn the lamb's head and front legs towards the passage. The ewe groaned and strained as she felt the movement inside her, power came back into her muscles, and she began to work with him. The hind legs began to present, and swiftly but cautiously he pulled against the ewe's heaving. Now, he thought, now! His hand moved in an arc, and the tiny body moved with it, so that the lamb's backbone was rolling underneath and the belly came uppermost. For a moment only he had need to fear it was pressing on its own life-cord, and then it was clear of the mother and lying red and sticky on the snow. He picked it up, marvelling as never before at the beauty of the tight-rolled gummy curls of fine wool patterning its sides and back. It appeared not to be breathing, so he scooped the mucus out of its mouth and nostrils, rubbed it with a piece of sacking, smacked it sharply on the buttocks, blew into the throat to start respiration, and with that the nostrils fluttered and the lungs dilated. 'Go on,' he said triumphantly to the prostrate ewe, 'see to him yourself. I'm no damned nursemaid for you, am I?' He licked the cold flecks of snow from around his mouth as the ewe began to lick her lamb, cleaned his hand and wrist, spat and spat again to rid himself of the hot fœtal smell in nose and throat.

Bending down to tidy her up, he marvelled at the strength and resilience of the ewe. 'Good girl,' he said approvingly, 'good girl then.' He would have spent more time over her but for the thickening snow. Soon he took the lamb from her and wrapped it in the sack which had been over his shoulders. She bleated anxiously when he offered her the sack to smell and started off along the ledge. He could hear her scraping along behind him and had time at the first bad corner to wonder what would happen if she nosed him in the back of the knees. Then he was at the second corner and could see the old man resting on his pole above him. He had been joined by an unshaven young labourer in a khaki overcoat. This was his brother-in-law. 'I near killed the ewe,' he told them, apologetic under the old man's inquiring eye. 'You better have a look at her.'

'It's a son,' said the brother-in-law. 'Just as I come home from work. I hurried over. And Jinny's fine.'

'A son. And Jinny!' His face contorted, and he turned hurriedly away from them. 'Hell,' he groaned, re-living the birth of the lamb; 'hell, oh hell!' The other two, embarrassed, knelt over the sheep, the old man feeling and muttering. 'Give me the titty-bottle,' he grunted presently. 'We'll catch you up.' The husband handed it over without speaking, and began to scuffle up the slope. Near the skyline they saw him turn and wave shamefacedly. 'He was crying,' said the brother-in-law.

'Better cry when they are born than when they are hung,' said the old man grumpily. The faintest whiff of sugared whisky came from the medicine-bottle. 'Not if it was to wet your wicked lips in hell!' he snapped upwards. He knew sheep: there was little he would need telling about what had happened on the rock platform. 'This pair'll do fine. But you'll have to carry the ewe when we come to the drifts.' He scowled into the descending snow, and eased the lamb into the crook of his arm, sack and all. 'You here for the night?'

Their tracks were well marked by this time. The man in khaki went ahead, flattening them further. The old man followed, wiry and deft. Two out of three, he was thinking; it might have been worse. His lips moved good-humouredly as he heard the black-backed gulls launch outwards from the scavenged cliff with angry, greedy cries. Unexpectedly, he chuckled.

Behind him the ewe, sniffing and baa-ing, her nose pointed at the sack, climbed wearily but determinedly up to the crest.

The Sun of Llanfabon [1]

In the days that are old and golden, Llanwonno church had a silver bell whose tongue splashed chimes of praises all over the land. None had more liking for its luscious jangle than the big-eared men of Llanfabon, and one night an assembly of them trod splay-footed through the river Taff to steal or (as they would prefer to say) to borrow it, knell, shell and clanger. It was necessary to complete the borrowing before sunrise, for at first light they might look to be observed and pursued by their big-eyed neighbours of Llanwonno.

Behold them then, late into the night, descending the stone-spangled slope of the Taff, their fretwork boots going crash-crash on the pebbles and their poles banging fireworks off the rocks. The bell alone was silent, for they had wound the clapper in velvet and straw before enfolding the whole sonorous dome in a cocoon of scarlet flannel nightshirts. However, just as they were crossing the river, the moon bolted out from behind cloud, alarming them greatly, for they mistook it for the sun. Their arms turned to jelly and they let the bell fall slap into a deep pool. It sank gurgling from sight, and not a note has been heard from it since.

But that is why the big-eyed men of Llanwonno call the moon the sun of Llanfabon, and the big-eared, bugle-nosed, barge-booted men of Llanfabon (who tell the whole story backwards) call the sun the moon of Llanwonno.

---

[1]Llanfabon . . . Llanwonno, contiguous parishes on the banks of the river Taff near Pontypridd, Glam.

IDWAL JONES (1895–1937)

The Way Up

When my family sent me to college
    I looked at those spires tall
And my head was buzzing with bits of advice,
    I couldn't remember them all;
But my uncle's advice I shall never forget,
    More precious than rubies to me:
'A supporter or two on a Council
        Is better than any degree.

'If it's Science or Maths, take it easy!
    Philosophy goes to your head,
Don't strain your brain with immoderate thought
    And don't take your text-books to bed.
Your first concern is with People!
    Set your sights on the top of the tree.
A supporter or two on a Panel
        Is better than any degree.

'Study how Influence ripples,
    Get to know how Appointments are made,
Temper your mind in the formative years
    And you'll master the tricks of the trade.
The prominent youth is the eminent man,
    Be headmaster at thirty-three!
A supporter or two on a Governing Board
        Is better than any degree.

'I hope your ambition's still wider,
    That this promising nephew of mine
Will treble the fame of the family name
    And end at the head of the line.
Grand will be your career –
    Think of mine and listen to me:
A supporter or two where it matters
        Is better than any degree.'

                              adapt. Wynne Roberts

JACK JONES (1884–1970)

The Light of the World

We had all been waiting hours for trams, and wondering what was the matter. Then one of the contractors who had been back to the pit-bottom to see what was the matter returned to tell us that something in the pit was broken, and that we would all have to find our way to the surface as best we could by way of the old return that would bring us out in Glyndyrus Wood, near the deep Glyndyrus Pond. 'I don't know what the state of the return is,' he said. 'But it's either that or stay down here all night doing nothing.'

So we all dressed, and dad whistled our Skye terrier bitch, whose name was Gyp, like all the others. We turned off the main underground roadway into some old workings, where in the old days the old-timers had worked coal on the pillar and stall system, not 'long-face' as we worked it. The old workings were in a bad state, and so was the return we had to travel to get to the surface now that the breakage of the guides or something in the pit-shaft made it impossible for us to get to the surface in the pit-cage.

Dad went confidently forward into the old workings, in which the almost rotten timber had grown whiskers of a sort of pit-moss – or is it called fungus? Anyway, the upright timbers along the footway were covered with it, and it made them look like shrouded sentries on guard. There was running water under our feet which had been dyed red either by the ironstone or some other dye in the rock of the roof. The background of continuous, but not loud, sound of the earth's unrest was punctuated by the snap of rotten timber, fall of stones, and droppings of water. There were also a faint whistling sound of straying air-currents, some of which were foul-smelling. In this decayed air the flames of our naked-light lamps weakened.

To scramble over falls of roof we had to fix our lamps in loops which most of us had sewn on the pokes of our caps. The lamp carried on our foreheads left us with both hands free to negotiate the difficult and dangerous passage over the many falls of roof, some of which were mountainous, and left only room for one to crawl over at a time. One false move would most likely start the roof above and bring another fall down to bury the crawler and those nearest him.

'Careful, son,' said dad, as he waited for me to come through the hole he had first crawled through. One fall of roof after another safely negotiated. Then we arrived at an expanse of water about the length of Pontyfyn Pond in the world above. The lamps we carried could not show us the far end of the expanse of water, which looked menacing to me. 'The swamp the old men used to talk about,' dad, who was in front with other men and boys behind, murmured. 'It's not too deep on the high right side.' He fixed his lamp with which he had been viewing the water in the loop of his cap again. Then he tutted down. 'Get on my back, son, and hold tight. Don't be frightened, and whatever you do – even if I stumble – don't put out your hand to touch the side-timber. Hold fast round my neck.'

I did, and dad waded into the water with me on his back, and our Skye Terrier bitch swimming in front. When the water was up above dad's middle I did get a bit frightened and my naked-light lamp fell into the water. 'My lamp.' 'Never mind the lamp now, son, you hold fast around dad's neck,' dad said in a way as calmed me.

Slowly he won his way through the expanse of ancient water, which at its deepest point, on the high right side along which our dad and the other men with boys on their backs travelled, was up to about our dad's chest. After they were all across safely, dad started up a steep incline. 'Shan't be long now,' he said. After we had climbed for some time he stopped, knelt, and pointed. 'Look, son.' There was what seemed to me to be a bright disc, about the size of a florin, on top of what appeared to be a distant mountain. 'That's what we've been looking for, son, the light of the world, the world where your mam is. Come on.' The disc of light grew in size as we climbed our way to the world's surface.

from *Unfinished Journey* (1937)

So long, Dad

Making conversation with a father who is dying on his feet is no easy job, but what can one do but talk? Presently our Mam appeared in the doorway, where she stood for a few seconds looking in at Dad and me, but she did not say anything, neither did Dad notice her standing there. The look on her face was one of loving concern. She went back to the visitors crowding the front room. I brought my new book, Dad. It's in the top little drawer of the chest of drawers in the front room. When you have quiet you'll be able to read a bit of it. Shall I fetch it for you to see? Yes, he said, I'd like to see it, my boy. I went and fetched it and he liked the jacket, but he didn't take the book into his hands. My hands are not very clean, he said. I took the book back to the top little drawer of the chest of drawers in the front room and tried to think what was best to say next to him. I don't suppose you are well enough for another of our little jaunts down town? I said. He chuckled weakly and looked sideways at me and then looked back into the fire. No, I don't suppose you are, I said; then Belle, my sister, came in and said: I'm warming you a drop of broth, Dad, and you're taking it so don't waste your breath to say no. Go on into the front room to Laura and the others, John. I'm all right here with Dad, I said.

I thought I was having the last few hours of Dad's company on this earth, and were it a hundred times more painful to sit there trying to think of something to say to him it would still have been a privilege if not a pleasure. So long, Dad, I said some hours later. So long, my boy. I kissed him, and feeling the tears coming to my eyes I took little David by the hand and walked out of the house with him. Your Father, said Laura when she and Mary and Bob, who was carrying little Norman, caught up with me. Your Father is – Yes, I know, I know, I almost shouted. I knew that before long he would be with King David, my brother David and all the other Davids gone before.

from *Me and Mine* (1946)

JOHN GWILYM JONES (1904–   )

The Plum Tree

My brother Wil and I are twins, conceived at the same moment in the same place, by the same love and the same desire. Mam ate the same food to strengthen us both, knew the same pain in carrying us. We moved inside her at exactly the same time. We were born together. The same hands received us and the same water bathed us. We gave exactly the same fright to my mother and the same pride to my father. Placed in the same cradle, we sucked at the same breasts. The same hand rocked us and, when we were weaned, we ate from the same bowl. We followed each other across the floor like shadows one of the other, and the same person taught us to say Mam and Dada and Sionyn and Wil and Gran and Grandad and bread-and-milk and trousers down and run-like-hell, and 'a' for apple and 'b' for baby, and who was the man who was beloved of God and twiceoneatwo, and Come into the garden Maud, and drink of this since this is my blood from the New Testament.

And yet, today, my brother Wil is in Egypt and I am working the land at Maes Mawr.

For years, I did not know that there was a difference between us. Wil was Sionyn and Sionyn was Wil. 'Sionyn, come here,' said Mam, and Wil ran to her as fast as his legs could carry him. 'Stop it, Wil, you little brat,' said Dad and I stopped that instant. When I was spanked and sent to bed without supper, Wil would take his trousers off as well, say his prayers and cry his eyes out, lying beside me under the bedclothes with his own stomach empty; and when Wil snipped off the top of his thumb with a scissors, I saw blood on the top of my thumb and had it bandaged, just like Wil.

It was the plum tree in the garden which began the tearing apart of Wil and me. God planted it there. And God said, let there be a plum tree at the top of the garden in Llys Ynyr, between the outside lav and the wall; and so it came to pass. I am not blaming God for this and I don't hold it against Him. After all, I am happy to enjoy the benefits He gives, and I must be content with the rest. God created the sun and moon, the stars, the sea and all things in it, and the earth with its animals, each according to its kind; cows to give us calves and milk, sheep to give us lambs and wool and warm clothing, and dogs to be friends to us. It is Him we must thank for fruit-bearing trees producing fruit according to their kind; oak trees showing us how to be strong and how to live to a ripe old age, giving acorns for the pigs; eating-apple trees and store-apple trees. And plum trees . . . small, dark plums with the white stuff inside as sweet as honey, melting to leave a clean stone between the tongue and the roof of the mouth, which can be shot out like a cork from an air gun. Yes, God planted the plum tree in our garden between the outside lav and the garden wall. I am planting this, He said, to make Wil into Wil and to make Sionyn Sionyn.

God is also responsible for creating man. Having breathed the breath of life into his nostrils, He created him in his own image. 'There you are now then,' He said, 'do as you like. If you prefer someone else to me, that's your business. You can be Nebuchadenazzer if you like, and silly enough to eat grass. Or you can be Daniel, praying with your face towards Jerusalem. You can believe that I will speak only to the Pope, or believe that Robin Puw, End House, knows me better than the Pope does. Bernard Shaw thinks that it's Robin Puw and the Pope's imagination which leads them to believe that I am talking to them. You're welcome to believe that as well. Or, if you so wish, you can believe, as Stalin does, that I am decorative enough, like a pretty little red flower on a tree, but that it is the tree which is important and which counts.'

That's not quite fair, God. I admit that Nebuchadenazzer was war-thirsty and thoughtless, but he did build Babylon into the most beautiful city the world had seen at that time. It's quite true that Daniel was an exemplary good boy, but he didn't lose a wink of sleep to try to mitigate the ordeal of his fellow slaves on the banks of the Euphrates. I don't know much about the Pope, but I do know that Robin Puw, End House, is the father of Neli Back Street and that he refuses to acknowledge her. I admit that Stalin's materialism killed five million peasants in the Ukraine, but he cannot be wholly bad; just consider how they are fighting today. Now then, I don't want you to think that I have lost sight of the plum tree in the garden; I haven't. God gave Wil the right to be Wil and me to be what I am, and although Wil wields a sword while I plough, Wil is a kinder sort than I, and I think the world of Wil and Wil thinks the world of me.

The plum tree was older than Gran. Although Gran is still alive, she was old even then. Her face was deeply lined, but she was as healthy as a firm nut except for the paralysed arm. She could reach you a fine clip on the ear with her left hand, but her right was as lifeless as the weights of a grandfather clock which had long since stopped. I used to think of Gran and the plum tree in the same breath. The two were alive before Gladstone died, and when Revivalist Evan Roberts was travelling up and down the country giving people odd experiences, some of which remain with us even now, blessed be his name, as John Huws, Pant, says . . . We do not know what Saviour and Mediator, Pardon and Repentance mean, but we believe in them, and that is what is important . . . .

I know very well that I latch on to every chance to digress, raising each red herring in turn so that I don't have to talk properly about the plum tree. And with good reason. In the very marrow of my bones, I hate to think about it. I sometimes think that the plum tree is my most deadly enemy. It was the tree taught me lifeless, dead things like Gran's right arm are more dangerous by far than live, healthy things like her left. It was the tree taught me that Satan is alive in the world today, and although it also taught me that nothing dies and that everlasting life is a fact and a reality, that is not wholly comforting.

You notice that I have talked about lifeless, dead things and then in the same breath I said that nothing dies. Inconsistency, you say? Perhaps you are right. A woolly mind? That could be equally true. Or then again, it could be that words change their meaning according to their context. That is how Members of Parliament justify themselves at any rate. You are not being fair, they tell their critics, you are quoting my words out of context.

Once, a long time ago, Wil and I went to see Vaughan, the Bronallt boy, in his coffin. I knew by this time that Wil was Wil. We were no longer the one in two and two in one, and although we went there together, I knew that we were now apart. Vaughan looked as if he was still alive: his cheeks were red and his teeth showed as if he was smiling. Someone had placed a bunch of flowers between his hands. Do you know what was the last thing he said? his mother asked us:

> My little hen is a white little hen
> All pink and yellow and red and black.

While I said to myself: today he is a member of the united Choir of the Paradise of Heaven whose blessed singing takes the angels of glory by surprise. I don't believe that today, mind you; that is, I don't believe exactly like that. Vaughan may not be singing but he is doing something. I believed once that he had achieved everlasting life because his mother and his sister Enid and I and others remembered him still. But his mother and Enid and I will die sometime and who will remember him then? It was only last week that I read an article on Karl Barth and I am now in the process of changing my mind yet again.

That night in bed I heard Wil crying as if his heart would break. I put my arm around him, 'What is it, Wil?' I said. 'I'm afraid of dying,' said Wil. 'You two go to sleep,' said my mother. We were still one to her.

Today Wil is in Egypt because he is afraid of death and I am ploughing the fields of Maes Mawr because I know that Wil will live for ever.

'We don't have it too bad,' said Wil, 'Our standard of living is high. We have nourishing food. Plenty of it. And we have freedom.'

'Quite so!' I retorted. 'At the expense of people living in Africa and in Malaya and India, whose own standard of living is lower than that of a pig in this country. Just think of Krupps in Germany and of his like in our own country.'

'It's easy enough for you to find fault with the rich,' Wil said. 'I know that they cheat the poor and starve them, but you must keep in mind that our own well-being is inter-related with theirs. What proof have you got that we would be better off if coal, the railways and the heavy industries were all nationalised? You can kill yourself trying to show the rottenness of society to that society, and what good would it do? Good and bad, my boy, are so much a part and parcel of each other that you just cannot separate them. We cannot think of other people all day long. Our business in life is to think a little more about our own duties and to justify ourselves in our own eyes. And if there's someone stopping us, well, there's only one thing for it. As you well know, Sionyn, I have very little patience with those who tie up nations in little parcels and say that all Frenchmen are immoral, all Germans military-minded, all Jews usurers, or that all Englishmen are arrogant and all Scots mean. They usually split up Wales into two parcels. If they're living in England and have made a little money by selling milk and satin, Wales is the Land of Song, the Land of the White Gloves and of strong, upright men, the salt of the earth. But to those of us who have stayed at home because we loved Wales, our nation is a pretty spineless one and hypocritical with it. And yet, there is a little truth in both versions. And at certain intervals all the immorality, the lust for war and the lust for money, all the arrogance, the meanness and the hypocrisy, break out like gore from a boil, and at those times it's every man for himself.'

I knew that there were answers to all these assertions but I could not for the life of me give them without feeling self-righteous and smug. The right answers are never smug or self-righteous. Psychologists say that ideas are very different from the impressions which caused them. Thus it follows that there exists a further difference when ideas are changed into words. I wonder if it's blasphemous to consider that this is why a sheep grows silent before its shearers.

'Eat up, for goodness sake,' says Mam. We are still the same to her. 'Eat,' she says, 'Sleep, get up, don't, hurry up, be quiet. . . . .' things which our legs and arms, our eyes and our ears can do. In her eyes we are flesh. . .flesh of her flesh.

We cause exactly the same anxiety to her. 'Do they give you enough to eat in Maes Mawr, Sionyn? Are there plenty of blankets on your bed? Take care that you've got plenty of warm things on. What sort of food do you get, Wil? Is it very cold in those tents? Remember to put enough on. That bitch, Mary Owen the Trucks, going on about our Sionyn not being in the army. 'If everyone was like Sionyn,' I said to her, 'there wouldn't be any war.' 'Such a pity that Wil didn't make a stand like Sionyn,' says Mr Williams the Minister. 'We're lucky to have people like Wil,' I said to him, 'or we'd all have been trampled underfoot a long time ago.'

From time to time, we are the same to one another:

'Do you remember the day, years ago, you knocked on Betsan Jones's door and ran away?'

'That wasn't me. It was you.'

'No, it wasn't, you did it.'

'No, it was you.'

'Remember us both learning the catechism and getting a shilling each from Gran?'

''Course I remember.'

'Can you remember which one of us fell off the plum tree?' And I reply, 'I did. I have no doubts about that.'

So we return to the plum tree, which is as inevitable as birth or death. As inevitable as the Day of Judgement, John Huws, Pant, would say, and perhaps he's right. The tree still stands between the lav and the garden wall, older by that much which has passed, the film of green on its bark a little denser. One day, Wil and I and I and Wil climbed up to its top. I sat on a branch that withered like Gran's right arm and I fell and broke my leg. I was stuck in the house for weeks with nothing to do except read, and read and read. Wil became friendly with Lias and little Harry at the Garage, and came back each evening talking of magneto, dynamo and clutch, changing gear and Bleriot and Terry H. I couldn't care less about a magneto or a dynamo and, even now, Wil picks up a book only when pushed to it.

trans. Elan Closs Stephens

J.R. JONES (1911–70)

Your Country Leaving You

It is said of one experience that it is among the most agonizing of all . . . namely that of having to leave the soil of your country for ever, of turning your back on your heritage, of being torn away by the roots from your homeland . . . I have not suffered that experience. But I know of another experience which is just as painful, and more irreversible (for you can always return to your home), and that is the experience of knowing, not that you are leaving your country, but that your country is leaving you, is ceasing to exist under your very feet, is being sucked away from you, as if by an insatiable, consuming wind, into the hands and possession of another country and another civilization. And as that is what is happening in Wales, we have to face something more terrible and more cruel than academic arguments, more or less, about how to avoid taxing the tolerance of the majority, or how to strike a balance between conflicting opinions and interests. What we have on our hands is *war* – the old war the Peoples have had to wage time and time again in the course of history: the struggle of the conquered for their very existence, the struggle to save their identity from being trampled into oblivion.

from *Gwaedd yng Nghymru* (1970), trans. Meic Stephens

Lewis Jones (1897–1939)

The Father of Jane's Baby

When they were all seated the official opened the conversation. 'Hmm,' he began ponderously, 'I believe I know what you have come about, James. I believe I am right in saying it is about your Jane, isn't it?' Receiving no reply to his question, he continiued, 'I have been told Jane is going to have a baby and that she do blame my son for it.'

Bridling at the sneer in his voice, Shane interrupted him. 'Yes,' she said, 'that be quite right. Jane be going to have a baby by your Evan.'

The outspoken assertion and the manner in which she made it startled the two men for a moment. Shane went on in a softer voice: 'We have come to ask you, as a God-fearing man, Evan, to make your son clean the gel he have dirtied. You have knowed me and James for many years now and, although James is only a collier and do like his drop of beer, you do know us to be 'spectable people not ashamed to look nobody in the face. Yes,' she went on proudly, 'we don't owe a penny to no man and nobody do need to be ashamed to have our Jane for a wife. I know we be poor, but she have been reared 'spectable and clean, thank God.' She paused a moment to swallow, then continued: 'Yes, Evan, we have come to ask you to make your son do the right thing.' Her voice faltered on the last sentence and it sounded like a plaint.

For some moments nothing else was said. Then the overman rose heavily to his feet and walked slowly to the door. He opened it and shouted, 'Evan, come here'. In a very short time the young man entered, sheepishly avoiding the eyes that scanned his face. 'You know what we have been talking about,' his father began. 'James and Shane do blame you for the baby that is coming to their Jane, and they want you to marry her. What have you got to say about it?' His words were a command.

Seconds elapsed before the youth made any response. The three parents anxiously watched him, each seeming ready to catch the words when they dropped from his lips. At last he started speaking. His voice was low and he kept looking at the floor. 'I do admit I have been with Jane,' he started, 'but only once and that was when we went away with the chapel.' He stopped a moment. No one moved and he continued, his breath quickening. 'She was courting regular with another chap before that. I have got witnesses to prove it.' He raised his head and looked at his father. Encouraged by the quick gleam of interest he saw in the latter's eyes, he failed to notice the horror in Shane's or the spasmodic twitching of Big Jim's face muscles. The young man chose his next words like bullets which he shot venomously at Jim and Shane. 'You can't trap me with this,' he rattled out in jerks. 'You have got the wrong bird this time. You are only blaming me because my father is an official. But it is no good looking for the right man in this house; he don't live here.'

Each word struck Shane with an impact that quivered through her body. She hid her drawn face in her hands. Hot tears trickled like molten glass through her fingers. Immersed in her own grief, she did not see Big Jim spring to his feet, his panting chest emphasising the magnitude of his bulk.

He stood motionless, the pallor of his face giving greater heat to the glow in his eyes. When he at last spoke the deep tremor in his voice made Shane shudder and raise her tear-stained face. 'Oh,' said Jim, with callous deliberation, 'so the son of Evan do class my gel a whore. Eh? The man who have used my daughter do now call her a prostitute.' He paused to battle with his passion, then spat out, 'Look well to yourself, man, before talking 'bout other people. Before you start to run other women down, look well to your own mother.'

Shane sensed the drift of his words and tried to stop him. She wailed through her tears, 'Don't say no more, James bach, for the sake of God.'

Jim waved her aside and paid no attention to Evan the Overman cowering in the chair. Completely dominating the situation, he nailed the trembling youth with his eyes and went on: 'Too late now. Too late. When you hurt my gel, you do put poison in my heart. Poison that have got to be spit out. And if it do kill anyone, who am I to try and stop it?' He paused again with a visible tremble, gulped hard and then continued: 'You say that your father is an official. Yes, that is true. But you don't tell us how he came to be one. Answer that, Evan bach, before you open your mouth again. But, there,' he went on raspingly, without waiting for a reply, 'perhaps you don't know.'

Apart from Jim's voice the room was silent. Shane sat rigid, her bottom jaw hanging loosely. Evan the Overman had buried his face in his arms, while his son stood motionless and helpless before the glaring eyes of Big Jim.

The young man trembled as Jim continued: 'Let me help you. Do you believe your father was made an official because he was a good workman. Ha-ha!' The laugh did not sound out of place. It was deep and bitter, giving coherence to the words that followed. 'No, of course not. I could work his hands off, but I have not been made an official. No, my boy, it is not *that* you have to brag about. Your father did not have the job of overman because of the work he have done himself.' Jim's voice began to rise as he said, 'No; it is not there you will find the answer. Your father was made an official because when Williams, the under-manager, come here first he did lodge with your father and mother. Yes,' he burst out passionately, his voice palpitating with the contempt that consumed him, 'your father did sell his wife's body for an overman's job.'

The usually arrogant colliery official slumped forward in the chair. His heaving shoulders betrayed what his covered face was hiding. Young Evan cowered, with staring eyes, against the door post. Big Jim lifted Shane from the settee and stood with her in the middle of the room.

Pride and passion deepened his voice: 'You do tell me to look somewhere else. Yes, I can. But you look first, my boy, to your own face and see if you can find the likeness of Evan the Overman there. Huh. That is one thing you will never see. I am sorry for you. The son of such a man as your father is not fit to enter the family of Jim the Big. I would sooner find the father of my gel's babby in the gutter than in this house.'

Jim's voice became softer as he said: 'But there be no need for me to look anywhere. I am man enough to father my daughter's babby as I have fathered her. I ask no man to make or to keep my children.'

Neither father or son opened their mouth as Jim made his terrible indictment. The room became cold as a vault of resurrected corpses. Shane, almost overcome by the ruthless, devastating words of her mate, trembled from head to foot. She was thankful when his great arm encircled her waist and he led her to the door, saying aloud. 'Come, Shane bach. Let us leave this painted muckhole and the rubbish that do live in it. Our Jane do still belong to us and her baby is ours.'

Big Jim paused as they passed the young man at the door. His voice vibrated with a sudden spasm of passion and hate. 'Do you hear me?' he shouted.

Neither of the stricken, shamefaced men looked up as he went on: 'Now both of you 'member this. The father of Jane's babby do not live in this house. If ever I hear a word that it do, that day I come back and pull it about your ears brick by brick.' With this he slammed the door, sternly bade Shane dry her tears, and with his arm through hers proudly marched past the neighbours who had seen them enter the house and had waited in anticipation of a rowdy scene.

Words were not necessary to explain the result of the interview. Shane's tear-stained face told it.

The couple found Len and Jane awaiting them when they arrived home. Jane looked in her mother's eyes and burst into sobs when she read the message they contained. Jim turned at the pitiful wail. 'That will do,' he said abruptly, 'there is to be no more crying in this house.' He waited until Jane had somewhat controlled herself, then added more softly, 'Sit down and wipe your eyes, my little gel. Now, listen to me. The little babby you are going to bring into the world belong to no one but the people in this house. It will be ours and no one else's. There will be no wedding before it is born, and its father is not Evan the Overman's son. Do you understand my words, Jane bach?' he queried, a world of love in his voice.

from *Cwmardy* (1937)

Jane in her Coffin

After dinner Mrs Thomas told Big Jim, 'We can go in now, James. You had better take the boy with you.' Jim rose from the table and caught Len's hand. As they approached the parlour door the boy felt he was on the verge of some great adventure. His heart missed a beat, then jumped more quickly into action at the sound of the raised latch. He thrust his perspiring hand more deeply into the engulfing fist of his father as they entered the parlour.

Len noticed immediately the two long candles wasting their flames in the daylight mellowed by the drawn window-blinds. The white-covered chairs puzzled him even while he wondered what the long yellow box on the table in the centre of the room was for. He instinctively knew that the funny-shaped plank of wood standing upright near the fire-grate belonged to the box. The shining shield near its top stared at him like a lonely glaring eye.

The lad pressed his body more tightly to the rigid leg of his father. He turned his head away from the shield and waited. Len knew something else was to come, but had no idea what it was until he heard Mrs Thomas murmur quietly, her apron to her eyes, 'Don't she look lovely, Mr Roberts?'

Like a flash Len knew what was in the box. Before he could say anything Big Jim bent down and lifted him from the floor. With awestruck eyes the boy looked down into the interior of what he now knew to be a coffin. Jane lay there, more still and silent than he had ever seen her.

Her body was clothed in a white lace and looked longer than when Len had last seen it. Her hands were waxy mirrors reflecting the blue tracery of all their veins. They were folded across her breast. One hand grasped a bunch of red roses that cast a blush over her smooth, white face, which seemed to smile into Len's downcast eyes.

Cuddled to Jane's side was the body of the baby that had killed her. Its tiny face looked like a blob of paste. Len felt a sudden urge to again caress Jane with his hands. He wanted to run them over the smooth contours of her breasts. Lumps of saliva rose to his throat. He swallowed them back in gulps and began to struggle hysterically in his father's grip. No tears came to his eyes as he continued the vain fight against Big Jim, but the feeling of impotence eventually conquered him and the emotional storm abated, leaving him panting on his father's shoulder.

Jim let him recover his breath, then slowly lowered him to the coffin until his lips touched those of his silent, smiling sister. Len shuddered at their cold clamminess. He tried to warm them with his breath. Jim saw the boy's hands wander through Jane's hair, and lifted him away before he could clasp her head.

Together father and son looked down for a few moments longer. Neither said a word. Their tears fused before reaching the dead face, whose smile seemed to soften at the burning touch. Big Jim turned away at last and the pair went quietly out, followed by Mrs Thomas, who closed the parlour door softly behind them.

Five days after Jane had died Len was again taken in to see her. This was to be the last occasion before they screwed the coffin down ready for the funeral next day. As before, Big Jim lifted his son above the edge. Len looked down and a look of horror filled his eyes. Jane's beautiful face was gone. In its place was a dirty yellow mask with snarling lips that curled back from shiny white teeth. A blackened penny grinned at him mockingly from each of her eyes. The roses had died and were now withered blotches on the white lace of her shroud. Dark blobs filled the places where her cheeks had been. The tiny shrunken form at her side was covered. A fusty smell rose from the coffin and reminded Len of the odour in his bed the night after Jane had died. An acid-tasting lump rose to his throat. It made him feel sick. Turning his head away he hid his burning face on Jim's neck. In this manner both went back into the kitchen.

All that night the horror of what he had seen sunk more deeply into Len's mind. The awful face chased him in his sleep. Always it was grinning before his eyes. It refused to go away. Fumes came from its mouth and entered his nose. He felt himself choking and screamed to Jane for help, pressing tightly to his body the pillow on which her head used to rest. But the horrid face with its coin-covered eyes and drawn lips followed him. He started fighting it away when he heard it say, 'Don't you know me, Len bach? I am Jane, your sister. Why do you drive me from you?'

Len stopped his frantic struggles and looked again.

The pennies melted and made way for bright blue eyes. The lips closed in and the cheeks filled out. Len's heart thrilled. He laughed happily and pressed the face of his sister to his lips. The short stiff hair on it hurt him. He looked again and found he had been kissing Evan the Overman's son. His body quivered with disgust and he threw the face from him with all his might. It rebounded back upon the bed and again it was the face of the coffin.

Len heard his father's voice ask from an interminable distance, 'What be the matter with you, Len bach? Perhaps you had better come to sleep with me and your mam'. Jim felt the steaming body of the lad dampen his flannel shirt as he carried him into Shane's bedroom. Finding comfort in his parents' presence, Len fell into a deep, lethargic sleep.

from *Cwmardy* (1937)

R. GERALLT JONES (1934–   )

Remember to Write

'Remember to write.' Clic-di-clac, clic-di-clac, clic-di-clac. The train's clattering wheels jangle mam's words in my mind as I sit in the corner and stare unseeing at the rain rushing by.

'Remember to write.'

I'm looking out of the dirty carriage window. The sea flows past in a hurry to get back to Pwllheli, to Llŷn, to Nain, and to Nefyn. God, I'd give a thousand pounds, two thousand, two thousand and dad's Morris car and the cricket book with Don Bradman's picture, to be playing football in Nefyn instead of going away to school. To be able to turn in my own time on Pwllheli platform after seeing someone else off to school, to walk through the wooden barrier, wait for as long as I like near the Wyman's bookstall and see the counter-full of

sweets, to buy a *Hotspur* and the *Sporting Record*, and then to saunter out into
the lovely rain. I'd stand then in the middle of Station Square and start getting
really wet, and I'd look up and down Pen Cob like an old farmer before
deciding which way to go. Then I'd turn to the left, in no hurry, and wander
slowly towards the bridge. I'd stand there for hours and hours in the rain,
watching the swans. Old snobs, swans are, pretending they don't know
anyone's looking at them. Down there they go swimming round and round like
lunatics for ages, their little black feet pumping like train's wheels underneath
them. Like a train. Clic-di-clac, clic-di-clac; remember to write. 'Dear Mam, I
don't like school. Please can I come home. At once. Yours in brief . . .'

But it will be ten weeks before I can walk Pen Cob again. Ten weeks. How
long is ten weeks? It's almost as long as from this very second to the end of the
world, from today to that time. Nain talks about when a drunken man kicked
the policeman's hat in Llanllyfni fair, it's like as-it-was-in-the-beginning-is-
now'n-for-ever-shall-be-world-without-end-amen. Nobody can see to the far
end of ten weeks. It's altogether too long for anyone to think about. I grab my
Hotspur and try to read about Cannonball Kidd, who can score a goal from
halfway against the best goalie in the world. But it's no use. I can't get
interested even in Cannonball Kidd. I can feel a great empty hole in my belly,
and I stare out through the window without seeing anything but the drizzle on
Pwllheli station. 'Dear Mam. Here's the letter. I've got a pain in my belly. Oh,
please can I come home . . .'

And now I was going as well. No more walking between the hedges to
school. What did 'away' mean? Was it farther than Pwllheli? Perhaps it was as
far as Bangor. Math said that the name of the place was Shwsbri, but that
meant nothing. It sounded a bit like strawberries, and strawberries could be
found in Llaniestyn, if only in Mr. Barret's garden. Would it be possible to fish
in the pond after being 'away', or to sit on the bridge, or to go to Felin Eithin
shop to buy fresh bread and eat all the crust on the way home? Could I play
trains in the front room? Clic-di-clac, clic-di-clac. Oh, Mam, I don't want to
go to Shwsbri. 'Dear Mam. I don't know where I'll be when you receive this
letter. I have jumped off the train. I am going to India because I don't want to
go to Shwsbri away to school. Yours truly . . .'

I fling down the *Hotspur*, stare indignantly at Criccieth station outside, and
attack my meat sandwich. It must be hours and hours since I had breakfast.

At Dovey Junction, when I have more or less forgotten the end-product of
the journey, and am poking around the platform happily enough, what do I see
in the middle of a crowd of people at the far end of the station but a school cap.
Exactly the same colour as the sparkling new cap which is safely tucked away in
my own pocket. I stand stock still. Then I creep back step by step round the
corner to the gents. I stand there for a minute, my heart pumping away and my
breath catching in my throat. Another boy going to the same place! Who is he?
He looks incredibly clever and beautiful in his cap. I peer around the corner of
the gents to look at him. He is standing still in the middle of the platform, with
a new, leather case by his side. And what is he doing? Reading a newspaper!

The only one I have ever seen reading a newspaper is my father. And my father is old. Do boys read newspapers in Shwsbri? Dear God, what sort of place am I going to?

When the Shwsbri train comes in, I jump smartly into an empty compartment near the back. Please God, I say, don't send that boy into this compartment. But I know perfectly well that it is no good. He arrives soon enough, swaggering his way down the corridor, cap over one ear. And in he comes. After flinging his bag up on the rack overhead and settling himself in a corner, he gives me the once-over, like a farmer at the stock-market.

'I see we're going to the same place,' he says off-handedly, pointing at the corner of my new cap that's peeping stupidly out of my coat pocket.

'I goin' to Shwsbri,' I volunteer.

'Yes, old son, we're all going there on this train,' he says, 'but you and I are going to the same school.'

'Oh. Yes.' There are too many English words chasing each other across his lips for me to follow properly. I can do nothing but sit and stare stupidly at his middle. Oh, Mam, I don't want to go away to school, where they talk funny and boys with newspapers and no damn anybody speaking Welsh. Diawl,[1] diawl, diawl, I say, leaning heavily on my lonely obscenity. I don't want to go to old school.

'I s'pose you're a new boy,' he offers, after a dreadful, long pause.

'Yes.'

'Mm. Well, you ought to be wearing your cap, you know. It's an offence not to wear your cap.'

'Oh.' I grab my black and yellow cap and stick it on my head. 'Offence?'

'Offence. Crime. Breaking the rules. What's the matter, don't you understand English?'

But this question does not require an answer, and he snuggles up behind his papers and comics to chew sweets and whistle tunelessly from time to time to show that he remembers I'm here. In Welshpool, three others decend on us, everyone laughing madly, thumping backs, pumping hands, and speaking a totally incomprehensible language, with words like 'swishing' and 'brekker' and 'footer' and 'prep'. After they've had their fill of taking each other's caps and kicking each other and flinging cases back and forth, someone notices me.

'What's this, Podge, freshie?'

'Yes,' says the veteran. 'Welshie as well. Can't understand a word of English.'

'Good God.' He gets up and stands in front of me and stares into my face. I can see the blackspots in the end of his nose. By this time, everyone is listening intently. He holds his face within three inches of mine. If I was brave, I would knock his teeth down his throat. If I was like Math or the Saint. But I'm not.

'Welshie are you? Welsh? Welsh?'

'Yes,' I say sadly, 'I am from Pen Llŷn.'

Everyone starts hooting with laughter, rolling around on their seats. The

[1] Diawl (lit. 'Devil'), an expletive.

questioner tries again.

'Going to Priestley School are you? School? School?'

'Yes.'

He turns triumphantly to the others.

'Bloody hell, fellers, we'll have some fun with this when we get there. All it can say is yes.'

And everyone starts rolling with laughter once again. I push myself far back into my corner for the remainder of the journey, feel the damn silly wetness in my eye, and try to think about Cannonball Kidd, about caravans, about Barmouth, about anything but about Mam and Pen Llŷn this morning. Clic-di-clac, clic-di-clac. 'Remember to write a letter.' Clic-di-clac, remember to write.

When the train reaches Shwsbri station, they all forget about me soon enough, and the whole gang rushes out on to the platform, their bags flying in all directions, caps shining new in the rain, everyone talking. On the platform, standing stiff as a poker, there's an ugly woman in a feathered hat, her lips one grim line, and a thin black walking stick in her hand. As each one of them sees her, he stops dead, pulls his cap straight, hauls trousers up, tries to get everything back into line.

'Well.' She looks at them as though she suddenly smells something unpleasant. 'Isn't there anyone else with you?'

Then she sees me standing in the carriage door, cap in hand, and my tie round the back of my neck.

'Oh.' With a come-and-gone smile flashing across her white teeth. 'Here he is. Are you Jones?'

'Yes, missus, My name is Joni Jones.'

'I see. Well, from now on you'll be Jones. Jones J. We don't use names like Johnnie at school, do we? And nice little boys don't say missus, Jones. My name is Miss Darby. Now boys, let's be on our way. We'll all be ready for our tea, I have no doubt.'

And off she goes along the platform, her stick clicking up and down, and her bottom waddling regularly from side to side like a duck's. And everyone follows her quiet as mice, and me following everyone else like Mrs. Jones the Post's little terrier dog.

I don't remember much about the next two days, thank God, only an occasional minute here and there. But I know very well that it's all far worse than any nightmare I've ever had about the place before I got here. And I had plenty of those. Everyone in this Priestley looks old and very experienced and talks a mouthful of English. The teachers have never heard of Wales, I don't think, and the cabbage is tough as string and black and green like watercress, and the bed is hard as sleeping on the floor, and the headmaster teaches something called Latin in a room with iron bars across the windows. Every night before going to bed I go to the lavatory to cry quietly and then go back to that old cold barn where everyone is pretending to sleep, and waiting to bait the Welshie.

On Sunday, we are all gathered together in the Latin room with a piece of paper and a small square envelope each, and the head tells us to write a letter home to say we are all right, have arrived safe and have had enough to eat. Well, I grab my brand new fountain-pen and start to write my letter.
Dear Mum and Dad,

I hope you are OK like me. I have arrived safe. The food is quite good and the school is quite nice. I am looking forward to the holidays. Remember me to Spot and to Llyn y Felin.

This in brief,
JONI.
from 'The Letter', trans. the author

ANONYMOUS

Hiraeth [1]

Tell me, men with wisdom gifted,
How hath *hiraeth* been created?
Of what stuff hath it been made,
That it doth not wear nor fade?

Gold and silver wear away,
Velvet too, and silk they say;
Weareth every costly raiment,
But *hiraeth* is a lasting garment.

Now a great and cruel *hiraeth*
In my heart all day endureth,
And when I sleep most heavily,
Hiraeth comes and wakens me.

Hiraeth, hiraeth, O! depart!
Why dost thou press upon my heart?
O! move along to the bed side,
And let me rest till morning tide.

trans. Aneirin Talfan Davies

---

[1] *Hiraeth*, longing

ROBERT AMBROSE JONES (Emrys ap Iwan; 1851–1906)

Keep Yourselves a Nation

Young Welsh people, while acquainting yourselves with the politics of the daily press, do not neglect to study the juster politics of the New Testament. Remember first of all that you are men and women, made of the same blood as the English and the Boers and the Kaffirs and the Chinese; for that reason, be prepared to accord them every privilege that you would claim for yourselves. Remember, secondly, that you are a nation, by God's ordinance; for that reason, do all you can to maintain your nation as a nation, by upholding its language, and all else valuable that pertains to it. If you are unfaithful to your country and your language and your nation, how can you be expected to be true to God and Mankind? Do not be ashamed of that which distinguishes you from other nations, and if you must imitate the nation which is your nearest neighbour, do so in that at which she excels over you, and not in her vanity, her treachery, her jealousy, her love of military and sporting exploits, her intellectual narrowness, and her lack of sympathy for other nations.

For inasmuch as God has made you a nation, keep yourselves a nation; because He took thousands of years to fashion a language especially for your purposes, keep that language; for in working together with God in his intentions for you, it will be easier for you to seek and discover Him. Who knows not that God has preserved the Welsh nation thus far for the reason that He has special work to be done through them in the world? Be that as it may, it would do no harm for you to believe as much. There is many a small nation which has grown influential in a short while, and many a mighty nation brought low as it were in a day. Nations, like human beings, have their allotted times. Let not the Welsh be found unready when their time is at hand.

from *Homiliau* (1906, 1909), trans. Meic Stephens

SALLY JONES (1935–   )

Ann Griffiths [1]

In little time I stake my claim
To all the panoply of fame.
My words are air, their manuscript
Forgetful flesh, a bony crypt
To lay these stillborn creatures in.

[1]Ann Griffiths (1776-1805), hymn-writer; her child lived only for a short while and she died soon after its birth.

This foolishness of light intent
I turn to praise, my patterns meant,
Poor gift, for Him by whose free gift
My life is bought; the seasons sift
Away my youth, my fear, my sin.

The fire upon my hearth is tame,
God's gentle creature; now my name
Is signed in polished oak and brass,
My soul is singing, clear as glass,
Pure as this babe I bear within.

My songs as light as ash are spent;
My hope's elsewhere, a long descent
In flesh and land – and yet the air
Stirs with fresh music, calls me where
Intricate webs of words begin.

Lord, let me not be silent till
All earth is grinding in Your mill!

T. GWYNN JONES (1871–1949)

Argoed [1]

Argoed, Argoed of the secret places . . .
Your hills, your sunken glades, where were they,
Your winding glooms and quiet towns?

Ah, quiet then, till doom was dealt you,
But after it, nothing save a black desert
Of ashes was seen of wide-wooded Argoed.

Argoed, wide-wooded . . . Though you have vanished,
Yet from the unremembering depths, for a moment,
Is it there, your whispering ghost, when we listen –

Listen in silence to the wordless speech
Where the wave of yearning clings to your name,
Argoed, Argoed of the secret places?

from *'Argoed'* (1927), trans. Anthony Conran

[1] Argoed, a remote part of Gaul, eventually laid waste by the Romans, according to the poet.

Ystrad Fflur [1]

The forest leaves at Ystrad Fflur
   Are rustling in the breeze,
And a dozen Abbots underground
   Are sleeping there at peace.

And there beneath the solemn yew
   Is Dafydd,[2] sweet his song,
And many a chief whose blade was keen
   In the grave's oblivion.

Though summer, when its time has come,
   Wakes leaves within the tree,
Man does not wake, and his handiwork
   Is crumbling tranquilly.

But though I see upon faith's ruins
   Sad death's oblivion,
When I walk the earth of Ystrad Fflur
   It eases me of pain.

                  trans. Joseph P. Clancy

T.H. JONES (1921–65)

Back?
(to R.S. Thomas)[3]

Back is the question
Carried to me on the curlew's wing,
And the strong sides of the salmon.

Should I go back then
To the narrow path, the sheep turds,
And the birded language?

Back to an old, thin bitch
Fawning on my spit, writhing
Her lank belly with memories:

[1] Ystrad Fflur, the abbey of Strata Florida, Cards.
[2] Dafydd, Dafydd ap Gwilym (*fl.* 1320-70), poet.
[3] R.S. Thomas (1913-   ), poet.

Back to the chapel, and a charade
Of the word of God made by a preacher
Without a tongue:

Back to the ingrowing quarrels,
The family where you have to remember
Who is not speaking to whom:

Back to the shamed memories of Glyn Dwr[1]
And Saunders Lewis's[2] aerodrome
And a match at Swansea?

Of course I'd go back if somebody'd pay me
To live in my own country
Like a bloody Englishman.

But for now, lacking the money,
I must be content with the curlew's cry
And the salmon's taut belly

And the waves, of water and of fern
And words, that beat unendingly
On the rocks of my mind's country.

Rhiannon

My daughter of the Mabinogion[3] name
Tells me Ayer's Rock is ten times higher than
A house, and she, being seven today,
Would like to see it, especially
To ride there on a camel from Alice Springs.
She also says she wants to be a poet –
Would the vision of that monolith
Stay in her mind and dominate her dreams
As in my mind and dreams these thirty years
There stands the small hill, Allt-y-clych,
The hill of bells, bedraggled with wet fern
And stained with sheep, and holding like a threat
The wild religion and the ancient tongue,
All the defeated centuries of Wales?

[1]Glyn Dwr, Owain Glyn Dŵr (c. 1354 – c. 1416), national hero, known in English as Owen
    Glendower.
[2]Saunders Lewis (1893-1985), writer and Nationalist leader, gaoled for his part in an arson
    attack on buildings belonging to the RAF at Penyberth, Caerns., in 1936.
[3]Mabinogion, a collection of medieval tales, in two of which Rhiannon is the principal character.

WILLIAM JONES (1896–1961)

Young Fellow from Llŷn

Young fellow from Llŷn, who's the girl of your heart,
You who wander so late in the evening apart?
My sweetheart is young and she comes from the Sarn,
And neat is her cottage that's under the Garn.

And what does she look like, the girl of your heart,
You who wander so late in the evening apart?
Dark, dark is my darling and dark haired is she,
But white shines her body like foam on the sea.

And what is she wearing, the girl of your heart,
You who wander so late in the evening apart?
In a long gown of shining white satin she goes
And red in her bosom there blushes a rose.

Young fellow from Llŷn, is she angry and flown,
That you wander so late in the evening alone?
Oh, never my sweetheart showed anger or pride
Since the very first time that we walked side by side.

Young fellow from Llŷn, why do tears then start
To your eyes as you wander so late and apart?
From her cheek Death has withered the roses away
And white is the wear in the cottage of clay.

trans. Harri Webb

LEWIS GLYN COTHI (*c.* 1420–89)

Lament for Siôn y Glyn

One boy, Saint Dwyn, my bauble:
His father rues he was born!
Sorrow was bred of fondness,
Lasting pain, lacking a son.
My two sides, dead is my die,
For Siôn y Glyn are aching.
I moan everlastingly
For a baron of boyhood.

A sweet apple and a bird
The boy loved, and white pebbles,

A bow of a thorntree twig,
And swords, wooden and brittle;
Scared of pipes, scared of scarecrows,
Begging mother for a ball,
Singing to all his chanting,
Singing 'Oo-o' for a nut.
He would play sweet, and flatter,
And then turn sulky with me,
Make peace for a wooden chip
Or the dice he was fond of.
Ah that Siôn, pure and gentle,
Cannot be a Lazarus!
Beuno once brought back to life
Seven who'd gone to heaven;
My heart's sorrow, it's doubled,
That Siôn's soul is not the eighth.

Mary, I groan, he lies there,
And my sides ache by his grave.
The death of Siôn stands by me
Stabbing me twice in the chest.
My boy, my twirling taper,
My bosom, my heart, my song,
My prime concern till my death,
My clever bard, my daydream,
My toy he was, my candle,
My fair soul, my one deceit,
My chick learning my singing,
My Iseult's chaplet, my kiss,
My strength, in grief he's left me,
My lark, my weaver of spells,
My bow, my arrow, my love,
My beggar, O my boyhood.
Siôn is sending his father
A sword of longing and love.

Farewell the smile on my mouth,
Farewell to my lips' laughter,
Farewell sweet consolation,
Farewell the begging for nuts,
Farewell, far-off the ballgame,
Farewell to the high-pitched song,
Farewell, while I stay earthbound,
My gay darling, Siôn my son.

trans. Joseph P. Clancy

ALUN LEWIS (1915–44)

The Mountain over Aberdare

From this high quarried ledge I see
The place for which the Quakers once
Collected clothes, my father's home,
Our stubborn bankrupt village sprawled
In jaded dusk beneath its nameless hills;
The drab streets strung across the cwm,
Derelict workings, tips of slag
The gospellers and gamblers use
And children scrutting for the coal
That winter dole cannot purvey;
Allotments where the collier digs
While engines hack the coal within his brain;
Grey Hebron[1] in a rigid cramp,
White cheap-jack cinema, the church
Stretched like a sow beside the stream;
And mourners in their Sunday best
Holding a tiny funeral, singing hymns
That drift insidious as the rain
Which rises from the steaming fields
And swathes about the skyline crags
Till all the upland gorse is drenched
And all the creaking mountain gates
Drip brittle tears of crystal peace;
And in a curtained parlour women hug
Huge grief, and anger against God.

But now the dusk, more charitable than Quakers,
Veils the cracked cottages with drifting may
And rubs the hard day off the slate.
The colliers squatting on the ashtip
Listen to one who holds them still with tales,
While that white frock that floats down the dark alley
Looks just like Christ; and in the lane
The clink of coins among the gamblers
Suggests the thirty pieces of silver.

I watch the clouded years
Rune the rough foreheads of these moody hills,
This wet evening, in a lost age.

[1]Hebron, a Nonconformist chapel.

In Hospital: Poona (1)

Last night I did not fight for sleep
But lay awake from midnight while the world
Turned its slow features to the moving deep
Of darkness, till I knew that you were furled,

Beloved, in the same dark watch as I.
And sixty degrees of longitude beside
Vanished as though a swan in ecstasy
Had spanned the distance from your sleeping side.

And like to swan or moon the whole of Wales
Glided within the parish of my care:
I saw the green tide leap on Cardigan,
Your red yacht riding like a legend there,

And the great mountains, Dafydd and Llewelyn,
Plynlimmon, Cader Idris and Eryri
Threshing the darkness back from head and fin,
And also the small nameless mining valley

Whose slopes are scratched with streets and sprawling graves
Dark in the lap of firwoods and great boulders
Where you lay waiting, listening to the waves –
My hot hands touched your white despondent shoulders

– And then ten thousand miles of daylight grew
Between us, and I heard the wild daws crake
In India's starving throat; whereat I knew
That Time upon the heart can break
But love survives the venom of the snake.

Goodbye

So we must say Goodbye, my darling,
And go, as lovers go, for ever;
Tonight remains, to pack and fix on labels
And make an end of lying down together.

I put a final shilling in the gas,
And watch you slip your dress below your knees
And lie so still I hear your rustling comb
Modulate the autumn in the trees.

And all the countless things I shall remember
Lay mummy-cloths of silence round my head;
I fill the carafe with a drink of water;
You say 'We paid a guinea for this bed,'

And then, 'We'll leave some gas, a little warmth
For the next resident, and these dry flowers,'
And turn your face away, afraid to speak
The big word, that Eternity is ours.

Your kisses close my eyes and yet you stare
As though God struck a child with nameless fears;
Perhaps the water glitters and discloses
Time's chalice and its limpid useless tears.

Everything we renounce except our selves;
Selfishness is the last of all to go;
Our sighs are exhalations of the earth,
Our footprints leave a track across the snow.

We made the universe to be our home,
Our nostrils took the wind to be our breath,
Our hearts are massive towers of delight,
We stride across the seven seas of death.

Yet when all's done you'll keep the emerald
I placed upon your finger in the street;
And I will keep the patches that you sewed
On my old battledress tonight, my sweet.

EILUNED LEWIS (1900–79)

The Birthright

We who were born
In country places,
Far from cities
And shifting faces,
We have a birthright
No man can sell,
And a secret joy
No man can tell.

For we are kindred
To lordly things,
The wild duck's flight
And the white owl's wings;
To pike and salmon,
To bull and horse,
The curlew's cry
And the smell of gorse.

Pride of trees,
Swiftness of streams,
Magic of frost
Have shaped our dreams:
No baser vision
Their spirit fills
Who walk by right
On the naked hills.

SAUNDERS LEWIS (1893–1985)

The Vineyard

God's nobleman, hearken,
A vineyard was set by a man on a sunlit hill,
He hedged her, and planted within her the noblest vines,
He enclosed her strongly, and built a tower in her midst,
And to his son he gave her, a goodly heritage,
That his name might be known among men from age to age.
But a herd of swine have broken into the vineyard,
Have trampled the fence, and root and devour the vines;
Is it not well for the son to stand in the breach
And to call his friends to his aid,
That the breach may be closed and the heritage made secure?
Garmon, Garmon,[1]
A vineyard placed in my care is Wales, my country,
To deliver unto my children
And my children's children
Intact, an eternal heritage:
And behold, the swine rush on her to rend her.
Now will I call on my friends,
Scholars and simple folk,
'Take your place by my side in the breach
That the age-old splendour be kept for ages to come.'
And this, my lord, is the vineyard of your Beloved too;
From Llan Fair to Llan Fair, a land where the Faith is established.

from *Buchedd Garmon* (1937), trans. D.M. Lloyd

The Deluge 1939

The tramway climbs from Merthyr to Dowlais,
Slime of a snail on a heap of slag;
Here once was Wales, and now
Derelict cinemas and rain on the barren tips;
The pawnbrokers have closed their doors, the pegging clerks
Are the gentry of this waste;
All flesh had corrupted his way upon the earth.

---

[1]Garmon (or Germanus; *c.* 378-448), a civil and military official in Gaul and, as bishop of
Auxerre, champion of Christian civilization against barbarian invaders.

My life likewise, the seconder of resolutions
Who moves from committee to committee to get the old country back on its
                                                                    feet;
Would it not be better to stand on the corner in Tonypandy
And look up the valley and down the valley
On the flotsam of the wreckage of men in the slough of despair,
Men and tips standing, a dump of one purpose with man.

Where there have been eyes there is ash and we don't know that we're dead,
Our mothers thoughtlessly buried us by giving us milk of Lethe,
We cannot bleed like the men that have been,
And our hands, they would be like hands if they had thumbs;
Let our feet be shattered by a fall, and all we'll do is grovel to a clinic,
And raise our caps to a wooden leg and insurance and a Mond pension;
We have neither language nor dialect, we feel no insult,
And the masterpiece that we gave to history is our country's M.P.s.

from 'Y Dilyw 1939', trans. Gwyn Thomas

The Eagles Depart

I, Paulinus[1] am old, at fifty I'm old,
And when I peer to the future it is not to this world I look;
My days here below almost over,
Enough for me to obey and to bide my hour.
And when I look back I behold how vainly I've striven.
Heavy my days have been,
Memories of youth remain my only delight.
Four years old was I in my father's arms in Caerleon
Gazing at the host of Maxen[2] and Helen the Arvonian Empress
Marching out of my city,
Under the eyes of the city,
Over the ringing stones of Sarn Helen out of the sound of the city.
Said my father, behold the world we have known is no more,
The long-established motion of the sun is no more,
Stability we shall know no more,
No more the carving of stones for the long-lasting dwellings,
The endless ages of Rome and her peace are no more.
And my father wept.

[1]Paulinus, a Roman governor.
[2]Maxen, Macsen Wledig (d. 388), Emperor of Rome in one of two historical tales in *The Mabinogion* . . . Helen, his wife.

But my mother replied:
When Rome's tranquillity is gone, the Peace of our Lord shall stand.
The daily oblations of Christian priests are the stones of our city's
                                                construction,
And our civilisation shall stand united and paved by the unshaken Creed.

Truly she spoke. For then,
Bereft of centurions and legions and the eagle banners,
And left in our weakness to hold the border,
The barbarians venturing nearer and ever nearer across the land,
And the Scots ever bolder and bolder from over the sea,
Yet in that hour it was that learning and piety
Blossomed like late spring in our land;
To our midst in Dyved and Gwent and Glamorgan
Came a constant stream of sages, teachers of letters and law
From the ravaged lands to the east and the burnt-out cities.
Our lime-washed churches and schools bloom like the cherry-tree's blossom,
And Ambrosius, lord of Caerleon and the South, eagerly welcomes
The heirs of Quintilian and Virgil, the fathers of language,
And the dejected pious disciples of Jerome of Bethlehem.

              from *Buchedd Garmon* (1937), trans. D.M. Lloyd

Ascension Thursday

What is up on the slopes this May morning?
Look at them, at the gold of the broom and laburnum
And the glowing surplice on the hawthorn's shoulders,
The alert emerald of the grass and the tranquil calves;

See the chestnut-tree's candelabra alight,
The bushes genuflecting and the mute birch nun,
The cuckoo's two notes across the stream's bright hush
And the mist's wraith curling from the censer of the dales:

Come out, people, from the council-houses before
The rabbits scatter, come with the weasel to see
The raising from the earth of a spotless host
And the Father kissing the Son in the white dew.

                              trans. Joseph P. Clancy

GWENETH LILLY (1920–   )

The Normans cross the Menai

The dawn broke slowly and miserably, with clouds hiding the hills and casting shadows over the whole countryside. Ieuan was aware of the hundreds of men at his back, as they stood there patiently in spite of their excitement and fear. He realized that he had one advantage over the others on the battlefield: as Father Thomas had said, he could see the enemy's manoeuvres.

And as the landscape gradually came into view, and the strait and the pontoon and the peninsula of Moel y Don emerged from the darkness, he said that Rhodri was right, and that their journey had not been in vain. The tide was low and the enemy was beginning to cross the pontoon of boats.

This was the most terrifying scene that Ieuan had ever witnessed. A mighty army was moving across the Menai: horsemen came first, for they were the leaders and the flower of the army in Anglesey. About fifteen of them were knights of some renown, bearing fine coats of arms on their shields, and their squires were at their sides with their pennants waving; red and blue, green and gold gleaming in the cheerless grey of November. The knights were clad in steel from head to foot and the horses were dressed in armour, too: large, heavy horses stepping ponderously from one boat to the next. Each knight had his company of horsemen, about thirty or more, mounted on strong horses that were armoured like their masters. Besides these, there was a huge regiment of foot-soldiers, many of them archers, as well as axe-men to cut trees and clear the ground for the horses. The procession was endless, and yet more were still waiting in orderly ranks beyond the pontoon on Moel y Don. From the large number of flags waving among the long spears it was evident that many important men and eminent soldiers were assembled here.

It was thrilling to see the powerful army shining in a long line that stretched from one shore almost to the other, silvery giants on huge horses relentlessly approaching the land of Arfon. This was Ieuan's first glimpse of the glory of French chivalry in all its glittering arrogance. He felt a dread that lifted him beyond ordinary fear. On each side and behind him there was total silence, not a man moving save the messengers who bore intelligence from one end of the field to the other. Ieuan looked over his shoulder and saw the waiting ranks for the first time. They were so drab, their everyday clothes blending with the grey of the field at the onset of winter: hardly any in steel, very many not even wearing a leather jerkin, with their arms having been made at home by the village smith and the soldiers themselves; on the field's flank there was a crowd of peasants carrying farm implements. For the most part they were infantry; there was only a small nucleus of horsemen mounted on ponies to the fore at mid-field, and a row of archers between them and the brow of the hill, with others to the right and left of them. But spears were the main weapon; the field looked like a forest of stakes. Ieuan noticed men as old as his grandfather, and boys as young as Gutun and himself. Every face wore the same look of surly determination. The thought had crossed Ieuan's mind that the horse and armour of one Norman knight would buy all the armoury of the scarecrows on this field. He was gripped by despair.

'Well, there's a fine lot of cocks for you,' said a soldier at the foot of the tree, as he gazed across the strait. He spat in the direction of the pontoon.

'Do the so-and-sos think they're going to a tournament?', asked his companion.

from *Rwy'n Cofio dy Dad* (1982), trans. Meic Stephens

RICHARD LLEWELLYN (1906–83)

In Blood, I say No

'Dada,' I shouted, 'are you near me?'

I hit my pick on stone and listened.

Only the growling up above, and voices from behind in the tunnel.

So on I went again, pick and pull, pick and pull and wasting more time getting the rock back, and scooping mud, and trying to shovel.

And then I found him.

Up against the coal face, he was, in a clearance that the stone had not quite filled.

I put my candle on a rock, and crawled to him, and he saw me, and smiled.

He was lying down, with his head on a pillow of rock, on a bed of rock, with sheets and bedclothes of rock to cover him to the neck, and I saw that if I moved only one bit, the roof would fall in.

He saw it, too, and his head shook, gently, and his eyes closed.

He knew there were others in the tunnel.

I crawled beside him, and pulled away the stone from under his head, and rested him in my lap.

'Willie,' I said, 'tell them to send props, quick.'

I heard them passing the message down, and Willie trying to pull away enough rock to come in beside me.

'Mind, Willie,' I said, 'the roof will fall.'

'Have you found him?' Willie asked me, and scraping through the dust.

'Yes,' I said, and no heart to say more.

My father moved his head, and I looked down at him, sideways to me, and tried to think what I could do to ease him, only for him to have a breath.

But the Earth bore down in mightiness, and above the Earth, I thought of houses sitting in quiet under the sun, and men roaming the streets to lose voice, breath, and blood, and children dancing in play, and women cleaning house, and good smells in our kitchen, all of them adding more to my father's counter-pane. There is patience in the Earth to allow us to go into her, and dig, and hurt with tunnels and shafts, and if we put back the flesh we have torn from her and so make good what we have weakened, she is content to let us bleed her. But when we take, and leave her weak where we have taken, she has a soreness, and an anger that we should be so cruel to her and so thoughtless of her comfort. So she waits for us, and finding us, bears down, and bearing down, makes us a part of her, flesh of her flesh, with our clay in place of the clay we thoughtlessly have shovelled away.

I looked Above for help, and prayed for one sweet breath for him, but I knew as I prayed that I asked too much, for how were all those tons to be moved in a moment, and if they were, what more hurt might be done to others.

Afraid I was, to put my hands with tenderness upon his face, for my touch, though with the love of the heart, might be an extra hurt, another weighing, for they were with dirt and cuts, and ugly with work that was senseless, not good to put before his eyes, for they were the hands of the Earth that held him.

His eyes were swelling from his head with pain and his mouth was wide, closing only a little as with weakness, and then opening wide again, and his tongue standing forth as a stump, moveless, dry, thick with dust.

And as the blood ran from his mouth and nose, and redness ran from his eyes, I saw the shining smile in them, that came from a brightness inside him, and I was filled with bitter pride that he was my father, fighting still, and unafraid.

His head trembled, and pressed against me as he made straight the trunk of his spine and called upon his Fathers, and my lap was filling with his blood, and I saw the rocks above him moving, moving, but only a little. And then they settled back, and he was still, but his eyes were yet beacons, burning upon the mountain-top of his Spirit.

I shut my eyes and thought of him at my side, my hand in his, trying to match his stride as I walked with him up the mountain above us, and I saw the splashings of water on his muscled whiteness as he stood in the bath, and the lamplight on his hands over the seat of the chair as he knelt in prayer at Chapel.

Air rushed from his throat and blew dust from his tongue, and I heard his voice, and in that strange noise I could hear, as from far away, the Voice of the Men of the Valley singing a plain amen.

So I closed his eyes and shut his jaw, and held him tight to me, and his bristles were sharp in my cuts, and I was heavy with love for him, as he had been, and with sadness to know him gone.

'We can move the rocks now, Wille,' I said.

'O Christ, Huw,' Willie said, 'is he out, then?'

'Yes,' I said, and feeling warmth passing from between my hands, 'my Dada is dead.'

'Hard luck, Huw, my little one,' Willie said, and coming to cry. 'Hard old bloody luck, indeed. Good little man he was.'

My mother sat in the rocking-chair with her hands bound in her apron, and looked through the open doorway up at the mountain-top.

'God could have had him a hundred ways,' she said, and tears burning white in her eyes, 'but He had to have him like that. A beetle under the foot.'

'He went easy, Mama,' I said.

'Yes,' she said, and laughed without a smile. 'I saw him. Easy, indeed. Beautiful, he was, and ready to come before the Glory. Did you see his little hands? If I set foot in Chapel again, it will be in my box, and knowing nothing of it. O, Gwil, Gwil, there is empty I am without you, my little one. Sweet love of my heart, there is empty.'

Well.

It is strange that the Mind will forget so much, and yet hold a picture of flowers that have been dead for thirty years and more.

I remember the flowers that were on our window-sill while my mother was talking that morning, and I can see the water dripping from a crack in the red pot on the end, for Bronwen was standing there, with her face in deep, dull gold from the sun on the drawn blind.

Thirty years ago, but as fresh, and as near as Now.

No bitterness is in me, to think of my time like this. Huw Morgan, I am, and happy inside myself, but sorry for what is outside, for there I have failed to leave my mark, though not alone, indeed!

An age of goodness I knew, and badness too, mind, but more of good than bad, I will swear. At least we knew good food, and good work, and goodness in men and women.

But you have gone now, all of you, that were so beautiful when you were quick with life. Yet not gone, for you are still a living truth inside my mind. So how are you dead, my brothers and sisters, and all of you, when you live with me as surely as I live myself?

Shall we say that the good Dr Johnson is dead, when his dear friend Mr Boswell brings him to thunder and thump before your very eyes? Is Socrates dead, then, when I hear the gold of his voice?

Are my friends all dead, then, and their voices a glory in my ears?

No, and I will stand to say no, and no, again.

In blood, I say no.

Is Ceinwen dead, then, and her beauty dear beside me again, and her eyes with jewels for me, and my arms hurting with the grip of her fingers?

Is Bronwen dead, who showed me the truth of the love of woman? Is she dead, who proved to me that the strength of woman is stronger than the strength of fists, and muscles, and the male shoutings of men?

Did my father die under the coal? But, God in heaven, he is down there now, dancing in the street with Davy's red jersey over his coat, and coming, in a moment, to smoke his pipe in the front room and pat my mother's hand, and look, and O, the heat of his pride, at the picture of a Queen, given by the hand of a Queen, in the Palace of a Queen, to his eldest son, whose baton lifted voices in music fit for a Queen to hear.

Is Mr Gruffydd dead, him, that one of rock and flame, who was friend and mentor, who gave me his watch that was all in the world he had, because he loved me? Is he dead, and the tears still wet on my face and my voice cutting through rocks in my throat for minutes while I tried to say good-bye, and, O God, the words were shy to come, and I went from him wordless, in tears and with blood.

Is he dead?

For if he is, then I am dead, and we are dead, and all of sense a mockery. How green was my Valley, then, and the Valley of them that have gone.

from *How Green was my Valley* (1939)

Alan Llwyd (1948–   )

The Welsh Language

Stand above the abyss, and shout into the cleft:
she's the thunder in the silence, the noise in the cold emptiness;
although fugitives grope for their splintered ropes on the cliff,
she's the one who prevents our fall into the great muteness.

She's the rain that refreshes the earth, the ruby's sheen,
the harvest breeze, rolling in the corn and the wheat;
the precious sapphire, the emerald in the grass that is green,
the restless rustling of barley, and bright gleam of light.

She protects from the mute edge, the fort that keeps enemies at bay,
and above the gaping abyss she is our tether;
she keeps our dignity, our home against all disarray,
the knot that unites; she gathers her people together.

Should the link shatter and break, what would be amiss?
Knot by knot the rope now opens above the abyss.

trans. the author

LLYWELYN GOCH AP MEURIG HEN (*fl.* 1350–90)

Lament for Lleucu Llwyd

For gay bard, barren summer,
Barren the world for a bard.
I was stripped bare, grief's comrade,
For choosing this month to tryst.
Today in Gwynedd[1] remains
No moon, no light, no colour,
Since one was laid, vile welcome,
Beneath hard earth, beauty's moon.

Fair girl in the chest of oak,
I'm bent on wrath, you left me.
Lovely form, Gwynedd's candle,
Though you are closed in the grave,
Arise, come up, my dearest,
Open the dark door of earth,
Refuse the long bed of sand,
And come to face me, maiden.
Here is, heavy cost of grief,
Above your grave, sun's radiance,
A sad-faced man without you,
Llywelyn, bell of your praise.
Wailing bard, I am walking
A foul world, priest of lust's bliss.
Dear one, whose worth grew daily,
Yesterday over your grave
I let tears fall in torrents
Like a rope across my cheeks.

But you, mute girl's fair image,
From the pit made no reply.
Sadly silent, lacking love.
You promised, speechless maiden,
Mild your manner, silk-shrouded,
To stay for me, pure bright gem,
Till I came, I know the truth,

---

[1]Gwynedd, a kingdom in north-west Wales (now a county).

Strong safeguard, from the southland.
I heard nothing, straight-spoken,
But the truth, slim silent girl,
Measure of maidens, Indeg,
Before this, from your sweet mouth.
Hard blow, why care where's my home,
You broke faith, and it grieves me.

You are, my cywydd[1] is false,
Truthful, words sweetly spoken:
It's I, grief's spilled-out language,
Who lie in sad harmonies;
I am lying, skimping prayer,
Lying the words I have cried.
I will leave Gwynedd today,
What care I where, bright beauty,
My fine flowering sweetheart:
If you lived, by God, I'd stay!
Where shall I, what care I where,
See you, fair moon's pure flower,
On Mount, Ovid's passion spurned,
Olivet, radiant maiden?
You've secured my place surely,
Lleucu, fair comely-hued nave,
Beautiful bright-skinned maiden,
Sleeper too long under stone.

Rise to finish the revels,
See if you thirst for some mead,
Come to your bard, whose laughter's
Long ended, gold diadem.
Come, with your cheeks of foxgloves,
Up from the earth's dreary house.
A wayward trail the footprints,
No need to lie, my feet leave,
In faltering from passion
About your house, Lleucu Llwyd.
All the words, Gwynedd's lantern,
I've sung, complexion of snow,
Three groans of grief, gold-ringed hand,
Lleucu, praised you, my precious.
With these lips, I ken praise-craft,
What I'll sing, life-long, in praise,

[1]cywydd, one of the major forms of Welsh prosody, of which this poem is an example.

My dear, foam's hue on rivers,
My love, will be your lament.

Lucid, sweet-spoken Lleucu,
My sweetheart's legacy was:
Her soul, Merioneth's treasure,
To God the Father, true vow;
Her slender, fine flour's colour,
Body to sanctified soil;
Girl mourned for, flour-white favours,
World's wealth to the proud dark man;
And yearning, lyric of grief,
This legacy she left me.

Two equal gifts, sad custom,
Pretty Lleucu, snow-spray's hue,
Earth and stone, bitter grief's gem,
Cover her cheeks, and oakwood.
Ah God, so heavy's the grave,
The earth on beauty's mistress.
Ah God, a coffin holds you,
Between us a house of stone,
Church chancel and stone curtain
And earth's weight and gown of wood.
Ah God, fair girl of Pennal,
A nightmare, buried your brow.
Hard lock of oak, bitter grief,
And earth, your brows were lovely,
And heavy door, heavy clasp,
And the land's floor between us,
A firm wall, a hard black lock,
A latch – farewell, my Lleucu.

                                    trans. Joseph P. Clancy

ALUN LLYWELYN-WILLIAMS (1913–)

When I was Young

All day and every day the sea shone, steeped in its blueness;
the sun foresaw no storms of tomorrow, wept no yesterday's guilt;
I walked the quay in the white morning, questioning masts,
prying and spying under the swoop of raucous gulls
till there was my *Gwennan Gorn*,[1] my spray whelp, my sea-spearer.

I would lie in the boat's prow and trail my hands in the water;
nearing the unbearable purity of the island lighthouse,
where the fish swayed and sped under the soundless rock;
how gaily the sail leapt to the blue heavens,
how prettily then it sank to the depth of my daring sinews!

The green land hung like a dream between the eyelids,
the furrows of the sea never counted the youthful hours of my course;
harsh, on returning, it was to tread the unheaving earth,
to traverse the heavy clay,
and to hear, now from its cell, the mortal knell of the flesh.

A return without returning: those suns wore
to their late long setting; but the darkling light over the bay
stays on, as though some miracle had snatched to that virginal tower
the warming eye of the world:
and, just as before time's watchmen besieged me, it shines
still on a voyage unfinished.

trans. Gwyn Williams

Yesterday's Illusion or Remembering the Thirties

Part of the regret is for adolescence in a period when enemies seemed
conveniently well defined . . . RICHARD HOGGART

In those painful days, we knew
who the enemy was: the sleek, corpulent capitalist,
the lunatic politician, and the guilty scientist:
it was easy to recognize the authors of our cancer and our disease.

On the edge of the city, the furrows of the unfinished street
fell into the rubble of the night, and the lovers

---

[1] *Gwennan Gorn*, the boat of Prince Madog ab Owain Gwynedd (*fl.* 1170).

disappeared there two by two, like anxious missionaries
into the barbarians' cauldron, into the ashes of the world.

In fear we awaited the apocalyptic judgement,
in fear – and in joy. For this were we born,
to confidence in the destruction of false idols; we were privileged
in our anger, and in our pity for the poor and lonely.

We did not see, at that time,
the Black Sow[1] lurking in the fierce bonfire,
nor the devil craving for the pigs' souls.

trans. R. Gerallt Jones

ARTHUR MACHEN (1863–1947)

An Enchanted Land

I shall always esteem it as the greatest piece of fortune that has fallen to me that
I was born in that noble, fallen Caerleon-on-Usk in the heart of Gwent[2]. . . .
The older I grow, the more firmly am I convinced that anything I may have
accomplished in literature is due to the fact that when my eyes were first
opened in early childhood they had before them the vision of an enchanted
land. As soon as I saw anything I saw Twm Barlwm, that mystic tumulus, the
memorial of peoples that dwelt in that region before the Celts left the Land of
Summer. This guarded the southern limit of the great mountain wall in the
west; a little northward was Mynydd Maen – the Mountain of the Stone – a
giant, rounded billow; and still to the north mountains, and on fair, clear days
one could see the pointed summit of the Holy Mountain by Abergavenny. It
would shine, I remember, a pure blue in the far sunshine; it was a mountain
peak in a fairy tale. And then to eastward the bedroom window of Llanddewi
Rectory looked over hill and valley, over high woods quivering with leafage like
the beloved Zacynthus of Ulysses, away to the forest of Wentwood, to the
church tower on the hill above Caerleon. Through a cleft one might see now
and again a bright yellow glint of the Severn Sea, and the cliffs of Somerset
beyond. And hardly a house in sight in all the landscape, look where you
would. Here the gable of a barn, here a glint of a whitewashed farmhouse, here
blue wood smoke rising from an orchard grove, where an old cottage was
snugly hidden: but only so much if you knew where to look. And of nights,
when the dusk fell and the farmer went his rounds, you might chance to see his

---

[1]Black Sow, an embodiment of the Devil in Welsh tradition, said to appear in the embers of a
bonfire.
[2]Gwent, a region (now a county) of south-east Wales.

lantern glimmering, a very spark on the hillside. This was all that showed in a vague, dark world; and the only sounds were the faint distant barking of the sheepdog and the melancholy cry of the owls from the border of the brake.

from *Far Off Things* (1926)

ROLAND MATHIAS (1915–   )

The Flooded Valley

My house is empty but for a pair of boots:
The reservoir slaps at the privet hedge and uncovers the roots
And afterwards pats them up with a slack good will:
The sheep that I market once are not again to sell.
I am no waterman, and who of the others will live
Here, feeling the ripple spreading, hearing the timbers grieve?
The house I was born in has not long to stand:
My pounds are slipping away and will not wait for the end.

I will pick up my boots and run round the shire
To raise an echo louder than my fear.
Listen, Caerfanell, who gave me a fish for my stone,
Listen, I am alone, alone.
And Grwyney, both your rivers are one in the end
And are loved. If I command
You to remember me, will you, will you,
Because I was once at noon by your painted church of Patricio?
You did not despise me once, Senni, or run so fast
From your lovers. And O I jumped over your waist
Before sunrise or the flower was warm on the gorse.
You would do well to listen, Senni. There is money in my purse.

So you are quiet, all of you, and your current set away
Cautiously from the chapel ground in which my people lie . . .
Am I not Kedward, Prosser, Morgan, whose long stones
Name me despairingly and set me chains?
If I must quarrel and scuff in the weeds of another shire
When my pounds are gone, swear to me now in my weakness, swear
To me poor you will plant a stone more in this tightening field
And name there your latest dead, alas your unweaned feeblest child.

ROBERT MINHINNICK (1952–   )

The Drinking Art

The altar of glass behind the bar
Diminishes our talk. As if in church
The solitary men who come here
Slide to the edges of each black
Polished bench and stare at their hands.
  The landlord keeps his own counsel.

This window shows a rose and anchor
Like a sailor's tattoo embellished
In stained glass, allows only the vaguest
Illumination of floor and ceiling,
The tawny froth the pumps sometimes spew.
  And the silence settles. The silence settles

Like the yellow pinpoints of yeast
Falling through my beer, the bitter
That has built the redbrick
Into the faces of these few customers,
Lonely practitioners of the drinking art.
  Ashtrays, a slop-bucket, the fetid

Shed-urinal, all this I wondered at,
Running errands to the back-doors of pubs,
Woodbines and empty bottles in my hands.
Never become a drinking-man, my
Grandmother warned, remembering Merthyr
  And the Spanish foundrymen

Puking their guts up in the dirt streets,
The Irish running from the furnaces
To crowd their paymaster into a tavern,
Leather bags of sovereigns bouncing on his thigh.
But it is calmer here, more subtly dangerous.
  This afternoon is a suspension of life

I learn to enjoy. But now
The towel goes over the taps and I feel
The dregs in my throat. A truce has ended
And the clocks start again. Sunlight
Leaps out of the street. In his shrine of glass
  The landlord is wringing our lives dry.

DEREC LLWYD MORGAN (1943–)

Trouble Registering my Daughter [1]

A sparkling girl, in Gwynfor's[2] year,
the bed produced another Welshwoman for his choir.
Drunk with joy I was, yes, there came
(the pain to independence)
quick as a thrill from a closed womb
to Carmarthenshire bright Elin.

Elin? Every maliceless scoundrel
of an Englishman will deny her blankly.
'She does not exist,' said the man of the living,
law belly, 'as such.
Do not give the little one
in her infanthood the challenge of an unhealthy language.'

O, the bother I had, a hellish quest,
honestly, let the Great God judge it,
with the man, the crown's mirror,
to get him to favour her,
until much later, until there came from Somerset House
the most lined fair certificate.

But for Elin now
her billingual right is nonsense.
What is a name worth to one who belongs,
Miss Being, to the cosmos without a name?

From the womb in her condition the fair one
was eighteen months without a name (officially)
an armied non-Elin,
daughter to a penalty, a cuckoo's nest.
One day, 'I'm Dafydd Iwan,[3]'
she said, 'and Japan.'
(She was a welfare missionary
in the dull greyhouse embassies of the exiled.)

---

[1]This poem refers to a campaign in the 1960s for the provision of bilingual birth-certificates,
     during which many parents refused to register the births of their children.
[2]Gwynfor, Gwynfor Evans (1912–), President of *Plaid Cymru*, elected as Member of
     Parliament for Carmarthenshire in 1966.
[3]Dafydd Iwan (1943–), folk-singer.

She's a boss. She is a music woman
on the outer side of her hide-and-seek.
She's the dance of an age's patience
around the Maypole of my life.
With the use of paint totally new to her,
she's a regular mock-Picasso.
She pretends she's mother, she's a cook by now,
she's the life of every party.
She's a bright flame of a dynamo,
she's a wizard of restlessness.
'I'm a train.' She is Venus,
she's the saint that polishes the stars.
She's the pope of divination:
last night
she conned love with her magic night-gown,
gave a service for a bride.
There was one day that went all to cock, whoops,
when she went berserk on the floor
claiming earnestly and happily
(the noise!) that she was Jesus meek and mild.

What is a name worth to one who belongs,
Miss Being, to the cosmos without a name?
The value (or worth) that there belongs to me
from a seed belly the whole world like this.

trans. the author

Robert Morgan (1921–   )

Blood Donor

The searching was easy and memory ripens
On the grey earth picture of Rees
In his grimy vest soaked in blood.
Forty-eight years under tense rock
Had stripped him like a tree with roots
In slag and marked him with texture of strain
And accident. But it was slow legs
And dust-worn eyes that were to blame.

The iron rock-bar was still in his hands
Held like a spear of a fallen warrior.
The rocks had dyed his silver hair red
And the heavy bar was warm and worn.

Blind flies swarmed in the blood-sweat
Air and the tough men with bruised
Senses were gentle, using distorted
Hands like women arranging flowers.

On the way out through roads of rocky
Silence you could sense images of confusion
In the slack chain of shadows. Muscles
Were nerve-tight and thoughts infested
With wrath and sharp edges of fear.
Towards the sun's lamp we moved, taking
Home the dark prisoner in his shroud of coats.

JAN MORRIS (1926–   )

The Welsh Republic

Six more centuries pass, and we imagine now, without benefit of bards, Wales
fulfilled once more, sometime in the twenty-first century perhaps. Let us see
how the country might look in the eye of another generation of visionaries,
cherishing still as Owain[1] did the idea of a Wales controlling its own destinies,
to its own tastes. We will fly into Wales this time, up the estuary of the Dyfi, the
Dovey, half-way along the Western coast, and there, clustered among green
water-meadows below the mountains, stands the national capital of Machynlleth. It is not a very big capital – the smallest in Europe, in fact, except possibly
Reykjavik – and it looks, as it always did, like a small market town: but the Red
Dragon[2] flies everywhere above its rooftops, a cosmopolitan crowd swarms
among its pubs and cafés, and sometimes a big black car with Corps
Diplomatique plates weaves a cautious way through the market stalls of Stryd
Marchnad. Here are assembled the central institutions of Welsh sovereignty.
Parliament meets on the very site where Owain's delegates assembled six and a
half centuries before. The Prime Minister's office occupies the fine old
building which has long been called the Royal House, and in which, it has
always been said, Glyndŵr kept some of his prisoners. The President of the
Republic lives in the eighteenth-century mansion, Plas Machynlleth, which the
Marquis of Londonderry gave to the municipality a century ago, and which has
fine staterooms for the entertainment of eminent visitors, and a balcony with

[1]Owain, Owain Glyn Dŵr (*c.* 1354 – *c.* 1416), national hero, known in English as Owen
Glendower.
[2]Red Dragon, the national flag of Wales.

flagpoles from which the President waves to the assembled populace on St David's Day (now combined with Independence Day), and each year declares by satellite the opening of the National Eisteddfod,[1] wherever it may be.

Offices of State are scattered piecemeal through the town – the Chancellery next door to the Wynnstay Arms, for instance, the Banc Cenedlaethol Cymru, the central bank of the Republic, occupying the somewhat enlarged premises of the old National Westminster, the Foreign Office in a long low building by the river (fishing strictly reserved, though, for members of the Dyfi Angling Society). Most of the accredited ambassadors of foreign Powers are based in London, but those who find it politic to have a legation in Wales occupy houses in the country round about – the English have lately bought Nanteos, for instance, the Americans have built a complex of air-conditioned bungalows on the seafront at Borth, and the Irish have been fortunate enough to acquire the former Brigands Inn at Mallwyd, which they have left fastidiously unaltered.

Though Machynlleth fulfils the normal functions of a capital, Wales is still not a centralist State. Most power is in the hands of the six regional councils. Most of the national bureaucracy is still in the former capital of Cardiff, much of the private sector business community too, while the National Library is at Aberystwyth still, the National University is divided into five campuses across the country, the National Museum has branches everywhere and the headquarters of the Defence Force is at Aberhonddu, Brecon. A new motorway (*Sarn Elen Newydd*) brings almost all these institutions within two hours of each other, and is being paid for by tolls (60 *ceiniog*[2] a passage).

Wales is a bilingual State, with priority being given to Welsh wherever possible, and only elderly citizens are now unable to speak Cymraeg. All civil servants, Members of Parliament and academics must be fluent in Welsh and English, and foreign students at the university are required to take courses in Welsh. Government business is conducted in both languages, and Members of Parliament may speak in either (though only a few veteran *Toriaid*[3] now choose to use English).

The single-chamber Parliament is elected by proportional representation. This has meant that the numerical preponderance of the south has never been great enough for an overall majority, and Wales is habitually governed by coalitions. Deliberations are entirely informal, the only concession to English parliamentary practice being the fact that division bells ring in the Wynnstay Arms, the Red Lion and (it is said) in the front parlour of the Irish Embassy. When the President opens the legislative session each year he is robed as an Archdruid, and attended by that matron with the horn of plenty.

Wales became a republic after a hotly disputed referendum, rigged some say by patriotic extremists. It is a member of the European Community, and a founder-member too of the Neutral League – in many parts of the world Wales is represented by the League's joint diplomatic corps. The emphasis of

[1]National Eisteddfod, the principal cultural festival of the Welsh people.
[2]*ceiniog*, penny.
[3]*Toriaid*, Tories.

Welsh foreign policy is on the European relationship, and the highest ambition of many of the cleverest young Welsh people is to represent their country in Brussels or Strasbourg. Relations with England are cordial: the border is open to travellers without passport, but there are strict regulations about the buying of property in Wales by foreigners, and this has vastly reduced the number of English residents. It is true that conservative English opinion still tends to look upon an independent Wales as a traitorous aberration, but the interests of the two nations seldom actually clash, and when the King of England recently paid a State visit to Machynlleth, except for a few catcalls he was kindly received, and at the Presidential banquet that evening made some amusing jokes about his boyhood impressions of Caernarfon Castle.

Economically Wales has thrived since the break from England. Freed from the restraints of British policies (and politics), the cooperatively owned steel-mills of the south, among the most productive in Europe, have dictated their own prices and found their own markets. The dozen or so surviving coal-mines devote their entire output to the coal-fuelled power stations that have replaced nuclear generators. Water and power are sold to England at a price agreed by independent arbitrators, oil coming by sea to the great refineries of the south and south-western coasts is subject to a special tax. Small industries have flourished as workers' co-operatives, with technical help from the Basques and the Jugoslavs, and even the least progressive of resort shopkeepers are obliged to admit that the independence of Wales, if it has somewhat inhibited mass tourism from England, has greatly increased the flow of more profitable categories from Europe and America: there are far fewer caravan sites, far more hotels of international standard – and the industry has been greatly helped, of course, by the recent inexplicable improvement in the Welsh climate.

The law of Wales, hammered out by constitutionalists in the years after independence, are an amalgam of English Common Law and the Laws of Hywel Dda,[1] embodied in an altogether new Code, *Cyfraith y Rhyddhad*, the Law of the Release. They are based upon the idea of contract, in both civil and criminal cases: keeping the peace and the faith is considered a universal contract between citizens, and its breach must be paid for, by cash payment, by service to the community, and only in extreme and obdurate cases by the punishment of the Republic. Judges are arbiters between claimants, and the principle of revenge, as against compensation or reconciliation, is abhorred. As for the national health services, under jurisdiction known as *Newid y Galon*, the Change of Heart, they are financed by that proportion of the national income reckoned to have been spent, under British administration, on the Crown, nuclear weapons, air defence and military intelligence, and are considered the most advanced in the Western world, inducing most of the best Welsh doctors, surgeons and nurses to remain in Wales, and offering completely free treatment and medicine of all kinds.

[1]Hywel Dda (d. 950), king and law-giver.

Wales being a neutral State, like Ireland, Sweden or Switzerland, it was only after long heart-searching that the founders of the Republic decided to have armed forces at all. The Defence Force that was finally decided upon, *Plant Owain*, is hardly an army really, but more a force of organized irregulars, wearing no uniform but camouflage fatigues, and trained solely for the guerrilla harassment of an occupying army: as such, it has been copied by small countries all over the world, and Welsh military instructors are much in demand abroad. Even so, it is embodied in the Welsh constitution that the republic should aspire towards a condition of absolute non-violence, and every seven years a public referendum decides whether the force shall be maintained at all (its members being guaranteed full pay for life if the people decide on abolition). There are no public military parades of any kind in Wales, and no pretensions to pomp, and the President and Prime Minister are guarded only by policemen in their denim dungarees. There are no official secrets whatsoever.

The strength of Wales has proved to be its smallness. A threat to nobody, a society of remarkable inner stability and contentment, its place among the nations is curious but admired. Welsh intermediaries are often invited to rule on international disputes, the Welsh voice in the United Nations, presented by a series of delegates of great intellectual force and wit, carries far more weight than might be expected. The bilingual newspaper *Cymru*,[1] which brought back to Wales many of the best Welsh journalists of Fleet Street, is quoted all over the world as a mouthpiece of enlightened opinion – the *Manchester Guardian* of its time, it has been called. As the very model of a non-nuclear, neutral, un-militarist ecological State, Wales is a lode-star for young idealists all over the world. And the psychological serenity of the Welsh people, freed at last from the old anxieties about identity and national purpose, is the envy of far richer Powers, and the despair of hostile ideologues.

It is only a fantasy, like Glyndŵr's perhaps: but which is the more improbable, the one that came true in 1404, or the one that is still just a fiction for the interlude?

from *The Matter of Wales: Epic Views of a Small Country* (1984)

[1] *Cymru*, Wales.

LESLIE NORRIS (1921–   )

Water

On hot summer mornings my aunt set glasses
On a low wall outside the farmhouse,
With some jugs of cold water.
I would sit in the dark hall, or
      Behind the dairy window,
Waiting for children to come from the town.

They came in small groups, serious, steady,
And I could see them, black in the heat,
Long before they turned in at our gate
To march up the soft, dirt road.
      They would stand by the wall,
Drinking water with an engrossed thirst. The dog

Did not bother them, knowing them responsible
Travellers. They held in quiet hands their bags
Of jam sandwiches, and bottles of yellow fizz.
Sometimes they waved a gratitude to the house,
      But they never looked at us.
Their eyes were full of the mountain, lifting

Their measuring faces above our long hedge.
When they had gone I would climb the wall,
Looking for them among the thin sheep runs.
Their heads were a resolute darkness among ferns.
      They climbed with unsteady certainty.
I wondered what it was they knew the mountain had.

They would pass the last house, Lambert's, where
A violent gander, too old by many a Christmas,
Blared evil warning from his bitten moor.
Then it was open world, too high and clear
      For clouds even, where over heather
The free hare cleanly ran, and the summer sheep.

I knew this; and I knew all summer long
Those visionary gangs passed through our lanes,
Coming down at evening, their arms full
Of cowslips, moondaisies, whinberries, nuts,
      All fruits of the sliding seasons,
And the enormous experience of the mountain

That I who loved it did not understand.
In the summer, dust filled our winter ruts
With a level softness, and children walked
At evening through golden curtains scuffed
        From the road by their trailing feet.
They would drink tiredly at our wall, talking

Softly, leaning, their sleepy faces warm for home.
We would see them murmur slowly through our stiff
Gate, their shy heads gilded by the last sun.
One by one we would gather up the used jugs,
        The glasses. We would pour away
A little water. It would lie on the thick dust, gleaming.

The Ballad of Billy Rose

Outside Bristol Rovers' Football Ground –
The date has gone from me, but not the day,
Nor how the dissenting flags in stiff array
Stuck bravely out against the sky's grey round –

Near the car park then, past Austin and Ford,
Lagonda, Bentley, and a colourful patch
Of country coaches come in for the match,
Was where I walked, having travelled the road

From Fishponds to watch Portsmouth in the Cup.
The Third Round, I believe. And I was filled
With the old excitement which had thrilled
Me so completely when, while growing up,

I went on Saturdays to match or fight.
Not only me; for thousands of us there
Strode forward eagerly, each man aware
Of tingling memory, anticipating delight.

We all marched forward, all except one man.
I saw him because he was paradoxically still.
A stone against the flood, face upright against us all,
Head bare, hoarse voice aloft, blind as a stone.

I knew him at once, despite his pathetic clothes;
Something in his stance, or his sturdy frame
Perhaps. I could even remember his name
Before I saw it on his blind man's tray. Billy Rose.

And twenty forgetful years fell away at the sight.
Bare-kneed, dismayed, memory fled to the hub
Of Saturday violence, with friends to the Labour Club,
Watching the boxing on a sawdust summer night.

The boys' enclosure close to the shabby ring
Was where we stood, clenched in a resin world,
Spoke in cool voices, lounged, were artificially bored
During minor bouts. We paid threepence to go in.

Billy Rose fought there. He was top of the bill.
So brisk a fighter, so gallant, so precise!
Trim as a tree he stood for the ceremonies,
Then turned to meet George Morgan of Tirphil.

He had no chance. Courage was not enough,
Nor tight defence. Donald Davies was sick
And we threatened his cowardice with an embarrassed kick.
Ripped across both his eyes was Rose, but we were tough

And clapped him as they wrapped his blindness up
In busy towels, applauded the wave
He gave his executioners, cheered the brave
Blind man as he cleared with a jaunty hop

The top rope. I had forgotten that day
As if it were dead for ever, yet now I saw
The flowers of punched blood on the ring floor,
As bright as his name. I do not know

How long I stood with ghosts of the wild fists
And the cries of shaken boys long dead around me,
For struck to act at last, in terror and pity
I threw some frantic money, three treacherous pence –

And I cry at the memory – into his tray, and ran,
Entering the waves of the stadium like a drowning man.
Poor Billy Rose. God, he could fight,
Before my three sharp coins knocked out his sight.

Elegy for David Beynon

David, we must have looked comic, sitting
there at next desks; your legs stretched
half-way down the classroom, while
my feet hung a free inch above

the floor. I remember, too, down
at The Gwynne's Field, at the side
of the little Taff, dancing with
laughing fury as you caught

effortlessly at the line-out, sliding
the ball over my head direct to
the outside-half. That was Cyril
Theophilus, who died in his quiet

so long ago that only I, perhaps,
remember he'd hold the ball one-handed
on his thin stomach as he turned
to run. Even there you were careful

to miss us with your scattering
knees as you bumped through
for yet another try. Buffeted
we were, but cheered too by our

unhurt presumption in believing
we could ever have pulled you down.
I think those children, those who died
under your arms in the crushed school,

would understand that I make this
your elegy. I know the face you had,
have walked with you enough mornings
under the fallen leaves. Theirs is

the great anonymous tragedy one word
will summarise. Aberfan.[1] I write it
for them here, knowing we've paid to it
our shabby pence, and now it can be stored

with whatever names there are where
children end their briefest pilgrimage.
I cannot find the words for you, David. These
are too long, too many; and not enough.

[1]Aberfan, a village near Merthyr Tydfil, Glam., where in 1966 part of a coal-tip slipped into the valley, killing 116 children in their school, and 28 adults.

JOHN ORMOND (1923–   )

Cathedral Builders

They climbed on sketchy ladders towards God,
With winch and pully hoisted hewn rock into heaven,
Inhabited sky with hammers, defied gravity,
Deified stone, took up God's house to meet Him,

And came down to their suppers and small beer;
Every night slept, lay with their smelly wives,
Quarrelled and cuffed the children, lied,
Spat, sang, were happy or unhappy,

And every day took to the ladders again;
Impeded the rights of way of another summer's
Swallows, grew greyer, shakier, became less inclined
To fix a neighbour's roof of a fine evening,

Saw naves sprout arches, clerestories soar,
Cursed the loud fancy glaziers for their luck,
Somehow escaped the plague, got rheumatism,
Decided it was time to give it up,

To leave the spire to others; stood in the crowd
Well back from the vestments at the consecration,
Envied the fat bishop his warm boots,
Cocked up a squint eye and said, 'I bloody did that.'

Salmon

first for, and now in memory of, Ceri Richards[1]

The river sucks them home.
The lost past claims them.
  Beyond the headland
It gropes into the channel
Of the nameless sea.
  Off-shore they submit
To the cast, to the taste of it.

[1]Ceri Richards (1903-71), painter.

It releases them from salt,
Their thousand miles in odyssey
For spawning. It rehearsed their return
    From the beginning; now
    It clenches them like a fist.

The echo of once being here
Possesses and inclines them.
    Caught in the embrace
Of nothing that is not now,
Riding in with the tide-race,
    Not by their care,
Not by any will they know,
They turn fast to the caress
Of their only course. Sea-hazards done,
They ache towards the one world
    From which their secret
    Sprang, perpetuate

More than themselves, the ritual
Claim of the river, pointed
    Towards rut, tracing
Their passion out. Weeping philosopher,
They reaffirm the world,
    The stars by which they ran,
Now this precise place holds them
Again. They reach the churning wall
Of the brute waterfall which shed
Them young from its cauldron pool.
    A hundred times
They lunge and strike

Against the hurdles of the rock;
Though hammering water
    Beats them back
Still their desire will not break.
They flourish, whip and kick,
    Tensile for their truth's
Sake, give to the miracle
Of their treadmill leaping
The illusion of the natural.
The present in torrential flow
    Nurtures its own
    Long undertow:

They work it, strike and streak again,
Filaments in suspense.
　　The lost past shoots them
Into flight, out of their element,
In bright transilient sickle-blades
　　Of light; until upon
The instant's height of their inheritance
They chance in descant over the loud
Diapasons of flood, jack out of reach
And snatch of clawing water,
　　Stretch and soar
　　Into easy rapids

Beyond, into half-haven, jounce over
Shelves upstream; and know no question
　　But, pressed by their cold blood,
Glance through the known maze.
They unravel the thread to source
　　To die at their ancestry's
Last knot, knowing no question.
They meet under hazel trees,
Are chosen, and so mate. In shallows as
The stream slides clear yet shirred
　　With broken surface where
　　Stones trap the creamy stars

Of air, she scoops at gravel with fine
Thrust of her exact blind tail;
　　At last her lust
Gapes in a gush on her stone nest
And his held, squanderous peak
　　Shudders his final hunger
On her milk; seed laid on seed
In spunk of liquid silk.
So in exhausted saraband their slack
Convulsions wind and wend galactic
　　Seed in seed, a found
World without end.

The circle's set, proportion
Stands complete, and,
　　Ready for death,
Haggard they hang in aftermath
Abundance, ripe for the world's
　　Rich night, the spear.

Why does this fasting fish
So haunt me? Gautama, was it this
You saw from river-bank
At Uruvela? Was this
 Your glimpse
 Of holy law?

In September

Again the golden month, still
Favourite, is renewed;
Once more I'd wind it in a ring
About your finger, pledge myself
Again, my love, my shelter,
My good roof over me,
My strong wall against winter.

Be bread upon my table still
And red wine in my glass, be fire
Upon my hearth. Continue,
My true storm door, continue
To be sweet lock to my key;
Be wife to me, remain
The soft silk on my bed.

Be morning to my pillow,
Multiply my joy. Be my rare coin
For counting, my luck, my
Granary, my promising fair
Sky, my star, the meaning
Of my journey. Be, this year too,
My twelve months long desire.

DANIEL OWEN (1836–95)

Will Bryan on the 'Fellowship'

Their surprise was no less when I informed them that Bob's case, and mine, and Bryan's, was to be 'brought before' the Fellowship that night. Beck, being 'Church', had only a hazy notion what was meant by 'Fellowship,' and 'bringing before' the Fellowship, until Bryan offered him the following explanation. Will had a remarkable gift for giving the gist of what he was superbly confident that he understood, and this is how he explained to Beck the nature and purpose of the Fellowship:

'It's like this,' said he, 'the Fellowship is a lot of good people thinking that they are bad, and meeting together every Tuesday evening to find fault with themselves.'

'I don't follow,' said Beck.

'Well,' said Will, 'look at it like this: You know old Mrs Peters, and you know Rhys's mother, – and it is not because Rhys is present that I mention her – but everybody knows that they are two good-living and godly women. Well, they go to the Fellowship; Abel Hughes goes to them, and asks them what they have to say. They say they are very wicked, and guilty of ever so many shortcomings, and Mrs Peters is often in tears as she says so. Then, Abel tells them they are not so evil as they think, and gives them counsel, and repeats lots of verses of Scripture, and then he goes to someone else, who in his turn says the same sort of thing, and they keep it up until half past eight when we all go home.'

'There's nothing like that in Church,' said Beck. 'We never hold a Fellowship and I never heard anyone there running himself down.'

'That's the difference between "Church" and "chapel",' said Will. 'You Churchpeople think yourselves good when you are bad, and the chapel people think themselves bad when they are good.'

from *Rhys Lewis* (1885), trans. D.M. Lloyd

Country Churchyards

It would be impossible to relate the story of the rural life of Wales in the present century (*i.e.* the nineteenth) without giving a prominent place to the chapel and the church. He that would attempt to tell the story otherwise would only succeed in showing how blind he was to its significance, or that he knew nothing of the 'land of song.' Let it be noted that I am referring to the present century. For to whatever commote of Wales one may go, wherever there is a human community, however small and scattered, on looking around, one of the first and most prominent objects that will meet the eye will be a chapel belonging to some religious denomination or other. The edifice will often be plain enough – four walls, a roof, a few windows and a door. If the human settlement is older than the present century, it is likely that there will also be a grey-looking church, and a churchyard with its sad yew tree casting a gloomy shade around. To this resting place generation after generation will have been brought in their turn, as can be seen from the tombstones, most of which will be tilted to one side as if by a stroke of paralysis. On some of these stones will be found an 'englyn,'[1] skilfully or indifferently composed, but I could not other than feel a sort of respect for the crudest of these brief metrical compositions; for the men who had felt the impulse to express their loss in these rude lines, and they who had carved them, now rest here alike, and maybe with no 'englyn' or even a stone above their heads.

I don't quite know why, but somehow I feel on visiting these places that it is the graveyard that makes the church holy rather than the opposite. And strong though my prejudice against the Establishment may be, and however worldly may have been some of those who, bareheaded and in white surplice, read in unseemly haste that magnificent burial service over hundreds of their fellow-men who now quietly rest, completely forgotten, under the green sod, my heart softens, and if it were in my power I would forgive them all their shortcomings and would canonize them every one. Whatever we may say, there is a spirit in these quiet old churchyards which creates a common fraternity, and a common and catholic humility before our Creator.

from *Gwen Tomos* (1894), trans. D.M. Lloyd

R. WILLIAMS PARRY (1884–1956)

Eifionydd [2]

Far from the scowl of progress,
   From drab industry afar,
There's a land of sea and wildness
   That bears no stain nor scar,
Save where the hillside plough lays bare
The sweet spring earth in the mountain air.

Far from the idiot violence
   Where wry new worlds repine,
Here is the dawnworld's fragrance
   That lingers like old wine,
Old, old the murmuring voice that dreams
About Rhoslan between two streams.

---

[1] *englyn*, a four-line verse written according to traditional rules of prosody.
[2] Eifionydd, a commote in north-west Wales.

And Lôn Goed's[1] a green heaven
   Where quiet is complete
From its roof of branches woven
   To the soft grass at my feet,
It leads to nowhere, the leafy lane
But none who linger there complain.

Ah, sweet to be arriving
   In that secluded vale,
Far from the scenes of striving
   And a world that's known and stale.
Alone I'd gladly wander there,
Or one with me, that peace to share.

trans. Harri Webb

The Fox

Near the mountain's summit, when the bells
of valley churches called all godly men,
and when the bright, still unspent sun of summer
called to the mountain, then – just then –
the silent movement of his thoughtless foot
pathed his rare beauty to our startled eye;
we did not move and did not wish to move,
frozen awhile, like a stone trinity
we stood, as with half-finished, careless stride
sudden he also stopped, the steady light
of the two eyes above the waiting paw
upon us. Then, without haste or fright,
over the ridge his ruddiness moved on,
and like a shooting star had come and gone.

trans. Gwyn Williams

Bluebells [2]

They come when the cuckoo comes,
   When she goes, they go too,
The wild nostalgic scent,
   The old enchanting hue;
Arriving, then bidding good-bye –
   Ah, but their days are few.

[1]Lôn Goed, a tree-lined road, celebrated for its quiet beauty.
[2]In Welsh bluebells are known as *clychau'r gog* ('cuckoo bells').

Under the trees of the hillslope
   On the steep flanks of the mount,
On meadow and dyke and bankside,
   But not on bare harrowed ground,
The blue blossoms are swelling
   That swell the cuckoo's sound.

Softer than Llandygái's
   Pealing at close of day,
They are tossing in the breezes,
   These silent bells of May,
Filling the mind with their chiming –
   Ah, but they fade away.

For when honeysuckle nightly
   Burdens the summer air,
And harebells in abundance
   Appear in the grass as before,
The cuckoo and her bells will
   Stir in the wind no more.

Trans. Joseph P. Clancy

T. H. PARRY-WILLIAMS (1887–1975)

These Bones

What shall we be, sweet, you and I,
When the flesh that clothed us is all laid by?

Desire must end when the blood grows chill,
Love and shame and the wayward will.

No joy of touch nor of sight again:
When the nerves have rotted there's no more pain.

No dream can stir, no sweet song rise
In a gaping skull with sightless eyes.

Of all that in you is now my pride
The white teeth only will then abide.

Naught of us when life is done
But bone and bone by speechless bone;

Mute heaps, under the laughing sky,
In fleshless slumber we two shall lie.

Bones only we are–yes, laugh, sweet face,
Till the white teeth flash from their lurking place;

Laugh loud and long; but, the laughter o'er,
Bones only you'll be for evermore,

Bones on bones, my beautiful maid,
And kite and raven about your head;

And none to ask of the flying year,
'Where is the flesh that rioted here?'

trans. H. Idris Bell

This Spot

Why should I give a hang about Wales? It's by a mere fluke of fate
That I live in its patch. On a map it does not rate

Higher than a scrap of earth in a back corner,
And a bit of a bother to those who believe in order.

And who is it lives in this spot, tell me that,
Who but the dregs of society? Please, cut it out,

This endless clatter of oneness and country and race:
You can get plenty of these, without Wales, any place.

I've long since had it with listening to the croon
Of the Cymry,[1] indeed, forever moaning their tune.

I'll take a trip, to be rid of their wordplay with tongue and with pen,
Back to where I once lived, aboard my fantasy's train.

And here I am then. Thanks be for the loss,
Far from all the fanatics' talkative fuss.

Here's Snowdon and its crew; here's the land, bleak and bare;
Here's the lake and river and crag, and look, over there,

The house where I was born. But see, between the earth and the heavens,
All through the place there are voices and apparitions.

I begin to totter somewhat, and I confess,
There comes over me, so it seems, a sort of faintness;

And I feel the claws of Wales tear at my heart.
God help me, I can't get away from this spot.

trans. Joseph P. Clancy

[1]*Cymry*, the Welsh people.

Hafod Lwyfog

One of the most daring things I ever did was to carve my name under that of Byron on the wall of Chillon Castle on the shore of Lake Geneva. I did it while the attendant's head was turned, since to add a name to the thousands that were on the walls already, was an offence by then. Carving one's name was an old custom among boys in times gone by, as it is among boys still. They would carve their names on everything, the bark of trees, lichen, a school bench, anything, especially if someone else's name was there already. It was some craving to make oneself immortal by innocent means, probably. There was something quite palaeographically interesting about this; boys whose names began with J always carved it like this – †. I once carved my name everlastingly deep on one of the joists of the Oerddwr cowshed. I am surprised on reflecting that I had enough patience to finish it.

But the last time I felt the whim was in Hafod Lwyfog a few years ago. I thought that I had completely rid myself of the habit, but one evening, after a day in the hay-harvest, I was slowly dragging my feet on the green hillock behind that ancient dwelling-place (the home of Ellis Wynne's[1] second wife, by the way) at the top end of Nantgwynant, when I saw a splendid place to hew my name in the smooth bark of a branch of a large holly-tree. And under the thrust of some urge I set about carving it with a knife, adding huge figures to denote the year. I prided myself on the artistic masterpiece, and yet I was a bit ashamed of being so boyish. I let the letters and the figures be, however, without trying to obliterate them; and there they are still, for all I know. After years of abstaining from the name-carving urge, it was rather strange that it 'broke out' suddenly like that on a summer's evening, and a fine holly-tree had to suffer as a consequence. I recalled that some *E LL* and *E* (a man and wife) had carved the initials of their names on one of the oak beams in the house, with the date 1638; but that man was one of the owners of the old mansion (which is a farmhouse by now) to be sure; and there was no significance for me, as far as I knew, in the memory of this. Expressing his right to the house, as his own property, was what that man was about. I had no right to the holly-tree, nor to anything else there, come to that. Yet, on reflection, perhaps I had a right to something, after all, and some vague stimulus had driven me to carve my name so definitely and confidently.

I had gone to Hafod Lwyfog at that time (with the kind permission of the two good people who farm there) in order to stop thinking and studying and writing – and to do nothing save work all I could with my body, and walk and eat and rest. And I succeeded wonderfully. There was excellent company to be had there; especially the man of the house. His experience of the world and people was wide and various, and there was no wisdom more mature than his. I forgot books and writing and 'cultural' things like that; and my favourite pastime (apart from going into the garden on a Sunday afternoon to see how big the fruit of that funny plant, the marrow, had grown, and how far across the border it had trespassed), my favourite pursuit was to go to the cart-house, that is the open building near the house where some of the machines and such-like were kept. A bench was to be found there, and every kind of tool for working in wood or iron. I spent many evenings there repairing an old gun that had come into my possession, and making it perfect; and then fashioning keys to fit the car. I had lost the original keys, and I made a lot of new ones from what I could remember of the old ones, and I succeeded so unexpectedly that I kept at it and made keys without number – and without need either. But after starting so successfully, it wasn't easy to give it up . . . An excellent place to mess about. It used to shock me to think that in years previous to that I had spent so much of my time bewildering my head with studies of all kinds – from Sanskrit to phonetics and from philology to physics; and worse even than that, spending years in studying and in writing, in collecting and preparing some kind of material for publication as books. What a fool I had been. When I wanted a bit of a change, I would go and fetch the gun, and walk across the meadows and the Wennallt bridge to the wood on the other side of the lake and the river for a pigeon, or perhaps a wild duck, with any luck. Glorious, natural, open-air, fine living.

And in the middle of all this one evening I set about carving my name on the holly-tree. It's possible that the old nature of the boy of yore had come to the surface for a while, for that nature is never completely buried. Perhaps it was the hand, unbeknown to me, that was protesting against disowning the craft that it had been taught. But this seems more probable to me – that in living 'naturally' like this and in trying to shake off 'cultural' things, I had discovered my true self in its elemental authenticity and in its bare naturalness, and that by the force of the discovery I had a sure, basic, personal right to my primitive, innate nakedness, and that I craved to record it somehow, although I had for the task only one of the tools of 'culture'. All that happened was that I carved my name and the date, as if I was insisting on silently declaring, 'I am myself now, anyway'. But the record remains as a pledge of a soul's return for a while to its proper temperament; and while that holly-tree remains without blemish at Hafod Lwyfog, I shall be helped to remember that and to comfort myself in thinking about the kenosis.

trans. Meic Stephens

IORWERTH C. PEATE (1901–82)

Nant yr Eira

There are owls tonight at Dôl-y-garreg-wen,
the grass covers the yard and the walls are grey with lichen,
and the cotton-grass spreads its sheet across the garden.

---

[1]Ellis Wynne (1671-1734), devotional writer.

The plumes are a white shroud, over Cwmderwen's bare peat-marsh,
and the two ricks are like two eyes aglow no longer,
and the stars a host of candles there on the hill's altars.

Frail white-topped dwellers on the moors, what sorry enchantment
turned each memory to a skeleton, and the ancient moor to a shrine?
None, save Time's tyranny that withers all that is fine.

The old voices will not come back to Beulah through the sore
burden of six feet of earth; too much for them to bear.
Be tranquil, bruised heart, and expect them no more.

The old gentleness you loved, it fled on unreturning ways,
it vanished with the summers, the sweetness of former days.
Nothing remains but the trembling of cotton-grass in the breeze.

trans. Joseph P. Clancy

THOMAS PENNANT (1726–98)

Portrait of a Lady

I must not omit the portrait of a lady, exceedingly celebrated in this part of Wales; the famous Catherine Tudor, better known by the name of Catherine of Berain,[1] from her seat in this neighbourhood. She was daughter and heiress of Tudor ap Robert Fychan, of Berain: she took for her first husband John Salusbury, heir of Llewenni, and on his death gave her hand to Sir Richard Clough. The tradition goes, that at the funeral of her beloved spouse she was led to church by Sir Richard, and from church by Morris Wynn, of Gwedir, who whispered to her his wish of being her second: she refused him with great civility, informing him that she had accepted the proposals of Sir Richard on her way to church, but assured him (and was as good as her word) that in case she performed the same sad duty (which she was then about) to the knight, he might depend on being her third. As soon as she had composed this gentleman, to shew that she had no superstition about the number three, she concluded with Edward Thelwall, of Plas y Ward, esq; departed this life August 27, and was interred at Llanyfydd on the 1st of September, 1591.

Her portrait is an excellent three-quarters, on wood. By the date, 1568, it seems to have been painted by Lucas de Heere; the only artist I know of in that period equal to the performance. I was told that in the locket she wore to the gold chain was the hair of her second and favourite husband.

from *Tours in Wales* (1778, 1781)

[1]Catherine of Berain (1534/5-91), known as 'The Mother of Wales' on account of her numerous children by four husbands.

The Red Bandits of Mowddwy

Return to Dinas y Mowddwy. On the road was informed of the place, not far from hence, where Lewis Owen, vice-chamberlain of North Wales, and baron of the exchequer of North Wales was cruelly murdered in the year 1555, by a set of banditti with which this county was over-run. After the wars of the houses of York and Lancaster, multitudes of felons and outlaws inhabited this country, and established in these parts, for a great length of time, from those unhappy days a race of profligates, who continued to rob, burn, and murder, in large bands, in defiance of the civil power, and would steal and drive whole herds of cattle, in mid-day from one county to another with the utmost impunity. To put a stop to their ravages, a commission was granted to John Wynn ap Meredydd, of Gwedir, and to Lewis Owen, in order to settle the peace of the country, and to punish all offenders against its government. In pursuance of their orders they raised a body of stout men, and on a Christmas Eve seized above four score outlaws and felons, on whom they held a jail delivery, and punished them according to their deserts. Among them were the two sons of a woman who very earnestly applied to Owen for the pardon of one: he refused; when the mother in a rage, told him (baring her neck) *These yellow breasts have given suck to those who shall wash their hands in your blood.* Revenge was determined by the surviving villains. They watched their opportunity when he was passing through these parts to Montgomeryshire assizes, to waylay him in the thick woods of Mowddwy, at a place now called, from the deed, Llidiart y Barwn; where they had cut down several long trees, to cross the road and impede the passage. They then discharged on him a shower of arrows; one of which sticking in his face, he took it out, and broke. After this they attacked him with bills and javalins, and left him slain, with above thirty wounds. His son-in-law John Llwyd, of Ceiswyn, defended him to the last, but his cowardly attendants fled on the first onset. His death gave peace to the country, for most rigorous justice ensued: the whole nest of banditti was extirpated, many suffered by the hand of justice, and the rest fled, never to return.

The traditions of the country respecting these banditti are still strong. I was told that they were so feared that travellers did not dare to go the common road to Shrewsbury, but passed over the summits of the mountains to avoid their haunts. The inhabitants placed scythes in the chimneys of their houses to prevent the felons coming down to surprise them in the night; some of which are to be seen to this day. This race was distinguished by the titles Gwylliaid y Dugoed and Gwylliaid Cochion Mowddwy, i.e. the banditti of the Black Wood, and the red-headed Banditti of Mowddwy.

from *Tours in Wales* (1778, 1781)

John Pook (1942–   )

In Chapel

I follow my mother in from the car
Under the side-arch, up the steps
And into the vestry schoolroom where
On Sunday afternoons we kept

The faith and flirted with the girls.
Though everything has changed, it all stays
Here exactly as it was; the smells
Of flowers, polished wood, the mops

Behind the piano in the corner,
The heavy Bible resting on the lectern.
Now, on Saturday night, my mother
Comes with dahlias, daffodils, her turn

On 'Flower Rota', ready for the morning.
Two decades and its faces flip
My mind while she spends time arranging
Flowers, watering from the tap.

Predictably, like time, the jar fills up.
Tomorrow will see her worship here
As usual. Beer-dry, I think of the cup
She'll drink from. I shall be elsewhere.

Caradog Prichard (1904–80)

Goodbye to a Friend

Little did I guess what Huw had to tell me when we met at the top of the new road.

'Jesus, boy, Mam was scared when she heard about Will Ellis the Porter,' Huw said.

Yes, I bet she was. My mother doesn't know yet, because she hasn't come home. I'm going up to my Grannie's to fetch her. She's sure to be there. Will you walk part of the way up the new road with me?

'Yes, sure. But, listen, you know those two men from the choir, the two in our house? Well, when I went home dinner time, they'd had good news. A telegram had come for the choir, to say the strike was over and telling them to hurry home.'

Go on!

'Yes, and my Dad stayed home from the Quarry today and went with our two, to meet the others in the choir in Salem chapel. They were going to have singing practice in Salem and that's where the telegram came. And d'you know what my Dad said when he brought them back to the house?'

No, I don't.

'Jesus, Mam and me nearly had a fit, I'm telling you.'

Well, what did he say then?

'Said he was going with them down to the South, to look for work in the coal pits.'

No, you don't say! He's not going?

'Yes, he is. Mam wouldn't agree for a long time and they were arguing about it all through dinner time. The two men from the South persuaded Mam in the end. Duw, they are kind. My father'll get twice as much money down there as he gets in the Quarry, see? And you know something else?'

What?

By this time we'd reached the cross roads, where Huw turned down to Stable Bridge and I was going up the hill to my Grannie's. We stopped by the wall to talk for another minute.

'He wants to take me with him,' Huw said, looking over the wall into the field.

Take you, Huw? I asked and something strange seemed to shoot through me.

'Yes,' Huw said, watching the field all the time.

Will they let you leave school, then?

'Yes, so my Dad says. Jesus, look, a rabbit!'

And there was a rabbit sitting in the field, watching us, with her two ears cocked.

'Damn it, I wish I had a gun,' Huw said.

Will they let you work down in the coal pit, Huw?

'Yes, why not?'

Lord, you'll be talking like Johnnie South when you come back.

'I won't be coming back, though.'

There we were, the two of us, leaning on the wall and staring like fools at that rabbit, and I could hear the sound of Huw's voice as if it was coming from some deep, echoing tunnel, 'I ... won't ... be ... coming ... back.' And neither of us saying a word.

But what will your mother do without either of you?

'Oh, we'll find a house down in the South and then she'll move down to us.'

When are you going, then, Huw?

'Tomorrow morning. On the eight o'clock train from the station.'

Tomorrow?

'Yes.'

You won't be in school tomorrow, then?

'Not on your life, boy.'

So I won't see you again?

'I'll write to you as soon as I've settled and found work and I'll give you all the news.'

You won't forget, will you?

'No, I promise. But I better be going now, look. We've got a lot of packing to do. So long, now, boy. I will write, honest, and you be sure to write back to me.'

I will, Huw. Goodbye now.

We shook hands for a long while and we kept repeating to each other to remember to write and then Huw made his way towards Stable Bridge and I set off for my Grannie's. I'd only taken a step or two when I turned round to have a last look at Huw before he went out of sight. And he had turned as well and he was running back towards me.

'Here,' he said, when he'd reached me, 'I'll give you this knife I got from the men from the South. It's got a sharp edge, mind.'

Jesus thanks, Huw. And, look, I'll give you this knife of mine, the one Humphrey Top House gave me. It's only a toy really, but p'raps you'll get some fun out of it.

'Yes, boy, I know I will. Well, goodbye now, then.'

Goodbye again, Huw, and remember to write. We shook hands again and he walked slowly towards Stable Bridge and I stood watching him till he'd gone out of sight. Then I, too, went slowly up the hill.

It's going to be strange in school tomorrow without Huw, I thought, and I began to brood about all sorts of things as I went up the hill. What if he's killed in the coal pits? Then I'd never see him again. But maybe I'll never see him again in any case, not after today. Then I remember that neither of us had said who would write first and I almost ran back to ask, but Huw had gone too far. I won't go to school tomorrow. I'll play truant. I can't bear going there without Huw. He'll write first, sure enough, because I won't know where to write to. South is a long way away. What'll I do now? Huw and Moi have gone and I'm all on my own. Jesus, I felt depressed when I reached Grannie's.

from *Un Nos Ola' Leuad* (1961), trans. Menna Gallie, *Full Moon* (1973)

Crying

In the end, the strange woman came back to the room, without my mother and carrying something in her hand.

'Here you are,' she said, 'you'll have to take these home with you.'

She put a small brown paper parcel tied with string into my hand.

What is it, then? I asked her.

'Your mother's clothes. And there are these, too. You'll have to take these as well.'

And she put the two rings in my other hand. One was Mam's wedding ring, worn thin, and the other one was the ring that had always been on my mother's finger.

I couldn't speak. I could only stare at the little parcel in my right hand and at the rings in my left. I kept trying to think how they could have got all Mam's clothes into such a small parcel.

It was then that I started to cry. But I didn't cry like I used to when I'd fallen and hurt myself long ago, and I didn't cry like I did at some funeral, nor the way I cried that time in Griff's bed when Mam went home and left me in Bwlch Farm years ago.

No, I was crying like throwing up.

Crying and not caring a damn who could see me.

Crying as if it were the end of the world.

Crying, howling, without a thought about who could hear me.

I enjoyed crying, like some people enjoy singing and others enjoy laughing.

Duw![1] I never cried like that before and I never have since, either. But I'd like to be able to cry like that just one more time.

I was still screaming crying as I went out through the door and down the stone steps and along the gravel path and through the gate to the road, till I sat down by the bank not far from the gates. I stopped crying after a while and began to groan like a cow in calf. Then to howl crying, again.

I was lying there, crying and groaning by turns when the motorcar from the Corner Shop came up to me. Little Will Policeman's father got out and helped me into the back seat with the strange woman. And after I'd been groaning there for a while and the motor going like the wind, the hum of the motor sent me to sleep. And I slept all the way home.

from *Un Nos Ola' Leuad* (1961), trans. Menna Gallie, *Full Moon* (1973)

[1]Duw!, God!

A.G. PRYS-JONES (1888–   )

Quite so

Within the whispering gallery of St Paul's
The merest whisper travels round the walls:
But in the parts where I was born and bred
Folk hear things long before they're even said.

A Ballad of Glyn Dŵr's[1] Rising

My son, the mist is clearing and the moon will soon be high,
And then we'll hear the thudding hooves, the horsemen speeding by,
With murmurs coming nearer, carried over on the breeze
Of the men who march in secret through the cloisters of the trees:
Tonight we two go riding, for the threads of fate are spun,
And we join Glyn Dŵr at Corwen at the rising of the sun.

For yesterday our leader was proclaimed the Prince of Wales,
His call to arms is sounding now among the hills and vales,
And Owain, heir of dynasties, in this auspicious year
May be our great deliverer, foretold by bard and seer:
And rumour runs that Arthur's[2] voice is heard along the west
Acclaiming this descendant of Cadwaladr[3] the Blest.

At last shall I unsheath again my father's two-edged sword,
And hand you mine to strike amain at Ruthin's tyrant lord,
Because I've waited, waited long throughout the bitter years
For this hour of freedom's challenge and the flashing of the spears:
So now we two must face as one the hazards of the night
To pledge our lives to Owain at the breaking of the light.

My son, go kiss your mother, kiss her gently, she'll not wake,
For an older mother calls you, though you perish for her sake:
The fabled Dragon banner flies once more above the Dee
Where the sons of Wales are gathering to set our people free
From wrong and dire oppression: pray, my son, for strength anew,
For widows will be weeping at the falling of the dew.

---

[1]Glyn Dŵr, Owain Glyn Dŵr (*c.* 1354 – *c.* 1416), national hero, known in English as Owen Glendower.
[2]Arthur (late 5th cent. – early 6th cent.), British military leader about whom there exist several tales which have been incorporated into English literature.
[3]Cadwaladr (d. 664), Prince of Gwynedd, a traditional hero.

GORONWY REES (1909–79)

The Hwyl

In memory I see myself now as a very small and rather stout child seated in the corner of our family pew. Facing me, at about the height of my eyes, is a small locker fixed in the corner of the pew, in which we kept our Bibles and hymn books, and where my brother and I secreted toys, sweets, and picture books which we had managed to smuggle into chapel. At this moment, I have just ceased playing with a long-eared mouse made out of my pocket handkerchief, and deprived of distraction I swivel my eyes half right to where, high in the pulpit, towering over me, a huge black figure, angry and eloquent, its arms outstretched like the wings of a great bird, is preaching endlessly on the tremendous themes of sin, grace, redemption, and eternal punishment.

In those days, it was usual for the Welsh preacher in the peroration of his sermon to enter into what is called in Welsh the *Hwyl*, which is a special form of impassioned utterance half-way between speech and song, and so rhythmical and emotional that sense gives way entirely to sound. A Welsh preacher in the *Hwyl* would not shrink from the most grotesque and bizarre effects; a simple appeal for funds for the mission field would become an elaborate play with the musical values of the words *Shilling, Patagonia*, and *Timbuctoo*. When the preacher moved into the *Hwyl*, it was formal notification that he had become possessed of the living Word, that the *afflatus* had descended upon him; he spoke as if with the gift of tongues, but the tongue was Welsh embellished with the most striking and esoteric words which happened to fit in with whatever rhythmical scheme the preacher was pursuing at the moment. This peculiar form of oratory, more closely allied to the tricks of tribal magic than the theology of Calvin and Augustine, could sometimes be strangely moving and impressive, even though the element of art and of artifice in it was always apparent. But every art has its decadence, and even as a child I was already living in the silver age of Welsh preaching; as practised by those who were merely performing a technical trick which was part of the stock-in-trade of every Welsh preacher, the *Hwyl* could seem merely cynical, a cold-blooded imitation of old masters in whom it had been the genuine voice of passion. In the mouths of novices merely following the style of their elders it could be ludicrous and embarrassing; but whatever form it took, the *Hwyl* was, for a child, terrifying.

One saw before one's eyes a man, whom one had taken to be a man like any other man, quite suddenly transformed into a kind of witch-doctor, demoniac and possessed; it was as if, without any warning, he had gone off his head. As a child I saw this happen on innumerable occasions and in a variety of forms; indeed, amongst our preachers, it was the rule and not the exception. Sometimes the trick was performed by one of the great popular artists of the Welsh pulpit, a man with the looks, the exquisitely arranged and silvered locks, the beautifully modulated voice, of a tragic actor; sometimes by men who had the violent passion and bitter eloquence of prophets; sometimes by some naïve, unlettered minister from an isolated chapel in the hills of Cardiganshire, whose sermon was quaint and touching like a primitive painting. But whatever form it took, the *Hwyl* inspired fear and terror in me, and a kind of shuddering shrinking from such a bare-faced, bare-breasted display of real or simulated emotion.

from *A Bundle of Sensations* (1960)

E. PROSSER RHYS (1901–45)

Wales

Sometimes I feel an impulse
To quit my native land, –
A land that loathes her burden
And will not make a stand;
A ready prey to raucous guile,
Wasting her substance all the while, –

And fly to sun-drenched islands
In the blue Southern Sea
Where prodigals with merry hearts
Live long and carelessly;
And join the dance in a green grove
To sweet guitars arousing love;

Where truth and right and duty
Are not the helpless prey
Of subtle words we would unlearn
In fear day by day;
Slogans, hysteria, come not there,
Nor weary hopes of a day more fair.

Men live in pure enjoyment
Of the simple things of life,
The sinister grip eluding
Of commercial greed and strife,
No currying favour or renown
By dragging their own country down.

Ah no! I can no other
Than stand here, come what may,
True to the land that bore me

Though sad her plight today;
With all her faults, my Wales has grown
Into the marrow of my bone.

And with the few who love her
Through every strain and shock,
Dreading no boorish insult,
Scorning the knaves who mock,
I call on our nation's youth
To come to terms with her ancient truth.

And when the supercilious
Uprooted, upstart crew
Maintain it is but folly
That moves our loyal few, –
Then come what may, I'll stand or fall
With the little band that gives her all.

trans. D.M. Lloyd

ALUN RICHARDS (1929–   )

Elmyra Mouth

Elmyra Mouth did not like *BBC Wales*. Either on the box or off it. Although she dutifully watched the programmes which involved her husband as assistant camera-man, she was always conscious of a great disparity between them and her. She did not like the announcers for a start. The women looked like something out of a Sunday School vestry and the men sounded phoney, half-London, half-Welsh, neither one thing nor the other, with the most unacceptable of getting-ahead acquisitions, posh accents.

Then again, on the few occasions when she went down from the valleys to Cardiff and waited for Davie in the staff canteen, Elmyra had increased her dislike for what went on behind the scenes. Take the bosses. They treated the more lowly technicians' wives like dirt, either looking through you, or rambling on amongst themselves in deep, book Welsh. Always jabber-jabber, it was, never mind whether you understood or not. They had no manners, Elmyra concluded, but that was not the worst. From what she had heard from Davie who was inclined to exaggerate to please her, the place was a hotbed of sex. You never knew who was sleeping with who, and for all the air of sanctity which somehow got on the air, behind the scenes, Elmyra was sure, the place was like a rabbit warren.

Wasn't it full of strangers? Glamorgan people lost out all the way along the line. You seldom came across anybody from the valleys, or Cardiff even, just the *in* Welshy-Welsh, catarrhal BA'd North Walians down for what they could get, Ministers' sons from everywhere, and girls from farms by the look of them, legs like bottles, all sitting around endlessly in the canteen, heads bent together and the hum of gossip rising like steam above a football crowd. Some of them *lived* in that canteen. It was an unhealthy atmosphere, Elmyra felt, and definitely not her style.

But there was another side to it. Her Davie had a good job by valley standards. On top of what he was geting in take-home pay, he always managed a few bob on top, what with car allowance, expenses and subsistence—it was as good as the Police from that point of view. But she had put her foot right down when there was any talk of moving down to Cardiff. Her grandmother had left her a furnished house, the corner one in the terrace, and where they lived, they had a view over the town that was worth waking up for.

From the bedroom window, she could see right down Dan y Graig Street, over the rows of terraced houses below them, right down to the memorial park where the trees formed an avenue beside the confluence of the Rivers Rhondda and Taff. Further away, familiar grey mountains and brown tumps stood sentinel over other valleys, and everywhere she looked, Elmyra felt at home. Here she had a position and status, and although they used to call her Elmyra Mouth because of her not being backward in coming forwards in that direction, she was well content to be at home. She was a valley girl, was she not? She knew every brick of Dan y Graig Street, every shadow of the courting gullies behind the terrace, every blade of grass and *cwtch* on the bare mountain and tip behind, and although now you didn't hear the tramp of miners' boots in the mornings and the little front parlour shop around the corner no longer sold lumps of chalk for the colliers to mark their drams as they did in her mother's day, it was still home and here she felt comfy. So when Davie'd proposed moving to Cardiff as it would cut down his travelling time, she had a cryptic and typical answer.

'Travel you bugger,' she said flatly. 'You'll not move me a inch!'

from 'The Scandalous Thoughts of Elmyra Mouth' in *Dai Country* (1973)

GRUFFUDD ROBERT (pre-1532 – post-1598)

Longing for Wales in Milan

Although fair the place where we are now and delightful it is to see the green leaves providing shade against the sun and pleasant to feel this northerly breeze blowing under the branches of the vine to gladden our hearts in this excessive heat, which is such a burden to one born and bred in a country as cold as Wales, yet I long for many things which were to be had in Wales and which helped to pass the time contentedly while sheltering from the heat on a long summer's day. For there, however hot the season, all manner of men could find their ease and diversion.

If you wanted entertainment, you could find a minstrel and his harp to play gentle airs, or a singer of sweet ditties to sing to the harp, whichever you desired, be it in praise of virtue or to revile misconduct. If you wished to hear about the customs of the country in our grandfathers' days, there would be grey-haired old men who would relate every remarkable and worthy deed which had been done in the land of Wales since time immemorial. But if it was meditation that you preferred, or to read in your own company, you could always choose a suitable place to do so, however hot the sun, either in green summer-houses, or beside running waters in a dale of saplings, or in a verdant valley, or on a clover-meadow's brow, or in a copse of birch or planted ash, or on an open, breeze-swept mountain, or in some other place, where the weather would cause neither weariness nor fatigue. But in this town there are no such things, for if you find a cave or nook where the sun never penetrates, you will catch a deadly chill by tarrying there. If, on the other hand, you stay in some open place, the heat will melt even the crows, and if you stay in the house, the sultriness will choke you. As for the vineyards, such as they are hereabouts, although they look beautiful enough and it is more pleasant to linger in them than anywhere else in these parts, yet a Welshman's heart does not respond to them, as it would to the banks of the Dee or the Vale of Clwyd, or to many places I could name from St David's to Holyhead in Anglesey. And even if this place were comparable to the finest spot in Wales, yet my heart would gladden sooner to hear the cuckoo sing in my own country than it would here on hearing the sweet notes of the nightingale, or the gentle voice of the thrush, or the bright song of the blackbird, or indeed if all the birds of the world were to join in harmony to sing the music of Paradise.

from the Preface to his *Welsh Grammar* (1567), trans. Meic Stephens

EIGRA LEWIS ROBERTS (1939–)

Deprivation

As Lisi Blodwen arranged the tinned salmon for her tea, she reflected that every old maid and widow should have a cat. Not that there was any great pleasure to be had from a relationship with an animal, but at least one could pet a cat or sulk at it without hurting its feelings or raising its hopes. And a cat, thank heaven, could not afford to sulk. On reflection there was more and more to be said for having one. What would be the best kind? A pedigree cat, perhaps, of princely blood; a cat to adorn a hearth. But no; a true blue-blooded cat would need such fussing. What a strain to have to treat a cat as an equal. No, a cat without a family tree would be best, one that could be kicked out of the way, and kept at a distance.

The salmon was good, so good indeed that she felt she could eat it all at once. And why not? She could afford to be greedy now, or lazy, or sluttish. She could afford to take the brake off all her weaknesses. She decided to clear the plate. She was about to settle down to it seriously when she heard the hard heels of her sister Jane on the back cobbles. This was Jane's third call today. Indeed, she'd been hovering around the house like the plague for days now. Trying to reason with Jane two or three times a day took all the strength she had. Every time she heard the sound of feet in the yard her inside would turn to water and she would have to hurry to the lavatory. Jane's refrain today was that Lisi Blodwen should take down the photograph of Huw Llewelyn from the mantelpiece. It was useless trying to explain to Jane that seeing Huw's face on the shelf was the next best thing to having him here with her.

She pushed the plate an arm's length away. She was just wiping her mouth with her handkerchief when Jane stepped into the kitchen, rigid with authority. Lisi half expected to see her waving a search warrant.

'Having your tea?'

'Just finished.'

'Don't take any notice of me.'

'No, I've done very well. What about you?'

'I could do with a bite.'

'There's a plate of salmon.'

'It looks good.'

'I've just opened it.'

'I don't want to take your meal.'

'I don't want it. It's too much for one.'

'I should think so indeed. There's enough here for three.'

Blodwen watched her sister digging into the salmon. Little pink streams ran down her chin and she pushed a large tongue out every now and then to catch them. So that was the end of her salmon. She didn't have much heart for it now in any case.

'Clear the plate.'

'Yes, I might as well. It won't keep in this close weather.'

'Excuse me. I've got to go to the back for a moment.'

'Again?'

'People do go.'

'Yes—within reason. Really I don't know what I wouldn't like to do to that old man, hurting you like this.'

'You talk of him as if he were an old pig or something.'

'A pig has more respect for its sty than he ever had for you. I never liked the man.'

'I never heard you criticize him before this happened.'

'I didn't want to hurt your feelings.'

'I've still got those. Anyway, there's no point in scratching old sores.'

'Not on a corpse there isn't. That gets cleaned up quickly enough. But this old skeleton is still breathing. And he'll be back from his honeymoon soon, and that wife of his hanging on to him. The baggage that she is!'

'So she's catching it now?'

'She knew very well that he belonged to you.'

'I had no more right to him than she had.'

'After twenty years of courting? You'd better go to the back. I'll expect a bit more sense from you when you get back.'

Lisi Blodwen sat on the lavatory seat. Thank goodness for a place to sit down out of sight and sound of Jane for a moment. Really there wasn't anywhere better than the lavatory for relaxing and contemplating life's problems. She'd settled dozens of problems sitting here. Nothing to distract one, nothing but the sound of water snoring in the pipes. Two more days and Huw Llewelyn and his new wife would be back in town. The pair of them would be shopping in Tesco's on Saturday afternoon (Huw Llewelyn had had plenty of practice carrying those silly little wire baskets). They would be there in the cross-seats in Salem on Sunday night (one seat away from the deacon's row); they would be welcoming people to their house and be welcomed to others' homes. Would there perhaps be an invitation to Llys Arthur? It would be an awful job to stay in the front parlour without slipping out to the kitchen every now and again to keep an eye on the food. Perhaps that woman would need help in carrying the dishes through. She would hardly know how to put her hand on every dish. Let's hope she'll take care of the hot water jug, at least. Sixty years old and still without a crack. Huw Llewelyn's mother had bought it in the church bazaar for sixpence ha'penny. And the jug had outlived her. What a pity that people had to go, while things so easy to replace stayed on.

But it would be easier to endure being with the two china dogs and the big Bible in the front parlour than to bear the good-byes. Huw Llewelyn standing on the step of Llys Arthur with his arm round his new wife's shoulder, instead of helping his sweetheart to avoid the holes in the road between Llys Arthur and here, as he had done for more than twenty years. But there wasn't much danger of that happening. Thank goodness there was another way between her house and the town, and that she had refused to turn Methodist with Huw Llewelyn.

'Blodwen, are you ill?'

There was no peace to be had, even in the lavatory.

'Hurry up, will you?'

Where did they go on their honeymoon? But nobody would believe they were on their honeymoon when they saw Huw Llewelyn with his hair thinning on the crown. He never had had a crop of hair like some boys. But what he had he kept neat, and he combed it as often as a girl.

'Lisi Blodwen, I shall have to get a move on.'

'I'm just coming.'

She could see Jane in the window watching her cross the yard. Her face looked comic through the lace curtains, the blue of one eye through one hole, the red of a lip in another and a lock of untidy hair like a coconut shy crowning the lot.

'You didn't have to wait.'

'Thanks for the welcome.'

'I was only thinking of you.'

'It would be better if you thought about yourself. I've got a husband to bear my burdens. What will you do now?'

'You didn't have to bother about the dishes.'

'I only cleared away a little. You'll have all evening to wash them, won't you? Well, what are you going to do?'

'I've got enough to live on.'

'I'm not talking about money. You yourself, inside, is what's important. A thing like this could shatter you at your age.'

'I'll get through it.'

'Do you remember how losing her sweetheart wrecked Emma Hughes?'

'She was only a girl.'

'She had more cause to pull herself together. A pretty girl like her can bring the boys running. You've still not got rid of that old picture.'

'And I don't intend to.'

'People who come to the house will have a shock seeing him baring his teeth at them.'

'Nobody comes here except you and your family.'

'Ugh! Look at those eyes of his, tiny and slit like a china cat. What did you ever see in him, tell me?'

'Where did they go on their honeymoon?'

'Someone in the shop said they'd gone to the tip of Lleyn.'

'Aberdaron perhaps.'

'Yes, perhaps that was what they said. But the whole country's full of some Aber this or that. Didn't the two of you go there once when you started courting?'

'We didn't go farther than Pwllheli.' Quietly.

'Really? Well, you have made a mess of things. Quarter of a lifetime down the drain to a dreg of a man like that. You're on the shelf now, anyway, do you realize that? And poor mother died worrying she wouldn't live to see your wedding. How long ago is that?'

'Twelve years.'

'And you're still without a man.'

'That's a gruesome thing to say.'

'I don't know that it wouldn't have been better to have lived in sin than hold hands like school kids. At least you'd have something to look back on.'

'Yes, I would.'

'Twenty years of courting. Walking down Betws road, and enough room to drive a cart between you.'

'End of term meetings and the Sunday School trip.'

'And an occasional night at the pictures—home at eight.'

'A quarter past. Then we'd sit here for hours talking.'

'What about?'

'What does one talk about?'

'About rents and shop bills and the future for the kids.'

'We always found something to talk about. That was his chair.'

'As if I didn't know. Did you change chairs sometimes?'

'Never. We'd take our coats off in the lobby and then straight to our chairs. Huw Llewelyn that side and me the other.'

'Good God, and the bedroom above you. Tell me, have you got any glands?'

Lisi Blodwen felt a cramp in her stomach.

'I've got to go to the back again, Jane.'

'God save us. There won't be any of you left. Is it all right for me to go home?'

'Yes, of course.'

'I don't really like leaving you.'

Jane went with her to the back and stood at the lavatory door. Lisi Blodwen stood there too. There was something unseemly in opening the door in Jane's presence.

'Do you know where I could get hold of a cat?' she asked hesitantly.

'So it's come to that, has it?'

'Come to what?'

'That you've got to have a cat instead of a man in your life?'

'A cat can be a lot more agreeable than a man, so they say.'

'Well, it's not likely to take off and leave you on the rubbish dump anyway. And you can talk to it if you don't have anyone else to talk to. Do you remember how Auntie Dora used to be?'

'Who wouldn't?'

'She used to carry on talking to herself night and day: question and answer, just like the catechism. Yes indeed, a cat, at once. It's lucky that cats aren't so hard to come by as lovers. I'll call later if I hear of one.'

Lisi already regretted mentioning the cat. It wouldn't dawn on Jane that there were cats and cats, just like men and men. Jane wouldn't mind bringing along any old skeleton in tow. One of those creatures that skulk from wall to hedge at night, perhaps, with its fur full of fleas. It would be a disgrace to her hearth to let in a creature like that. Ugh, she had never had much to say for cats. But she could manage. Great God, she would have to manage.

She didn't have to go to the lavatory after all. Her inside steadied as soon as she said good-bye to Jane. She went back to the house and the kitchen. She looked Huw Llewelyn straight in the eye. It wasn't fair to judge people from the colour and shape of their eyes. Huw had old Ifan Llewelyn's eyes, and everyone testified to the fact that Ifan was as safe as the bank. And she'd never had any cause to doubt Huw Llewelyn. In fact his word was as good as a vow on the Bible. But it was a pity that he'd taken that woman to Lleyn, of all places. He must have remembered that little hotel he had fancied so long ago. 'I'll come here on my honeymoon,' he had said. There must have been a lot of changes in that hotel by now, but perhaps the inside would be like it was, old and solid, and its coolness like a balm on the flesh. She had lain the other side of the wall from her sweetheart, and the groan of his bed as he turned had sent the strangest shivers through her. She would have run to him had there been a welcome for her. She'd suggested it tentatively, but not tentatively enough to prevent shame from spreading in a blush on Huw Llewelyn's pale cheeks. 'We'll do everything properly,' he said. 'A ring first, and then bed; that's the way I was taught.' Of course Huw Llewelyn was right—cautious, wise Huw Llewelyn, the truest of men. She had done her best to be worthy of him.

Had he cooled towards her perhaps, after that night? But he'd courted her faithfully, without ever mentioning it. 'It would have been better if you'd lived in sin,' Jane had said. That's what she would have done. Jane was one to step first and look later. And Lisi couldn't remember her ever tripping up. And she herself, like a fool, watching every step. But she would have slept with him. One night in a little old-fashioned hotel, and the moon dangling outside the window, teasing them. One night she could have turned to now as to a book and read over and over again. On winter evenings with an empty chair opposite her, passing the summer night at the tip of Lleyn, lying safe and warm, shoulder to shoulder, thigh to thigh with her only lover ever.

Sometime in the evening Jane called again.

'Still sitting here,' she said sympathetically.

'There's no hurry.'

'Well I'm blowed. That picture's gone.'

'I put it on the fire just now.'

'You did a sensible thing, Lisi. The place is healthier already. I've got a cat for you.'

'What kind is it?'

'Just like any other cat for all I know. It hasn't opened its eyes yet. It will grow up with you.'

Splendid. She could put her foot down with it before it got cheeky.

'Don't give it too much room. I was thinking that perhaps that was what you did with that man.'

'Perhaps indeed.'

'Didn't he use to stretch out on the hearth as if he was the man of the house? But more fool you for offering him everything and getting nothing.'

'Nothing. When shall I have the cat?'

'The day after tomorrow if you like. They'll be glad to get rid of it. It would end up in the river otherwise. Not many people need a cat nowadays.'

Apart from old maids and widows, thought Lisi Blodwen. Especially old maids, for whom there was no point in looking forward or back.

'Damn that Huw Llewelyn,' she said aloud.

'Thank heaven,' said her sister Jane.

                                                        trans. Enid R. Morgan

KATE ROBERTS (1889–1985)

The Condemned

It was in the house with Laura that he liked to be. Before long, Laura and the house became an essential part of him, as the quarry had been before that. He gave up asking his sons about the quarry. When his friends came to call on him, to hear about the quarry had given him too much pain at first. But gradually his interest lessened, and he gave up asking questions. He grew accustomed to being at home.

He came to think more about Laura. Did she know the doctor's verdict? He did not want to ask her, for fear that she would by some sign betray the fact that she knew. To hear the verdict, for the second time and in his own home, would be too much for him. He would have to endure the same feeling as he had endured when he heard for the first time; and he was too cowardly for that. By now, he had no feeling of any kind at all about the doctor's verdict. The agitation of that moment had worn away, and he did not feel ill enough now to live through the moment again, or to think about his end. There was pleasure in life as it was now: he could have a cup of tea with Laura, about three o'clock, and on baking-day some dough-cake with currants in it, to eat while it was still hot. The doctor had said he could eat anything.

How much did Laura know? She looked as though she knew nothing. She went about her work happily as usual, and talked to him about the business of the farm and the matters of the district. Sometimes he caught her looking at his face and his eyes between her and the light, as though she were looking at their colour. Laura drew closer to him, and came to mean more to him than she had done since their courting days. She was a pretty little thing then, with her brown curly hair: and really, she carried her years well still, though she was fifty-two, the same age as himself. He could remember the time he first saw her, on the day of the May Fair, when she was changing her place, and he was in town with his father, selling a cow. He remembered how he had been mad about her until she promised to marry him. He used to go to see her every chance he got, and he could see her before his eyes everywhere throughout the day. After they married, the smallholding and the business of living took their whole interest, and like so many country people, they thought there was no need to show affection after marriage. After marrying, people begin to live, not to love. They quarrelled sometimes, and since they were not emotional people they became friends again in a quiet casual way, by talking about the pigs or the cattle; they did not return to the subject of their quarrel. And there was never a place or a time, somehow, for lover-like talk. In the spring and the summer there would be work to do in the fields after he came home from the quarry, and in the winter there were continual meetings in the chapel, and there was no time to do anything but read the newspaper.

By now, Dafydd was sorry that he had not spent more time talking to Laura. How much better it would have been: she would have had that friendliness when he was gone, it would be something for her to remember. When they looked back on their life, what had they had of it? Only a cold, casual life, which reached its summit of pleasure when the month's wage happened to be good. They did not draw nearer to each other when the wage was small. Indeed, a poor month made them silent and casual. He would make amends for the past now. He was going to enjoy life at home like this with Laura, to go for a motor trip round Anglesey alone with her. They had never gadded about much after marrying. They had been looking forward to a better time continually, and had let life go past without their having seen the world. Yes, it was fine in the house with Laura. He liked looking at her; he knew now, what he hadn't known before, how many buttons there were on her bodice, what the pattern of her woollen shawl was, how many pleats there were in her apron. It was a pity he could not be like this for ever. He came to realize that when his pain began to increase. He could not enjoy his food so much; there was not so much pleasure in watching the bread rising by the fire, nor in smelling it baking. When he was just going to lose something, he had begun to enjoy it. He saw the Indian summer of his illness slipping away from him. He could not get up by dinnertime, and he began to long for the chimney-corner. He would get up towards the evening so as to be able to sleep better. The pain increased. He could not take interest in things around him. The doctor came more often, and gave him drugs to ease his pain. He would fall asleep, and feel sick and disheartened when he woke. Sometimes he would drop off into a coma. He would forget the things around him. What did he care for the doctor in Liverpool now? It was his illness that was important, not the doctor's verdict. The verdict had nothing to do with his illness. He wanted to get rid of a little of the pain, so that he could talk to Laura. She was at his bedside whenever she got a chance. He had a better day now and then, and got up in the afternoon, but he did not enjoy his tea. But soon he became too ill to get up at all, and Laura left him only when he was asleep.

And on that hay-harvest day in July he was very ill. Outside, the neighbours were carrying his hay, and he was too ill to take any interest in that. He did not care this year whether he got a big rick or a little one, whether the hay was good or bad. He was conscious of people coming to and fro to the house to get food. He was more wide awake than usual, and he wanted Laura more. She was there as often as she could be, running back and fore between the dinner-table and the bed. He wanted to talk to her, to talk about their courting days, when they used to go for walks along the White Road, and see lapwings' nests in the holes on the mountain. He wanted to talk to her about the time he saw her first, at the fair, when she was disheartened because she was changing her place. How happy those days were when they could press tightly against each other as they came home from the eisteddfod[1] at the Rock Chapel! How they enjoyed the journey home from a preaching festival: he would have been burning to see the sermon ending, and have found himself looking at Laura more often than

[1] *eisteddfod*, a cultural festival, usually organized on a competitive basis.

at the preacher! He wanted to tell her all these things. Why hadn't he told her them on those afternoons when they had had their little tea together? Why was his shyness lessening as his body weakened? The next time Laura came into the bedroom he would see that he told her.

When she came, the last meal was over, and the house was quiet. They could not hear any of the noise from the yard behind the house. The smell of hay came into the bedroom through the window. There was a smell of sickness about the bed, and an unpleasant taste in Dafydd's mouth. He was half-lying, with pillows behind him. Laura came to him.

'Will you take a little bit of something to eat?' she said. 'Everybody's cleared away from the house now.'

'No,' said he, 'I can't eat anything now.' And then he added, 'I'm getting weaker, you know.'

But having said that, he noticed Laura, and saw that her tired face bore the marks of weeping.

'Laura,' he said, 'what's the matter?'

'Nothing,' said she, turning the side of her face to him.

He took hold of her and turned her to him; and in her glance he saw the knowledge that the doctor had given to him. His words left him. He could not remember anything that he wanted to tell her, but he took hold of her, and pressed her to him; and she felt his hot tears running down her cheek.

from 'The Condemned', trans. Dafydd Jenkins

No Letter from Twm

The news that Twm was in France came as a great blow to Jane and Ifan Gruffydd. They had never imagined this would happen and had kept thinking the war would be over before lads like Twm had to go.

From then on it was as if a cloud hung over their heads, waiting to break. Somehow they could not believe it would lift of its own accord. The most painful thing was waiting for the post, expecting a letter to come. When they got one they would be happy for a few days; then they would begin to worry again.

The mother made cakes, and twice a week sent off a parcel to France; it was the only thing she did in the week that she put her whole heart into; and it hurt her to see her husband bringing cigarettes to put in the parcel when he was so much against them. Their neighbours used to do the same thing: 'As you're sending a parcel, put these cigarettes in for Twm' they would say quite often, until their *own* children went off to the army.

There was no work at all in Moel Arian. The men, both young and middle-aged, went off either to the army or the munitions factories, or else to work on the docks in Liverpool and other places. Every now and then Ifan Gruffydd would do a spell of work at Holyhead, unloading ships, after which he would come back to do things on the farm. When he was working there he was allowed to come back every Sunday. It was a blessing that by now their grandson Eric was living with them.

People at home now began to ask themselves–and to ask each other–what exactly was happening. They had often before known bad times. They had suffered wrong and injustice in the quarries, the oppression of managers and owners, oppression through favouritism and corruption. They had seen their friends and children killed at work, but they had never before had their boys taken away from them to be killed in war. Since they could not now discuss things up in the huts on the quarry, it was when they met at Sunday School that they searched for explanations.

They had by now wholly given up believing that the war was a war to protect the rights of small nations, that it was a war to end wars; nor did they believe that one country was more to blame than another; but they came to believe that in every country there were people who were glad of the war and who were using their boys for their own profit. These were 'y bobol fawr',[1] the very same people who squeezed the life out of them in the quarry, who sucked their blood and turned it into gold for themselves. People now believed in the depths of their hearts that somebody was making money out of the war, just as somebody made money out of their bodies in the quarry; and they believed that these people wanted to put off the day of peace. They knew that if their children refused to go to the war, *they* would come to get them and force them away.

If God existed, why did he not intervene? Why did he always let the poor suffer? This was the great problem for them in Sunday School. And as the world outside changed, so their opinions changed. Their faith in preachers and political leaders was undermined. Preachers who previously were like gods to them, they now condemned because these now argued in favour of the war. Indeed, some people stayed away from chapel for months after a preacher had preached the just war. By the same token preachers who attacked the war rose in their estimation. And names of some well-known statesmen had come to stink in everyone's nostrils.

But the war went on. More of the boys came home in uniform, and the news of the first deaths arrived.

In Treffrwd, Owen worried about these same things. He was tired to death of the stupid, empty talk you got everywhere from people who were considered intelligent. People in that proud little town talked of the glory of war and the bravery of our boys, and they believed every single word that was in the newspapers. It was true that they made great efforts to send things out to the soldiers, and to give them a welcome home, but the soft, empty talk and the unending clichés were enough to drive one mad. Their children came home from the army camps, and if these were officers, they turned up their noses at people like Owen who dared to walk about the streets safe in their civilian clothes. These lads were well-enough looked after, thought Owen, grammar-

[1] Y bobol fawr, lit. 'the big people'.

school boys who had been coddled throughout their lives, never been short of anything. If they were suffering now, it was the first time they ever *had* suffered. As for his own people, they had known hardship all their lives, and as if that was not enough, war had now come like an invisible hand and flattened them with the ground. He wanted to go up to these stiff, polished officers, and tell them this. But what good would it do? What could they know, living in this rich valley in the middle of plenty, what could they understand of a small place like Moel Arian with its poor scab of earth that was not even good enough to support the kind of cows they were familiar with? What did they know about wrenching a living from land that was all peat and clay, land that sometimes, nevertheless, bred a little intelligence.

Some of the women teachers at school began to reproach Owen for not joining up. He was too contemptuous to explain that he had been temporarily exempted on account of his health. The only thing that would have made him join up was a feeling of fidelity to the friends and relatives who already had: if they were suffering, he should be with them; not out of sympathy for the war but out of sympathy for the boys. This came to worry him more as Twm's letters began to arrive. It was not that his brother complained, but rather the absence of complaint when there was good reason for it, that made Owen feel he should be there suffering alongside Twm. And then he rememberd his parents at home. He knew how they felt, and how they would feel if he too joined up. But then the next minute he would feel that his duty to Twm was greater.

There was a young teacher at the school called Ann Elis – a girl from Meirionydd. She and Owen had never done more than pass the time of day. She was extremely quiet, and on certain days had a most terribly sad look. One day a telegram came for her, and people said that her young man had been killed in the war. When she came back to school after a few days she looked like someone who had been seriously ill for months. Owen wanted to go up to her and say how sorry he was, but now she walked past him, and past everyone else, without saying a word.

A month later a telegram arrived calling Owen home. He did not need to be told why.

That morning, at the beginning of July 1916, Jane Gruffydd was expecting a letter from Twm. She had not had one for six days. She was fairly worried, but not too much so, since once before she had had to wait a long time and had then got two letters together. These days all she could manage was to do the milking and get Eric ready for school before the postman came, and he was sometimes late. He was late to-day, or else he had gone. But she still sat waiting instead of getting up and starting on her work. No; *there* he was, blowing his whistle at the gate. She was pleased and ran down. But it was not a letter from Twm, nor from any other of the children; instead a long envelope with the Government stamp on it.

'Drat', she said. 'More of these forms to answer. You'd think we had a thousand acre farm'.

But when she opened it she found that these were not the same sort of forms. These were in English. She saw Twm's name and his number in the army, and there was another stiff white piece of paper with only a little written on it – also in English.

She ran down to the shop with the letter.

'Some old papers in English have come through the post, Rhisiart Huws. You wouldn't like to tell me what they say, would you? It's something to do with Twm, anyhow'.

The shopkeeper read it, and held it in his hand for a while.

'Sit down, Jane Gruffydd', he said gently.

'What's the matter?' she said, 'nothing's happened, has it?'

'Yes, I'm afraid so', he said.

'Is he alive?'

'No, I'm afraid not. Ann —', he shouted back from the shop to the kitchen, 'bring some water straight away'.

'Come through to the kitchen, Jane Gruffydd', said the wife, and took hold of her arm.

Later, she took her home to Ffridd Felen.

Ifan was working at the time on one of the nearby farms where they had started on the hay earlier than at Moel Arian. When he saw a man crossing the field to find him, he too knew why he was being called home.

Before nightfall all the children arrived. The neighbours came and did the work. They showed every kindness. And that night, when the last of them had gone, the children and their parents huddled together by the fire, feeling that this was the best way for them to be on the night when the first breach had been made in the family.

As she put her head on the pillow and tried to close her eyes on the pain, scores of sad thoughts came to the mother's mind. But among them all there flashed one other thought – that she would not have to fear the sound of the postman tomorrow.

from Traed mewn Cyffion (1936), trans. Ned Thomas

Old Age

Next evening I went to Llain Wen. Gwen had asked me to go, for by this time she was getting very anxious. Once again the old woman failed to recognise me. And when she did realise who I was, she took no interest in me or in my affairs.

It was a night of hard frost, clear moonlight, and not a breath of air stirring. The ice crunched under my feet as I walked along the road towards Llain Wen.

'It's blowing up for a gale, isn't it?' said the old woman, to no one in particular.

'How long is it till Christmas?' she asked, before I had a chance of correcting her about the wind.

'Two months,' I replied.

'Dear, dear,' she said, 'I remember as if it was yesterday me and my sister Aels making toffee on Christmas Eve when the two of us were working at Gwastad Faes. And would you believe it?' she asked, putting her hand on my knee, 'we put the toffee out to cool, and as soon as we'd done it we heard a terrible screech. And what was it but a hen running over the toffee and burning herself. Her claws came off her, poor creature!' She burst out laughing.

'Stop that nonsense, mother!' said Gwen sharply, and then, in a gentler tone, to me, 'How was Twm?'

'Pretty poorly,' I replied, 'pretty poorly, much worse than when I saw him before.

'Yes,' said Gwen, 'I saw him much worse the day I was there. Something's got him, I'm afraid.'

'Goodness me!' said the old woman, 'strange things used to happen in the old days.'

'Mother, be quiet,' said Gwen impatiently. 'Didn't you hear Wil saying how ill Twm is?'

'Twm?' asked the old woman. 'Ah, oh yes.' Then she resumed: 'I remember Aels and me coming home over Gwredog bridge with our sweethearts from the Autumn Fair, and when we were on the bridge we saw a ghost and off we went, back almost to the town, and came home round by the road. She was a smart girl, Aels. She could have anyone she wanted for a sweetheart.'

As I looked at her sitting there, an old old woman, my mind went back to the time when I used to call at Llain Wen for Twm on the way to school. She was then a round red-cheeked apple-dumpling of a woman, moving briskly about the house. She thought the world of Twm. He was the youngest boy, and she coddled him. All through the winter, and for most of the summer, she made him wear a mustard-flannel on his chest, and a flannelette scarf round his neck and crossed over his chest beneath his braces. Not until he nearly melted in the heat of July was he allowed to discard these things. She could hardly bear to let the wind blow on him. I thought of that hard-working mother, and of this old woman sitting by the fire with folded hands.

I think she still wore the same clothes. I couldn't remember ever seeing her without her white cap under her black straw hat. And it wasn't a goffered cap like the one Betsan Ifan wore when I was a boy, but a frilled cap, with a little round black hat turned down, its brim bound with velvet and a feather round the crown. I never saw her wearing any other, and I never once saw her without it in the house. She wore a homespun petticoat, a flannel bodice, and a blue and white apron; on her feet a pair of clogs with shiny clasps. 'The same kind of clothes,' I said to myself, 'but a different face and a different pair of arms. These weren't the arms I used to see long ago kneading a panfull of dough until it heaved like a bog under her hands. There was little of her face to be seen, for she tied the strings of her cap under her chin, and that little was crinkled like mud after rain. Her hands yellow and mottled like damp-stained wallpaper, a drop of water in the corner of her eye. She shook her head all the time, sometimes up and down, sometimes sideways.

'The wind's rising, isn't it?' she said.

'It is that,' I replied. 'And it's time I was going.'

As I opened the door upon the quiet night, with the moon shining on the doorstep, I could hear her saying 'The wind's rising to a gale.' I turned home, sadly.

I went to see Twm several times after this, and each time he seemed to be getting worse. On Winter Fair day I went to town early in the morning, but even at that hour one of Twm's neighbours who knew how friendly we were was looking for me. I could tell by his face that he had bad news to break. Twm was very ill, he said, much worse than the night before, and he doubted whether he'd find him alive when he got back. I turned my back on the Fair and set out, determined to see him once again. But I was too late. He had died an hour ago, and it was left to me to break the news at Llain Wen. I walked every foot of the way, and by the time I reached Llain Wen the one o'clock hooters were sounding in the quarries.

As I opened the gate of the path leading to the house I saw the old woman in the doorway, her head peering out round the door post. Before I opened the gate a passer-by asked me if he was on the right road for Llanberis. She obviously saw him, for her first question to me was: 'What did he want?'

'He wanted to know if he was on the right road to Llanberis.'

'Oh!'

She stared at me again.

'Who are you?' she asked.

'Wil,' I replied, 'Wil, Twm's friend.'

'Oh?' I could not tell whether or not she knew me. I leant against the wall of the house, wondering how best to break the news to her.

'I came to the door to have a look round before dark,' she said.

'Did you?' I said, and then I went on, clumsily, 'It's bad news I have for you, you know. Twm, poor fellow – well, he's gone.'

'Twm?' she asked. 'Which Twm?'

'Twm your son, your youngest son,' I answered.

She looked at me uncomprehendingly as she replied:

'Don't know him.'

From 'Old Age', trans. Ll. Wyn Griffith

DAFYDD ROWLANDS (1931–   )

Joseph the Milk

In a milk-bottle you only get the exact measure that you have paid for – the justice of the scales, the fairness of perfect balance. You pay for a pint, you get a pint – no more, no less. It was not like that when Joseph the Milk was around.

'Who is Joseph, my children?' asked the preacher in the Children's Service, referring to the lad in his coat of many colours. It was my impetuous brother who answered giving mother a twinge of embarrassment. 'He delivers milk to our house'. Joseph the Milk, from Rhyd-y-fro, one of the many faces that dapple the fresco of my childhood. Those were long days. Between dawn and sunset there was a sweeping stage of laughter and tears in the sunshine and the rain. Now the days are short, insufferably short, and each hour a momentary flash. Minutes don't exist any more in this acceleration. But a child's hours were long and endless when the warm season of the fern was like a limitless century.

Early on Saturday morning I would sit on a low wall at the top end of the street. There was in that wall – in fact there still is – a smooth stone shaped like a small seat, and in the snugness of that seat I would sit, my sharp ears straining to measure the distance between me and the faint sound of horseshoes in another street. The distance would grow less and less, the sound louder and clearer. The sweetness of that anticipation cannot be described, that peculiar and pleasurable sweetness which is a quivering in the stomach, akin to the thrill felt by the youngster on his way to his first date with a new sweetheart. But it was not a fair-complexioned girl that I was waiting for on those sunny Saturdays. The focus of my infatuation was Joseph the Milk's horse-and-cart, and the milkman's 'Wo-w' when he reached the end of the street was music to my ears. The aged mare would stop and allow a happy lad to step with a stretch up onto the dizzy floor of the cart before setting off again on the round of adventure.

But the highlight of the pleasure was not the ride, not the proud stance between the heavy churns as we progressed along the streets like Caractacus in Rome, head held high and eyes sparkling with courage. The climax of those Saturday mornings was to hold the small milk-can in my hand and be for a few minutes a real milkman, a miniature Joseph, and to pour the white, wholesome liquid from the can into the measuring-cup, and from the metal measure into the earthenware jug on the windowsill. And then the silent rite, the devotional supplement, the communion after the meeting – the pouring of a few extra drops, drops of generosity. I had seen Joseph himself administering that sacrament as he poured into our jug and I did not doubt that he did the same at every house. And I followed his example. You paid for a pint, but it wasn't a pint that you got. More was received than the just measure, in a small flow of unassuming kindness.

Joseph went the way of all flesh before the advent of meticulous bottles, filled with precision, that clatter in the rush of the busy little man from the big united Company in whose white sea there are no drops of the lost generosity. . . . Yes, Joseph is now dead, and the charitable milk-can is rusting in the rain. The army of bottles is taking over; they stand on the window-sill, a row of shiny little soldiers, where once was administered the homely sacrament of kindness.

'Who is Joseph, my children?' A symbol of that giving which is more than the asking, an emblem of kind-hearted selling and neighbourly living, an embodiment of the value which vanished with the fading of the echoing horseshoes in the harsh sound of the poisonous machines. He who was cast into a pit.

from *'Joseff'*, trans. the author

A Child's War

September 1939. I was eight years old and I had a snug bed under the stairs. To me and children of my age the thing that was called 'the war' was nothing more than a new setting for our games and the unreal phenomenon which gave a special slant to our playing. Learning birds' names became learning the names of aeroplanes, geography a theatre of war. The silent Sundays became noisy Sundays as Captain Mainwaring and his regiment of doddering old men, each with a broom-handle on his shoulder and the letters LDV on his arm, practised their manoeuvres in the fern of Barley Hill and tested their military boots around the houses. We had new friends, little foreigners from Walthamstow and Chatham. We went as families to the vestry, like someone going to market to buy a budgie or a tortoise, to get an evacuee. 'Please, mam, can we have two?' The evacuee in the house next door used to wet the bed every night, but nobody was cross with him. And the nights grew darker. In the Pavilion, week after week, there was *Flash Gordon* with his head, at the end of each instalment, in the mouth of the ugliest beast imaginable. And from the spine-chilling terror of those fanged jaws we would emerge into the night, and there wasn't a single lamp to comfort us in the utter darkness of the blackout. We used to go to Sunday School, and on the plain windows of the puritannical vestry the beautiful patterns of sticky paper held the glass against the shock of bombs. A new hymn was learned in a strange language to make the little Londoners happy: 'Take my life and let it be consecrated, Lord, to thee . . .' After tea, we would gaze at the map of Europe on the wall, and watch grandpa move the small flags – the Union Jack and the Swastika – and in the moves the fortunes of war. We went to school with a square box dangling from our necks, a box which was opened when we practised the drill – learning, in the rubber mask, to breathe through the long perforated nose that resembled the snout of the legendary black pig, and our breath steaming inside the celluloid window. Smothering was just as bad as choking.

Then came the forties; the war drew closer and became more real. I had company under the stairs. The night was lit up by the flames of Swansea and the long rays of searchlights probing the valley ceiling for the metal birds of the enemy. And in the morning, on our way to school, we collected the jagged shrapnel, the cold remnants of a hot night. We stole apples from Annie May's garden and were surprised that the house was so quiet and that nobody ran after us. We heard later that her brother had been killed in an aeroplane. We took the apples back and placed them like flowers under the tree. Women found jobs on the buses and carried on with the drivers – or so it was said. Americans came to Mynydd y Gwair and gave us small packets of coffee and peculiar balloons that could not be inflated and at the sight of which my mother would faint. The war went on and our games became more cruel and fiendish. My cousin came home from Burma, from forests crawling with invisible Japanese, and he was quiet and had little to say. And the war went on. I got tired of it, and went to sleep under the stairs.

from '1939', trans. the author

HOWARD SPRING (1889–1965)

Errand Boy

When winter set in I became engaged as a regular Saturday errand boy at the greengrocer's and fishmonger's. Before there was light in the sky I would be at the shop where a natty little pony was pawing the ground, harnessed to a light cart. The greengrocer was a woman, and a devil of a driver. Already she would be waiting, reins in her fingers, and no sooner had I leapt up beside her than we were off with a jingle of harness and a brisk cloppity-clop of the pony's hoofs.

I loved those rides, though to this day I can feel the bittter tingling in my feet that did not reach down to the friendly straw strewn on the floor. The sharp air cut like whips, but what of that when such a gallant drive was forward! Over the river bridge we went before a soul was stirring, and into the heart of the town. There in Custom House Street, which is Cardiff's Covent Garden, I held the pony while the woman chaffered over boxes of kippers and crates of oranges, sacks of potatoes and all the ingredients of her picturesque calling.

Dead though the city might be elsewhere, Custom House Street was wide awake, full of champing horses, and rattling harness, and shouting men; and the pavements exhaled into the still frosty air their unforgettable smell of trodden vegetable garbage.

Back then we would rattle as briskly as we had come, the lash lightly stroking the pony's flank as he tore past the grey face of the workhouse behind the elms that were winter-bare. Then, after a cup of tea in the parlour behind the shop, we would open up for business, and the day degenerated into a prosaic lugging of baskets about the streets, delivering the threepenn'orths of this and that which housewives 'were too lazy or too proud to carry for themselves.

At eleven p.m., while the gas-flares were still sizzling in the shop, I would be sent home after a sixteen-hour day with a shilling for wages and a couple of herrings for charity. I had no complaints to make, for a sumptuous midday dinner was thrown in, too.

I liked that job, but lost it through ambition. A scholarship examination was held one Saturday, and in order to sit, my employer having refused me permission, I took French leave. I did not win the scholarship, but I was given the sack.

from Heaven Lies About Us (1939)

Poverty

How on earth was that family kept together? I received four shillings for my five and a half day week at the Docks. Older than I were one brother and two sisters. All were earning some pittance; but then there were another brother and two more sisters still at school.

As I see it, only the indefatigable realism of my mother kept us afloat. She was a little five-foot woman who could read the simplest things, but made a great to-do if she had to sign her name. She was not often called upon to do so; but when she was, the occasion was elevated to such dignity, the operation was performed with such care and circumspection, that one would think no document she signed could have less importance than Magna Charta.

She worked her fingers to the bone. Screwing her 'coarse apron' into a roll, she would set off with a brisk step, wearing rather jauntily a man's cap. She scrubbed and charred, while the younger children were at school; and when they were at home she found time to do her own housework, to run piles and piles of other people's linen through the mangle and to wash the clothes which it was my business to collect from our clientele, and to take back when they were laundered. I would gather the bundles on the way home from the Docks, huge loads done up in sheets that I heaved on to my back, then staggered off like Christian before his sins rolled away.

These things troubled me. I was bitterly ashamed of being seen lugging those bundles. The boys used to yell: 'Your mother takes in washing!' and, by Heaven, she did! But these things worried her not at all. She was a realist. There was a family to be, somehow, 'brought up'. She set about it in the only way she knew.

She acquired in those years a sort of terrific momentum, so that, long after it was necessary for her to do such things, she could not stop; and when the rest of us were lying abed we could hear her downstairs laying into the beginning of the day's washing. A woman would be coming in to do it, but she couldn't be restrained. She would be up early on the specious pretence of 'putting things ready'. It was never possible to get a maid to suit her. Her own dogmatic views about how things ought to be done were too deeply planted. In those early days she cared nothing what anybody thought of her, and when I complained that boys were yelling after me in the street, she replied with a favourite saying of hers: 'Let them call you what they like so long as they don't call you pigeon-pie and eat you.'

It cost her much to bring up her sons. She lost two of them; and for the one she lost in the war she was awarded five shillings a week. It was I who had to be the realist then. She was very small, very grey, but fierce and energetic as ever. 'They can keep it!' she said. 'They can keep it! He was worth more than that.'

Her only relaxation in those arduous days was on Sunday nights. We carried on with the readings – and it was only during those few hours that I read anything that was good. We went through book after book by Dickens. He pleased my mother immensely. 'I'll tell you all about *my* life, some day,' she used to say to me. 'Then you can write a book that'll make people laugh.'

I don't know where the idea came from that I would write books, or whence she got the notion that her life had been comic. Certainly, she refused to consider it tragic. It was just a job like any other and she put all she knew into it.

One night there was illness in the house. I was told to run for the doctor. I was to say to him: 'Come at once. It will be all right. We can pay you.'

It seemed to me horrible to have to say any such thing to the doctor. For the first time I realized in a concrete way how poor we were.

from *Heaven Lies About Us* (1939)

ANONYMOUS

A Reminder

When a man's turned forty, though
His outward show is brave,
One sound will wipe his smile away –
The digging of a grave.

trans. Glyn Jones

Dylan Thomas (1914–53)

Fern Hill [1]

Now as I was young and easy under the apple boughs
About the lilting house and happy as the grass was green,
    The night above the dingle starry,
        Time let me hail and climb
    Golden in the heydays of his eyes,
And honoured among wagons I was prince of the apple towns
And once below a time I lordly had the trees and leaves
        Trail with daisies and barley
    Down the rivers of the windfall light.

And as I was green and carefree, famous among the barns
About the happy yard and singing as the farm was home,
    In the sun that is young once only,
        Time let me play and be
    Golden in the mercy of his means,
And green and golden I was huntsman and herdsman, the calves
Sang to my horn, the foxes on the hills barked clear and cold,
        And the sabbath rang slowly
    In the pebbles of the holy streams.

All the sun long it was running, it was lovely, the hay
Fields high as the house, the tunes from the chimneys, it was air
    And playing, lovely and watery
        And fire green as grass.
    And nightly under the simple stars
As I rode to sleep the owls were bearing the farm away,
All the moon long I heard, blessed among stables, the nightjars
        Flying with the ricks, and the horses
            Flashing into the dark.

And then to awake, and the farm, like a wanderer white
With the dew, come back, the cock on his shoulder: it was all
        Shining, it was Adam and maiden,
        The sky gathered again
    And the sun grew round that very day.
So it must have been after the birth of the simple light
In the first, spinning place, the spellbound horses walking warm
        Out of the whinnying green stable
            On to the fields of praise.

---

[1]Fern Hill, a farm near Llangain, Carms., where the poet spent holidays as a child.

And honoured among foxes and pheasants by the gay house
Under the new made clouds and happy as the heart was long,
   In the sun born over and over,
     I ran my heedless ways,
   My wishes raced through the house high hay
And nothing I cared, at my sky blue trades, that time allows
In all his tuneful turning so few and such morning songs
   Before the children green and golden
     Follow him out of grace,

Nothing I cared, in the lamb white days, that time would take me
Up to the swallow thronged loft by the shadow of my hand,
   In the moon that is always rising,
     Nor that riding to sleep
   I should hear him fly with the high fields
And wake to the farm forever fled from the childless land.
Oh as I was young and easy in the mercy of his means,
     Time held me green and dying
   Though I sang in my chains like the sea.

Memories of Christmas

Years and years and years ago, when I was a boy, when there were wolves in Wales, and birds the colour of red-flannel petticoats whisked past the harp-shaped hills, when we sang and wallowed all night and day in caves that smelt like Sunday afternoons in damp front farmhouse parlours, and we chased, with the jawbones of deacons, the English and the bears, before the motor-car, before the wheel, before the duchess-faced horse, when we rode the daft and happy hills bareback, it snowed and it snowed. But here a small boy says: 'It snowed last year, too. I made a snowman and my brother knocked it down and I knocked my brother down and then we had tea.'

'But that was not the same snow,' I say. 'Our snow was not only shaken from whitewash buckets down the sky, it came shawling out of the ground and swam and drifted out of the arms and hands and bodies of the trees; snow grew overnight on the roofs of the houses like a pure and grandfather moss, minutely white-ivied the walls and settled on the postman, opening the gate, like a dumb, numb thunderstorm of white, torn Christmas cards.'

'Were there postmen then, too?'

'With sprinkling eyes and wind-cherried noses, on spread, frozen feet they crunched up to the doors and mittened on them manfully. But all that the children could hear was a ringing of bells.'

'You mean that the postman went rat-a-tat-tat and the doors rang?'

'I mean that the bells that the children could hear were inside them.'

'I only hear thunder sometimes, never bells.'

'There were church bells, too.'

'Inside them?'

'No, no, no, in the bat-black, snow-white belfries, tugged by bishops and storks. And they rang their tidings over the bandaged town, over the frozen foam of the powder and ice-cream hills, over the crackling sea. It seemed that all the churches boomed for joy under my window; and the weathercocks crew for Christmas, on our fence.'

'Get back to the postmen.'

'They were just ordinary postmen, fond of walking and dogs and Christmas and the snow. They knocked on the doors with blue knuckles. . . . '

'Ours has got a black knocker. . . . '

'And then they stood on the white Welcome mat in the little, drifted porches and huffed and puffed, making ghosts with their breath, and jogged from foot to foot like small boys wanting to go out.'

'And then the Presents?'

'And then the Presents, after the Christmas box. And the cold postman, with a rose on his button-nose, tingled down the tea-tray-slithered run of the chilly glinting hill. He went in his ice-bound boots like a man on fishmonger's slabs. He wagged his bag like a frozen camel's hump, dizzily turned the corner on one foot, and, by God, he was gone.'

'Get back to the Presents.'

'There were the Useful Presents: engulfing mufflers of the old coach days, and mittens made for giant sloths; zebra scarfs of a substance like silky gum that could be tug-o'-warred down to the galoshes; blinding tam-o'-shanters like patchwork tea cosies and bunny-suited busbies and balaclavas for victims of head-shrinking tribes; from aunts who always wore wool next to the skin there were moustached and rasping vests that made you wonder why the aunts had any skin left at all; and once I had a little crocheted nose bag from an aunt now, alas, no longer whinnying with us. And pictureless books in which small boys, though warned with quotations not to, *would* skate on Farmer Giles' pond and did and drowned; and books that told me everything about the wasp, except why.'

'Go on to the Useless Presents.'

'Bags of moist and many-coloured jelly babies and a folded flag and a false nose and a tram-conductor's cap and a machine that punched tickets and rang a bell; never a catapult; once, by mistake that no one could explain, a little hatchet; and a celluloid duck that made, when you pressed it, a most unducklike sound, a mewing moo that an ambitious cat might make who wished to be a cow; and a painting book in which I could make the grass, the trees, the sea and the animals any colour I pleased, and still the dazzling sky-blue sheep are grazing in the red field under the rainbow-billed and pea-green birds.

'Harboileds, toffee, fudge and allsorts, crunches, cracknels, humbugs, glaciers, marzipan, and butterwelsh for the Welsh. And troops of bright tin soldiers who, if they could not fight, could always run. And Snakes-and-Families and Happy Ladders. And Easy Hobbi-Games for Little Engineers, complete with instructions.

'Oh, easy for Leonardo! And a whistle to make the dogs bark to wake up the old man next door to make him beat on the wall with his stick to shake our picture off the wall.

'And a packet of cigarettes: you put one in your mouth and you stood at the corner of the street and you waited for hours, in vain, for an old lady to scold you for smoking a cigarette, and then with a smirk you ate it. And then it was breakfast under the balloons.'

'Were there Uncles like in our house?'

'There are always Uncles at Christmas.

'The same Uncles. And on Christmas mornings, with dog-disturbing whistle and sugar fags, I would scour the swatched town for the news of the little world, and find always a dead bird by the white Post Office or by the deserted swings; perhaps a robin, all but one of his fires out. Men and women wading or scooping back from chapel, with taproom noses and wind-bussed cheeks, all albinos, huddled their stiff black jarring feathers against the irreligious snow.

'Mistletoe hung from the gas brackets in all the front parlours; there was sherry and walnuts and bottled beer and crackers by the dessertspoons; and cats in their fur-abouts watched the fires; and the high-heaped fire spat, all ready for the chestnuts and the mulling pokers.

'Some few large men sat in the front parlours, without their collars, Uncles almost certainly, trying their new cigars, holding them out judiciously at arms' length, returning them to their mouths, coughing, then holding them out again as though waiting for the explosion; and some few small Aunts, not wanted in the kitchen, nor anywhere else for that matter, sat on the very edges of their chairs, poised and brittle, afraid to break, like faded cups and saucers.'

Not many those mornings trod the piling streets: an old man always, fawn-bowlered, yellow-gloved and, at this time of year, with spats of snow, would take his constitutional to the white bowling green and back, as he would take it wet or fine on Christmas Day or Doomsday; sometimes two hale young men, with big pipes blazing, no overcoats and wind-blown scarfs, would trudge, unspeaking, down to the forlorn sea, to work up an appetite, to blow away the fumes, who knows, to walk into the waves until nothing of them was left but the two curling smoke clouds of their inextinguishable briars. Then I would be slap-dashing home, the gravy smell of the dinners of others, the bird smell, the brandy, the pudding and mince, coiling up to my nostrils, when out of a snow-clogged side lane would come a boy the spit of myself, with a pink-tipped cigarette and the violet past of a black eye, cocky as a bullfinch, leering all to himself.

I hated him on sight and sound, and would be about to put my dog whistle to my lips and blow him off the face of Christmas when suddenly he, with a violet wink, put *his* whistle to *his* lips and blew so stridently, so high, so exquisitely loud, that gobbling faces, their cheeks bulged with goose, would press against their tinselled windows, the whole length of the white echoing street. For dinner we had turkey and blazing pudding, and after dinner the Uncles sat in front of the fire, loosened all buttons, put their large moist hands over their watch chains, groaned a little and slept. Mothers, aunts and sisters scuttled to and fro, bearing tureens. Auntie Bessie, who had already been frightened, twice, by a clock-work mouse, whimpered at the sideboard and had some elderberry wine. The dog was sick. Auntie Dosie had to have three aspirins, but Auntie Hannah, who liked port, stood in the middle of the snowbound back yard, singing like a big-bosomed thrush. I would blow up balloons to see how big they would blow up to; and, when they burst, which they all did, the Uncles jumped and rumbled. In the rich and heavy afternoon, the Uncles breathing like dolphins and the snow descending, I would sit among festoons and Chinese lanterns and nibble dates and try to make a model man-o'-war, following the Instructions for Little Engineers, and produce what might be mistaken for a sea-going tramcar. . . .

Always on Christmas night there was music. An uncle played the fiddle, a cousin sang 'Cherry Ripe', and another uncle sang 'Drake's Drum'. It was very warm in the little house.

Auntie Hannah, who had got on to the parsnip wine, sang a song about Bleeding Hearts and Death, and then another in which she said her heart was like a Bird's Nest; and then everybody laughed again; and then I went to bed. Looking through my bedroom window, out into the moonlight and the unending smoke-coloured snow, I could see the lights in the windows of all the other houses on our hill and hear the music rising from them up the long, steadily falling night. I turned the gas down, I got into bed. I said some words to the close and holy darkness, and then I slept.

from 'A Child's Christmas in Wales'

After the Funeral

(In memory of Ann Jones)[1]

After the funeral, mule praises, brays,
Windshake of sailshaped ears, muffle-toed tap
Tap happily of one peg in the thick
Grave's foot, blinds down the lids, the teeth in black,
The spittled eyes, the salt ponds in the sleeves,
Morning smack of the spade that wakes up sleep,
Shakes a desolate boy who slits his throat
In the dark of the coffin and sheds dry leaves,
That breaks one bone to light with a judgement clout,

[1]Ann Jones (d. 1933), the poet's aunt, who lived at Fern Hill.

After the feast of tear-stuffed time and thistles
In a room with a stuffed fox and a stale fern,
I stand, for this memorial's sake, alone
In the snivelling hours with dead, humped Ann
Whose hooded, fountain heart once fell in puddles
Round the parched worlds of Wales and drowned each sun
(Though this for her is a monstrous image blindly
Magnified out of praise; her death was a still drop;
She would not have me sinking in the holy
Flood of her heart's fame; she would lie dumb and deep
And need no druid of her broken body).
But I, Ann's bard on a raised hearth, call all
The seas to service that her wood-tongued virtue
Babble like a bellbuoy over the hymning heads,
Bow down the walls of the ferned and foxy woods,
That her love sing and swing through a brown chapel,
Bless her bent spirit with four, crossing birds.
Her flesh was meek as milk, but this skyward statue
With the wild breast and blessed and giant skull
Is carved from her in a room with a wet window
In a fiercely mourning house in a crooked year.
I know her scrubbed and sour humble hands
Lie with religion in their cramp, her threadbare
Whisper in a damp word, her wits drilled hollow,
Her fist of a face died clenched on a round pain;
And sculptured Ann is seventy years of stone.
These cloud-sopped, marble hands, this monumental
Argument of the hewn voice, gesture and psalm,
Storm me forever over her grave until
The stuffed lung of the fox twitch and cry Love
And the strutting fern lay seeds on the black sill.

The Outing

The charabanc drew up outside, and when the members of the outing saw my uncle and me squeeze out of the shop together, both of us cat-licked and brushed in our Sunday best, they snarled like a zoo.

'Are you bringing a *boy*?' asked Mr Benjamin Franklyn as we climbed into the charabanc. He looked at me with horror.

'Boys is nasty,' said Mr Weazley.

'He hasn't paid his contributions,' Will Sentry said.

'No room for boys. Boys get sick in charabancs.'

'So do you, Enoch Davies,' said my uncle.

'Might as well bring *women*.'

The way they said it, women were worse than boys.

'Better than bringing grandfathers.'

'Grandfathers is nasty too,' said Mr Weazley.

'What can we do with him when we stop for refreshments?'

'I'm a grandfather,' said Mr Weazley.

'Twenty-six minutes to opening time,' shouted an old man in a panama hat, not looking at a watch. They forgot me at once.

'Good old Mr Cadwalladwr,' they cried, and the charabanc started off down the village street.

A few cold women stood at their doorways, grimly watching us go. A very small boy waved good-bye, and his mother boxed his ears. It was a beautiful August morning.

We were out of the village, and over the bridge, and up the hill towards Steeplehat Wood when Mr Franklyn, with his list of names in his hand, called out loud: 'Where's old O. Jones?'

'Where's old O?'

'We've left old O behind.'

'Can't go without old O.'

And though Mr Weazley hissed all the way, we turned and drove back to the village, where, outside the Prince of Wales, old O. Jones was waiting patiently and alone with a canvas bag.

'I didn't want to come at all,' old O. Jones said as they hoisted him into the charabanc and clapped him on the back and pushed him on a seat and stuck a bottle in his hand, 'but I always go.' And over the bridge and up the hill and under the deep green wood and along the dusty road we wove, slow cows and ducks flying by, until 'Stop the bus!' Mr Weazley cried. 'I left my teeth on the mantelpiece.'

'Never you mind,' they said, 'you're not going to bite nobody,' and they gave him a bottle with a straw.

'I might want to smile,' he said.

'Not you,' they said.

'What's the time, Mr Cadwalladwr?'

'Twelve minutes to go,' shouted back the old man in the panama, and they all began to curse him.

The charabanc pulled up outside the Mountain Sheep, a small, unhappy public-house with a thatched roof like a wig with ringworm. From a flagpole by the Gents fluttered the flag of Siam. I knew it was the flag of Siam because of cigarette cards. The landlord stood at the door to welcome us, simpering like a wolf. He was a long, lean, black-fanged man with a greased love-curl and pouncing eyes. 'What a beautiful August day!' he said, and touched his love-curl with a claw. That was the way he must have welcomed the Mountain Sheep before he ate it, I said to myself. The members rushed out, bleating, and into the bar.

'You keep an eye on the charra,' my uncle said; 'see nobody steals it now.'

'There's nobody to steal it,' I said, 'except some cows,' but my uncle was gustily blowing his bugle in the bar. I looked at the cows opposite, and they looked at me. There was nothing else for us to do. Forty-five minutes passed, like a very slow cloud. The sun shone down on the lonely road, the lost, unwanted boy, and the lake-eyed cows. In the dark bar they were so happy they were breaking glasses. A Shoni-Onion Breton man, with a beret and a necklace of onions, bicyled down the road and stopped at the door.

'Quelle un grand matin, monsieur,' I said.

'There's French, boy bach!' he said.

I followed him down the passage, and peered into the bar. I could hardly recognize the members of the outing. They had all changed colour. Beetroot, rhubarb, and puce, they hollered and rollicked in that dark, damp hole like enormouse ancient bad boys, and my uncle surged in the middle, all red whiskers and bellies. On the floor was broken glass and Mr Weazley.

'Drinks all round,' cried Bob the Fiddle, a small, absconding man with bright blue eyes and a plump smile.

'Who's been robbing the orphans?'

'Who sold his little babby to the gyppoes?'

'Trust old Bob, he'll let you down.'

'You will have your little joke,' said Bob the Fiddle, smiling like a razor, 'but I forgive you, boys.'

Out of the fug and babel I heard: 'Come out and fight.'

'No, not now, later.'

'No, now when I'm in a temper.'

'Look at Will Sentry, he's proper snobbled.'

'Look at his wilful feet.'

'Look at Mr Weazley lording it on the floor.'

Mr Weazley got up, hissing like a gander. 'That boy pushed me down deliberate,' he said, pointing to me at the door, and I slunk away down the passage and out to the mild, good cows. Time clouded over, the cows wondered, I threw a stone at them and they wandered, wondering away. Then out blew my uncle, ballooning, and one by one the members lumbered after him in a grizzle. They had drunk the Mountain Sheep dry. Mr Weazley had won a string of onions that the Shoni-Onion man raffled in the bar. 'What's the good of onions if you left your teeth on the mantelpiece?' he said. And when I looked through the back window of the thundering charabanc, I saw the pub grow smaller in the distance. And the flag of Siam, from the flagpole by the Gents, fluttered now at half mast.

The Blue Bull, the Dragon, the Star of Wales, the Twll in the Wall, the Sour Grapes, the Shepherd's Arms, the Bells of Aberdovey: I had nothing to do in the whole, wild August world but remember the names where the outing stopped and keep an eye on the charabanc. And whenever it passed a public-house, Mr Weazley would cough like a billygoat and cry: 'Stop the bus, I'm dying of breath!' and back we would all have to go.

Closing time meant nothing to the members of that outing. Behind locked doors, they hymned and rumpused all the beautiful afternoon. And, when a policeman entered the Druid's Tap by the back door, and found them all choral with beer, 'Sssh!' said Noah Bowen, 'the pub is shut.'

'Where do you come from?' he said in his buttoned, blue voice.

They told him.

'I got a auntie there,' the policeman said. And very soon he was singing 'Asleep in the Deep.'

Off we drove again at last, the charabanc bouncing with tenors and flagons, and came to a river that rushed along among willows.

'Water!' they shouted.

'Porthcawl!' sang my uncle.

'Where's the donkeys?' said Mr Weazley.

And out they lurched, to paddle and whoop in the cool, white, winding water. Mr Franklyn, trying to polka on the slippery stones, fell in twice. 'Nothing is simple,' he said with dignity as he oozed up the bank.

'It's cold!' they cried.

'It's lovely!'

'It's smooth as a moth's nose!'

'It's *better* than Porthcawl!'

And dusk came down warm and gentle on thirty wild, wet, pickled, splashing men without a care in the world at the end of the world in the west of Wales. And, 'Who goes there?' called Will Sentry to a wild duck flying.

They stopped at the Hermit's Nest for a rum to keep out the cold. 'I played for Aberavon in 1898,' said a stranger to Enoch Davies.

'Liar,' said Enoch Davies.

'I can show you photos,' said the stranger.

'Forged,' said Enoch Davies.

'And I'll show you my cap at home.'

'Stolen.'

'I got friends to prove it,' the stranger said in a fury.

'Bribed,' said Enoch Davies.

On the way home, through the simmering moon-splashed dark, old O. Jones began to cook his supper on a primus stove in the middle of the charabanc. Mr Weazley coughed himself blue in the smoke. 'Stop the bus,' he cried, 'I'm dying of breath!' We all climbed down into the moonlight. There was not a public-house in sight. So they carried out the remaining cases, and the primus stove, and old O. Jones himself, and took them into a field, and sat down in a circle in the field and drank and sang while old O. Jones cooked sausage and mash and the moon flew above us. And there I drifted to sleep against my uncle's mountainous waistcoat, and, as I slept, 'Who goes there?' called out Will Sentry to the flying moon.

from 'A Story'

ANONYMOUS

Lament in Old Age

Before I was crook-backed, I had word-craft:
    My exploits were honoured.
    Argoed's men feasted me always.

Before I was crook-backed, I was bold:
    I was welcomed in the mead-halls
    Of Powys,[1] Wales' paradise.

Before I was crook-backed, I blazed:
    My spear was frontmost, first-piercer.
    I'm hunchbacked, downcast, heavy-hearted.

Wooden crook, here's harvest-time:
    Red the bracken; yellow the grass.
    I've done with what I'm fond of.

Wooden crook, here's winter-time:
    Men are loud over liquor.
    Uncheered is my bedside.

Wooden crook, here is springtime:
    Red cuckoos; bright for banquets.
    Mine no more, love from a maiden.

Wooden crook, here's summer-time:
    Red furrow; furling tendrils.
    I loathe the look of your beak.

Wooden crook, familiar stick,
    Prop up one old and heartsick,
    Llywarch,[2] forever babbling . . .

This leaf, the wind carries it away:
    Ah, sorry its lot.
    It is old; it was born this year.

What I loved as a lad is now my loathing,
    Girl, stranger, untried steed.
    For me they are not fitting.

---

[1]Powys, one of the principal kingdoms of early Wales (now a county).
[2]Llywarch, Llywarch Hen, an old man who is the chief character in a cycle of *englynion* written in the 9th or 10th century.

The four I've ever most hated
Combine forces all at once,
Cough and age, sickness and grief.

I'm old, I'm alone, I'm misshapen, cold,
    Whose bed once was honoured.
I'm grief-struck, I'm bent in three.

I'm old, bent in three, I'm weak and witless.
    I'm sudden, I'm savage.
Those who loved me love me not . . .

Sorry the lot allotted to Llywarch
    On the night of his birth:
Long labour, with no relief.
    from the 'Llywarch Hen Saga' (9th/10th cent.), trans. Joseph P. Clancy

GWYN THOMAS (1913–81)

The Jazz Band

Somewhere outside my window a child is whistling. He is walking fast down the hill and whistling. The tune on his lips is 'Swanee'. I go to the window and watch him. He is moving through a fan of light from a street lamp. His head is thrown back, his lips protrude strongly and his body moves briskly. 'D.I.X.I.–Even Mamee, How I love you, how I love you, my dear old Swanee . . .' The Mississippi and the Taff kiss with dark humming lubricity under an ashen hood of years. Swanee, my dear old Swanee.

The sound of it promotes a roaring life inside my ears. Whenever I hear it, brave ghosts, in endless procession, march again. My eyes are full of the wonder they knew in the months of that long, idle, beautifully lit summer of 1926.[1]

By the beginning of June the hills were bulging with a clearer loveliness than they had ever known before. No smoke rose from the great chimneys to write messages on the sky that puzzled and saddened the minds of the young. The endless journeys of coal trams on the incline, loaded on the upward run, empty and terrifyingly fast on the down, ceased to rattle through the night and mark our dreams. The parade of nailed boots on the pavements at dawn fell silent. Day after glorious day came up over the hills that had been restored by a quirk of social conflict to the calm they lost a hundred years before.

When the school holidays came we took to the mountain tops, joining the liberated pit-ponies among the ferns on the broad plateaux. That was the pic-

---

[1] 1926, the year of the General Strike.

ture for us who were young. For our fathers and mothers there was the inclosing fence of hinted fears, fear of hunger, fear of defeat.

And the, out of the quietness and the golden light, partly to ease their fret, a new excitement was born. The carnivals and the jazz bands.

Rapture can sprout in the oddest places and it certainly sprouted then and there. We formed bands by the dozen, great lumps of beauty and precision, a hundred men and more in each, blowing out their songs as they marched up and down the valleys, amazing and deafening us all. Their instruments were gazookas,[1] with a thunderous bringing up of drums in the rear. Gazookas: small tin zeppelins through which you hummed the tune as loudly as possible. Each band was done up in the uniform of some remote character never before seen in Meadow Prospect. Foreign Legionaries, Chinamen, Carabinieri, Grenadiers, Gauchos, Sultans, Pearl-divers, or what we thought these performers looked like, and there were some very myopic voters among the designers. There was even one group of lads living up on the colder slopes of Mynydd Coch, and eager to put in a word from the world's freezing fringes who did themselves up as Eskimos, but they were liquidated because even Mathew Sewell the Sotto, our leading maestro and musical adviser, could not think up a suitable theme song for boys dressed up as delegates from the Arctic and chronically out of touch with the carnival spirit . . .

At the carnival's end Gomer and Cynlais said we would go back over the mountain path, for the macadamed roads would be too hard after the disappointments of the day. Up the mountain we went. Everything was plain because the moon was full. The path was narrow and we walked single file, women, children, Matadors, Sons of Dixie and Britannias. We reached the mountaintop. We reached the straight green path that leads past Llangysgod on down to Meadow Prospect. And across the lovely deep-ferned plateau we walked slowly, like a little army, most of the men with children hanging on to their arms, the women walking as best they could in the rear. Then they all fell quiet. We stood still, I and two or three others, and watched them pass, listening to the curious quietness that had fallen upon them. Far away we heard a high crazy laugh from Cynlais Coleman, who was trying to comfort Moira Hallam in their defeat. Some kind of sadness seemed to have come down on us. It was not a miserable sadness, for we could all feel some kind of contentment enriching its dark root. It may have been the moon making the mountain seem so secure and serene. We were like an army that had nothing left to cheer about or cry about, not sure if it was advancing or retreating and not caring. We had lost. As we watched the weird disguises, the strange, yet utterly familiar faces, of Britannias, Matadors and Africans, shuffle past, we knew that the bubble of frivolity, blown with such pathetic care, had burst for ever and that new and colder winds of danger would come from all the world's corners to find us on the morrow. But for that moment we were touched by the moon and the magic of longing. We sensed some friendliness and forgiveness

[1]Gazookas, home-made tin instruments which, when hummed into, produced a plaintive, monotonous sound.

in the loved and loving earth we walked on. For minutes the silence must have gone on. Just the sound of many feet swishing through the summer grass. Then somebody started playing a gazooka. The tune he played was one of those sweet, deep things that form as simply as dew upon a mood like ours. It must have been 'All Through the Night' scored for a million talking tears and a basic disbelief in the dawn. It had all the golden softness of an age-long hunger to be at rest. The player, distant from us now, at the head of the long and formless procession, played it very quietly, as if he were thinking rather than playing. Thinking about the night, conflict, beauty, the intricate labour of living and the dark little dish of thinking self in which they were all compounded. Then the others joined in and the children began to sing.

from *Gazooka* (1957)

Over the Mountain

The mind, the body move in shrinking circles. My being has never edged more than a few inscrutable inches from the kitchen of the house where I lived as a boy, a teeming and tempestuous place, cocoon of myths and spinning absurdities. From its seemingly always open door we had a mountain in full view. It was called Arthur's Crown. Once, long ago, we had a sad and noble king called Arthur. This mountain had a sad and noble shape. So we called it Arthur's Crown. It was very beautiful. It was bare except for a fringe of stunted trees across its top, bent and crouched by the winds that blew in from the sea.

I felt sorry for those trees and I was relieved when I climbed the slope for the first time, touched them and found them stronger and happier-looking than they had ever looked from the valley-bed. That mountain became the centre of my heart and imagination. My father often pointed to it. He said that one day he would take us over it.

Beyond the mountain, with its magical velvet paths moving through the high summer ferns, in another valley, there was a town called Mountain Ash. There, said my father, we had a lot of aunts and cousins.

'They are beautiful,' he said, 'those aunts and cousins. As beautiful as that mountain. But shorter, you understand. And they are kind. They have a big house. Tall windows and flowers in them all. They will be waiting for us. They will see us coming down the hillside. They will come out to meet us. They have money. They will give you money.'

That last sentence clinched it. Things were tough. We were even borrowing from the mice. And they were appealing for protection to the International Bank.

A Sunday morning came when my father took us for the first time on the long hill-top walk to Mountain Ash. The path to the mountain-top was steep and treacherous underfoot. My father walked fast. To our small untrained legs the mountain seemed like a wall and we seemed like flies. Short of clutching my father's jacket and boarding him like a bus we could never have kept up.

Fortunately my father knew everyone who passed and talked to them, discussing their problems without being able to do much to solve them.

As we approached the top we were full of a sense of an enchantment about to be revealed, touched, tasted. Enchanted it was. That sea of ferns, endless to the eye of a child. A world of kind and golden light. Larks singing with a force that made it seem they were trying to burst their way into one of the local choirs. And we would sing back at them. Larks and sheep looking so gentle and intelligent one spoke to them and got answers of a kind.

It was and is the land of my emotions. To the north stretch the ranges of mountains that make Wales a land of mysterious and exclusive valleys; to the south the channel that divides us from England, full, as dusk fell, of the winking, tempting lights of ships going to or coming from the great waters of the West.

A dozen times we started on that Sunday walk with my father. But we never got to Mountain Ash. We never got to see those aunts and cousins whose goodness and beauty would have brought new dimensions of joy into our lives.

Halfway across the plateau there is a village called Llanwonno. In the village is a pub called The Tavern of the Fountain. Near the pub was a spring and its water was sweet. This made no appeal to my father. He always considered water-drinking an inferior experience. By the time he got to the village he had developed a thirst it would have taken two fire-brigades to put out. He knew the landlord and landlady of the pub.

Although the pub was officially closed on Sunday my father was always welcomed in, and for three or four hours in the cool, stone-flagged bar he would sip beer and talk to his friends about the people they had known who now rested in the grave-yard just over the road from the pub.

'I can't think of a healthier place to be buried,' my father would say. 'No noise, no smoke, no traffic. A treat.'

As my father drank and chatted the afternoon away, the talk grew less solemn with the passing of every pint, and we heard the gales of laughter come rocking through the pub's closed door. We stayed outside, drinking lemonade and watching the wind make a kind of visual music among the ferns. If it were a day of great heat we would go to the shadowy banks of an ice-cold stream nearby. We would fish and catch nothing. Or we would bathe and catch colds. But even sneezing we never lost the sense of being in an unsmirched paradise.

We never managed to complete the journey to the neighbouring valley, to the big house where the group of fair and benevolent women and maidens would be watching for us in their flowered windows, to accord us a warm and silver welcome. After a session in the pub my father would be too weary even to start the second leg of his journey.

Using my brother and myself as two short crutches he would make his uneven way back to our house. There he would sit by the kitchen window, staring at the lovely mountain, a look of sad remorse on his face, vowing that one day, like a latter-day Moses, he would lead us all the way to that promised land in Mountain Ash where the cousins and aunts would be waiting to usher us into a heaven of affection, a blinding shower of tarts, toffees and threepenny bits. He never did.

I was at the Fountain Inn one evening last summer. Our intention was to cross the plateau all the way to Mountain Ash and fix once and for all the location of that shrine of loveliness that had slipped furtively in and out of my father's talk and dreams so many years ago.

The whole day had been a throne of sweet sensations. The walk over the mountain-top had been exquisite, the air and the grass a matching velvet. We had meat and wine in the dining-room. We were in a fine, rare mood of abdication. We talked of the futility of power and spoke with relish of Edward II who had been betrayed, captured in a dingle nearby and trundled to some English fortress, there to be abominably executed. So we were told by our teacher in the Primary School whose authority was total, and who had compiled a bulging dossier on local treacheries.

Then the inn filled up with a rush. It was a visit by the whole of the Pendyrus Male Voice Choir, singers of matchless passion from the Little Rhondda. There was a pause for a drink of welcome and the pianist struck a rich chord for silence. A quartet of ancients were discussing parliamentary government with such gall the fabric of Westminster must have winced. Alongside them two men were trying to recall the year in which a brilliant black sheep called Caradoc had outsmarted a whole panel of sheep-dogs. It took three more rich chords to make these debators fall still.

The choir roared into a piece about the irrelevance of death and the certain prospect of renewal. They then eased the strain and brought all our doubts back with a very negative item called 'Ten Green Bottles'. Then, the midsummer dusk out-standing, they sang one of the loveliest of the quiet carols. The night put on a cap of gold. I was home, at my earth's warm centre. The scared monkey was back in the branches of his best-loved tree. I've never had any truly passionate wish to be elsewhere.

from *A Few Selected Exits* (1968)

Love in the Terraces

In the Terraces, we never opposed love. The way we viewed this question was that love must be pretty deeply rooted to have gone on for so long. One would have to be very deep to tinker with so deep a root, deeper than we were. Also, love passes on the time. That is a prime feature in any place where there is a scarcity of work for the local men and women to do, a state which prevailed on a high plane indeed during the dark years now being spoken of. Also, love, properly used, keeps people warm. That is a fact of some importance when coal has to be considered as part of the groceries. Also, love possessing the power of making its subjects see things in a clearer light, creates a desire for beauty. This was interesting to us because if there was one thing the Terraces lacked more than any other it was that very beauty.

Our group which met nightly on the wall at the bottom of our backyard was agreed that never had so little beauty been compressed into so large a space as we saw in the Terraces. It was a clumsy bit of packing altogether. We took this in our solemn way to mean that when men consent to endure for too long the sadness of poverty and decline, beauty sees no point in staying, bows its head and goes. There was much poverty in the Terraces, nearly as much as air, weather or life. It achieved a variety of flavours and shapes that did credit to our orginality and patience. Beneath its layers beauty lay in a mess and, no doubt, very dead. Men like artists who gallop after beauty should make a new set of divining rods, find out where hell is and put poverty in. Then beauty, rising like a rainbow from man's new dreams, would be pervasive as the mist of pettiness among us now and would come galloping after them for a change.

Among us, in the Terraces, love sometimes broke out. Love, making people see things in a clearer light, had a depressing effect. The Terraces, seen in a dim light that softened the curves, could give a man a bellyache that nothing short of a hot water bottle atop the belly could ease. Therefore, to see the Terraces in any hard, revelatory light such as would be given off by a kerosene flare or passion, would make the lover wish for the very opposite of the Terraces. That opposite would be beauty. So beneath the dark waters of the stream along whose banks we lived, pinched, scraped and pondered, there would sometimes flash the forms of beauty desired and we got much joy from watching these flashing, brief, uncatchable forms. They were the promise of life in a community that had come as near to a general stoppage of living as any community can come without staging a mass execution.

'But the most important thing about love, though,' said my friend Walter, 'is that it keeps people warm. That's more important even than love considered as a means to breeding to a man who hasn't got the means to go filling his outhouse with coal. To that man, anything that puts him in a position not to care about the state of his outhouse is a very big thing. That's a bigger thing even than man's having been descended from the apes.'

And, with the exception of my friend Ben, who had seen a chimpanzee in Bostock's menagerie and who thought that it was a very great achievement to have worked one's way up from being just an ape, we were all pretty much of this love-is-warmth school of thought for which my friend Walter always took up the tongs. We thought this the more interesting because we ourselves were too old, plain or politically conscious to be in the running for any love that might be knocking about. My friend Walter was a very cold subject except about the brain where he always had a spout of deep ideas that kept his skull warm. My friend Ben was married. My friend Arthur had some stomach trouble that seemed to him to be a fair summing up of all that was wrong with the world, and the viewpoint of my friend Arthur was pretty dark on most topics. There was nothing particularly wrong with me. My stomach was in order. I was single. But women, to me, never seemed to be more than just me all over again. A bit quicker to become mothers, I being a man, and a bit slower to use the vote, but with no more difference than that. We shared the floor space of a zoo and kept the place as tidy as we could during our journey through it. I could never look upon women with the zeal that came so easily to the bulk of my fellow-voters.

This did not prevent us from taking a keen interest in those of our neighbours who were visited by love. Sometimes, the love worked out all wrongly and made a mess of these neighbours, such a mess as caused my friend Walter to say that if men wanted to weep as much as they had good reason to, they would have to carry a tengallon reserve tear tank strapped to their back to be brought into play for special sessions of this weeping business. Sometimes it would make these neighbours slightly dafter than they had been, and this meant that we would be a bit busier than ever going around explaining to these neighbours whose minds had been laid waste in patches by passion, such facts as the rising cost of living and the weaknesses of a competitive society which we thought should rank as high in the consideration of these neighbours as the itch for union of bodies in love. Or, love would leave them as it found them, which did not say much for them or for the brand of love they went in for. Or it would set them alight and the warmth from their burning would be very pleasant to such sad and continually frozen types as ourselves.

from *The Alone to the Alone* (1947)

GWYN THOMAS (1936–)

Horses

Suddenly there were forms there:
Heads bright of eye
Leapt out of the alien dark,
Out of the night into the headlights' gleam.

The twentieth century braked
And in the tousled manes before us
Pieces out of the past were
Gazing at us brightly.

Neighing and snorting nostrils,
Legs teeming with terror;
Scattering then. After the hooves
Stopped threshing the darkness: stillness.

After the nerves of seeing
Stopped twitching with the imprint of the flurry
Of the forms that came before our faces
Like a fist, the light was full of quietness.

Shifting into gear and moving
On a road that wound along the face of the world
In a wide night where time was untied
And let loose in a fearful roaming.

trans. Joseph P. Clancy

An Old Thing

When she came to the bus courtesy stopped
All but the children from turning round
And staring at her, a wreck of a woman,
But everyone noticed.

She is old, but battling the transformation
Called time by a struggle to hide
What is taking place about her bones,
The slackening there and the wizening.

It is hard to believe, but once she was lovely.
Some remember desire spreading in them
Like a rose, a purple wound through their flesh
From a sultry yearning for her thighs.

And now it's come to the point where that feeder
On fevers, he that lives on the sickly warmth of old maladies
And new blood breaking foully out of young veins
Is hesitating to lie with her.

There was life among her years, there was beauty.
It was there, time cannot deny it.
And what remains of the indelible is the vain
Folly of the rouge and the liquid cosmetic.

I'll say that she is brave,
At least that there is more than loathsome old vanity
In the struggle to subvert the colour of the years.
But I was none too pleased, especially in a public place,
To have her sitting beside me the way she was.

trans. Joseph P. Clancy

NED THOMAS (1936–   )
The Black Cloud

'How much longer can it last?' asked the teacher, and we all knew what he was talking about for, with all our differences, the six of us were joined together by the daily and lifelong neurosis of the Welsh language, and it was this, together with the advisers of Her Majesty's Government, that had drawn us together. We had all been nominated to one of those official Welsh committees that does more than its critics will concede but never enough, and which met six times a year in different towns in Wales.

This time we were at a seaside resort in Meirionydd. The meeting was over. Our Secretary had rushed back to be at the Welsh Office the next day. Two other members of the committee were driving south together. Though one of them was a Welsh-speaker, both of these would have found our discussion a strain, for they were relaxed characters, for whom the scene as they drove out along the prom was one of late summer afternoon carelessness. It was approaching the hour of wet towels and fractious children and high tea. Soon the lights would go on in Bellevue and Glan-y-Môr and the last cruise boat would come breasting homewards on a reddish oily swell.

But we were walking along the shore away from the crowds and had spotted the clouds coming up over Cardigan Bay. 'And always the South darkening for rain, and the wind rising,' said the professor, who was sometimes too ready with literary quotation. The beach below us was clear except for one ball-game on the sands. Half a dozen men in black trousers, light shirts and braces, and a dozen assorted children were seemingly dancing around the beach in that light of spectral and immortal sunshine that sometimes precedes night and storm. Portly ladies were coaxing the smallest children with immense gentleness towards the lone white motor-coach: *'Dere, Non fach.'*[1] It was probably a Sunday School trip from Cardiganshire that brought to our ears the first Welsh we had heard that afternoon, in or out of committee.

'I sometimes think,' continued the teacher, 'that we are just cheering ourselves up. Every week we read in our Welsh papers that there's a new Government form in Welsh, that signs are going to be bilingual, that a group of Tibetan immigrants are showing interest in learning Welsh. You know that I am not someone who enjoys being pessimistic. I want people to learn Welsh; and every small linguistic right is worth fighting for. I support *Cymdeithas yr Iaith*[2] and *Plaid Cymru*[3] and *Adfer*.[4] But I also teach in what the Welsh Department of Education calls a "naturally Welsh" primary school. And I don't believe such places exist any more. Only at the level of the smallest

---

[1] *'Dere, Non fach'*, 'Come along, Non dear'.
[2] *Cymdeithas yr Iaith*, the Welsh Language Society.
[3] *Plaid Cymru*, the Welsh Nationalist Party.
[4] *Adfer*, a group calling for the establishment of officially designated Welsh-speaking districts in west and north Wales.

hamlet in Wales will you find today a unit that lives wholly and naturally in Welsh, at least when not watching television, or reading the local paper. I don't even give these communities more than ten years as things are going. Farms change hands at prices no local people can afford, houses become holiday cottages, and the councils are usually so slow and blind and led by the supposed expertise of outsiders, that they actually help these processes along. Do you find any Welsh secondary schools in really Welsh-speaking areas? No, it only happens when an area has become so anglicized that a special option for a few parents cannot possibly affect the basic Englishness of the community.

'You know that line in one of Dafydd Iwan's[1] songs: "*Dyw'r werin ddim digon o ddynion, bois*"?[2] As an objective statement of the condition of ordinary people in the Welsh-speaking areas, it's terribly true. Down the centuries they've seen the Welsh language and themselves beaten every time they raised their heads, so that they've almost forgotten what it is to win ground. But the line also sounds like a moral judgement on them, and *there* it is terribly unfair, because it is always up to educated and privileged people to show ordinary people that they can win. And now we come to the terrible weakness of our position. So many of the educated professional Welsh-speakers are down in the anglicized South running television and the national institutions, busy converting the English-speaking population to take up Welsh at least as a hobby, establishing Welsh schools where the children play in English in the yard. If we had all the time in the world I'd say, "You get on with the work there, and we'll get on with it here and we'll end up with one Welsh Wales." But can't they see that when the last geographically concentrated Welsh-speaking communities go, all the learners and bilingual secondary schools in Glamorganshire won't keep Welsh going? When I speak to people down there I sometimes think they don't know what is happening to the Welsh-speaking areas. They think we are there like mountains securing their retreat. But it seems more likely to me that we are going to die separate deaths. Those of us in the Welsh-speaking countryside will end up as a few half-crazed individuals speaking Welsh to our dogs and English to everyone else, the very opposite of what our grandfathers did, while the steel ribbon of cars winds down the valleys to the marinas and chalet-villages where Welsh will be in evidence all over the place, mis-spelt and misused. It's happening already. Somebody put it well the other day: "More and more Welsh signs lead to fewer and fewer Welsh places".'

'Meanwhile down in Cardiff they are going to end up like the Parsees, sending their children to the same schools, marrying each other, speaking Welsh on certain circuits, among people with certain middle-class mores, and if you stray out of the fold, bang! you are into English.

'But you can't say this to people and get through to them because what you are really saying is, "Give up your job and come back and live in the Welsh areas at half your salary or on the dole." And who are we to say it, we who

---

[1]Dafydd Iwan (1943-   ), folk-singer.
[2]"*Dyw'r werin . . .*', 'The common people are not men enough, lads'.

already have the few teaching and other professional jobs in these areas. Do you know, I sometimes think that if every Welsh-speaking child decided to go on the dole when he left school until he got work in his own area, we'd have a really Welsh-speaking community here—of sorts. But "getting on" is so built in to our culture.'

The black cloud had moved in over the bay and we all felt the strength of the teacher's melancholia which expressed itself not just in the words he said, but in their cadence, in the suffering deepset eyes, the white hair and bony expressive hands. He was much more completely Welsh than the rest of us – one of us had learned our language and another had only a residual grasp – and if *he* was so hopeless, where should the rest of us find strength? So many of us have a myth of someone or somewhere that is really and truly Welsh that it comes as a shock to find that there is no firm ground. Perhaps the myth has to be shattered before we can understand that everything depends on each one of us, all the time.

from 'Six Characters in Search of Tomorrow', *The Welsh Language Today* (ed. Meic Stephens, 1973)

R.S. THOMAS (1913–   )

The Welsh Hill Country

Too far for you to see
The fluke and the foot-rot and the fat maggot
Gnawing the skin from the small bones,
The sheep are grazing at Bwlch-y-Fedwen,
Arranged romantically in the usual manner
On a bleak background of bald stone.

Too far for you to see
The moss and the mould on the cold chimneys,
The nettles growing through the cracked doors,
The houses stand empty at Nant-yr-Eira,
There are holes in the roofs that are thatched with sunlight,
And the fields are reverting to the bare moor.

Too far, too far to see
The set of his eyes and the slow phthisis
Wasting his frame under the ripped coat,
There's a man still farming at Ty'n-y-Fawnog,
Contributing grimly to the accepted pattern,
The embryo music dead in his throat.

A Blackbird Singing

It seems wrong that out of this bird,
Black, bold, a suggestion of dark
Places about it, there yet should come
Such rich music, as though the notes'
Ore were changed to a rare metal
At one touch of that bright bill.

You have heard it often, alone at your desk
In a green April, your mind drawn
Away from its work by sweet disturbance
Of the mild evening outside your room.

A slow singer, but loading each phrase
With history's overtones, love, joy
And grief learned by his dark tribe
In other orchards and passed on
Instinctively as they are now,
But fresh always with new tears.

Welsh History

We were a people taut for war; the hills
Were no harder, the thin grass
Clothed them more warmly than the coarse
Shirts our small bones.
We fought, and were always in retreat,
Like snow thawing upon the slopes
Of Mynydd Mawr; and yet the stranger
Never found our ultimate stand
In the thick woods, declaiming verse
To the sharp prompting of the harp.

Our kings died, or they were slain
By the old treachery at the ford.
Our bards perished, driven from the halls
Of nobles by the thorn and bramble.

We were a people bred on legends,
Warming our hands at the red past.
The great were ashamed of our loose rags
Clinging stubbornly to the proud tree
Of blood and birth, our lean bellies
And mud houses were a proof
Of our ineptitude for life.

We were a people wasting ourselves
In fruitless battles for our masters,
In lands to which we had no claim,
With men for whom we felt no hatred.

We were a people, and are so yet.
When we have finished quarrelling for crumbs
Under the table, or gnawing the bones
Of a dead culture, we will arise,
Armed, but not in the old way.

Kneeling

Moments of great calm,
Kneeling before an altar
Of wood in a stone church
In summer, waiting for the God
To speak; the air a staircase
For silence; the sun's light
Ringing me, as though I acted
A great rôle. And the audiences
Still; all that close throng
Of spirits waiting, as I,
For the message.
                Prompt me, God;
But not yet. When I speak,
Though it be you who speak
Through me, something is lost.
The meaning is in the waiting.

THOMAS JACOB THOMAS (SARNICOL; 1873–1945)

Dic Siôn Dafydd

He scorned his land, his tongue denied;
Nor Welsh nor English, lived and died
A bastard mule—he made his own
Each mulish fault, save one alone:
Dic somehow got, that prince of fools,
A vast vile progeny of mules.

trans. H. Idris Bell

JOHN TRIPP (1927–86)

Diesel To Yesterday

There is downpour, always,
   as the carriages inch into Newport:
perhaps six times in ten years
   of a hundred visits to custom,
the entry to my country is uncurtained
   by rain or mist. I look
at the shambles of sidings and streets,
   the rust of progress and freight wagons,
the cracked façade of bingo cinemas.
   Sometimes I expect to see
the callous peaked caps and buttons
   of visa-checkers, cold sentries
on a foreign border, keeping out the bacillus
   in hammering rain and swirling fog.
Often I wish it were so, this frontier sealed
   at Chepstow, against frivolous incursion
from the tainting eastern zones.

Patience vanishes with frayed goodwill
   at the sight of the plump bundles
tumbling into Wales.
   They bring only their banknotes
and a petrol-stenched lust for scenery
   to shut in their kodaks,
packing out the albums of Jersey
   and the anthill beaches of the south.
They stand in line for pre-heated grease
   in the slums of crumbled resorts,
nose their long cars into pastureland
   and the hearts of ancient townships
that now are buried under chromium plate.

I catch myself out in error, feel
   ignoble in disdain.
The bad smell at my nostril
   is some odour from myself –
a modern who reeks of the museum,
   not wanting his own closed yesterday
but the day before that,
   the lost day before dignity went,
when all our borders were sealed.

Separation

But this night is the same
as any other night. The clocks bang.
It will pass like other nights,
while the squirrel twitches in his sleep,
the farmer sags bone-weary to his cot.

I will watch another sunset, clear and tangerine,
as cattle trail to their barns,
another dawn break through the west.
Somewhere the fox will stir in his loneliness,
a fieldmouse camp in an ancient boot.

If only we had been a simpler pair,
engaged in piecemeal tasks
on some outlying croft,
instead of the busy unimportant ones
everyone told us were correct.

Days will melt into days
when not even the shape of your hands
will be remembered,
not even the curve of the mouth
or the quiet sentences of disgust.

The lady in the shop still has her gout,
the neighbour hoses and hoses his car,
the tits land on the milk-tops,
the baker delivers one Hovis and sliced.
Calamity on the radio does not touch us.

So I shall wait for more trains,
move from this point to that,
write you a last line about property.
I will observe it all as before
and wish we'd been simpler as the nights close in.

ANONYMOUS

The Death of Saint David [1]

And after he had bestowed his blessing on all, he spoke these words: 'Noble brothers and sisters, be glad, and guard your faith and religion, and do the little things which you have heard from me, and which I have shown you. And I shall go the way which our fathers go. And fare you well,' said David, 'and may your conduct be steadfast on the earth. For we shall never meet here again.' And then was heard a cry arising from all, a wail and lamentation and weeping, and people exclaiming 'Woe to us that the earth does not swallow us, that fire does not burn us, would that God would raise the sea over the land, and cause the mountains to fall on us,' and almost all that were present were near unto death. From the Sunday to the Wednesday after David's death they took no meat or drink, but prayed piteously. And Tuesday night, close on cock-crow, lo, a host of angels filled the city, and all places in the city were filled with song and joy. And in the morning hour, behold, Jesus Christ came, accompanied by the nine orders of heavenly beings, as when He is surrounded by them in majesty. And the brilliant sun shone over the whole host. And that Tuesday the first day of March, Jesus Christ bore away David's soul in great triumph and gladness and honour. After his hunger, his thirst, and cold, and his labours, his abstinence and his acts of charity, and his weariness, and his tribulation, and his afflictions, and his anxiety for the world, the angels received his soul, and they bore it to a place where the light does not fail, and there is rest without labour, and joy without sadness, an abundance of all good things, and victory, and brilliance, and beauty; where Christ's champions are commended, and the undeserving rich are ignored, where there is health without sickness, youth without old age, peace without dissension, glory without vain ostentation, songs that do not pall, and rewards without end. . . .

from *The Book of the Anchorite of Llanddewibrefi* (1346), trans. D.M. Lloyd

ALED VAUGHAN (1920–   )

The White Dove

It was a Saturday, always in that age gone by a magic day. No school, the whole countryside to roam in, my secret self the captain of the top-of-the league football team, scoring all the goals and leaving every man on the field breathless with my dash and skill. Or perhaps I was the last of the Welsh Kings, alone on a moonlit moor after a fierce battle with the English, and striding the heather savagely as I planned a campaign that would crush the

[1] David, Dewi Sant (6th cent.), the patron saint of Wales.

enemy into powder. My faithful followers would carry me shoulder high, victorious through the village; in passing I would knock the spotless black bowler off Evans the schoolmaster's head, knock it into the mud because the week before he had given me six canes for uprooting two of the best school apple-trees to make stilts.

But that day, that hour, I was playing with my best friend, Emyr, in the stackyard at home. Emyr wasn't there, but I had to have him with me because it was a competition to see who would be the first to hit the empty salmon tin stuck on top of the garden fence. Emyr was my left hand and had six stones; I was my right hand, and I too had six stones – except when I was losing, and then I would look up at the sky and sneak an extra one. I was winning most of the time because I'm a right-handed person.

'A wonderful aimer you are!' I made Emyr say. 'Four times you've hit it! And only once have I got it.'

'I practise almost every night,' I answered modestly.

'So do I,' Emyr admitted.

There was nothing else I could say. I shrugged my shoulders and smiled shyly. Then I hit the tin twice running. My heart trembled in my throat.

It was a grey afternoon. Black clouds dragged across the valley, so low that they just missed our chimney that had a slate on top to stop the wind turning the smoke back. The sky was wide and flat. The mountains were covered. In the fields the green grass had been washed with soot, and the trees were strange animals with bare and dry horns stabbing the sky. The two or three withered leaves clinging crisply to them were sensitive ears. Everywhere was like the picture of the Great War in the classroom, the picture that made me sweat and crumble inside every time I looked at it. Horses, men, guns and bayonets were plastered across one another on a canvas of blood and flame.

There was an emptiness on my left side. Emyr had gone. The salmon tin was the helmet of a German as he peeped over the edge of a trench, and I was a French Field-Marshal throwing cannon balls at him.

I had hit him three times without killing him, and I knew I was getting tired of being a French Field-Marshal, when a white dove came curving swiftly and silently out of the black clouds. It made three smooth circles round the stackyard and then, with a little flutter, it settled on the high rib of our barn roof.

I was transformed. I was no longer myself, a boy with two arms, two legs, and a face. I was the earth, everyone, everywhere, and I drifted silently around the barn, my eyes always on the white dove. It stood delicately on the roof, carved in snowflakes, a dazzling light that made a joke of the sombre world. Its small unblemished breast rose and fell evenly in confident challenge to the threatening sky. Time had gone, and I was standing in the centre of eternity.

A howling gust of wind rode menacingly across the black and grey countryside. It struck cruelly at the side of the dove. The white form lost its grace; wings screamed, and feathers were chaotic with fright. My omniscience shrivelled; I was aware again of the sombreness of the afternoon.

The bird regained its dazzling beauty, but my peace was destroyed. Time was back, pressing callously. I was now full of a trembling desire to hold the dove safely in my hands. Before peace could return I would have to possess it, to protect it, to have it with me always. I ran to the cart shed and my eagerness gave me strength to carry the long ladder which I placed against the barn wall. When I reached the roof the dove was still there, almost within reach. My joy was back; but not calm and strong as before. I climbed higher to balance precariously on the top stave, my knees pressed against the hard tile coping of the roof. But I was beyond the vicious hand of danger: the dove had exterminated it. Making endearing noises my tongue had never discovered before I pushed my hand along the cold slates. The bird turned its head, and examined my crawling fingers with round flat eyes the colour of new pennies. And then, just as I was about to touch it, it fluttered gently, swooped above the sloping roof, and flew straight through the open doorway of the cart shed. I clutched at the slates. They had suddenly become the jagged teeth of danger grinning at me. I descended the ladder with painful care.

In the enclosed shed the dove had perched itself on a high rafter, and as I closed the giant doors to trap it I knew I was bordering on evil.

With ancient cunning I examined every possible way of reaching the bird. But it was up beyond anything I could climb, and I knew the ladder was too long to stand upright in the shed. Then the evil gripped me completely, and I relished it. Outside, after making sure that no one was looking, I helped myself to a pocketful of stones. I returned, fastened the doors, and took aim. The first stone missed. It exploded against the galvanized roof, and the dove inclined its head towards the noise, asking a silent question. But the second stone struck home and my prey threw itself helplessly against its harsh prison wall. I was jubilant. But there was something terrifying about the way the bird had not uttered a sound when the stone violated it. I struck again, and in a hysterical attempt to escape the dove crashed into a steel girder. As it fell into my waiting arms its wings thrashed ecstatically.

And oh, the searing joy of holding it, of feeling its softly curving feather-covered body filling the hollows of my hands! Its heart ticked sharply against my palms as if the life of it were thrusting itself forward to communicate and immerse itself in mine. And it succeeded in its quest, for at that moment I was as one with the dove, a white flash of happiness, free to fly over the cumbersome world to explore the smooth sky. The evil had never been. 'Oh my lovely, lovely, lovely dove!' I crooned. 'My beautiful white dove!'

I carried it out of the prison. The moment it saw the sky and fields it tried to escape. It struggled in my hands and its startled eyes blinked with alarm. I shrank with unhappiness. It didn't want me, didn't understand me. 'I won't hurt you!' I sobbed, holding it directly in front of me so that it could understand by the look on my face. 'I won't hurt you! I'll be your greatest friend! I'll spend every evening and all Saturday and Sunday feeding you!'

It struggled again, and I had to hold it firmly. Everything was confused because I didn't want to force it to do anything against its will, and yet I wanted to keep it. After it had settled and I was thinking it had understood I wanted to be its friend, its beak opened and a small ball of blood rolled off its creamy tongue and broke on the back of my hand. Stunned, I watched it trickling warmly down to my wrist. Then came a terrible remorse. 'Forgive me! Forgive me!' I cried, holding its warm body firmly to my breast. 'I didn't mean to hurt you! I only wanted to be your friend! Will you forgive me? Am I forgiven?' I held it away from me and opened my hands, hoping that if I were to offer it its freedom my crime would be redeemed, and that if it didn't fly away it would be proof that it had forgiven me. But my fingers had scarcely broken away from the feathers when the wings opened and without a sound its white form streaked through the air and climbed towards the black clouds. It vanished.

The world was now an endless cave and I was alone, lost, as lonely as the sea on a stormy night. My heart could hold no more and I wept as I ran towards the grey house.

HENRY VAUGHAN (1621–95)

They are all Gone into the World of Light!

They are all gone into the world of light!
    And I alone sit lingring here;
Their very memory is fair and bright,
    And my sad thoughts doth clear.

It glows and glitters in my cloudy brest
    Like stars upon some gloomy grove,
Or those faint beams in which this hill is drest,
    After the Sun's remove.

I see them walking in an Air of glory,
    Whose light doth trample on my days:
My days, which are at best but dull and hoary,
    Mere glimmering and decays.

O holy hope! and high humility,
    High as the Heavens above!
These are your walks, and you have shew'd them me
    To kindle my cold love.

Dear, beauteous death! the Jewel of the Just,
    Shining nowhere, but in the dark;
What mysteries do lie beyond thy dust;
    Could man outlook that mark!

He that hath found some fledg'd bird's nest, may know
  At first sight, if the bird be flown;
But what fair Well, or Grove he sings in now,
  That is to him unknown.

And yet, as Angels in some brighter dreams
  Call to the soul, when man doth sleep:
So some strange thoughts transcend our wonted theams,
  And into glory peep.

If a star were confin'd into a Tomb
  Her captive flames must needs burn there;
But when the hand that lockt her up, gives room,
  She'll shine through all the sphære.

O Father of eternal life, and all
  Created glories under thee!
Resume thy spirit from this world of thrall
  Into true liberty.

Either disperse these mists, which blot and fill
  My perspective (still) as they pass,
Or else remove me hence unto that hill,
  Where I shall need no glass.

Peace

My Soul, there is a Countrie
  Far beyond the stars,
Where stands a winged Centrie
  All skilfull in the wars,
There above noise, and danger
  Sweet peace sits crown'd with smiles,
And one born in a Manger
  Commands the Beauteous files,
He is thy gracious friend,
  And (O my Soul awake!)
Did in pure love descend
  To die here for thy sake,
If thou canst get but thither,
  There growes the flowre of peace,
The Rose that cannot wither,
  Thy fortresse, and thy ease;
Leave then thy foolish ranges;
  For none can thee secure,
But one, who never changes,
  Thy God, thy life, thy Cure.

HILDA VAUGHAN (1892–1985)

Megan Lloyd

To her neighbours she was known as Megan Lloyd. In my memory she lives as Saint Anne. Years after I had lost her, I was wandering through the Louvre, and came upon the picture attributed to Leonardo. I stood before it, happy; and my eyes filled with tears. Megan Lloyd, when I knew her, was older than this wise and gracious mother of the Virgin. Her hair was white as lamb's wool; her face, like a stored apple, seamed with fine wrinkles. Yet there was her familiar smile, full of tenderness and understanding. She is in my mind now, seated, like Leonardo's homely saint, in the open. Often I saw her moving about the farmhouse kitchen, or sitting beside the whitewashed hearth, her fingers, as she stooped to warm them, cornelian red in the glow of a peat fire. Sometimes she had a grandchild in her lap, and another in the cradle that her foot was rocking with slow rhythm. But I remember her best as I saw her often during my last summer in Wales, out of doors, her faded lips parted a little to the hill wind. She sat on an oaken chair upon the stretch of sward surrounding Cwmbach homestead, where hissing geese paddled to and fro, bobbing their heads on long necks. From the neighbouring buildings, white as mushrooms in the green landscape, came the cheerful noises of a farmyard and a house full of lusty children. Her eldest son, dark and dour, clothed in earth-brown corduroys, her busy shrill daughter-in-law, her tribe of swarthy grandchildren, to me were present only as a background to Saint Anne. They and their home were like the walled towns, the cavalcades of horsemen, the plumed trees, behind the central figure of the Madonna in some fifteenth-century altar piece. They had no connection with my tranquil saint. Their toil and clatter, their laughter, quarrelling and crying did not disturb us, who were the only two human beings of leisure in the countryside. I was idle and self-tortured throughout that long hot summer. The harsh gales of spring were raging through my mind, unemployed and as yet empty of experience. She was profoundly calm; serene as an autumn evening after a tempestuous day, when the wind has fallen and the dead leaves lie still. It was with difficulty that she dragged herself abroad. Her fingers were twisted with rheumatism; she could no longer work. She could not even see to read her Bible. So, during these last months of her life, she sat, content to wait for death, with hands folded, while she watched the shadows of the hills on either side of Cwmbach as they stole across the narrow valley. The shade of the eastern hill dwindled behind the house as the sun reached its zenith; that of the western hill advanced when the sun began to sink. Little Cwmbach was so strait that only for an hour at noon was its whole width lit by sunshine. The mountains rose like walls on either side, shutting out the world. Down in the dingle lay the solitary farm and a stern chapel, square and grey, with the caretaker's cottage clinging to its side, as a white shell to a strong rock. An angry stream, hurling itself against boulders, foamed between these two dwelling places, and a thin ribbon of road wound its empty length up over the pass, where the hills converged. Day after day I climbed across a waste of heather, moss and bog, and, scrambling down the channel of a waterfall, flung myself at Saint Anne's feet. I was eighteen. The universe to me was the stage upon which my own tragedy was being acted. I talked by the hour about myself and my important emotions. She listened with inexhaustible patience. When I told her that no one had ever loved or suffered as I did, she smiled, not with derision, but sadly, as one who knew better. If I looked up at her and found her smiling in that fashion, I fell silent. Then, after a while, she would begin to talk. It was thus I came to know her lover, her husband and her child. Her words were few, but they had magic to conjure up the dead. I knew so well their looks, their manner of speech, their gestures; it is hard to believe that never in my life did I see them, save through her eyes, or hear their voices except as an echo in her memory.

from *A Thing of Nought* (1934)

RICHARD VAUGHAN (1904–83)

A Country Wedding[1]

I turned to have a last look at the old place as Justin and I drove out of the yard. The morning sun struck full on the front of the house. The sycamore threw its large-leafed shadows over the flagstones and the cropped green in front of the parlour window; and as I sat there in the cart while Justin got down to close the yard gate, I felt a great love well up inside me. In a way I was saying goodbye to something, though in every splash of sunlight and behind every blue shadow there trembled the half-glimpsed impression of Grett's face. And it was back here for a week or a fortnight that I was bringing my bride. Grett Ellis was coming home to us, the Peeles of Trewern ...

I noticed every tree, every flower, every blade of grass that morning. The dew was webbed on the bramble bushes, and the blackberries were blue and shiny. Justin was starched and brushed up to his ears. He had done his best to curl the brim of his bowler back into shape. It had never been the same since the night he had fallen off the cob. Despite his efforts, it still gave him a rakish, shonny-like air, the brim coming down flatter than it should over his left temple. We both had a red clove in our buttonholes and our shirt cuffs were like snow around our red wrists.

We waited some minutes below the Allt so that father and mother could lead the way into the village. It was not long before we heard the crunch of the wheels coming down the red road. Father and mother sat stiffly side by side.

[1]The background to the wedding is a long-standing feud between the bridegroom's family, the Peeles of Trewern, and the Ellises, the family of the bride.

Mother was in a black silk dress and wore a hat trimmed with a thin white band around it. Her lace gloves came up over her wrists, and she carried a large bunch of late roses, carnations and chrysanthemums in her lap. As was customary with father, he was carefully dressed and well-groomed. There wasn't a speck of dust or dandruff on the shoulders of his square-shouldered black coat. His collar was snow-white (mother had ironed all our collars and cuffs the night before and had strung them along the brass rod underneath the mantelpiece until the morning) and his large black stock with its gold horseshoe served only to accentuate its glazed whiteness and the smooth texture of his chin above it. The trap gleamed in the sun, the yellow spokes of the wheels and the shining brass on the harness caught the beams that slanted through the hedge. Suspended by its curved handle over the back of the seat was his silver-mounted walking-stick. Daniel Peele of Trewern was going to his son's wedding in style anyway!

Everyone was out in the village to meet us. Waiting at the cross-roads were Lewsin, Elias the Carpenter and old Howells. We adjusted the seat for them to ride behind father and mother.

Then, as we set off again, I nearly jumped out of my skin as a volley of fowling-pieces sounded from behind the hedge. So I was having a good send-off from the village. Everyone who had a gun was carrying it; and there, stretched across the road, was the rope to impede our progress to the church. Father nodded his approval at this: it was part of the traditional ritual of the parish. Justin and I had to unhitch the rope and it was some minutes before we were on our way again . . .

From time to time I kept thinking of Grett's family. Would they dare at the last minute to keep Grett from coming and make us the laughing-stock of the parish?

'Don't worry,' Justin assured me. 'They wouldn't dare. And, remember, for all they know – they've only got Grett's word for it – she might be in the family way. They daren't risk it, Ned.'

There were a score or more traps outside the church when we came up. Justin tapped out his pipe on his heel.

'A good crowd,' he said. 'There's Moc over there. Duw Mawr![1] Look at that white chrysanthemum he's wearing! And there's Llew and Dic from Brynamman . . . Don't forget, Ned, we are all with you!'

I followed Justin through the kissing-gates and into the porch. There were smiles everywhere for me. I had one look round before going in. Then, with the eternal blue of the Van Rocks and the dazzle of the sun for ever imprinted on my eyes, I followed Justin up the shadowy aisle.

The sun streamed through the stained glass, and the altar-cloth seemed woven of divine blue, red, and gold, and other half-tones. Vases of flowers had been placed in the windows. Anne Lewis was in her seat at the organ, and I could hear people walking into the church behind me . . .

[1] *Duw Mawr!* Great God!

Justin took out his watch and showed me the time. It was not quite eleven. I could hear the whispering behind me, and a bird outside sang as if it hadn't a care in the world. My legs trembled, and every now and again I had to wipe the palms of my hands. Then, suddenly but quietly, here was the vicar with his white surplice freshly washed and ironed for the occasion, and with his book in his hand, coming up to the altar. He gave a nod to Anne Lewis, and as she started to play the congregation rose to its feet.

I stood up, Justin beside me, and saw Grett coming up the aisle on her father's arm. Behind them came her mother and Jeff. All I saw in that moment was that Grett was in a white frock and that she carried a mass of flowers in her hands. The whole family sat in the stalls facing father and mother. The vicar waited until the organ stopped, then he beckoned me out to the aisle. It was then that I saw Grett face to face. She was a little pale, her dark hair just showing under the large brim of her yellow hat. Where or when she had bought her white frock and hat, I had no idea; all I knew was that I had never seen her so lovely. Her eyes held me for a moment and I was suddenly aware that all the nervousness had left me.

Together we knelt on the red carpet in front of the altar. I tried hard to photograph everything around me on my mind. Yet, try as I would, it was only the small, insignificant things that I saw: the flannel sleeves of the vicar protruding under his coat-sleeves giving the lie to his white collar and surplice; the gold candle-sticks flashing where the sun caught their bevelled edges . . . Then there was a shuffling of feet as some latecomer pushed into a pew, someone coughed, and a fly buzzed against the closed window.

The minutes passed. I heard myself repeating the words after the vicar, a note of exultation creeping into my voice. Then Grett's voice came to me, and I was proud that the whole parish was there to hear the words she said. The vicar gave us every help, whispering to each of us as our turn came to repeat after him. In answer to his question as to who was giving Grett away, a silence fell on us all as John Ellis stepped forward and gave her to me. Then followed my avowed troth to Grett Ellis, and as I heard her say that she, Margaretta Anne, did take me to be her husband, I fought hard with myself to restrain the happy sob that rose in my throat, and only its mist touched my eyes. I felt Grett tremble a little and put my arm round her to give her strength.

Justin was ready with the ring, and as I placed it on Grett's finger her eyes held me with all the passion and courage that was in her nature . . .

The service over, the vicar led the way to the vestry. I did not kiss Grett, knowing that she did not expect me to do so in front of such a large crowd. Mother, however, put her arms around her and kissed her cheek; father shook hands with her. The Ellises did nothing. Mrs Ellis stood behind Jeff and her husband, crying quietly into her handkerchief.

The vicar made the entry in the church register in his beautiful small hand, and then handed the pen to Grett and to myself.

He looked at father.

'You'll witness it, Daniel Peele, just there. Put your name there.'

Father examined the broad relief critically and removed a minute hair from it. That done, he wrote his name carefully in his copperplate.

There was a half-challenge in the vicar's voice as he turned to John Ellis: 'Now, John Ellis, you sign here!'

Grett's father took the pen and wrote his name under father's, looping his signature underneath with a flowing line and two little circles which he dotted carefully.

As we walked down the aisle, Anne Lewis played something that was light and gay in six-eight time. Behind Grett and myself came father and mother, John Ellis and Mrs Ellis, with Justin, Jeff, the vicar and others behind them. A stinging hail of rice met us as we came out of the porch into the sunshine. Moc had got hold of the bell rope, and was in his shirt-sleeves pulling and bending for all he was worth.

The people crowded around us. The squire shook my hand and then took off his hat and kissed Grett on her cheek.

'Good luck! Good luck!' he repeated over and over. Then he chuckled and whispered in my ear. 'You have beaten them all, well done!'

Many jokes were levelled at us. Lloyd Parry shouted out that I was pale enough already; Berthlwyd told me to remember that the corn harvest was still to come and put his hand on the small of his back to illustrate his meaning. Grett took all this in good part. She was wise enough not to show any false prudery in front of them, and only when the jokes became a little too broad did she bend her head, raise a protesting hand, and turn aside.

We stood in a half-circle outside the porch waiting for father to give the word to start off. The old man beamed at everyone. He gave the impression that he was the proudest man there.

'Now, vicar,' he said jocularly, 'off with that surplice and into your coat and hat!' He turned to the crowd: 'A welcome to you all at Trewern! Plenty of food and drink for everyone.'

So far Grett's father and his family had not addressed a word to me or Grett. Mrs Ellis was still crying. Jeff stood by her holding his bowler in his hand. Father crossed over to John Ellis. I saw John Ellis shake his head stubbornly.

'But you must,' insisted father. The talking and laughter around us ceased abruptly. Father went on: 'You, Mrs Ellis, and Jeff must come. I won't take no!'

John Ellis looked across at Grett. Then a smile broke on his face and he came over to us and took her arm.

'Well, well! So you are Mrs Peele now!' He turned to me. 'Be good to her,' he said quietly. 'She's got courage. I wish you well!' He turned to Mrs Ellis: 'Come on, Mary; and you Jeff, get the trap ready. We'll go to the breakfast.' . . .

What a journey it was down the breast of the hill to the river and up to the village! Behind us came the traps and the singing of the hymns and old folk-songs. This was something I had never dreamed of – this participation of the parish in my wedding.

At last, the Allt rose into view.

'Home!' I said.

Grett pressed against me, and desire and warmth went coursing through me as she touched me with her knee. She held her gloves in her hand and every now and then I glanced at her ring.

The last half-mile was taken in style. Justin gave the horses their heads and the dust rose behind us. We waited by the yard gate until the others came up.

Father came hurrying up to us and held his arms out to Grett and lifted her down to the ground.

'Welcome!' he said. 'Welcome to Trewern!'

He then helped Grett's mother down and led her to the house.

By this time about a dozen traps were pulled up in the yard. Those on foot were still to come.

'Come upstairs!' Mother took Grett's arm; and so, holding her frock above her ankles, Grett passed over the threshold of my home.

'Food in half an hour!' shouted father. 'We must wait for the rest to come.'

From inside the kitchen came the sound of women's voices, mother fretting and fussing about the food; and there, coming from the barn, was Justin with a four and a half in his arms. He was sweating, and bits of hay clung to his clothes.

'There's four more like this,' he shouted as he passed us, 'and port and rhubarb wine for the ladies.' . . .

Justin need not have taken his boots off to come upstairs that night, for Grett and I were awake. We heard him coming up over the Allt – it was well after two o'clock – but before coming in the yard, he unsaddled the cob and turned her loose in the field behind the barn; then he opened the front door quietly. He crept upstairs, missing the step near the top that always creaked, and went softly past our door. In a minute or so, we heard his bed creak, and then the house was still and quiet again.

Glory to the night and its stillness, to the loveliness it concealed and made more lovely; glory to the rivers of Wales that night so that our blood caught their wild singing and flashing tumult. Glory to the petalled smoothness of a woman's body, glory to her hair that is like silk, to the arms that reach out in the darkness to draw one to her mouth and her kisses; glory to each false dawn that gave us another hour of Eden, to the wakened bird that sang and was silent again because it was still night. Glory to the Van Rocks brooding over the parish; glory to every river and brook whispering their litanies under the soft stars; glory to the corn that awaited our scythes, and to the hay that filled our barns. Glory to all the singers and the choirs, to every hymn and chant caught in the rafters and stones of the old church. Glory for ever and ever to my mother for her quiet sadness and to the old man for his strength and the demon that possessed him at times; glory to Justin for his oaths and the earthy richness of his heart. Glory to the Plough and Orion and the Evening Star and to every pool in Sawdde that caught their gold and held it until the glassy alders came between them and their running mirror. Glory to Dafydd ap Gwilym[1] and his dream of Morfudd's[2] hair and Dyddgu's eyes; glory to Trebor Mai[3] and his moon in the cold waters of Llyn-Caer-Hafnant. Glory to the mill at Brecon, to Dai Probert the boxer, and to Moc Mihartach. And glory, too, to the moment when desire can want no more, when the burning sword is lowered and the night is still and dark and filled with peace. Glory, glory to Grett, and glory to Justin my brother; a Gogoniant yn y goruchaf i'r Tad, ac i'r Mab, ac i'r Ysbryd Glan.[4]

from *Moulded in Earth* (1951)

VERNON WATKINS (1906–67)

Ode to Swansea

Bright town, tossed by waves of time to a hill,
Leaning Ark of the world, dense-windowed, perched
High on the slope of morning,
Taking fire from the kindling East:

Look where merchants, traders, and builders move
Through your streets, while above your chandlers' walls
Herring gulls wheel, and pigeons,
Mocking man and the wheelwright's art.

Prouder cities rise through the haze of time,
Yet, unenvious, all men have found is here.
Here is the loitering marvel
Feeding artists with all they know.

There, where sunlight catches a passing sail,
Stretch your shell-brittle sands where children play,
Shielded from hammering dockyards
Launching strange, equatorial ships.

Would they know you, could the returning ships
Find the pictured bay of the port they left
Changed by a murmuration,
Stained by ores in a nighthawk's wing?

---

[1]Dafydd ap Gwilym (*fl.* 1320-70), poet.
[2]Morfudd . . . Dyddgu, women celebrated by Dafydd ap Gwilym.
[3]Trebor Mai, Robert Williams (1830-77), poet
[4]*a Gogoniant yn y goruchaf . . .*, 'and Glory in the highest to the Father, and to the Son, and to the Holy Spirit'.

Yes. Through changes your myth seems anchored here.
Staked in mud, the forsaken oyster beds
Loom; and the Mumbles lighthouse
Turns through gales like a seabird's egg.

Lundy sets the course of the painted ships.
Fishers dropping nets off the Gower coast
Watch them, where shag and cormorant
Perch like shades on the limestone rocks.

You I know, yet who from a different land
Truly finds the town of a native child
Nurtured under a rainbow,
Pitched at last on Mount Pleasant hill?

Stone-runged streets ascending to that crow's nest
Swinging East and West over Swansea Bay
Guard in their walls Cwmdonkin's
Gates of light for a bell to close.

Praise, but do not disturb, heaven's dreaming man
Not awakened yet from his sleep of wine.
Pray, while the starry midnight
Broods on Singleton's elms and swans.

Returning to Goleufryn

Returning to my grandfather's house, after this exile
From the coracle-river, long left with a coin to be good,
Returning with husks of those venturing ears for food
To lovely Carmarthen, I touch and remember the turnstile
Of this death-bound river. Fresh grass. Here I find that crown
In the shadow of dripping river-wood; then look up to the burning mile
Of windows. It is Goleufryn, the house on the hill;
And picking a child's path in a turn of the Towy I meet the prodigal town.

Sing, little house, clap hands: shut, like a book of the Psalms,
On the leaves and pressed flowers of a journey. All is sunny
In the garden behind you. The soil is alive with blind-petalled blooms
Plundered by bees. Gooseberries and currants are gay
With tranquil, unsettled light. Breathless light begging alms
Of the breathing grasses bent over the river of tombs
Flashes. A salmon has swallowed the tribute-money
Of the path. On the farther bank I see ragged urchins play

With thread and pin. O lead me that I may drown
In those earlier cobbles, reflected; a street that is strewn with palms,
Rustling with blouses and velvet. Yet I alone
By the light in the sunflower deepening, here stand, my eyes cast down
To the footprint of accusations, and hear the faint, leavening
Music of first Welsh words; that gust of plumes
'They shall mount up like eagles', dark-throated assumes,
Cold-sunned, low thunder and gentleness of the authentic Throne.

Yet now I am lost, lost in the water-wound looms
Where brief, square windows break on a garden's decay.
Gold butter is shining, the tablecloth speckled with crumbs.
The kettle throbs. In the calendar harvest is shown,
Standing in sheaves. Which way would I do you wrong?
Low, crumbling doorway of the infirm to the mansions of evening,
And poor, shrunken furrow where the potatoes are sown.
I shall not unnumber one soul I have stood with and known
To regain your stars struck by horses, your sons of God breaking in song.

Peace in the Welsh Hills

Calm is the landscape when the storm has passed,
Brighter the fields, and fresh with fallen rain.
Where gales beat out new colour from the hills
Rivers fly faster, and upon their banks
Birds preen their wings, and irises revive.
Not so the cities burnt alive with fire
Of man's destruction: when their smoke is spent,
No phoenix rises from the ruined walls.

I ponder now the grief of many rooms.
Was it a dream, that age, when fingers found
A satisfaction sleeping in dumb stone,
When walls were built responding to the touch
In whose high gables, in the lengthening days,
Martins would nest? Though crops, though lives, would fail,
Though friends dispersed, unchanged the walls would stay,
And still those wings return to build in Spring.

Here, where the earth is green, where heaven is true
Opening the windows, touched with earliest dawn,
In the first frost of cool September days,
Chrysanthemum weather, presaging great birth,

Who in his heart could murmur or complain:
'The light we look for is not in this land?'
That light is present, and that distant time
Is always here, continually redeemed.

There is a city we must build with joy
Exactly where the fallen city sleeps.
There is one road through village, town and field,
On whose robust foundation Chaucer dreamed
A ride could wed the opposites in man.
There proud walls may endure, and low walls feed
The imagination if they have a vine
Or shadowy barn made rich with gathered corn.

Great mansions fear from their surrounding trees
The invasion of a wintry desolation
Filling their rooms with leaves. And cottages
Bring the sky down as flickering candles do,
Leaning on their own shadows. I have seen
Vases and polished brass reflect black windows
And draw the ceiling down to their vibrations,
Thick, deep, and white-washed, like a bank of snow.

To live entwined in pastoral loveliness
May rest the eyes, throw pictures on the mind,
But most we need a metaphor of stone
Such as those painters had whose mountain-cities
Cast long, low shadows on the Umbrian hills.
There, in some courtyard on the cobbled stone,
A fountain plays, and through a cherub's mouth
Ages are linked by water in the sunlight.

All of good faith that fountain may recall,
Woman, musician, boy, or else a scholar
Reading a Latin book. They seem distinct,
And yet are one, because tranquillity
Affirms the Judgment. So, in these Welsh hills,
I marvel, waking from a dream of stone,
That such a peace surrounds me, while the city
For which all long has never yet been built.

Taliesin[1] in Gower

Late I return, O violent, colossal, reverberant, eavesdropping sea.
My country is here. I am foal and violet. Hawthorn breaks from my hands.
I watch the inquisitive cormorant pry from the praying rock of Pwlldu,
Then skim to the gulls' white colony, to Oxwich's cockle-strewn sands.

I have seen the curlew's triangular print, I know every inch of his way.
I have gone through the door of the foundered ship, I have slept in the winch of
                                                                    the cave
With pine-log and unicorn-spiral shell secreting the colours of day;
I have been taught the script of the stones, and I know the tongue of the wave.

I witness here in a vision the landscape to which I was born,
Three smouldering bushes of willow, like trees of fire, and the course
Of the river under the stones of death, carrying the ear of corn
Withdrawn from the moon-dead chaos of rocks overlooking its secret force.

I see, a marvel in Winter's marshes, the iris break from its sheath
And the dripping branch in the ache of sunrise frost and shadow redeem
With wonder of patient, living leaf, while Winter, season of death,
Rebukes the sun, and grinds out men's groans in the voice of its underground
                                                                    stream.

Yet now my task is to weigh the rocks on the level wings of a bird,
To relate these undulations of time to a kestrel's motionless poise.
I speak, and the soft-running hour-glass answers; the core of the rock is a
                                                                    third:
Landscape survives, and these holy creatures proclaim their regenerate joys.

I know this mighty theatre, my footsole knows it for mine.
I am nearer the rising pewit's call than the shiver of her own wing.
I ascend in the loud waves' thunder, I am under the last of the nine.
In a hundred dramatic shapes I perish, in the last I live and sing.

All that I see with my sea-changed eyes is a vision too great for the brain.
The luminous country of auk and eagle rocks and shivers to earth.
In the hunter's quarry this landscape died; my vision restores it again.
These stones are prayers; every boulder is hung on a breath's miraculous birth.

Gorse breaks on the steep cliff-side, clings earth, in patches blackened for
                                                                    sheep,
For grazing fired; now the fair weather comes to the ravens' pinnacled knoll.
Larks break heaven from the thyme-breathing turf; far under, flying through
                                                                    sleep,
Their black fins cutting the rainbow surf, the porpoises follow the shoal.

[1]Taliesin (*fl.* late 6th cent.), a poet and character in folk-tale.

They are gone where the river runs out, there where the breakers divide
The lacework of Three Cliffs Bay in a music of two seas;
A heron flaps where the sandbank holds a dyke to the twofold tide,
A wave-encircled isthmus of sound which the white bird-parliament flees.

Rhinoceros, bear and reindeer haunt the crawling glaciers of age
Beheld in the eye of the rock, where a javelin'd arm held stiff,
Withdrawn from the vision of flying colours, reveals, like script on a page,
The unpassing moment's arrested glory, a life locked fast in the cliff.

Now let the great rock turn. I am safe with an ear of corn,
A repository of light once plucked, from all men hidden away.
I have passed through a million changes. In a butterfly coracle borne,
My faith surmounting the Titan, I greet the prodigious bay.

I celebrate you, marvellous forms. But first I must cut the wood,
Exactly measure the strings, to make manifest what shall be.
All earth being weighed by an ear of corn, all heaven by a drop of blood.
How shall I loosen this music to the listening, eavesdropping sea?

Anonymous

Pwyll, Prince of Dyfed

Pwyll prince of Dyfed[1] was lord over the seven cantrefs of Dyfed; and once upon a time he was at Arberth, a chief court of his, and it came into his head and heart to go a-hunting. The part of his domain which it pleased him to hunt was Glyn Cuch. And he set out that night from Arberth, and came as far as Pen Llwyn Diarwya, and there he was that night. And on the morrow in the young of the day he arose and came to Glyn Cuch to loose his dogs into the wood. And he sounded his horn and began to muster the hunt, and followed after the dogs and lost his companions; and whilst he was listening to the cry of the pack, he could hear the cry of another pack, but they had not the same cry, and were coming to meet his own pack.

And he could see a clearing in the wood as of a level field, and as his pack reached the edge of the clearing, he could see a stag in front of the other pack. And towards the middle of the clearing, lo, the pack that was pursuing it overtaking it and bringing it to the ground. And then he looked at the colour of the pack, without troubling to look at the stag; and of all the hounds he had seen in the world, he had seen no dogs the same colour as these. The colour that was on them was a brilliant shining white, and their ears red; and as the exceeding whiteness of the dogs glittered, so glittered the exceeding redness of

[1]Dyfed, a region of west Wales (now a county).

their ears. And with that he came to the dogs, and drove away the pack that had killed the stag, and baited his own pack upon the stag.

And whilst he was baiting his dogs he could see a horseman coming after the pack on a big dapple-grey steed, with a hunting horn round his neck, and a garment of brownish-grey stuff about him by way of a hunting garb. And thereupon the horseman drew near him, and spoke to him thus. 'Chieftain,' said he, 'I know who thou art, but I will not greet thee.' 'Why,' said he, 'perhaps thy dignity is such that it should not do so.' 'Faith,' said he, 'it is not the degree of my dignity that keeps me therefrom.' 'Chieftain', he replied, 'what else then?' 'Between me and God,' said he, 'thine own ignorance and discourtesy.' 'What discourtesy, chieftain, hast thou seen in me?' 'Greater discourtesy I have not seen in man,' said he, 'than to drive away the pack that had killed the stag and to bait thine own pack upon it. That,' said he, 'was discourtesy, and though I will not take vengeance upon thee, between me and God,' said he, 'I will do thee dishonour to the value of a hundred stags.' 'Chieftain,' said he, 'if I have done thee wrong, I will redeem thy friendship.' 'How,' he replied, 'wilt thou redeem it?' 'According as thy dignity may be; but I know not who thou art.' 'A crowned king am I in the land whence I come.' 'Lord,' he replied, 'good day to thee, and from what land is it thou comest?' 'From Annwn,'[1] answered he; 'Arawn king of Annwn am I.' 'Lord,' said he, 'how shall I win thy friendship?' 'This is how thou shalt,' he replied. 'There is a man whose domain is opposite to mine for ever warring against me. That is king Hafgan, from Annwn; and by ridding me of his oppression, and that thou easily mayest, thou shalt win my friendship.' 'That will I do,' said he, 'gladly. But show me how I may do it.' 'I will,' said he. 'This is how thou mayest. I will make with thee a strong bond of friendship. This is how I will do it: I will set thee in Annwn in my stead, and the fairest lady thou didst ever see I will set to sleep with thee each night, and my form and semblance upon thee, so that there shall be not a chambermaid, nor an officer, nor any other man that has ever followed me shall know that thou art not I. And that,' said he, 'till the end of a year from tomorrow, and our tryst then in this very place.' 'Aye,' he replied, 'though I be there till the end of the year, what guidance shall I have to find the man thou tellest of?' 'A year from tonight,' said he, 'there is a tryst between him and me, at the ford. And be thou there in my likeness,' said he. 'And one blow only thou art to give him; that he will not survive. And though he ask thee to give him another, give it not, however he entreat thee. For despite aught I might give him, as well as before would he fight with me on the morrow.' 'Aye,' said Pwyll, 'what shall I do with my kingdom?' 'I will bring it about,' said Arawn, 'that there shall be neither man nor woman in thy kingdom shall know that I am not thou; and I shall go in thy stead.' 'Gladly,' said Pwyll, 'and I will be on my way.' 'Without let shall be thy path, and nothing shall impede thee till thou arrive in my domain, and I myself will bring thee on thy way.'

[1] Annwn, the Celtic Otherworld.

He brought him on his way till he saw the court and the dwellings. 'There,' he said, 'the court and the kingdom in thy power. And make for the court. There is none within that will not know thee, and as thou seest the service therein thou wilt know the usage of the court.'

He made for the court. And in the court he could see sleeping-rooms and halls and chambers and the greatest show of buildings any one had ever seen. And he went into the hall to pull off his boots. There came squires and chamberlains to pull them off him, and all as they came saluted him. Two knights came to rid him of his hunting garb and to apparel him in a robe of gold brocaded silk. And the hall was made ready. Here he could see a warband and retinues entering in, and the most comely troop and the best equipped any one had seen, and the queen with them, the fairest woman any one had ever seen, dressed in a robe of shining gold brocaded silk. And thereupon they went to wash and drew near the tables, and they sat in this wise: the queen one side of him, and the earl, as he supposed, the other side.

And he began to converse with the queen. And of all he had ever seen to converse with, she was the most unaffected woman, and the most gracious of disposition and discourse. And they passed their time with meat and drink and song and carousal. Of all the courts he had seen on earth, that was the court best furnished with meat and drink and vessels of gold and royal jewels.

Time came for them to go to sleep, and to sleep they went, he and the queen. The moment they got into bed, he turned his face to the bedside and his back towards her. From then till morning not one word did he speak to her. On the morrow tenderness and amiable discourse was there between them. Whatever affection was between them during the day, not a single night to the year's end was different from what that first night was.

The year he spent in hunting and song and carousal, and affection and discourse with his companions, till the night the encounter should be. On that appointed night, the tryst was as well remembered by the man who dwelt furthest in the whole kingdom as by himself. And he came to the tryst, and the gentles of the kingdom with him. And the moment he came to the ford a horseman arose and spoke thus. 'Gentles,' said he, 'give good heed! It is between the two kings that this meeting is, and that between their two bodies. And each of them is a claimant against the other, and that for land and territory; and each of you may stand aside, and let the fight be between them.'

And thereupon the two kings approached each other towards the middle of the ford for the encounter. And at the first onset the man who was in Arawn's stead struck Hafgan on the centre of his shield's boss, so that it was split in two and all his armour broken, and Hafgan was his arm and his spear's length over his horse's crupper to the ground, with a mortal wound upon him. 'Ha, chieftain,' said Hafgan, 'what right hadst thou to my death? I was bringing no claim against thee; moreover I knew no reason for thee to slay me. But for God's sake,' said he, 'since thou hast begun my death, make an end.' 'Chieftain', he replied, 'I may repent doing that which I have done to thee. Seek who may slay thee: I will not slay thee.' 'My trusty gentles,' said Hafgan, 'bear me hence. My death has been completed. I am in state to maintain you no longer.' 'Gentles mine,' said the man who was in Arawn's stead, 'take guidance, and discover who ought to be my vassals.' 'Lord,' said the gentles, 'all men should be, for there is no king over the whole of Annwn save thee.' 'Aye,' he replied, 'he who comes submissively, it is right that he be received; they that come not humbly, let them be compelled by dint of swords.'

And thereupon he received the homage of the men, and he began to subdue the land, and by mid-day on the morrow the two kingdoms were in his power. And thereupon he made for his trysting-place, and came to Glyn Cuch.

And when he came there, Arawn king of Annwn was there to meet him. Each of them welcomed the other. 'Aye,' said Arawn, 'God repay thee thy friendship. I have heard of it.' 'Aye,' he replied, 'when thou comest thyself to thy country thou wilt see what I have done for thee.' 'What thou hast done for me,' said he, 'may God repay it thee.'

Then Arawn gave to Pwyll prince of Dyfed his proper form and semblance, and he himself took his proper form and semblance; and Arawn set off for his court in Annwn, and he rejoiced to see his retinue and his war-band, for he had not seen them for a year. Yet they for their part had known nothing of his absence and felt no more novelty at his coming than of yore. That day he spent in mirth and merriment, and in sitting and conversing with his wife and gentles. And when it was more timely to seek slumber than to carouse, to sleep they went.

He got into bed, and his wife went to him. The first thing he did was to converse with his wife and indulge in loving pleasure and affection with her. And she had not been used to that for a year, and it was of that she thought. 'Alas, God,' said she, 'what different thought is there in him to-night from what has been since a year from to-night!' And she meditated a long time, and after that meditation he awoke and spoke to her, and a second time, and a third, but no answer thereto did he get from her. 'Why,' he asked, 'dost thou not speak to me?' 'I tell thee,' she said, 'for a year I have not spoken even so much in such a place as this.' 'Why now,' said he, 'we have talked closely together.' 'Shame on me,' said she, 'if since a year from yesternight, from the time we were enfolded in the bedclothes, there has been either delight or converse between us, or thou hast turned thy face towards me, let alone anything that would be more than that between us.' And then he fell a-thinking. 'O lord God,' said he, 'a man steadfast and unswerving of his fellowship did I find for a comrade.' And then he said to his wife, 'Lady,' said he, 'do not blame me. Between me and God,' said he, 'I have neither slept nor lain down with thee since a year from yesternight.' And then he told her the whole of his story. 'By my confession to God,' said she, 'strong hold hadst thou on a comrade, for warding off fleshly temptation and for keeping faith with thee.' 'Lady,' said he, 'that was my thought too when I was silent with thee.' 'Nor was that strange,' she replied.

Pwyll prince of Dyfed came likewise to his domain and land. And he began to inquire of the gentles of the land how his rule had been over them during the past year, compared with what it had been before that. 'Lord,' said they, 'never was thy discernment so marked; never wast thou so lovable a man thyself; never wast thou so free in spending thy goods; never was thy rule better than during this year.' 'Between me and God,' he replied, 'it is proper for you to thank the man who has been with you. And here is the story, even as it was'–and Pwyll related the whole of it. 'Aye, lord,' said they, 'thank God thou hadst that friendship; and the rule we have had that year, surely, thou wilt not withhold from us?' 'I will not, between me and God,' answered Pwyll.

And from that time forth they began to make strong the bond of friendship between them, and each sent the other horses and grey-hounds and hawks and all such treasures as they thought would be pleasing to the heart of either. And by reason of his sojourn that year in Annwn, and his having ruled there so prosperously and united the two kingdoms in one by his valour and his prowess, the name of Pwyll prince of Dyfed fell into disuse, and he was called Pwyll Head of Annwn from that time forth.

from *The Mabinogion* (1948), trans. Gwyn Jones and Thomas Jones

HARRI WEBB (1920–)

Big Night

We started drinking at seven
And went out for a breather at ten,
And all the stars in heaven
Said: *Go back and drink again.*

Orion was furiously winking
As he gave us the green light
So went back in to our drinking
Through the breakneck Brecknock night.

We were singers, strongmen and sages,
We were witty and wise and brave,
And all the ghosts of the ages
Applauded from Crawshay's[1] grave.

The tipsy Taff was bawling
A non-traditional tune
And the owls of Pontsarn were calling
Rude names at the frosty moon,

[1] Crawshay, Richard Thompson Crawshay (1817-79), iron-master, who is buried at Faenor, near Merthyr Tydfil, in a tomb inscribed with the words 'God forgive me'.

And homeward we were staggering
As the Pandy clock struck three
And the stars of the Plough went swaggering
From Vaynor to Pengarnddu.

Thanks in Winter

The day that Eliot died I stood
By Dafydd's[1] grave in Ystrad Fflur,[2]
It was the depth of winter,
A day for an old man to die.
The dark memorial stone,
Chiselled in marble of Latin
And the soft intricate gold
Of the old language
Echoed the weather's colour
A slate vault over Ffair Rhos
Pontrhydfendigaid, Pumlumon,
The sheep runs, the rough pasture
And the lonely whitewashed houses
Scattered like frost, the dwellings
Of country poets, last inheritors
To the prince of song who lies
Among princes, among ruins.
A pilgrim under the yew at Ystrad Fflur
I kept my vow, prayed for my country,
Cursed England, came away

And home to the gas fire and televison
News. Caught between two languages,
Both dying, I thanked the long-dead
Minstrel of May and the newly silent
Voice of the bad weather, the precise
Accent of our own time, taught
To the disinherited, offering
Iron for gold.

---

[1]Dafydd, Dafydd ap Gwilym (*fl.* 1320-70), poet.
[2]Ystrad Fflur, the abbey of Strata Florida, Cards.

A Crown for Branwen [1]

I pluck now an image out of a far
Past and a far place, counties away
On the wrong side of Severn, acres
Of alien flint and chalk, the smooth hills
Subtly, unmistakeably English, different,
I remember, as if they were China, Sinodun,
Heaven's Gate and Angel Down, the White Horse
Hidden from the eye of war, Alfred at Wantage,
His bodyguard of four Victorian lamp-posts
And his country waiting for another enemy
Who did not come that summer. Everything
Shone in the sun, the burnished mail of wheat
And hot white rock, but mostly I recall
The long trench.

    A thousand years from now
They'll find the line of it, they'll tentatively
Make scholarly conjectures relating it
To Wansdyke, the Icknield Way, Silbury.
They'll never have known a summer
Of tense expectancy that drove
A desperate gash across England
To stop the tanks.

    Most clearly I see
The tumbled ramparts of frantic earth
Hastily thrown up, left to the drifting
Seeds of the waste, and the poppies,
Those poppies, that long slash of red
Across the shining corn, a wound, a wonder.

Lady, your land's invaded, we have thrown
Hurried defences up, our soil is raw,
New, shallow, the old crops do not grow
Here where we man the trench. I bring
No golden-armoured wheat, the delicate dance
Of oats to the harvest is not for me nor
The magic spears of barley, on this rough stretch
Only the poppies thrive. I wreathe for you
A crown of wasteland flowers, let them blaze
A moment in the midnight of your hair

---

[1]Branwen, a heroine in *The Mabinogion*

And be forgotten when the coulter drives
A fertile furrow over our old wars
For the strong corn, our children's bread.
Only, princess, I ask that when you bring
Those bright sheaves to the altar, and you see
Some random poppies tangled there, you'll smile,
As women do, remembering dead love.

D.J. Williams (1885–1970)

Earliest Recollections

I, David John Williams, was born, they say, in Penrhiw, in the parish of Llansawel in Carmarthenshire, between four and five o'clock in the morning on the 26th of June, in the year 1885, and Margaret Anne, my sister Pegi, between three and four o'clock in the morning on the 21st of January 1887. My mother used to say that Pegi got up an hour before me ever afterwards. We got our alien names from our grandparents, Jaci and Marged Penrhiw and Dafydd and Ann Rhiw'r Erfyn (later Gwarcoed), who were all Welsh people. Three of them hardly knew a word of English, as far as I am able to ascertain, and the fourth, Jaci, had only fairground English, enough of it to keep accounts, in a battered way, in his daybook. A brother, the first-born of the marriage, died at birth through my mother's having run down the steep slope of Cae Dan Tŷ, when her time was near, in her excitement on hearing that a cow had got into the bog at the bottom of Cae Du.

I heard them say that, if it were not for this accident, I, as the second son, should have been named Jâms after Uncle Jâms, my father's youngest brother, a young man not then married, living with us as one of the family. In that case I should most likely have been Jim Penrhiw to the people of the neighbourhood, so that there should not be two Jâmses in the same house. My mother had a brother Jâms, and Jâms was a name in the family on my father's side. Uncle Jâms was named after an uncle of his, Jâms Williams, Jemi Cilwennau, my grandfather's brother, one of the sons of Llywele. My father's mother's maiden name was Jâms, too. She was one of the Jâmses of Cwm Gogerddan, Caeo.

Difficulties arise when one searches back in memory's earliest cells and records what one finds. First, it is a hard task to put the incidents in their time sequence because they tend to fuse into the one static image that remains so clear in the minds of most people. During these years the normal child, brought up in normal circumstances, does nothing but happily and contentedly exist. Day and year and eternity are the same length and mean the same to him as far as he is conscious of them. It is all one endless day. His yesterday and tomorrow dawn on him slowly with the increasing interplay of their joys and sorrows. Again, one's imagination is very much alive during these years, and fact and fancy are easily woven together. When a child hears people speak time and again of an incident, especially if their relation of it is lively and dramatic, it is quite possible for him to come to believe that he was there at the time, hearing and seeing it all. That is why some children from three to six years old go through a stage of fibbing that is frightening to their parents in their solicitude for their children's integrity from the cradle, the father or the mother perhaps having completely forgotten such a period in his or her own life. A naturally poor memory is another matter; and still another is that moral laxity where the boundary between truth and falsehood is throughout life a matter of personal convenience only.

As it happens, I have one clear division in my life that gives me an advantage in dating my earliest memories. This division ever remains clear and definite in my mind. Nothing passes over it, either backward or forward.

On the rate-book the name of my earliest home is Penrhiw Fawr – that is, Great Penrhiw – so called obviously not on account of its size, but to distinguish it from another Penrhiw in the same parish, Penrhiw Drummond, as it was sometimes called, as it belonged to the estate and family of Sir James Drummond of Plas Rhydodyn, who owned the tithes of the whole parish at that time, as well as most of the land, and the richest land, therein. At the beginning of October 1891, Michaelmas Day being the end of the year of tenure generally, my parents moved from Penrhiw Fawr, to give it its official name for the time being, and went over Cwmcoedifor bank to a little place on the other side of the hill called Abernant, at the side of the road that runs from Llandeilo, in the Tywi valley, to Llanybydder, in the Teifi valley. My age at the time was six years and three months.

The day we moved still remains to me one of the most important days of my life. I have long been of the opinion myself – apart from everything that psychologists say to confirm it – that a child's observation and memory of what goes on around him in his very early days are very much deeper and more intense than people in general have believed them to be. I heard Deio'r Llether when he was over eighty years old relating to us in a corner of a hayfield, quite soberly, that he remembered 'as if it were yesterday' how his mother put her hand into her big pocket under her petticoat and counted out twenty gold sovereigns on the palm of his father's hand for him to go and buy a horse in St Barnabas Fair in Llandeilo – and that was three days before he was born! Deio was an old fellow who had his own sly way of putting things, and I would not go as far as affirming the literal truth of that testimony! But I will say this: I think I could write a sizeable book of my recollections of life in Penrhiw before I left that place at the age of six without drawing upon my imagination at all – at least, not consciously. As I have said, it is a kind of static image I have of my life up to that time, and I haven't as much as one objectively established date to hand to support or to correct my memory of it. It was all one long to-day, dateless, endless, and carefree. The only definite point of time I have is the day we left Penrhiw at the beginning of October 1891.

from *Yr Hen Dy Fferm* (1953), trans. Waldo Williams, *The Old Farmhouse* (1961)

The Square Mile

To me this is the most excellent of all possible homelands. I learnt to love it, I believe, before I learnt to walk. I have never travelled this part of the country from Bwlch Cae Melwas to Bwlch Cefen Sarth and from Craig Dwrch to Y Darren Fawr without feeling strangely stirred in my nature, like one who feels the full tide of his terrestrial and spiritual inheritance surging through his soul. This, actually, is the land of my fathers. It took possession of me, and I have taken possession of it in accordance with that simple property of my nature that responds. I have hardly ever failed to visit it on my holidays. I have often longed to return to it to live and work, for I felt that I could do my best work there, among my own people – a dream now that will never come true. Although I have spent three-quarters of my life far out of sight of it, and have lived in a kind and engaging society, my heart has never once left its homeland. Only here have I a spiritual home. This close homeland love, if you will have it that way, concentrated upon the square mile in the old locality of my boyhood where I saw the fairest things in life, has made me an irredeemable 'Shir-gâr.'[1] It is the heart of my patriotism, if I may use a word that has been so much traduced throughout the generations without sullying it further. To me the patriotism of those broadminded 'internationalists' we have in our nation, zealous for the rights of every nation except their own, is but superficial and meaningless rigmarole, paper patriotism to be carried on the strongest wind blowing at the time, whether from London or Moscow or any other centre of wind. The danger these people run, as some one said, is to be so wide that they have no sides to contain anything. But woe to us Welsh people if in our moral turpitude and soul-rotting materialism we give anyone, who ever he be, the right to trample on the beauty of our childhood's homeland and to destroy the values of its past days. If it may be said that there is a divine right to anything on earth, the right over the land of Wales belongs to the Welsh nation, and not to any alien, whoever he be.

from *Yr Hen Dy Fferm* (1953), trans. Waldo Williams, *The Old Farmhouse* (1961)

A Good Year

The rent of Pant y Bril was fifty shillings a year, and as Rachel relied upon a calf to provide the money, the day the cow calved was one of the great days of her year: not the greatest of all, for that honour fell to the day of sale. Once only did the cow fail her, and it took the best part of her life to recover from that disaster.

She talked so much about the price she hoped to get that the neighbours – some of them owning many calves – could almost reckon their profit or loss for

[1] '*Shir-gâr*', lit. 'Carmarthenshire', here used to denote a man of that county.

the year according to the price of Rachel's calf. If she got fifty-two and six, it would be a good year and everyone paid his way; fifty-five shillings meant a year of prosperity, and some unexpected weddings. But if the bargain were struck on Rachel's small hard hand at forty-seven and six, a lean year followed, and if the price fell as low as forty-five shillings, it was high time to hold a service of intercession.

Rachel pondered deeply upon these matters as she knit her stocking in the garden immediately after dinner, the fleeting warmth of an April day quickening her ruddy complexion. Her dog, Cora, with her tail curled into a small yellow ring on her back, sniffed here and there, finding more delight in this riot of smells than in the scraps of dinner she had just finished. Spring and its magic were in the air: wherever she looked, Rachel saw young growth, on currant bush, gooseberry, and the red rose climbing up the house. She looked at it all, this miracle of sudden birth, as if she saw it for the first time, unconsciously drawing it all into her own life. Could she hope for spring in herself, or must she dwell for ever in that long autumn that cut short the summer of her youth, fifteen years ago, when she was left a childless widow mourning the gentlest of husbands? Fifteen years of hard scraping for food, of sacrifice of body and of soul. She had made the best of it, in spite of lapses. But had not King David himself sinned and repented and found forgiveness, as the preacher said on Sunday? And now she felt so cheerful and contented, untroubled by her past, that she knew that her sins were forgiven her.

She glanced at her clothes: a short white shawl on her shoulders, a well-ironed check apron neatly pleated, and her brightly shining shoes. Before coming out, she had looked into her mirror and found that the crowsfeet under her eyes were less noticeable than usual. In the gentle warmth of the day, with young life budding round her and permeating the world, she felt ten years younger.

A moment later her mind went back to the sermon, and she blushed a little, without knowing exactly why. And then came another impulse, equally inexplicable, to return to the house for her coarse apron and her clogs and to clean the pigsty. None too soon, as she had noticed in the morning when she fed the pig. But before she made up her mind, a gruff voice greeted her over the garden gate and startled her, and she turned cold and virtuous within.

'And how's my bonny today?' The words came thickly, with a beery richness. 'Here I am again .... I'll buy your calf from you.'

'I might have known that this lump of a fellow would turn up,' said Rachel to herself as she tried to hide behind a currant bush, and her eyes fell guiltily upon her neat black shoes.

'Ah-ha! Playing hide and seek, my pretty? Let's have a look at you ... aren't we grand today? Just look at her!' said Tim as he placed his elbows on the bar of the gate. He knew well enough that he commanded the garden, and he thought of the gold that lay snugly in the long grey purse in his trouser pocket. A cunning rogue, turning up each spring, long before the snowdrops, to inquire into the fate of the first-born calf.

'I'm not selling the calf this year, to you or anybody else,' said Rachel. She had been forced to leave the shelter of the currant bushes, and her anger had driven the blood to her cheeks. 'Clear off. . . . I'm finished with you!'

'Did you ever hear the like? Going to retire and live on your means like Griffiths Tŷ Sych, I suppose! But maybe you're going to rear him . . . Rachel Ifans, Pant y Bril, Mark One X Bull!' Tim roared with laughter at his own joke.

'You fool! It isn't a bull calf, and as the cow's getting old, I'm going to rear it.'

'I don't know about the cow,' said Tim, his small black eyes twinkling dangerously. 'I know you're getting younger each year. Let's have a look at your new shoes . . . let me see if they fit properly. And I want to see how you got those pleats in your apron,' he added as he tried clumsily to open the gate.

'If you come one step nearer, I'll set the dog on you!' shouted Rachel. But Cora was too intent upon her own business in the hedge even to protect her mistress.

'No use calling Cora . . . she knows me well enough,' said Tim. 'Come, my beauty, let's have a squint at your calf. We'll strike a bargain soon enough.' He nodded his head towards the cowhouse.

Suddenly a clod of earth flew past him, followed by a second and a third.

'Just you dare to come here again until I send for you, you scoundrel,' shouted Rachel, ablaze with righteous indignation. And Tim, cunning as he was, saw that he was on the wrong tack this time. He retreated, mumbling to himself about the strange ways of women.

As soon as she saw that he had gone, Rachel went into the house, relieved at her success in casting Satan out of the garden, but weeping a little in her excitement. Sitting by the fire, she succeeded even in conquering that uneasy conscience which had pricked her ever since last Sunday's sermon. But in her joy she forgot that the devil is never so dangerous as in defeat; before the warmth of her gratitude had cooled, new thoughts began to stir. A vision of Tim, dark and ungainly, striding up the lane with the soil falling about his ears. She began to laugh riotously at the thought that a slip of a creature like herself had sent him flying. What would the neighbours say?

But after all, why should they know? Many worse than he, all said and done, although his tongue was as rough as his beard. But he had no right to comment on the fact that she was wearing her best shoes . . . she wore them for her own pleasure, not for his. If he came back that night – as he might well do, for he never bought a beast without going away once or twice or even thrice, to screw down the price by a few coppers – if he returned, she'd salt him well in the matter of money.

The lamp was on the table, and Rachel sat meditating in the dusk. Perhaps she had been over-hasty and had missed her market: the rent was long overdue. Suddenly she was roused by noises in the cow-house. Walking along the passage from the kitchen to the stalls, she saw Tim feeling the calf's ribs. The calf arched his back in gratitude.

'Not a bad calf, Rachel, I must say,' said Tim as he came out, ignoring the events of the afternoon.

'He's all right, but his price is beyond you,' Rachel replied significantly.

'Come now, don't be awkward. Tell me your price and we'll make a deal of it. It's getting late, and I've a long way to go.'

'No need for you to have come back,' said Rachel briskly.

'Don't waste time. I know you're dying to get rid of the calf . . . you wouldn't have slept tonight if I hadn't turned up. Seeing it's you, I'll give you fifty shillings.'

Rachel was surprised at his opening bid. 'I won't get forty for it,' he continued, 'not after I've dragged it twenty miles to Carmarthen fair next Saturday . . . not a chance.'

'Fifty-five,' she answered stiffly.

'Tell you what I'll do . . . we'll split. Give me half a crown and a cup of tea. . . . I've a great thirst on me.'

'Fifty-five,' said Rachel obstinately. 'And not a penny will I bate even if you stay the night.'

'No, no . . . never mind the half-crown. A cup of tea is all I want.'

'You're talking nonsense,' she replied.

They haggled long over the remaining half-crown, although Rachel was anxious to close.

'Since you're so obstinate, you can have your half-crown,' said Tim, tired of it all. 'Give me your hand, and we'll close it on fifty-five.'

She snatched her hand away.

'You and your dirty tricks . . . fifty-five? I said sixty-five all along. Fifty-five, indeed!' She laughed into his face and ran back into the house.

'You fool,' she continued, holding the door half open. 'If you hadn't been so cheeky about my best shoes, you'd have had the calf for fifty shillings, and luck-money as well. Did you think I put my best clothes on because you were coming?'

'Heaven alone knows,' Tim replied.

'I know well enough, I'm telling you. And it's my turn now . . . you can have the calf for sixty, and maybe I'll throw in a cup of tea. Make up your mind quickly before I shut the door.'

'You can keep your calf till his horns grow through the roof,' said Tim.

She slammed the door.

Tim had not gone far before he was caught in a heavy shower. He turned up the collar of his coat and took shelter beneath a holly tree, his mind in a turmoil: angry with Rachel for fooling him, still more angry with himself. The sky darkened and the wet clouds raced. More rain to come. On his right, long miles of cross-country trudging over moor and marsh. On his left, an arm of lamplight reaching out towards him and the rain falling across it. There was Rachel in her clean apron and her bright new shoes that cost her so much, laying the table for tea. Pride, Avarice and Ambition struggled within him as the rain poured down upon his head.

Suddenly he heard the click of the door-latch, and a wide shaft of light penetrated through the rain. He saw Rachel peering into the dark, her hand shading her eyes.

'Three pounds is a terrible price to pay for a wee thing like that,' said Avarice.

They still talk of it as the most prosperous year the country ever knew.

trans. Ll. Wyn Griffith

ANONYMOUS

The Hall of Cynddylan [1]

The hall of Cynddylan is dark tonight,
    No fire, no pallet.
  I'll keen now, then be quiet.

The hall of Cynddylan is dark tonight,
    No fire, no candle,
  Who but God will keep me tranquil?

The hall of Cynddylan is dark tonight,
    No fire, no bright gleaming.
  For your sake my heart's aching.

The hall of Cynddylan, dark is the roof,
    Gone the fair assembly.
  One should do good when able.

The hall of Cynddylan, your beauty's gone,
    In the grave's your buckler.
  While he lived, not a fissure.

The hall of Cynddylan is lorn tonight,
    Gone is the master.
  Ah death, why let me linger?

The hall of Cynddylan is still tonight
    Atop the rock's fastness.
  No prince, no people, no prowess.

[1] Cynddylan, King of Powys in the early 7th century, the destruction of whose court is here lamented by his sister Heledd.

The hall of Cynddylan is dark tonight,
  No fire, no singing.
My cheeks are worn from weeping.

The hall of Cynddylan is dark tonight,
  No fire, no household.
Free flow my tears where night falls.

The hall of Cynddylan, the sight stabs me,
  No rooftop, no fire.
Dead my lord, myself alive.

The hall of Cynddylan's laid bare tonight,
  Gone the steadfast swordsmen,
Caewg, Cynddylan, Elfan.

The hall of Cynddylan's lifeless tonight,
  Gone the honour owed me.
No men, no women to guard it.

The hall of Cynddylan is tame tonight,
  Having lost its ruler.
God of mercy, what shall I do?

The hall of Cynddylan, dark is the roof,
  Since the Saxon cut down
Powys' Cynddylan and Elfan.

The hall of Cynddylan is dark tonight,
  No sons of Cynddrwynyn,
Cynon and Gwiawn and Gwyn.

The hall of Cynddylan hurts me each hour,
  Gone the great assembly
I once saw at your hearthside.

from the 'Heledd Saga' (9th/10th cent.), trans. Joseph P. Clancy

Gwyn Williams (1904–   )

Easter Poem

It's night. I stroke the cotoneaster
above my head in the hedge
as I used to stroke a girl's hair.
Am I falling in love with the earth
I'll be mated with before long
or is it an easy urge to belong
more to the things about me? From birth
we drift away from the lair
of rank nature, cadge
a brief freedom, but this Easter
catches me with its quick switch
from sun to snow. Earth, you bitch!

Herbert Williams (1932–   )

The Old Tongue

We have lost the old tongue, and with it
The old ways too. To my father's
Parents it was one
With the *gymanfa ganu*,[1] the rough
Shouts of seafarers, and the slow
Dawn of the universal light.
It was one with the home-made bread, the smell
Of cakes at missionary teas,
And the shadows falling
Remotely on the unattempted hills.

It is all lost, the tongue and the trade
In optimism. We have seen
Gethsemane in Swansea, marked
The massacre of innocents. The dawn
Was false and we invoke
A brotherhood of universal fear.
And the harbour makes
A doldrum of the summer afternoon.

[1] *gymanfa ganu*, a singing festival.

Even the hills are diminished.
They are a gallon of petrol,
There and back. The old salts
Rot. And the bread
Is tasteless as a balance sheet.

Oh yes, there have been gains.
I merely state
That the language, for us,
Is part of the old, abandoned ways.

And when I hear it, regret
Disturbs me like a requiem.

ISLWYN WILLIAMS (1903–57)

Will Thomas's Cap

Talking about football, I wonder how many of you remember Will Thomas's first game for Wales? It was the game against England at Swansea. Wales won, you remember: Will Thomas scoring under the posts two minutes from the end. Well, how many of you took particular notice of Will that day? If you noticed, he was different in *one* thing from every other Welsh player: he was the only player on the Welsh side . . . but half a minute; I'm beginning at the wrong end. . . .

It began one night when Will Thomas came home from college with a black eye.

'Hullo!' said his father. 'What on earth have your been doing?'

'Playing football,' was the answer. 'Is supper ready?'

His mother stopped dead on her way to the back kitchen and turned round.

'Playing football?' she said. 'Well, indeed! That's a nice thing to learn at college, I must say!'

And there you have Jane Thomas to the T; 'a woman of few words' as the Bible says, and the strictest Puritan in the place. Mind you, she was a good woman; a better woman never lived. I ought to know; I live next door to her. But there you are, we all have our little faults; and Jane Thomas's was narrow-mindedness. She was – well – *terribly* narrow. She was down on everything that gave a man a little bit of enjoyment. She wouldn't go to a concert or an eisteddfod; they were places where Satan tempted the weak, she said. And of course, everyone who took a drop of beer now and again, or even went to the pictures, was a wicked man. As for boxers, well, according to her, they were going at top speed to hell. And from what I could see, her opinion of football and footballers wasn't much better.

But that was all she said to Will that night: and as it turned out, she never said another word to him about it. Only, every time the subject was mentioned after that, she'd either get up suddenly from her chair and stalk out of the room, or else go on furiously with her knitting with her lips shut very tight and her head down. Of course, she was always asking him about his lessons in the college: her great ambition was to see Will pass his B.A. with first-class honours.

Mind you, his father wasn't much better. But it wasn't narrow-mindedness in him. Oh, no: old Evan was too good-natured for that. The big drawback there was that he didn't know anything about the game; he knew absolutely nothing at all about football. Really, he was pathetic: he didn't even know the difference between soccer and rugby. That's hard to believe I know, but it's as true as I'm sitting here. But fair play to the old man: he had never taken any interest in the game, poor dab. Books and reading had been Evan's hobby all his life. Give him a book and he was satisfied. Oh, Evan was an intelligent man in his way: he was the backbone of the Literary Society with us here in Saron. But as I said, he didn't know the first thing about football, poor chap.

Mind you, between you and me, he became quite proud of Will–on the sly. But remember, he didn't dare show or say anything about that in the house. Oh, no: that would have been fatal. There was an awful row that time when Jane found the *Football Echo* under the cushion in the parlour.

Well, pity for Will, you say. Well, yes, in a way. But if his mother was sour and his father ignorant, he had *one* friend who was ready to roll his sleeves up all the way: and that was his uncle Jack, his father's brother. If books had been Evan's hobby, football had been Jack's ever since he was a small boy. There's a difference between two brothers. Mind you, Jack was a tidy chap too: a splendid collier and chapel every Sunday like clockwork. But he was a little bit more rough than Evan–you know what I mean. Well, football had always been his greatest delight. *Der*, he had a wonderful memory to begin with. Jack could tell you who was playing on such and such a ground at such and such a time, who had scored, and how, how many caps so and so had had–and all those things, back for many years. He could tell you what kind of stockings Percy Bush[1] was wearing in 1905, what Gwyn Nicholls's' father's work was, what was the name of Dicky Owen's' grandmother, and all those little details.

Well, you can imagine what he thought of Will. I never saw such a fuss in my life. Only 'Will, our Evan's boy' was to be heard from him:

'Hey, did you hear about our Evan's boy? He's playing for the college, look. He'll make a good forward too. He's big, he's fast, he's got hands like a pair of shovels, *and* there's brains there. Mark my words, he'll go far. Watch what I'm telling you!'

And, fair play to old Jack, the truth he spoke too. Will was playing for Swansea long before he finished in college. *Der*, his uncle Jack was crazy about him! He was down in Swansea every Saturday, in the stand, too, if you please.

---

[1]Percy Bush . . . Gwyn Nicholls . . . Dicky Owen, famous names in the annals of Welsh rugby.

And I don't know how many shifts he lost going up to Coventry and Gloucester and all those places, just to see Will play.

He took Evan with him once, to see a game at St Helen's. Mind you, Jane Thomas didn't know anything about that stunt: I don't think she knows to this day. Going down to buy an axe was the excuse, I remember. Anyhow, Jack took Evan with him to see Newport at St Helen's. He'd been trying to teach Evan a few things by this time, but from what he told me the following Sunday after chapel, he hadn't been very successful.

'I'll never take him again,' he said to me that night. 'I had enough of him yesterday. *Diawch*,[1] our Evan is slow learning, you wouldn't believe. He's hopeless, hopeless! Talk about ignorance! I don't know how many times he asked me what the *strum* was for – yes, *strum*, if you please! And he asked me several times if their Will was a wing. After all I had said to him about trying to use his intelligence! I ask you: what's the using of knowing your Bible inside out, and how to write *englynion*,[2] if you can't show a bit of gumption on a football field? I must say, I had to tell him in the end, "Listen here, Evan; be quiet. You are making me blush here. And for goodness' sake, don't let on to anybody that you are Will's father, or the poor dab will never lift his head again!" So he shut up after that for a while. But he was at it again before the end. . . .

And fair play to old Jack: he tried his best with Jane Thomas, too, but it was hard work. He came to me with his grouse then too. 'Now, there's a headstrong woman for you! She's worse than Evan; fair play for our Evan – he isn't narrow; ignorant our Evan is, and slow learning. But I don't know what to say about that woman he's got. She isn't human. No indeed, I've asked her several times to try and take a mother's interest in her child: nothing doing. . . . "John," she said to me, "listen here, one word is as good as a hundred. I'm not willing for him to play that old game. What I want is to see the boy get on!"

'"But Jane, fach," I told her, "be reasonable, girl: the boy *is* getting on famously. He's playing for Swansea now; and you watch what I'm telling you, he'll get his cap too!"

'"What cap?" she said.

'"His cap for playing for Wales of course."

'"Go on, you and your old cap," she said. "An old cap indeed. Silly rubbish I call it!" . . . Yes, "silly rubbish", that's how she was talking, look, about Will getting his cap – a woman well over sixty. Oh, Jane Thomas is a very strange woman. It's so unnatural, somehow; her son playing for Swansea, and her treating it so lightly. No, indeed, it makes you think sometimes that she hasn't been to the far end of the oven!'

And that's how things went on for months: Will improving his chances in every game, his mother shutting up like a box every time the thing was mentioned, and his father, poor dab, trying to learn the ins and outs on the sly.

---

[1] *Diawch!*, By the Devil!
[2] *englynion* (sing. *englyn*), a four-line verse written according to tradition rules of prosody.

Jack of course was up to his ears in paste, keeping a scrap-book of everything the critics were saying about Will.

Well, I shall never forget the night the Big Five were meeting to pick the team against England. Something had gone wrong with my set, and Evan had asked me over the wall to come into their house to hear the nine o'clock news. Jack had been on the phone to 'Old Stager', and had been put to understand that the team would be announced at the end of the news. So I went in about half past eight, to make sure like.

Evan was reading by the fire, and Jane was knitting as usual. Mind, I don't think she had any idea what was up, and of course, I didn't say a word. Well, the news came on, and at last the Welsh team was given out. When he came to the forwards, Evan's face was like a piece of chalk, and when Will was named, he turned to Jane.

'Did you hear what he said, Jane?'

'What?'

'Our Will has been capped.'

She didn't say a word. She just looked as if she'd heard that Will had been sent to jail, and out she went to the back kitchen without looking at one of us. With that, we heard someone running like mad outside, and in through the door he came like a bull. It was Jack, of course, with all his breath in his fist. He tried to say something, and there: he failed to say another word; he went to cry like a baby. He wasn't in work the next day; his nerves all in rags, the doctor said. . . .

You remember the game, of course. In my opinion, that's the best game Will Thomas ever played. But the funny thing is this: the night before the match Jack and I thought he wouldn't be playing at all. He was in an awful state. He wouldn't say what was the matter at first, but at last we got it out of him.

'Mother's carrying on as if I'm going to be hanged. Not a word all these months, only a long face. I tell you, I don't feel like playing at all!'

Jack was furious about it. He took me out to the back door. He was almost crying in his temper.

'Damn that woman!' he said savagely. 'Isn't she *wicked*? Isn't she *terrible*? It's – it's – it's sinful, that's what it is. She's going to spoil one of the best boys who ever played for Wales. Mark my words, Wales will lose tomorrow simply through the antics of that wicked woman!'

Anyhow, there wasn't much better shape on us when we were ready to leave the house the next morning: Will and his father looking exactly as if they were going to an inquest, and Jack with his teeth clenched looking as if he was ready to murder someone.

When we were moving towards the door, Jane Thomas called very quietly from the back kitchen:

'William!'

'Yes, mother?'

'Come here.'

Will turned back. 'You go on,' he said. 'I'll be after you now.'

But wait we did, outside the house, with Jack as white as a sheet, biting his nails. At last, Will came out, grinning from ear to ear, carrying a little parcel.

'What's that you've got?' said Jack, all excited.

'What do you think?' answered Will, still grinning broadly. 'A pair of stockings my mother has knitted for me!'

Jack was dumbfounded. '*Duw Mawr!*[1] Don't – don't tell your lies!' he stuttered. 'What colour are they?' he added quickly. 'Red they must be, mind; red, the same colour as the jerseys!'

'What does it matter what colour they are!' said Will. 'I'm going to wear them whatever happens!'

And that's why, as I was going to say at the beginning, every player on the Welsh side that day wore red stockings – all, that is, except Will Thomas.

As Jane Thomas said to her sister Elizabeth that evening: 'I'm very fond of navy blue, especially for men.'

trans. the author

RAYMOND WILLIAMS (1921–　)

You Got a Boy, Harry

More and more often, during the last weeks of waiting, Mrs Lucas moved across the lane and stayed with Ellen. The warm spring had matured into an unusually hot summer. The hay was cut, in the fields across the valley, and horses dragged the loaded gambos through the narrow lanes, to the barns where the dusty heat, even near the gables, was almost unbearable. Eira, when Mrs Lucas was at the cottage, lay in a cradle in the open porch, and usually stretched out beside her was Rex, the Lewises' collie, old and smelling in the heat. In the cottage, everything was made ready for the birth, and still the meals were prepared, and the men came at their odd times from work and ate them, going out quickly again, leaving the women on their own. At first, Morgan still ate in his own house, but as Mrs Lucas stayed more with Ellen he would often come to the cottage and take his meals there, while the house across the road stood temporarily unused. On the line, traffic was heavy, with the big summer shifting of coal. Several Sundays were worked, and the men were more often away.

It was on a Sunday, late in July, that the birth came. Ellen did not get up in the morning, and Harry fetched Mrs Lucas early. She at once got Ellen up and made her walk around the room, in which the big tester bed left only a narrow space. Morgan was at work, and Harry, due to relieve him at two that afternoon, stayed around the cottage, often standing near Eira, who was sleeping peacefully in the porch. Mrs Lucas had expected to cook Sunday

[1] *Duw Mawr!*, Great God!

dinner, but she could not leave Ellen for more than a few minutes, and Harry, under her directions, put the food on the stove. He wanted the birth to come before he had to go to work, but when he went up, soon after one, he found Ellen still being roughly walked about the room, then stopping and leaning on the end of the bed, looking across at him with the distant eyes of a child in pain. He said what he could, and went reluctantly back down. Soon after, he had to leave for the station.

Morgan promised, when he relieved him, to come back up when there was news, but Harry sat all afternoon and evening in the box, which on Sundays was always lonely, and no message came. At ten he closed up, for Meredith to reopen at five, and rode as fast as he could down the village, and up the steep dark lane. The yellow lamp shone out from the bedroom window; only a candle was burning downstairs. Eira was back in her own bed, and Morgan in his own kitchen. Harry stood in the garden, hearing a scream from the window open above him. He could not say he heard Ellen – the voice was strange and barely human – but he could hear Mrs Lucas's urgent voice, and knew that still he must wait. Above the garden and the trees, the summer sky was drawing into an intense deep mauve. Over the line of the Cefn, to the east, hung the pale full moon. Harry walked to the big water-butt, which was almost empty. He could smell, from the drying wood, a sourness which stayed separate from the night-sweet scent of the stocks and roses under the red wall. Above him the tall chimney stack seemed distorted and elongated. The screaming came again.

He went indoors and along the passage to the foot of the stairs. Then he knew he must turn back, and walked slowly out through the porch to the back-kitchen. He lit the hand-lamp, and stoked the fire of the copper, in which the water was still hot. There was a step at the door, and Morgan was looking across at him. They nodded, but hardly spoke. Harry saw suddenly how tense Morgan was. He looked away without speaking and put a kettle on the stove for tea. They sat opposite each other, in the poor light, sipping the scalding tea. Above them, the bedroom was silent. After some while, they heard footsteps down the stairs and along the passage. Harry stood, expecting to see Mrs Lucas, but it was Mrs Hybart. He had not known she was in the house. She came in, looked at them both, and smiled.

'You two making yourselves comfortable then?'

'How is she?' Morgan asked. Harry had asked only with his eyes.

'Not a she, a he,' Mrs Hybart said roughly. 'You got a boy, Harry.'

Harry smiled, looking past her shoulder.

'Don't you want to know how your wife is?' she went on, watching him with amused eyes.

'She's all right, is she?'

'Yes boy, all right and all over.'

'It's been such a time.'

'Aye, the first, and too big he is, see. What you want a boy like that for?'

'Big?'

'Aye. Now don't stand there gaping but let me have some of that water. You let the copper fire out?'

'No, I stoked it.'

'Thank goodness you're some use. Standing there, the two of you. Like dogs in the wet you are. Mind then, let me fill this bowl.'

The men stood obediently aside. They were used to this.

'Eira asleep?' Mrs Hybart said over her shoulder to Morgan.

'Aye,' Morgan said, gruffly.

'Mind then,' she said, as she came with the filled bowl from the copper and walked back out through the porch.

The birth had been difficult, but there were no complications, although Ellen was very weak. Harry saw her briefly that night, and she smiled and looked for him to go to see the child. Harry went across, awkwardly, and stared down into the cradle. Mrs Lucas lifted the lamp, and the yellow light fell across the tiny wrapped head.

'Right, get off to bed now,' Mrs Lucas whispered. Harry turned and smiled again at Ellen, who did not notice him. Then he went tiptoe out of the warm room. He did not go to bed until Mrs Hybart came down on her way back to her own house. He thanked her, and then took a candle and went up alone to the end room.

from *Border Country* (1960)

Black Mountains

1

See this layered sandstone among the short mountain grass. Place your right hand on it, palm downward. See where the sun rises and where it stands at noon. Direct your middle finger midway between them. Spread your fingers, not widely. You now hold this place in your hand.

The six rivers rise in the plateau of the back of your hand. The first river, now called Mynwy or Monnow, flows at the outside edge of your thumb. The second river, now called Olchon, flows between your thumb and the first finger, to join the Mynwy at the top of your thumb. The third river, now called Honddu, flows between your first and second fingers and then curves to join the Mynwy, away from your hand. The fourth river, now called Grwyne Fawr, flows between your second and third fingers, and then curves the other way, joining the fifth river, now called Grwyne Fechan, that has been flowing between your third and your little finger. The sixth river, now called Rhiangoll, flows at the outside edge of your little finger. Beyond your hand are the two rivers to the sea. Mynwy carrying Olchon and Honddu flows into the circling Wye. Grwyne and Rhiangoll flow into the Usk. Wye and Usk, divided by the Forest of Gwent, flow to the Severn Sea.

It was by Wye and Usk, from the Severn Sea and beyond it, that men first came to this place.

The ridges of your five fingers, and the plateau of the back of your hand, are now called the Black Mountains. Your thumb is Crib y Gath or Cat's Back. Your first finger is Haterall. Your second finger is Ffawyddog, with Bal Mawr at the knuckle. Your third finger is Gader, with Gader Fawr at the knuckle. Your little finger is Allt Mawr, and its nail is Crug Hywel, giving its name to Crickhowell below it. On the back of your hand are Twyn y Llech and Twmpa and Rhos Dirion and Waun Fach. Mynwy and Olchon flow from Twyn y Llech. Honddu flows from Twyn y Llech and Twmpa. Grwyne Fawr flows from Rhos Dirion. Grwyne Fechan and Rhiangoll flow from Waun Fach.

You hold the shapes and the names in your hand.

2

It was by Wye and Usk, from the Severn Sea and beyond it, that men first came to this place.

We have no ready way to explain ourselves to you. Our language has gone utterly, except for the placename which you now say as Ewyas. The names by which we knew ourselves are entirely unknown to you. We left many marks on the land but the only marks that you can easily recognize are the long stone graves of our dead. If you wish to know us you must learn to read the whole land.

3

The long barrows of the first Black Mountain shepherds are clustered on flat grasslands between the steep northern scarp, at your wrist, and on one side the wide valley of the Wye, on the other the valley of the Usk and the basin of Llyn Syvadon, now called Llangorse Lake.

When the first shepherds came there was thick oak forest from the rivers to the level of these grasslands. Then the forest thinned, and there was good pasture among the scattered trees. On the ridges above them, in the climate of that time, there were great winter bogs in the peat above the deep sandstone, but there was some summer grazing on the slopes. They lived at that chosen level, at first only in the summers, going back to the rivers in the winters, but later yearthrough.

These are still flat grasslands, grazed by thousands of sheep and hundreds of ponies. Below them and above them the land has changed and been changed.

4

We can count in generations. Say two hundred and twenty generations from the first shepherds to us. Then a new people came. Say one hundred and sixty generations from them to us. They came when the climate was changing. Winters were much colder and summers hotter and drier. While elsewhere in the island men were moving down from chalk uplands, because the springs were failing, here the sandstone ridges and the plateau were drying, and there was new summer grazing. Surviving tracks show the change. To every ridge, now, there are long, transverse, sometimes zigzag, tracks from the middle heights to the crests. They are often sunken, making a characteristic notch where they break the ridge. The local name for such a track is *rhiw*. Along these tracks, sheep and cattle were driven for the summer grazing. Meanwhile, below the old grasslands, the forest was changing. The damp oak forest fell back, and new clearings were made among the more diverse woods. And this people felled along the slopes of the ridges. There was then more grass but also the heather began to spread. They lived and worked in these ways for sixty generations.

5

New peoples came. Say a hundred generations from them to us. And again the climate was changing. Winters were milder, summers cooler and wetter. They settled a little higher than the first shepherds, and in new ways. They built folds and camps at the ends of ridges: at Pentwyn, Y Gaer, Crug Hywel, Castell Dinas. There were summer pastures behind them, along the lower ridges, for their sheep and cattle and horses. And still they cleared towards the valleys, in small square fields. There were peaceful generations, but increasingly, now, more peoples were coming from the east. The folds and steadings became armed camps. The names of history begin with the Silures. But then a different arrival: an imperial people: Romans. These said of the Silures: 'non atrocitate, non clementia mutabatur': changed neither by cruelty nor by mercy. Literate history, imperial history, after more than a hundred generations of history.

6

In literate history the Black Mountains are marginal. They are still classified today as marginal or as waste land. After the Silures no new people settled them. The tides of conquest or lordship lapped to their edges and their foothills, leaving castles facing them – Ewyas Harold, Ewyas Lacy, Grosmont, Skenfrith, White Castle, Abergavenny, Crickhowell, Bronllys, Hay, Clifford – to command their peoples. Romans drove military roads at their edges. Normans pushed closer, but had no use for land above seven hundred feet. In the mountains and their valleys the people were still there, with their animals. They were the children of the first shepherds and of the upland people and of the camp-builders. Roman governors wanted them to come down and live in new towns. Some went, some stayed. When the Romans left the island, some came back to the mountains. By at latest the sixth century, in modern reckoning, the Black Mountains were a kingdom, which lasted, precariously, until the twelfth century. Twenty generations of Roman rule and its aftermath. Twenty-five generations of a small native kingdom. They called the kingdom by a very old name: Ewyas.

7

Where then are the Black Mountains? The physical answer is direct. The literate and administrative answer is more difficult.

At a certain point on the narrow and winding road which we drive in summer for shopping – past Pentwyn and Parc y Meirch, below the source of the Mynwy and over the brooks of Dulas and Esgyrn – at a certain point on this secluded road between high banks and hedges of hazel and holly and thorn, at this indistinguishable point there is a ridged bump in the roadway, where the roadmen of Brecon (now Powys) and the roadmen of Hereford (now Hereford and Worcester) have failed to see eye to eye. It is a trivial unevenness, deep within this specific region. It is the modern border between England and Wales.

And this is how it has gone, in literate and administrative history. The small kingdom of Ewyas – not small if you try to walk it, but politically small – was often, while it still had identity, redrawn or annexed or married into the neighbouring kingdoms of Brycheiniog or Gwent or Erging (Archenfield). Its modern political history is differently arbitrary. A dispute between the London court and a local landowning family, at the time of the Act of Union between England and Wales, led to a border which follows no natural feature or, rather, several in an incomprehensible series. In the twentieth century, three counties had lines drawn across and through the Black Mountains: lines on maps and in a few overgrown and lichened stones. Brecon pushed one way, Monmouth-shire another, Hereford a third. The first was part of Wales, the third part of England; Monmouthshire, until it became Gwent, anomalous between them. A national park boundary followed these amazing administrative lines. Then Brecon was incorporated into the new Powys. Monmouthshire in name became the old Gwent. Hereford and Worcester, unwillingly joined, considered and rejected the name of West Mercia. It was almost, even in name, a very old situation: this marginal, this waste land, taken in at the very edges of other, more powerful, units.

Within the Black Mountains, these lines on the map mean nothing. You have only to stand there to see an unusually distinct and specific region. Or go on that midsummer Sunday – Shepherds' Sunday – when they drive the tups from above the Usk to above the Monnow and track down unmarked sheep. An old internal organization, in the region's old activity, still visibly holds. Later, of course, the externally drawn lines and their consequences arrive, administratively, in the post. They are usually bills.

8

How to see it, physically? At first it is to strange. You need your hand on the stone to discern its extraordinary structure. Within the steep valleys, or from any of the ridges, this basic shape of the hand is not visible. And of course at every point there are minor features: cross valleys, glaciated cwms, rockfalls (*darens*), steeply gouged watercourses. It is so specific a country, yet its details take years to learn.

Black mountains? From a distance, like others, they are blue. From very close they are many colours: olive-green under sunlight; darker green with the patches of summer bracken; green with a reddish tinge when there are young leaves on the whinberries; dark with the heather out of flower, purple briefly in late summer; russet in the late autumn bracken; a pale gold, often, in the dead winter bracken, against the white of snow. Black? Entirely so, under heavy storm clouds. Very dark and suddenly solid under any thick cloud. The long whaleback ridges can be sudddenly awesome.

But then their valleys are so different. Now Mynwy and Olchon and Honddu and Rhiangoll are farmed; Grwyne Fawr is forested and dammed; Grwyne Fechan is farm, a little forest and then upland pasture. The oldest modern farms are half-way up each slope from the valley beds, where the springs mostly rise. The old valley roads are at this level. But there are now roads and farms right down by the rivers, where there can be some flat fields. Then from these and the others the cleared fields climb the slopes, to uneven heights. Ash and thorn and rowan and cherry are still felled, bracken ploughed, to enclose a new field from the mountain. Others, once cleared, have gone back to scrub and bracken. At the farthest points, often surprisingly close, are old ruined stone farms, thick now with the nettles marking human occupation. In the Napoleonic wars there was this high and intensive settlement. It fell back with the decline of the Welsh woollen industry. The fields have been taken in to other farms. The rest of the story is what is called depopulation.

But the valleys are bright green, under the different colours of the mountains. Trees flourish in them. From some ridges the valleys still look like woodland, with the farms in clearings. But there is always a sharp contrast between the bleak open tops, with their heather and whinberry and cotton sedge and peat pools, their tracks which dissolve into innumerable sheep tracks, their sudden danger, in bad weather, in low cloud and mist with few landmarks, and the green settled valleys, with the fine trimmed farm hedges, the layered sandstone houses – colours from grey and brown towards pink or green, the patchwork of fields. At midsummer the valleys are remarkable, for on the trimmed hedges of thorn and holly and hazel and ash and field maple there is an amazing efflorescence of stands of honeysuckle and pink or white wild roses, and on the banks under them innumerable foxgloves. It is so close to look up from these flowers to the steep ridges. By one of the ruined farms there was once a whole field of foxgloves. It is now back to bracken and thistle.

But in the next field they are felling and clearing again, and the ploughed earth above the sandstone goes through a range of colours from wet dark red to dried pink among the bright grass.

So this extraordinarily settled and that extraordinarily open wild country are very close to each other and intricately involved. Either, with some strictness, can be called pastoral, but then with very different implications. As the eye follows them, in this unusually defining land, the generations are distinct but all suddenly present.

9

It is a place where you can stand and look out. From Haterall there is the vast patchwork of fields of the Herefordshire plain, across to the Malverns and the Clees. From Twmpa there is distance after distance of upland Wales, from Radnor and Eppynt to Plynlimmon and Cader Idris and the neighbouring Beacons. From Allt Mawr there is the limestone scarp, on the other side of the Usk, where the iron industry came, and in the valleys behind it, Rhymney and Taff and Rhondda, the mining for coal.

Land, labour, and history. It can be cold standing there. The winds sweep those ridges. You go back down, into the settled valleys, with their medley of map names.

Different views, different lives. But occasionally, laying your right hand, palm downward, on the deep layered sandstone, you know a whole, intricate, distinct place. The Black Mountains. Ewyas.

from *Places: an anthology of Britain* (ed. Ronald Blythe, 1981)

Anonymous

Death

One night as I lay on my bed,
And sleep on fleeting foot had fled,
Because, no doubt, my mind was heavy
With concern for my last journey:

I got me up and called for water,
That I might wash, and so feel better;
But before I wet my eyes so dim,
There was Death on the bowl's rim.

I went to church that I might pray,
Thinking sure he'd keep away;
But before I got on to my feet,
There sat Death upon my seat.

To my chamber then I hied,
Thinking sure he'd keep outside;
But though I firmly locked the door,
Death came from underneath the floor.

Then to sea I rowed a boat,
Thinking surely Death can't float;
But before I reached the deep,
Death was captain of the ship.

                                        trans. Aneirin Talfan Davies

WALDO WILLIAMS (1904–71)

What is Man?

What is living? Finding a great hall
Inside a cell.
What is knowing? One root
To all the branches.

What is believing? Holding out
Until relief comes.
And forgiving? Crawling through thorns
To the side of an old foe.

What is singing? Winning back
The first breath of creation:
And work should be a song
Made of wheat or wood.

What is statecraft? Something
Still on all fours.
And defence of the realm?
A sword thrust in a baby's hand.

What is being a nation? A talent
Springing in the heart.
And love of country? Keeping house
Among a cloud of witness.

What is this world to the great powers?
A circle turning.
And to the lowly of the earth?
A cradle rocking.

                                        trans. Emyr Humphreys

In Two Fields

Where did the sea of light roll from
Onto Flower Meadow Field and Flower Field?
After I'd searched for long in the dark land,
The one that was always, whence did he come?
Who, oh who was the marksman, the sudden enlightener?
The roller of the sea was the field's living hunter.
From above bright-billed whistlers, prudent scurry of lapwings,
The great quiet he brought me.

Excitement he gave me, where only
The sun's thought stirred to lyrics of warmth,
Crackle of gorse that was ripe on escarpments,
Hosting of rushes in their dream of blue sky.
When the imagination wakens, who calls
Rise up and walk, dance, look at the world?
Who is it hiding in the midst of the words
That were there on Flower Meadow Field and Flower Field?

And when the big clouds, the fugitive pilgrims,
Were red with the sunset of stormy November,
Down where the ashtrees and maples divided the fields,
The song of the wind was deep like deep silence.
Who, in the midst of the pomp, the super-abundance,
Stands there inviting, containing it all?
Each witness' witness, each memory's memory, life of each life,
Quiet calmer of the troubled self.

Till at last the whole world came into the stillness
And on the two fields his people walked,
And through, and between, and about them, goodwill widened
And rose out of hiding, to make them all one,
As when the few of us forrayed with pitchforks
Or from heavy meadows lugged thatching of rush,
How close we came then, one to another –
The quiet huntsman so cast his net round us!

Ages of the blood on the grass and the light of grief,
Who whistled through them? Who heard but the heart?
The cheater of pride, and every trail's tracker,
Escaper from the armies, hey, there's his whistling –
Knowledge of us, knowledge till at last we do know him!
Great was the leaping of hearts, after their ice age.
The fountains burst up towards heaven, till,
Falling back, their tears were like leaves of a tree.

Day broods on all this beneath sun and cloud,
And Night through the cells of her wide-branching brain –
How quiet they are, and she breathing freely
Over Flower Meadow Field and Flower Field –
Keeps a grip on their object, the fields full of folk.
Surely these things must come. What hour will it be
That the outlaw comes, the hunter, the claimant to the breach,
That the Exiled King cometh, and the rushes part in his way?

trans. Anthony Conran

Preseli[1]

Wall of my boyhood, Foel Drigarn, Carn Gyfrwy, Tal Mynydd,
Backing me in all independence of judgment,
And my floor from Y Witwg to Wern and down to Yr Efail
Where the sparks spurted that are older than iron.

And in the yards, on the hearths of my people –
Breed of wind, rain, and mist, of sword-flag and heather,
Wrestling with the earth and the sky and winning
And handing on the sun to their children, from their stooping.

Memory and symbol, a reaping party on their neighbour's hillside,
Four swaths of oats falling at every stroke,
And a single swift course, and while stretching their backs
Giant laughter to the clouds, a single peal of four voices.

My Wales, land of brotherhood, my cry, my creed,
Only balm for the world, its message, its challenge,
Pearl of the infinite hour, pledge given by time,
Hope of the long journey on the short winding way.

This was my window, the harvesting and the shearing.
I beheld order in my palace there.
A roar, a ravening, is roaming the windowless forest.
Let us guard the wall from the beast, keep the well-spring free of the filth.

trans. Joseph P. Clancy

[1]Preseli, hills in northern Pembrokeshire.

Remembrance

One blissful moment as the sun is setting,
A mellow moment ere the night comes on,
To bring to mind things which are long forgotten,
Now lost in dust of eras that are gone.

Now like the foam breaking on lonely beaches,
Or the wind's song and no one there to hear,
I know they call on us in vain to listen, –
The old forgotten things men loved so dear.

Things wrought through cunning skill in early ages,
Neat little dwellings and resplendent halls,
And well-told stories that are lost for ever,
And olden gods on whom no suppliant calls.

The little words of languages once living,
Lively was then their sound on lips of men,
And pleasing to the ear in children's prattle,
But now, no tongue will fashion them again.

O countless generations of earth's children,
Of dreams divine, and fragile godlikeness,
Is there but stillness for the hearts that quickened,
That knew delight and knew grief's bitterness?

Often when evening falls and I am lonely
I long once more to bring you all to mind,
Pray, is there no-one treasures and holds dear
The old forgotten things of humankind?

trans. D.M. Lloyd

WILLIAM WILLIAMS (Pantycelyn; 1717–91)

I Gaze across the Distant Hills

I gaze across the distant hills,
    Thy coming to espy;
Beloved, haste, the day grows late,
    The sun sinks down the sky.

All the old loves I followed once
    Are now unfaithful found;
But a sweet sickness holds me yet
    Of love that has no bound!

Love that the sensual heart ne'er knows,
   Such power, such grace it brings,
Which sucks desire and thought away
   From all created things.

O make me faithful while I live,
   Attuned but to thy praise,
And may no pleasure born of earth
   Entice to devious ways.

All my affections now withdraw
   From objects false, impure,
To the one object which unchanged
   Shall to the last endure.

There is no station under heaven
   Where I have lust to live;
Only the mansions of God's house
   Can perfect pleasure give.

Regard is dead and lust is dead
   For the world's gilded toys;
Her ways are nought but barrenness,
   And vain are all her joys.

trans. H. Idris Bell

Guide me, O thou great Jehovah [1]

Guide me, O Thou great Jehovah,
   Pilgrim through this barren land,
I am weak, but Thou art mighty;
   Hold me with thy powerful hand:
     Bread of heaven, bread of heaven,
   Feed me till I want no more.

Open now the crystal fountain,
   Whence the healing stream doth flow,
Let the fire and cloudy pillar
   Lead me all my journey through:
     Strong Deliverer, strong Deliverer,
   Be Thou still my strength and shield.

---

[1]This hymn is sung to the tune 'Cwm Rhondda', as is Ann Griffiths' 'Lo, between the Myrtles'.

When I tread the verge of Jordan,
  Bid my anxious fears subside;
Death of deaths, and hell's Destruction,
  Land me safe on Canaan's side:
    Songs of praises, songs of praises,
  I will ever give to Thee.

trans. the author and Peter Williams

ACKNOWLEDGEMENTS

The Publishers would like to thank the following for permission to reproduce copyright material:

Carcanet Press Ltd for 'Lunchtime Lecture', 'Harvest at Mynachlog' and 'Birth' from *Selected Poems* by Gillian Clarke (1985).

Robert Morgan for 'Blood Donor' © Robert Morgan 1967.

Idris Christopher Bell for translations by H.I. Bell.

Poetry Wales Press for 'Little of Distinction' by Ruth Bidgood from *Lighting Candles* (1982), 'Summer 1984' by Duncan Bush from *Salt* (1985), 'Preparations' by Tony Curtis from *Selected Poems 1970-1985* (1986), 'The Bridge' by John Davies from *The Visitor's Book* (1985), 'Water', 'The Ballad of Billy Rose' and 'Elegy for David Beynon' by Leslie Norris from *Selected Poems* (1986).

Glyn Jones for 'The Meaning of Fuchsias', extracts from *The Valley, The City, The Village* (J.M. Dent 1956) and *The Learning Lark* (J.M. Dent 1960) and the translation from *Honeydew on the Wormwood* (Gwasg Gregynog 1984).

Gwyn Williams and Alun Books for 'Easter Poem' from *Choose Your Stranger* (1979).

Vivian Idris Davies for extracts by B.L. Coombes from *These Poor Hands* (Gollancz 1939).

Jane Edwards for 'Blind Date', translated by Derec Llwyd Morgan.

Derec Llwyd Morgan and Gwasg Gomer, Llandysul for 'Trouble Registering my Daughter'.

Gwyn Jones and Mair Jones for the translations by Gwyn Jones and Thomas Jones in *The Mabinogion* (J.M. Dent 1948).

Gwyn Jones for the extract from *A Prospect of Wales* (Penguin 1948).

Oxford University Press for pieces from *Selected Short Stories* by Gwyn Jones, © Gwyn Jones 1974, *Welsh Legends and Folk-tales* retold by Gwyn Jones, © Gwyn Jones 1955, *The Matter of Wales* by Jan Morris, © Jan Morris 1984, *Definition of a Waterfall* by John Ormond, © OUP 1973, *Places: an Anthology of Britain* chosen by Ronald Blythe © Oxfam 1981.

J.M. Dent for the extract from *The Railway Game* by Clifford Dyment (1962).

Harrap Ltd for extracts from *The Old Farmhouse* by D.J. Williams, translated by Waldo Williams.

Chatto & Windus for the extract from *Border Country* by Raymond Williams.

George Ewart Evans for the extracts from *The Voices of the Children*, originally published in 1947 by The Penmark Press, Cardiff.

Dr Pennar Davies, author, Gwilym Rees Hughes, translator, Gwasg Gomer, publishers, and *International Poetry Review* for 'Gravity'.

The estate of Caradoc Evans for 'Be This Her Memorial' by Caradoc Evans from *My People* (Andrew Melrose 1915).

Lady Jones for the extract by E. Tegla Davies from *Nedw*, translated by Meic Stephens (Hughes a'i Fab 1922).

Christopher Davies Ltd for extracts from: *The Secret Room* by Marion Eames, translated by Margaret Phillips (1975), *Spring of Youth* by Ll.Wyn Griffith (1935), *Cerddi'r Cyfannu* by Alan Llwyd and translated by Alan Llwyd (1980), *Native Ground* by Robert Minhinnick (1979), *High Heritage* by A.G. Prys-Jones (1969), *Collected Poems 1958-1978* by John Tripp (1978) and *Requiem and*

Celebration by John Ormond (1969).

Gee & Son Ltd, Denbigh, Clwyd, for extracts from: *Gŵr o Baradwys* by Ifan Gruffydd (1963), translated by Meic Stephens, *Ancestor Worship* by Emyr Humphreys (1970), *Adar Rhiannon* by William Jones (1947), translated by Harri Webb and *Y Goeden Eirin* by John Gwilym Jones (1946), translated by Elan Closs Stephens.

Allen & Unwin for 'The Mountain over Aberdare' from *Raiders' Dawn* and 'Goodbye' and 'In Hospital: Poona (1)' from *Ha! Ha! Among the Trumpets* by Alun Lewis.

Lady Anglesey and Mr Roger Morgan for the extract by Hilda Vaughan from *A Thing of Nought* (Lovat Dickson & Thompson 1934).

C. Julia C. Jones for the extract by J.R. Jones from *Gwaedd yng Nghymru*, translated by Meic Stephens.

Plaid Cymru for the extracts by Kate Roberts from *A Summer Day* (Penmark Press 1946), translated by Ll.Wyn Griffith and Dafydd Jenkins, and from *Planet*, translated by Ned Thomas.

Indiana University Press for 'For my Ancestors' by Rolfe Humphries from *Collected Poems* (1966).

Lawrence & Wishart Ltd for the extracts by Lewis Jones from *Cwmardy* (1937).

Penguin Books Ltd for the extracts from Geoffrey of Monmouth: *The History of Britain*, translated by Lewis Thorpe (Penguin Classics 1966), © Lewis Thorpe 1966.

Faber & Faber Ltd for 'Dai's Boast' by David Jones from *In Parenthesis* (1937).

Aled Vaughan for 'The White Dove' (*Faber Book of Stories*, edited by Kathleen Lines 1960).

Eben Morris for 'One Day by the Sea' (*The Angry Summer* Faber 1943), 'Do You Remember 1926?' and 'Consider Famous Men, Dai Bach' (*Gwalia Deserta* Dent 1938) by Idris Davies.

Alexander Cordell and Hodder & Stoughton Ltd for the extract from *The Fire People* (1972).

Hugh Wyn Griffith for 'Silver Jubilee 1939' by Ll.Wyn Griffith from *The Barren Tree* (Penmark Press 1945).

University of Wales Press for 'The Deluge 1939' by Saunders Lewis from *Presenting Saunders Lewis*, translated by Gwyn Thomas (1973).

Mrs Gwyn Thomas for the extracts from *Gazooka* (Gollancz 1957) and *The Alone to the Alone* (Nicholson & Watson 1947) by Gwyn Thomas.

Kent State University Press for the translation by Rolfe Humphries of 'The Girls of Llanbadarn' by Dafydd ap Gwilym from *Nine Thorny Thickets* (1969).

D. Brown & Sons Ltd for 'Quite so' by A.G. Prys-Jones from *A Little Nonsense* (1984).

Herbert Williams for 'The Old Tongue', first published by The Triskel Press (1966).

Curtis Brown Ltd on behalf of the estate of Rhys Davies © Rhys Davies 1969.

The estate of Gwyn Thomas and Felix de Wolfe for the extract by Gwyn Thomas from *A Few Selected Exits* (Hutchinson 1968).

Ned Thomas and B.S. Johnson for their translation of 'Glamorgan and Carmarthenshire' by D. Gwenallt Jones which appeared in *Planet*.

Joseph P. Clancy for his translations from *The Earliest Welsh Poetry* (Macmillan 1970) and *Medieval Welsh Lyrics* (Macmillan 1965).

Gomer Press for for: 'The Swan' (*Twentieth Century Welsh Poems*, translated by J.P. Clancy) and 'Blackthorn' (*Poems*) by Euros Bowen; 'A Cywydd for Kate' by J.P. Clancy (*The Significance of Flesh*); 'A Girl's Hair' by Dafydd ab Edmwnd (*To Look for a Word*), translated by Gwyn Williams; 'Land of my Mothers' by Idris Davies (*Collected Poems*); 'A Prayer' by J. Kitchener Davies (*Twentieth Century Welsh*

Poems), translated by J.P. Clancy; 'Rebel's Progress' by Tom Earley (*Rebel's Progress*); 'Agincourt', 'Anthem for Doomed Youth' (*A Sense of Time*) and 'Matters Arising' (*A Sense of Europe*) by Raymond Garlick; the extract from *The Years of the Locust* by W.J. Gruffydd, translated by D.M. Lloyd; 'Exultation' by Hywel ab Owain Gwynedd (*To Look for a Word*), translated by Gwyn Williams; 'Portrait of a Pregnant Woman' and 'Having our Tea' by Bobi Jones (*Twentieth Century Welsh Poems*), translated by J.P. Clancy; 'The Dead' by D. Gwenallt Jones (*Twentieth Century Welsh Poems*), translated by J.P. Clancy; 'The Common Path' by Glyn Jones (*Selected Poems*); 'Ann Griffiths' by Sally Jones (*The Forgotten Country*); 'Ystrad Fflur' by T. Gwynn Jones (*Twentieth Century Welsh Poems*), translated by J.P. Clancy; 'Back?' and 'Rhiannon' by T.H. Jones (*Collected Poems*); the extract from *Rwy'n cofio dy Dad* by Gweneth Lilly, translated by Meic Stephens; 'When I was Young' (*To Look for a Word*, translated by Gwyn Williams) and 'Yesterday's Illusion or Remembering the Thirties' (*Poetry of Wales 1930-70*, translated by R. Gerallt Jones) by Alun Llywelyn-Williams; 'The Flooded Valley' by Roland Mathias (*Burning Brambles*); 'Eifionydd' (*A Crown for Branwen*, translated by Harri Webb), 'The Fox' (*To Look for a Word*, translated by Gwyn Williams), and 'Bluebells' (*Twentieth Century Welsh Poems*, translated by J.P. Clancy) by R. Williams Parry; 'This Spot' (*Twentieth Century Welsh Poems*, translated by J.P. Clancy) and the essay from *Casgliad o Ysgrifau* (translated by Meic Stephens) by T.H. Parry-Williams; 'Nant-yr-Eira' by Iorwerth C.Peate (*Twentieth Century Welsh Poems*), translated by J.P. Clancy; 'In Chapel' by John Pook (*That Cornish Facing Door*); the extract by Ned Thomas from *The Welsh Language Today* (edited by Meic Stephens); 'Returning to Goleufryn' and 'Taliesin in Gower' by Vernon Watkins (*Unity of the Stream*); 'Big Night', 'Thanks in Winter' (*The Green Desert*) and 'A Crown for Branwen' (*A Crown for Branwen*) by Harri Webb; 'A Good Year' by D.J. Williams (*Storiau'r Tir Glas*), translated by Ll.Wyn Griffith; 'Preseli' by Waldo Williams (*Twentieth Century Welsh Poems*), translated by J.P. Clancy; 'Deprivation' by Eigra Lewis Roberts (*Storiau'r Dydd*), translated by Enid R. Morgan; the extract by Hugh Evans from *The Gorse Glen* (Brython Press), translated by E. Morgan Humphreys; the extract by T. Rowland Hughes from *Out of their Night* (Gwasg Aberystwyth), translated by Richard Ruck.

Emyr Humphreys for the extracts from *Miscellany Two* (Poetry Wales Press 1981), *A Toy Epic* (Eyre & Spottiswoode 1958) and *Outside the House of Baal* (Eyre & Spottiswoode 1965).

David Higham Associates for extracts by: Goronwy Rees from *A Bundle of Sensations* (Chatto & Windus 1960); Geraint Goodwin from *Heyday in the Blood* (Cape 1936); Richard Hughes from *The Wonder Dog* (Chatto & Windus 1977); Elisabeth Inglis-Jones from *Peacocks in Paradise* (Faber 1950); Dylan Thomas from *Collected Poems* (Dent 1952), *The Collected Stories* (Dent 1983) and *A Prospect of the Sea* (Dent 1955); Howard Spring from *Heaven Lies About Us* (Collins 1939).

Gwyn Thomas for 'An Old Thing' (*Y Weledigaeth Haearn*, Gee 1965), 'Horses' (*Enw'r Gair*, Gee 1972), translation by J.P. Clancy in J.P. Clancy and Gwyn Thomas: *Living a Life* (Bridges Books 1982).

The Executors of the estate of J.O. Francis.

Mrs Mattie Prichard for extracts by Caradog Prichard from *Full Moon* (Hodder & Stoughton 1973), and the translator, Menna Gallie.